Themes of
Contemporary Art

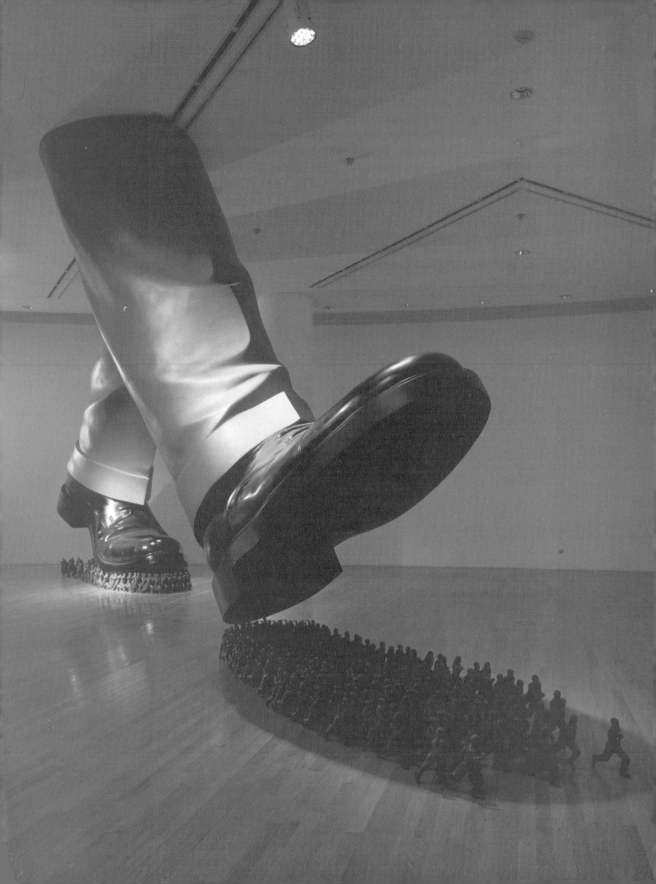

Themes of Contemporary Art

VISUAL ART AFTER 1980

Second Edition

JEAN ROBERTSON
HERRON SCHOOL OF ART AND DESIGN
INDIANA UNIVERSITY–PURDUE UNIVERSITY INDIANAPOLIS

CRAIG McDANIEL
HERRON SCHOOL OF ART AND DESIGN
INDIANA UNIVERSITY–PURDUE UNIVERSITY INDIANAPOLIS

New York   Oxford
OXFORD UNIVERSITY PRESS
2010

Oxford University Press, Inc., publishes works that further Oxford University's
objective of excellence in research, scholarship, and education.

Oxford   New York
Auckland   Cape Town   Dar es Salaam   Hong Kong   Karachi
Kuala Lumpur   Madrid   Melbourne   Mexico City   Nairobi
New Delhi   Shanghai   Taipei   Toronto

With offices in
Argentina   Austria   Brazil   Chile   Czech Republic   France   Greece
Guatemala   Hungary   Italy   Japan   Poland   Portugal   Singapore
South Korea   Switzerland   Thailand   Turkey   Ukraine   Vietnam

Published by Oxford University Press, Inc.
198 Madison Avenue, New York, New York 10016
http://www.oup.com

Library of Congress Cataloging-in-Publication Data

Robertson, Jean, 1950-
   Themes of contemporary art : visual art after 1980 / Jean Robertson,
Craig McDaniel. — 2nd ed.
      p. cm.
   Includes bibliographical references and index.
   ISBN 978-0-19-536757-7
      1. Art, Modern—20th century—Themes, motives. 2. Art, Modern—21st century—
Themes, motives. I. McDaniel, Craig. II. Title.

N6490.R5487 2010
709.04--dc22

                                                                    2008048622

Printing number: 9 8 7 6 5 4 3 2

Printed in the United States of America
on acid-free paper

Frontispiece: Detail of 2-11

FOR OUR FAMILIES
KEEPERS OF OUR PAST AND FUTURE

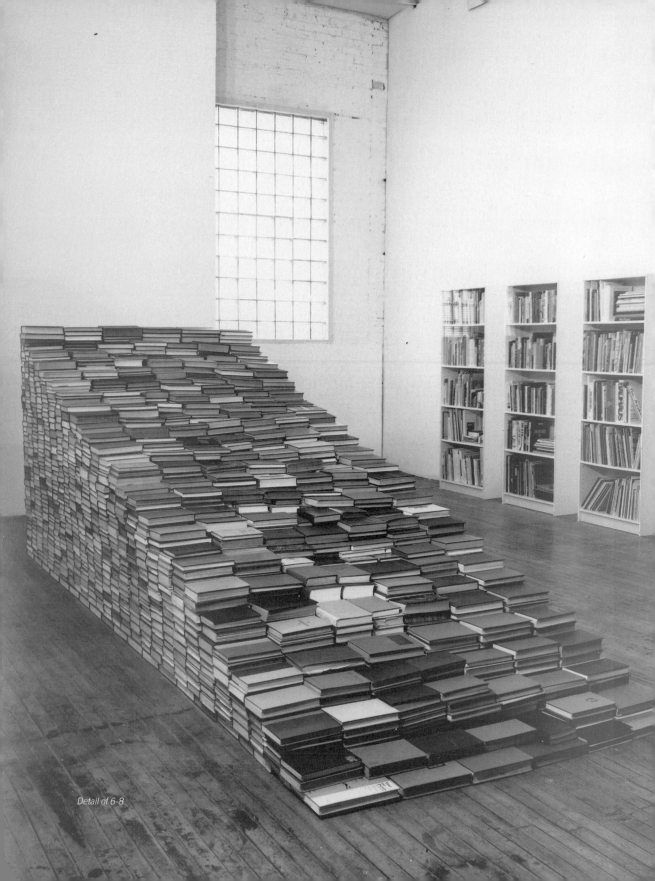

Detail of 6-8

Contents

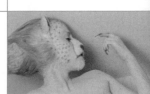
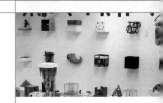
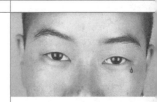

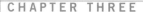
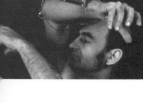
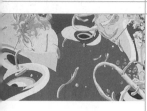

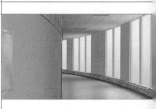
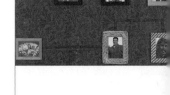

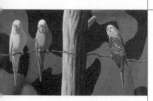

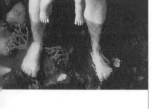

Color plate section follows page 176

Preface

Contemporary art is a vast arena of diverse styles, techniques, materials, subjects, forms, purposes, and aesthetic traditions. Viewers of the art of today and the recent past find themselves in the presence of objects and images that can range from the lighthearted to the soul searching, from the monumental to the ephemeral, from the highly recognizable to the strangely alien. To provide a cohesive gateway for those who are encountering this art with little advance knowledge or experience, we offer an approach that concentrates on seven themes that have been widespread in artistic practice during the past three decades: identity, the body, time, place, language, science, and spirituality. After an initial chapter that provides an overview, the seven themes are explored in as many chapters.

We chose to write about seven themes, rather than fifteen or twenty, because we want to provide a sufficient analysis of each theme so as to reveal something of the depth of thinking and intensity of practice within that arena. More themes, within a compact-size publication, would necessarily have meant curtailing our treatment of any one theme. As the chapters will document, each of the themes we selected has received significant attention by contemporary artists, critics, curators, and art historians. Furthermore, each theme we chose to examine has an enduring lineage in art history as well as widely recognized importance in daily life. Thus, we believe that our choices of thematic topics are valid, enduring, and vital, even though not exhaustive of all possible significant themes.

But why use themes as the structure for this book? An introductory text on recent art could have been organized around media disciplines (painting, sculpture, and so forth); in our view, however, such a treatment would tilt the discussion too heavily toward materials, techniques, and formal concerns. Of course, media distinctions remain important, and no more so than in the academy, where most studio art programs still offer a media-specific focus in the range of courses and majors in the curriculum. We believe that a balanced view of artists' diverse approaches to materials and techniques can be presented by discussing examples from virtually all the major media (as well as some that are idiosyncratic) within the structure of a thematic focus. Each chapter presents work in a variety of media that explore aspects of the theme being analyzed.

Furthermore, by focusing on thematic content, the structure of this volume fosters a cross-disciplinary approach that reflects an increasing trend in how artists and curators of new art function today.

Arguably an emphasis on theoretical concerns could also provide the structure for a text on contemporary art. Indeed, a number of edited collections of theoretical writings by artists and critics already exist. (An instructor with a strong interest in theory might opt to assign one of these collections of writings in tandem with our volume.) However, in terms of an introductory text on contemporary art, if just one text is used, one organized into theoretical chapters strikes us as a less effective choice than a thematic organization. Theory directly propels some, but not all artists. Still, we recognize the influential role of theory in the art of our time, and a concise assessment of some of the theoretical underpinnings of each theme is provided in every chapter, while a brief overview of the influence of theory vis-à-vis art after 1980 is presented in chapter 1.

A thematic approach, it seems to us, provides a judicious balance between discursive thinking and careful looking. By emphasizing the analysis of artworks thematically, our volume prioritizes the process of cognitive interpretation alongside attentive perception. The interpretations that we offer are never construed as the only possible interpretations. On the contrary, a primary pedagogical principle of our book is that meanings of any artwork are flexible: the same work can be presented so as to reveal alternative interpretive stances. Interpretations, mirroring the culture at large, are constructed by an interweaving of factors that are brought into play by the artist, society, and the viewer.

Within the analysis of the seven themes, we introduce artists working in a diverse range of media disciplines. Disciplines include those that are ancient (painting, sculpture), those that became central to the work of advanced artists during modernism (photography), those that have gained widespread attention within the past several decades (installation, performance, and video), and disciplines that depend on recently developed technologies (digital art).

The presiding context of the book is contemporary art in the West. The book is informed by our understanding that current art in the West is indebted to and embedded in heritages from many cultures around the world and that numerous influential artists who are working in the United States and Europe are immigrants. This introductory text provides a look at the vigorous involvement in contemporary art by artists from a wide variety of cultural and geographic backgrounds, including some artists living outside the West who are engaged in exhibitions, publications, and/or events that are finding an international audience.

Themes of Contemporary Art is not a traditional survey in the sense of providing a chronological history of art since 1980. We believe that trying to sort the most recent art into "movements" or "styles" is premature and most likely impossible at this point. Many present tendencies are just commencing or are in midstream, and we cannot see their full shape clearly or predict their future course and significance. It is not even certain that the old-style linear narrative of one movement influencing and leading into the next is adequate anymore. In our view, attempting to sort the diverse directions of contemporary art into a chronological structure would be confusing for readers and needlessly arcane. Instead, what we provide is an extended look at themes that are prevalent right now (and, in looking at themes, we provide a context for examining an assortment of the issues and practices that are currently vital). We also provide focused studies of a range of recognized artists, thereby offering students insights and a critical perspective on the rapidly evolving state of contemporary art. Our book is a kind of snapshot of where artists and critics are today in their thinking and activities.

Structure of the Book

The introduction orients the reader to the primary focus of the book: a thematic engagement with contemporary art. The term *theme* is defined and then applied immediately as a framework for analyzing two works of art, a photograph by Richard Misrach and a sculpture by Roxy Paine.

Chapter 1, "The Art World Expands," provides an overview of key aspects of contemporary art using broad strokes (concepts, issues, and terms of engagement) and an introduction to a (brief) history of the United States and the world 1980–2008. The chapter clarifies five characteristics of artistic practice over the past three decades: old media have thrived while new media made waves; a spectrum of diverse artistic voices emerged within individual societies and across international borders; increasing globalization impacted art practice and economics; theoretical writings provided a strong influence; and art met (and, at times, melded with) contemporary popular culture in all its manifestations. Furthermore, each of these five developments continues to define the present.

Chapters 2 through 8 form the core of this intellectual project: to chart contemporary artistic practice through the lens of key themes. Each of these chapters follows a similar format, including an introduction to the thematic topic, a concise look at historical precedents and influences, and a detailed analysis of key points that characterize how contemporary artists have responded to and embodied aspects of the theme in specific works. The chapter closes with a more in-depth profile of two artists who, we argue, have devoted significant energy within the parameters of the theme under discussion.

Artists who came of age in the 1980s and 1990s tend to be conceptually oriented. Readers of this volume will gain insights into how and why many contemporary artists place a great emphasis on creating meaningful work that connects to the world outside art, including intellectual debates from a wide array of discourses. An emphasis on thematic meaning has not come at the expense of the importance of form. Indeed, the analyses of specific artworks throughout these chapters will reveal that form remains a primary carrier of content. By providing a clearly structured approach, the student/reader will *learn how to learn* about new art, including artworks that are not discussed.

A range of issues and influences that are pervasive in current art discourse are examined, including the impact of social agendas and the rise of new media. A look at these topics within the context of artworks exploring the themes under review should give readers insights into the current dialogue that surrounds the creation, exhibition, and discussion of new works of art. Theoretical concepts—including feminism, postmodernism, poststructuralism, multiculturalism, and postcolonialism—are introduced at appropriate junctures as powerful analytical tools. Issues involved with our potential aesthetic engagement with art are raised as well. Within the discussion of the thematic categories and in the artists' profiles, the various roles that artists assume—including the artist as visionary and the artist as social activist—will provide students with an opportunity to consider how, when, and why art can be created.

The Audience for the Book

Themes of Contemporary Art: Visual Art After 1980 is designed to be a core text in introductory-level courses on the recent history of contemporary art. It can serve as the text for introductory courses that begin with art of the 1980s, perhaps supplemented by an edited book of theoretical writings on contemporary art or by a packet of readings selected by the instructor. We hope that this volume will serve as a resource that is intellectually engaging without being intimidating for diverse student populations.

Themes of Contemporary Art could also be used as a resource to supplement instruction in art appreciation courses at the university level (to provide a way to extend the discussion of art appreciation concepts to the art of our own era). Indeed, many art appreciation texts include substantial discussions of themes in art over time, but with only a cursory examination of the art of the present. The structure of our book would parallel how students are learning about art of the past while introducing them to current practices.

In addition, this book is designed to function as a pedagogical resource for introductory, intermediate, and advanced undergraduate-level studio art classes, since the discussion of thematic content can be utilized as a springboard for studio projects in virtually any media. Studio art instruction is challenged increasingly to offer systematic approaches to conceptualizing content, in order to engage students in the kind and quality of thinking that underpins the studio practice of professional artists. This volume can serve as a text to supplement in-class instruction in techniques, tools, materials, and formal concerns.

We also wrote this volume with the aim that general readers, who are not enrolled in a university class, would find it to be a useful, thoughtful, and thought-provoking guide to exploring the curious, and often challenging, landscape of contemporary art.

Alternate Paths Through the Book

The chapters may be read in sequence, following the order in which they appear. Alternatively, each chapter may be approached individually and in any order. Some teachers may prefer to have their students read all or some of the seven thematic chapters prior to the first chapter. Chapter 1, offering a condensed analysis of key developments that characterize the entire past three decades, including the role of theory, may be taken up after students have explored some (or all) of the thematic chapters. Teachers of studio art may want to select those chapters—in any order—that dovetail with the content of studio projects that are being explored during a particular semester. Teachers of art appreciation may want to assign chapters in the order in which thematic topics are being studied in the overall course.

Acknowledgments

This book would not exist except for the support we received. Our work was aided by the many individuals who generously shared with us their encouragement and expertise and those numerous institutions that provided us with resources.

Professional peers from the United States and England reviewed the text in manuscript form of both editions at several stages in the process of its preparation. We thank the following for insightful criticism that strengthened our thinking as well as our writing: Elissa Auther, University of Colorado at Colorado Springs; Terry Barrett, Ohio State University; Catherine Caesar, University of Dallas; Claude Cernuschi, Boston College;

Constance Cortez., Texas Tech University; Kathy Dambach, Florida International University; Kathleen Desmond, University of Central Missouri; Cecilia Dorger, College of Mt. St. Joseph; Tracy Featherstone, Miami University; Pamela Fletcher, Bowdoin College; Mary Francey, University of Utah; Gerar Edizel, NYSCC at Alfred University; Paul E. Ivey, University of Arizona; Elizabeth Lee, Dickenson College; Dana Leibsohn, Smith College; Jean Miller, Marshall University; Robert Nauman, University of Colorado at Boulder; Barbara Nesin, Spelman College; Jo Ortel, Beloit College; Kirstin Ringelberg, Elon University; Kristine Stiles, Duke University; Timea Tihanyi, University of Washington; and, Tim van Laar, University of Illinois. We benefited from the expert assistance of a fine staff at Oxford University Press, and thank the following for their contributions: Cory Schneider, Assistant Editor, and Marianne Paul, Production Editor.

We extend our appreciation to our talented colleagues at Indiana University's Herron School of Art and Design, on the campus of Indiana University-Purdue University Indianapolis. We extend particular thanks to Dean Valerie Eickmeier at Herron for her ongoing encouragement of faculty research projects, including her support of a sabbatical for Jean Robertson during which the preliminary stage of planning and researching this book was conducted. An Indiana University President's Arts and Humanities Initiative Award and a Clowes Fellowship from the Vermont Studio Center provided valuable support for work on this project for Jean and Craig respectively, and an Indiana University New Frontiers in the Arts and Humanities award, funded by Lilly Endowment, provided additional support for researching this second edition. We also thank our students for helping us hone many of the ideas presented in this volume during class discussions.

The artists and their dealers who made available the materials and permissions for illustrations have added an invaluable component to this volume. Thanks to the Indiana University Press for permission to reproduce, in altered form, sections of a previously published essay by Jean Robertson, woven into sections of chapter 3 in this volume. Thanks to the School of Fine Arts Gallery, Indiana University-Bloomington for permission to reproduce altered sections of a previously published essay by Jean Robertson, woven into sections of chapter 7. We appreciate the contributions of Dr. James D. Robertson and Professor Alan Jones, who reviewed sections in chapter 7, science, and were especially helpful in suggestions to clarify the definition of science.

Lastly we want to thank three individuals who have made irreplaceable contributions to the preparation and completion of this book project. First and foremost, we thank Janet Beatty, Executive Editor at Oxford University Press, for her acumen in shepherding us wisely through the development of our writing from the beginning of the project through the completion of this second edition. Significant changes in approach and conception occurred along the way, and we acknowledge Jan's guidance to bring greater clarity to our writing and to steer us to a more effective organization of the entire book. Secondly, we thank Martha Morss, a long-term friend of ours, for her editing expertise. Martha helped us produce a book that, we hope, will be thought-provoking without being mind-boggling and full of needless jargon. Lastly, we owe our gratitude to Colleen Tulledge, who joined the project for the second edition in key capacities: as research assistant, illustration and permissions researcher, timeline researcher, and general assistant in preparing the project for submission to our publisher.

A world without art is unimaginable.

J.R. and C.Mc.

Themes of
Contemporary Art

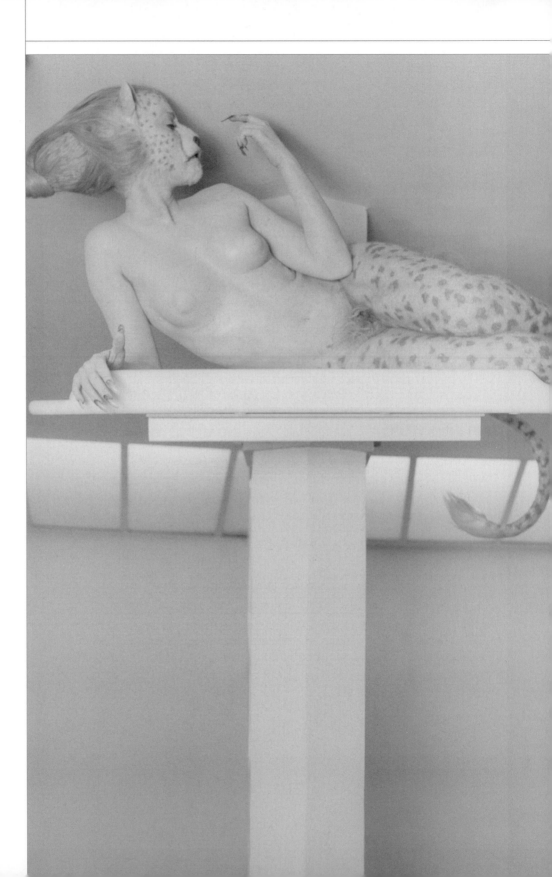

Detail of 3-7

Introduction

In writing *Themes of Contemporary Art: Visual Art After 1980,* we aimed high: to offer you, our readers, an accessible, engaging, and wide-ranging introduction to the world of recent art. Within these pages, we explore work by hundreds of contemporary artists who, we believe, have succeeded in giving memorable substance to their creative visions. The artworks illustrated and discussed in the chapters that follow function in a plenitude of ways, arousing our curiosity, delighting our senses, evoking our emotions, and provoking questions and debate. In the pages that follow, you should expect to find some of your notions about art—about its definitions, its purposes, and its manifestations—turned in new directions, perhaps, at times, even topsy-turvy. This learning won't come without effort. We need you to engage actively in your pursuit of fresh knowledge.

This book explores a segment of history—a history of some significant achievements in visual art over the past three decades. However, you will discover that this volume avoids one of the usual routes taken in the study of history: the march in step with chronology. Rather than proceed through the period under discussion in strict linear fashion, we prefer to concentrate primary attention on a selection of seven prominent themes that have recurred in art during recent decades: identity, the body, time, place, language, science, and spirituality. Each chapter considers artworks made throughout the entire period from the point of view of that chapter's theme.

What do we mean by a theme in a work of art? A theme is a clustering of ideas around a particular topic. In discussing a theme, we are concerned with the overarching ideas that are embodied and expressed by the artwork's totality. Looking at themes, we focus on the meaning of a work of art examined as a whole, including the impact that materials, techniques, form, and subject matter make on content.

A thematic approach provides a judicious balance between discursive thinking and careful looking. By emphasizing the thematic analysis of artworks, this text gives priority to the process of interpretation. While we offer interpretations of the artworks that are presented, we recognize that the meanings of any artwork are multiple and complex and that all interpretations are negotiable.

We believe that an engagement with thematic ideas will prepare the reader to face both familiar and unfamiliar works of art with intellectual excitement. Indeed, our goal is to empower the reader/viewer with an enlarged mental perspective. The future will offer much that is unfamiliar. Learning to think about new art will provide tools for adapting to all manner of future events and can be a pleasure in and of itself.

Themes of Contemporary Art: What, Why, and How

Imagine you are an art critic whose mission is to compare the meanings you find in a wide variety of individual artworks. How would you proceed with this task? One way to begin is to examine the materials that each artist selected in producing an object, image, video, or event. The decision to cast a sculpture in bronze, for instance, inevitably affects its meaning; the work becomes something different than if it had been cast in gold or plastic or chocolate, even if everything else about the artwork remains the same. Next, you might examine how the materials in each artwork have become an arrangement of shapes, colors, textures, and lines. These, in turn, are organized into various patterns and compositional structures. In your interpretation, you would comment on how salient features of the form contribute to the overall meaning of the finished artwork.

The meaning of most artworks, however, is not exhausted by a discussion of materials, techniques, and form. Most interpretations also include a discussion of the ideas and feelings that the artwork engenders. For example, a photograph of a stretch of landscape in the American West by Richard Misrach [I-1] is defined only partially by the fact that it is a color photograph carefully composed to accentuate the sense of deep space in the view. The meaning is also in the subject matter of the photo, an orderly arrangement of tables and chairs within a barren landscape. But what does all this mean? Why did the photographer frame this view through the camera lens, and what effect does the photograph have on you as a viewer?

By examining other photographs by the same artist and reading some of the literature on his work, you would discover that this particular artwork is one in a series that Misrach calls his *Desert Cantos* series. Like all the works in the series, this one focuses on an outdoor location in the American West. Entitled *Outdoor Dining, Bonneville Salt Flats, Utah* (1992), this photo records the strange beauty in a scene of empty chairs and tables. Photographs in the series show how the western landscape has been transformed by human actions, including bomb craters produced by explosions at nuclear test sites. Every work in the *Desert Cantos* series appears to stem from one basic idea: that humans have made nature subservient to our needs and wishes and that continuing to do so endangers not only nature's health, but our own. Variations on this theme are explored throughout Misrach's *Desert Cantos*.

This text looks at art after 1980 in terms of selected themes that have been prevalent in the period. In many works of art, the artist conveys a theme by investing a subject with emotional significance or implying a moral value. In some works of art, the theme is expressed by a set of symbols (e.g., a rose may symbolize romantic love, while thorns represent pain). In the study of art history, an interrelated, conventional set of symbols is called *iconography*. When using a thematic approach, we construct a mental framework for making sense of the ideas that are expressed in the artwork and their embodiment in certain materials, forms, and iconography.

It is important to note that while the subject matter of a work of art contributes to the overall cognitive content, the subject matter is not usually equivalent to the

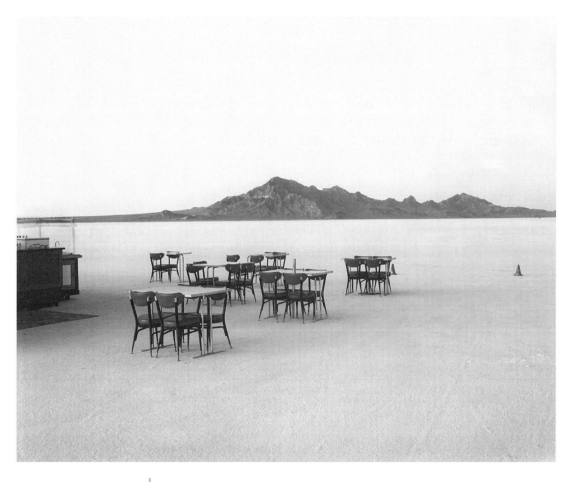

I-1 Richard Misrach | *Outdoor Dining, Bonneville Salt Flats, Utah,* 1992

Color photograph, 40 x 90 inches

Courtesy of Fraenkel Gallery, SF Marc Selwyn Fine Art, LA and Pace/MacGill Gallery, NY

theme. For example, artist Roxy Paine's *Crop* (1998) [I-2] is a sculptural re-creation of a six-by-eight–foot plot of garden soil. Appearing to grow out of the soil are Paine's painstakingly rendered simulations of poppy plants. In addition to its literal subject matter—a patch of poppies—*Crop* is freighted with meaning that derives from our recognition that the poppy plant ultimately becomes salable as opium or heroin. We may interpret the artwork as a metaphor for a world full of dangers, tensions, temptations, and condemnations and define its theme as having something to do with the health of the planet. (The artwork may take on an additional level of meaning for viewers who recognize that much of the world's heroin supply originates in the poppy fields of Afghanistan.)

Exploring the chapters in this volume, you should bear in mind that our selection of seven primary themes does not exhaust the broad range of content found in contemporary art.[1] Furthermore, these thematic categories do not necessarily reflect those that the artists who made the works would name. Artists' intentions regarding content

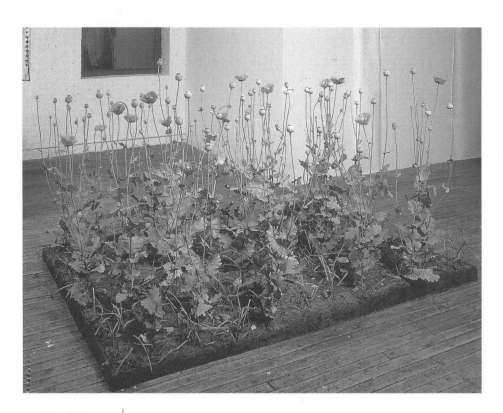

I-2 Roxy Paine | *Crop,* 1997–1998
Lacquer, epoxy, oil paint, pigment, 58 x 96 x 72 inches
Photo by John Lamka
Courtesy of James Cohan Gallery

are complex, reflecting both conscious and unconscious ideas, and often involve more than one theme. Moreover, while contemporary artists are engaged in thinking about the content of the works they create, not all artists think about themes in a precisely defined manner.

These seven thematic categories allow us to present a sample of artworks from which you can grasp influential concepts that stretch across much of the art of our time. Each theme functions as an interpretive lens, an analytical tool for exploring the various levels of meaning that artworks embody. Ultimately, almost all works of art can be viewed from the perspective of more than one theme. As you may have observed, the two artworks we just discussed—the photograph of the Salt Flats in Utah by Misrach and the sculpture of a poppy patch by Paine—are related to each other in that both involve aspects of our (human) relationship to the land. Both works would fit easily into chapter 5, in which we focus on the theme of place. But both could be analyzed in terms of other themes as well. It may be appropriate to explore the works in terms of spirituality, the topic of chapter 8, discussing them as metaphors for an apocalyptic end to human life and the loss of ability to find spiritual renewal. That an artwork can be approached from multiple interpretive contexts does not diminish the relevance or value of any one of them. The seven themes are broad and multileveled, and intersect in multiple ways.

A Brief Orientation

Chapter 1 presents a broad introduction to important developments in art and to ideas and events that influenced art in the period from 1980 through 2008. It introduces ideas that apply to all the themes discussed in subsequent chapters. Chapters 2 through 8 delve into the themes themselves, one theme to each chapter in the following order: identity, the body, time, place, language, science, and spirituality.

Chapters 2 through 8 follow a similar format. An introduction situates the theme within a broad social and cultural matrix, a brief historical overview discusses artistic approaches to the theme and related concepts in earlier eras, recent artists' treatments of the theme are evaluated in terms of key theories and strategies of art production, and the theme is examined in terms of subcategories that have received critical attention in contemporary exhibitions and publications. Following an in-depth discussion of the theme, each chapter provides two profiles of individual artists. Each profile presents a concise examination of the ideas and approaches of an artist who has devoted a substantial portion of his or her creative energies to exploring aspects of the theme under discussion.

By approaching the landscape of contemporary art from the perspective of the seven themes selected for this text, we believe that our readers will benefit from two familiar footholds. First, these themes of art overlap in significant ways with the concerns of contemporary living. Each reader already possesses knowledge, ideas, and terms for thinking about topics, such as place, time, and the body. To this degree, each chapter starts on familiar ground, which is inherently meaningful to everyone. Second, the themes demonstrate that the achievements of contemporary artists have a historical context. Readers can see that the art of our own period connects with and draws from the rich traditions of past art. We expect that all our readers possess at least a modicum of knowledge of the traditions of art (e.g., they can recognize a landscape painting or a portrait), and so we build on this as a way of anchoring new learning to the bedrock of previous knowledge.

Note

1. While numerous themes are prevalent in the discourse on contemporary art, it is a curious fact that other themes that are important to the public, such as sports and marriage, are examined only rarely by notable contemporary artists and the art critics and historians who focus on contemporary art.

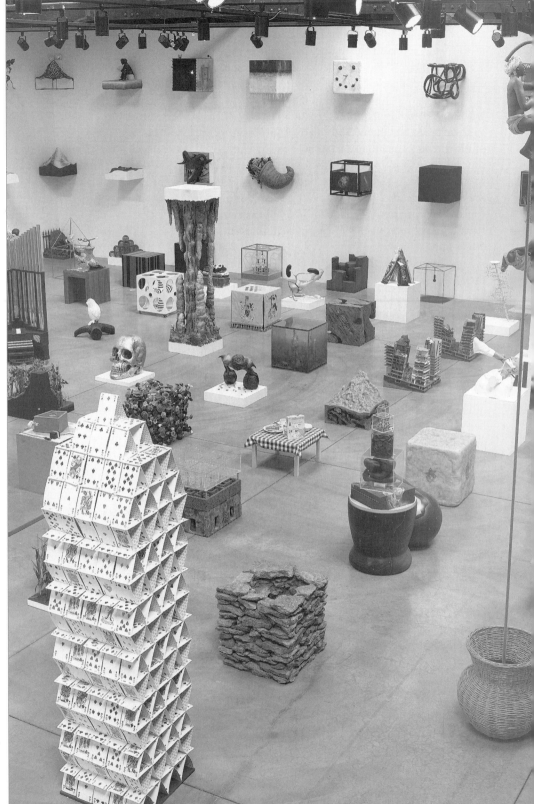

Detail of 1-7

CHAPTER ONE

The Art World Expands

In our travels and visits to exhibitions of contemporary art over the past several years, we've encountered many unusual and challenging works of art. Here is a sampling:

- *Inopportune: Stage One* (2004) [1-1] by Cai Guo-Qiang, an installation showing nine identical white cars suspended in midair and positioned to create the impression of successive stages of a car flipping over in an explosion from a car bombing, while long tubes radiating colored light burst out in all directions from the windows (seen in the midcareer survey of the artist's work shown at the Guggenheim Museum in New York City in 2008).
- *The Eighth Day* (2001) [color plates 17 and 18], a "transgenic" artwork by Eduardo Kac, brought together living, bioengineered, glow-in-the-dark mice, plants, and fish and a biological robot ("biobot") in an environment housed under a clear four-foot-diameter Plexiglas dome (seen at the Institute for Studies in the Arts, Arizona State University, Tempe).[1]
- An impressively large painted triptych by Li Tian Yuan (2001), based on a satellite image, shows progressively closer views of the artist and his infant son on the Great Wall of China (included in an international exhibition of art dealing with the interface of art and science at the National Museum, Beijing, China).
- A re-creation of Gino de Dominicis's controversial 1972 *Second Solution of Immortality: The Universe Is Immobile*, staged by the Wrong Gallery, situated a woman with Down's syndrome in a nearly empty gallery, where she sat staring at a simple arrangement of symbolic objects (seen at the 2006 Frieze art fair in London, where the stillness of the performance piece stood in stark contrast to the frenetic sensory overload elsewhere at the fair).[2]

As these examples hint, the world of contemporary art is rich, diverse, and unpredictable. Although painting, photography, sculpture, drawing, and the crafts still attract a large number of practitioners, these familiar forms of art no longer subsume the field. Film, video, audio, installation, performance, texts, and computers are common media

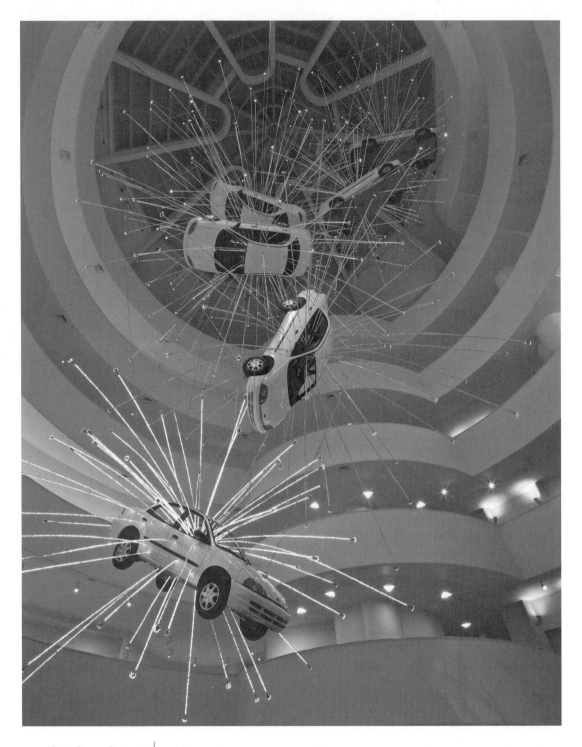

1-1 **Cai Guo-Qiang** | *Inopportune: Stage One,* **2004**

Nine cars and sequenced multichannel light tubes, Dimensions variable. Seattle Art Museum, Gift of Robert M. Arnold, in honor of the 75th Anniversary of the Seattle Art Museum, 2006. Exhibition copy installed at Solomon R. Guggenheim Museum, New York, 2008. Photo by David Heald

Photograph © The Solomon R. Guggenheim Foundation

today, and artists are often fluent in several media. Artists freely mix media or may practice a medium with a long lineage in an unconventional way, such as making paintings that look like pixilated computer images or drawing with unconventional materials, such as chocolate syrup.

Contemporary art is in flux. Old hierarchies and categories are fracturing; new technologies are offering different ways of conceptualizing, producing, and showing visual art; established art forms are under scrutiny and revision; an awareness of heritages from around the world is fostering cross-fertilizations; and everyday culture is providing both inspiration for art and competing visual stimulation. The diversity and rapid transformations are intriguing but can be daunting for those who want to understand contemporary art and actively participate in discussions about what is happening.

Along with the dynamic nature of contemporary art, content matters. Looking back at the history of modern art, it is debatable whether the idea of "art for art's sake" truly took over the thinking of modernist theorists and artists. But certainly there were periods in the twentieth century, especially just after World War II, when critics (famously the American Clement Greenberg, who died in 1994) and some influential avant-garde artists advocated *formalism*, an emphasis on form, rather than content, when creating and interpreting art. Those who are invested in formalism were and are concerned mainly with investigating the properties of specific media and techniques, as well as the general language of aesthetics (the role of color or composition, for instance). But formalism is inadequate for interpreting art that expresses the inner visions of artists or art that refers to the world beyond art. When pop art appeared in the 1960s, with its references to cartoons, consumer products, and other elements of shared culture, the limitations of formalism became evident, and a broader range of theories surfaced, including postmodernism, poststructuralism, feminism, and postcolonialism, as we discuss later in this chapter.

Throughout the period we discuss—1980 to the present—artists have engaged deeply with meaningful content. Artists who have been active since 1980 are motivated by a range of purposes and ideas beyond a desire to express personal emotions and visions or to display a mastery of media and techniques. Political events, social issues and relations, science, technology, mass media, popular culture, literature, the built environment, the flow of capital, the flow of ideas, and other forces and developments are propelling artists and providing content for their artworks.

Overview of History and Art History: 1980–2008

The past three decades have been eventful in virtually every area of human activity, including politics, medicine, science, technology, culture, and art. In the 1980s, fax machines and compact-disc players entered widespread use, the first laptop computers were introduced, and cordless telephones became available. Also in the 1980s, for the first time in the United States, a woman was appointed to the Supreme Court, a woman traveled in space, and a woman headed a major party ticket as a candidate for vice president. The Berlin Wall was dismantled, and Germany reunified in 1989, presaging the collapse of communism in Eastern Europe. In the 1990s, numerous controversies raged over threats of global warming and genetic engineering of plants and animals; a sheep was successfully cloned in 1997. Also in the 1990s, a brutal civil war led to the breakup of Yugoslavia into several independent republics, ethnic massacres devastated the African state of Rwanda, and nationalist conflicts broke out in the new states of Georgia and Azerbaijan in the former Soviet Union. Early in the 1990s, apartheid officially ended in South Africa. By the mid-1990s, the Internet system linked millions of users. In 1995, the Federal Building in Oklahoma City was destroyed by American terrorists. The 2000s so far have been extremely violent. In September 2001, the World Trade Center in New York was destroyed and the Pentagon in Washington, D.C., was attacked by Islamist terrorists. The U.S.-led invasion of Afghanistan commenced later that fall, and in 2003, the United States led an invasion of Iraq that toppled the government of Saddam Hussein. Years later, the wars in Afghanistan and Iraq continue. Civil unrest and even open warfare have plagued many regions, including the Darfur region of Sudan, Jewish and Palestinian settlements in the Middle East, and Chechnya, on the border of Russia. Food shortages and famines; new infectious diseases, such as bird flu; the rising costs of oil; and increasing evidence of climate change offer a bleak outlook to people worldwide, especially in the poorest nations. Meanwhile, new economic powerhouses, including China and India, are exerting influence on the global economy. Technological changes continue to have a social impact, including new medical and scientific discoveries, new forms of instant communication like text messaging and blogging, and other growing capabilities and influence of computer technologies.

The demographics of various parts of the world have changed dramatically since 1980. Just in the United States, "the US experienced a profound demographic shift in the 1980s, with an influx of over 7 million immigrants from Latin America, the Caribbean, and Asia. By 1990, 25 per cent of Americans (population 247 million) claimed African, Asian, Hispanic, or Native American ancestry."[3] Every year, across the globe, the relocation of vast numbers of people occurs in response to wars, famines, ethnic violence, and economic pressures and opportunities. Alterations in national boundaries and distributions of power are commonplace.

The art world itself underwent major changes during the period covered in this text. Major art centers lost some of their dominance as art activities became more decentralized. The changed artistic landscape led to a significant cross-fertilization of ideas among locations across the globe. While New York City remained a primary destination on the contemporary art world map, other urban centers—including London, Los Angeles, Tokyo, Shanghai, Dubai, Mumbai, Istanbul, Berlin, São Paulo, and Johannesburg—ratcheted up their support and presentation of new art to such a degree that anyone who expected to remain knowledgeably informed felt pressured to research current activities in these locations.

The art scene exploded after 1980, with a marked increase in artists, dealers, collectors, publications, and exhibition spaces. The formation of new institutions, as well as new or revamped facilities at existing institutions, expanded the number, size, and quality of locations where the latest in visual art could be seen by a growing public, including tourists seeking entertainment. Of these projects, several are notable not only for offering intriguing possibilities for the exhibition of art, but because the architectural structures assert themselves as works of art in their own right. Topping the list in terms of publicity were the Guggenheim Museum's new branch in Bilbao, Spain (1997), designed by architect Frank Gehry, and the spectacular transformation of an enormous power station along the Thames River in London into Tate Modern (2000).[4] Other notable new venues include MASS MoCA (1999), which offers a vast 100,000 square feet of exhibition space in a converted nineteenth-century factory building in North Adams, Massachusetts, and the more modestly scaled but boldly designed Wexner Center (1989) on the campus of Ohio State University in Columbus, a project by Peter Eisenman.

The fortunes and misfortunes of contemporary artists take shape, to a large degree, within the sphere of the commercial galleries that present new art. Reputations are built by the support of prominent gallery dealers and the approval of the critics, curators, and collectors who carefully monitor and judge the quality of the art featured in highly publicized exhibitions. During the era, there were frequent shifts in the zones of concentrated art activity (such as the reduction of galleries located in New York's SoHo area and the dramatic influx of galleries into the historic meat-packing district known as Chelsea by the mid-1990s), as well as numerous gallery openings and closings, which reflected fluctuations in national economies. The rise of neo-expressionism in the early 1980s, for instance, was tied to a boom in the U.S. stock market, while an economic recession later in the decade was responsible, in part, for retrenchment and attention to more modestly scaled artistic projects. In the first decade of the twenty-first century, the art market boomed again and grandiose projects were under way once more. All this, of course, is not without precedent. General forces at work in society, including politics, demographics, and economics, have always influenced the history of art.

In addition to an enormous range of activities, including exhibitions, performances, film and video screenings, and lectures, presented by public institutions within facilities devoted to contemporary art, the contemporary period witnessed a surge of *public art*—visual arts activities in public settings, such as city streets, plazas, parks, and commercial facilities. Public dollars funded many of these activities, a fact that turned out to be something of a double-edged sword. The support of contemporary art with government dollars was a crucial means of enlarging the funds available to artists and institutions; in the United States and Britain, such support was often a percentage of the amount budgeted for new government-funded public construction projects.

The use of public dollars increased attention to contemporary public art (taxpayers were interested to know how their money was being spent), but the increased attention also resulted in more controversy whenever a vocal core trumpeted their outrage over a specific project. Maya Lin's *Vietnam Veterans Memorial* (1981–84), located on the Mall in Washington, D.C.; Richard Serra's *Tilted Arc* (1981), installed in a public plaza near a government office building in Manhattan; and Mark Quinn's *Alison Lapper Pregnant* (2005), a monumental sculpture of the nude, pregnant body of disabled artist Lapper (born with no arms and shortened legs), displayed on the fourth plinth in London's Trafalgar Square, are examples of public art projects that galvanized public opinion, both pro and con. The *Vietnam Veterans Memorial* was ultimately embraced even by its original opponents. A more conservative outlook prevailed for *Tilted Arc*: Serra's work was removed in 1989 after a lengthy legal battle. Quinn's sculpture was always intended to be temporary (the fourth plinth is used for an ongoing series of contemporary sculptures), and was on view there for only eighteen months.

In the United States, art by feminists, queers, and artists perceived to be unpatriotic or sacrilegious were particular targets of public uproar, fueling the so-called culture wars that erupted in the late 1980s and early 1990s over public funding and freedom of expression. Highly publicized controversies accompanied a traveling exhibition of photographs by Robert Mapplethorpe in the early 1990s that included some photos showing homosexual activities; the exhibition of *Piss Christ* (1987) by Andres Serrano, a photographic image of a plastic crucifix submerged in urine, which was deemed blasphemous by some religious spokespersons; the offer in 1990 by feminist artist Judy Chicago to donate her monumental collaborative creation *The Dinner Party* (1979) to the University of the District of Columbia, a plan blocked by conservative members of Congress who called the work pornographic because some interpreted the imagery as representing female genitalia; and the exhibition Sensation showing works by young British artists, which caused a furor and media frenzy when it opened at the Brooklyn Museum in 1999, with much of the attention centering on Chris Ofili's painting *The Holy Virgin Mary*, which featured a black Madonna decorated with resin-covered lumps of elephant dung. Also under pressure from Congress, the National Endowment for the Arts eliminated fellowships to individual artists in 1995.

Political considerations influenced some contemporary artists to engage in institutional critiques. Such critiques took aim at both art institutions, with artists attempting to reveal how museums, commercial galleries, and other organizations control how art is produced, displayed, and marketed, and institutions within the wider society; for example, feminists critiqued the social structures and hierarchies that limit female potential. Politically motivated art projects were particularly prevalent in the late 1980s and first half of the 1990s.

Activist art addressed social realities that were heard and seen in the news and experienced directly by the artists involved. Art about AIDS provides a key example. AIDS began its destructive growth in the early 1980s, when the disease was first recognized and named. In the 1980s, before treatments had been developed and refined, an AIDS diagnosis was like a death sentence. "Life was lived with that bell tolling all the time," recalls writer Stephen Koch.[5] The association of AIDS with homosexual men at that time brought forth a wave of virulent homophobia. In response to the crisis and to massive losses from AIDS within the arts community, numerous artists, including David Wojnarowicz, Keith Haring, and the art collective known as Gran Fury, put their art in the service of AIDS activism. Other arenas that provided serious political content for contemporary art included feminist politics and issues of race, homelessness, corporate capitalism, consumerism, and militarism.

In the past decade, there has been something of a stalling of artistic political activism. Although survivors of the culture wars and occasional younger artists still court controversy (sometimes for shock value more than for ideological reasons), many more artists want to engage the public, rather than challenge social and political institutions and practices. A notable trend is the supersizing of art, found in the production of spectacular, often highly crafted and technically complex, works that require teams of assistants, specialist consultants, and big budgets to realize. For example, Kac's *The Eighth Day* [color plates 17 and 18] and Cai's *Inopportune: Stage One* [1-1] were made with the help of consultants and assistants.

The history of contemporary art is not entirely a story of young artists bursting onto the scene with new ideas. While many previously unknown artists emerged after 1980, the presence and influence of older artists was important as well. For example, Joseph Beuys died in 1986, Andy Warhol in 1987, Louise Nevelson in 1988, Roy Lichtenstein in 1997, Agnes Martin in 2004, Allan Kaprow and Nam June Paik in 2006, and Robert Rauschenberg in 2008. Most of these artists were making vital work up until their deaths, so that even an art movement, such as pop art, which we normally associate with the 1960s, was evolving within the ongoing production of the oeuvres of Warhol and Lichtenstein. A retrospective exhibition of work by Louise Bourgeois toured internationally in 2008–09, when the influential artist was 96 and still active.

Themes of Contemporary Art is not a traditional survey in the sense of providing an in-depth chronological history of art since 1980. The history of art over the past thirty years is fantastically rich and involves many diverse stories, motivations, influences, ideas, and approaches. Attempting to map recent art into a tight chronological structure of movements or even of collections of major artists would be premature and, in fact, would misrepresent the contemporary period. Whereas the art world before 1980 is distant enough that we can perceive some sequence of trends (really multiple intersecting and interacting trends), more recent art practices are much more pluralistic and amorphous in character. Many of the artists we discuss are in midcareer and still defining their practices. Many present tendencies are just commencing or are in midstream, and we cannot see their shape clearly or predict their future course and significance. The old-style linear narrative of one movement influencing and leading into the next is not adequate anymore. (It is debatable whether a linear model really was ever historically accurate.) As artist Haim Steinbach said (remembering the 1980s, although his statement applies to the entire contemporary period), "I see [the period] as an archipelago, in which different things were going on, on different islands. They were going on concurrently but not always moving in the same direction."[6]

Old Media Thrive, New Media Make Waves

If we cannot place contemporary art into neat compartments or a series of movements, we can still make a few broad observations about developments and tendencies in art since 1980.

Painting didn't die in contemporary art, despite predictions to the contrary made in the 1970s. Indeed, painting enjoyed something of a rebirth in the United States in the early 1980s, during the heyday of neo-expressionism, "an international movement dominated by oversized canvases and emotional gestures, and by a bustling commercial market."[7] Young Americans making bold, gestural paintings, including Julian Schnabel, David Salle, and Eric Fischl, were celebrated and compared to dramatic painters who had emerged in Europe in the 1970s, such as the German neo-expressionist Anselm Kiefer. While enormously popular, neo-expressionism had its detractors, who saw the artists as opportunists who simulated emotion in order to appeal to the market. By 1990, the neo-expressionist momentum had died down, but in its wake painting continued to attract critical attention, although with some rising and falling in its influence (especially when examined on a regional basis) and changes in the concerns of its practitioners. Neo Rauch, who was born in 1960 in Leipzig, East Germany, has gained great notoriety in the twenty-first century as an oil painter who continues the grand tradition of large-scale history painting. Rauch's ambiguous narratives, layered imagery, and appropriated styles conjure up a range of historical influences and references, from surrealism to Soviet-era social realism to the satires of Russian Sots Art to the neo-expressionism of the generation just before him [1-2]. In addition, like the work of many acclaimed current painters, Rauch's paintings critique the art of painting, cleverly manipulating painting's language of representation.

Like other traditional media, such as drawing and sculpture, the practice of painting saw its boundaries stretched and took on new life in the contemporary period. What

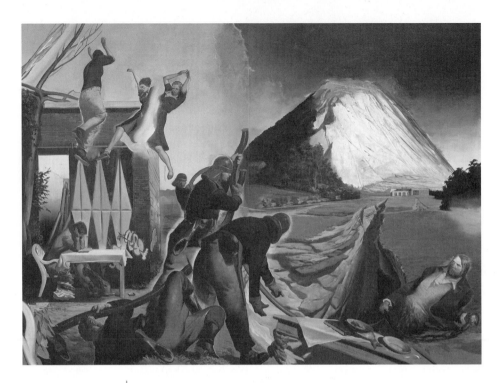

1-2 Neo Rauch | *Die Fuge,* **2007**
Oil on canvas, 300 x 420 cm
Kunsthalle Hamburg
Photo by Uwe Walter
Courtesy of Galerie EIGEN + ART Leipzig/Berlin and David Zwirner, New York

defines a painting? Can we still recognize one when we see one? Thousands upon thousands of paintings are created each year in the familiar portable, rectangular, paint-on-canvas format. But exciting work has pushed painting into areas where it embraces unconventional materials and often overlaps with sculpture and installation art. For example, Fred Tomaselli makes "paintings" that are collages of plants, pills (over-the-counter and prescription), insect wings, and catalog clippings [color plate 19]. Kara Walker cuts silhouettes from paper to make large-scale murals [4-9]. Guillermo Kuitca and Fabian Marcaccio, two artists from Argentina, exemplify the push to open the venerable queen of the arts up to new possibilities that embrace the third dimension. Kuitca has painted maps on full-size mattresses, while Marcaccio trusses his paintings at odd angles between the walls and floor. Brazilian Adriana Varejão assembles wall-based reliefs using tiles, oil, and foam [color plate 5].

Photography became a player. Even as brushy neo-expressionist painting garnered headlines, the 1980s saw a rising tide of photo-based art. Artists had used photography as a medium from its officially announced invention in 1839, but it was in the 1980s that photography really escaped its secondary status and "moved to the very centre of avant-garde art practices…, rivalling painting and sculpture in size, spectacular effects, market appreciation, and critical importance."[8] Large-scale color printing of photographs became feasible for the first time in the early 1980s, propelling the interest of museums and collectors. Photography also exerted a noticeable influence on other forms of art, particularly some genres of painting, which sometimes seemed to be playing catch-up in striving to create a convincing illusion of the way the world "really" (i.e., photographically) looks.

Photography also expanded its own boundaries as artists gave free rein to experimentation, adopting new technologies, such as the computer, and hybridizing with other forms of art, including installation and performance. More and more photographers turned to elaborate fabrications, constructing staged scenes that they then photographed or manipulating and altering camera images after shooting. The widespread leap into digital photography in the twenty-first century facilitated and accelerated the manipulation of photographs, with computer programs, such as Photoshop, replacing the hands-on darkroom procedures needed to alter analog negatives. An example of photography's use as a tool for fabricating convincing portrayals of imaginary realms is Japanese photographer Yoshio Itagaki's intriguing concoction *Tourists on the Moon #2* (1998) [1-3].

Sculpture as an art form widely expanded its sphere of influence, and the range of content and forms within the genre expanded as well. In the 1970s, during the reign of minimalism, pared-down abstract sculpture predominated. Such minimalist sculpture emphasized simplified abstract volumes (what some critics referred to as "primary forms"). In the 1980s, and extending into the present, sculptors dramatically broadened the forms, techniques, and materials they selected. In addition to creating sculptures from traditional materials, such as bronze, marble, and wood, artists made sculptures from a wide array of materials as well as found objects. British sculptor Tony Cragg, for instance, became widely known in the 1980s for his wall-mounted, multipart sculptures created by arranging found plastic objects (e.g., packaging materials, throwaway plates, and plastic containers), often all of the same color, into pictographic patterns.

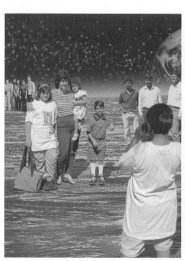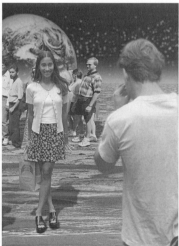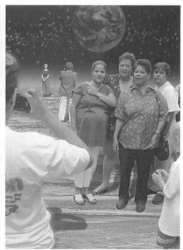

1-3 Yoshio Itagaki | *Tourists on the Moon #2*, 1998
Triptych, color photograph, 40 x 90 inches
Courtesy of the artist and Jack the Pelican Presents, New York

Furthermore, while sculptors continued to carve, cast, and construct discrete, unique objects, others expanded their practice so that sculpture overlapped with other art forms. Artists, such as Robert Gober in the United States and Dinos and Jake Chapman in England, produced works that incorporated multiple sculptural objects within their multimedia installations.

The ready-made became the remix. Early in the twentieth century, Dada artist Marcel Duchamp famously exhibited unaltered found objects, such as a urinal and a snow shovel, as what he called *ready-mades*, or found sculptures. Numerous artists since then have experimented with found objects and images, including other Dada artists, the surrealists, the so-called junk sculptors of the 1950s, pop artists, and a range of artists who are interested in techniques of assemblage or the conceptual implications of the ready-made. Performance artists likewise have mixed everyday movements, sounds, props, and behaviors with more conventionally theatrical elements.

In the 1980s, in line with then up-to-the-minute theories of postmodernism, visual artists adopted *appropriation* as an approach to using ready-made objects and images. Appropriation artists comb both art history and vernacular culture for found objects, styles, images, subjects, and compositions and recombine details borrowed here and there into eclectic visual pastiches. Schlock and kitsch borrowings are readily combined with details from high art, architecture, and design.[9]

American Jeff Koons references the slick refinement and packaging of mass-produced consumer products in the creation of his art. Koons's gleaming *Rabbit* (1986) [1-4] is an appropriation of a novelty Mylar balloon, which the artist had cast in polished stainless steel. Koons knowingly fuses and confuses commercial glitz with the polished forms of earlier modern art and the everyday subjects of pop art sculptures. Like many of his other sculptures, in which the artist appropriates actual consumer objects (e.g., kitsch statuary and toys) and remakes them in a new medium as highly crafted luxury objects for wealthy collectors, Koons's *Rabbit* appears to warmly embrace our consumer lifestyle while, at the same time, coolly appraise the shallowness of a civilization that is devoid of deeper meaning.

In the twenty-first century, new terminology has begun to emerge to capture expanded practices and ideas around the concept of the ready-made. Borrowed from hip-hop culture and the world of music, the terms *sampling* and *remixing* are sometimes substituted for the older terms *appropriation* and *collage*. The use of such terms recognizes that found-object practices now encompass the new media and data networks of the digital age, which give artists instant access to an endless supply of images, sounds, and data, as well as the tools to recombine and reconfigure them at will. What this all means for the future of artistic production and the value of old and new media is open to debate.

New media attract artists. Video technology attracted experimenters within the field of art, notably Nam June Paik, as soon as it became available in the 1960s. During the 1990s, video became a prominent medium, in part because its time-based character supports a renewed interest in telling stories in art and exploring narrative structures. Also in the 1990s, numerous artists adopted digital technologies as small, powerful computers became affordable and software programs facilitated sophisticated graphic manipulations. Artists used digital tools both in the service of traditional media, designing the structure for a sculpture on a computer, for instance, and as a new formal and conceptual arena in itself. With the widespread use of DVD recording technology in the early 2000s, artists, and the gallery system that derives its profits from the sale

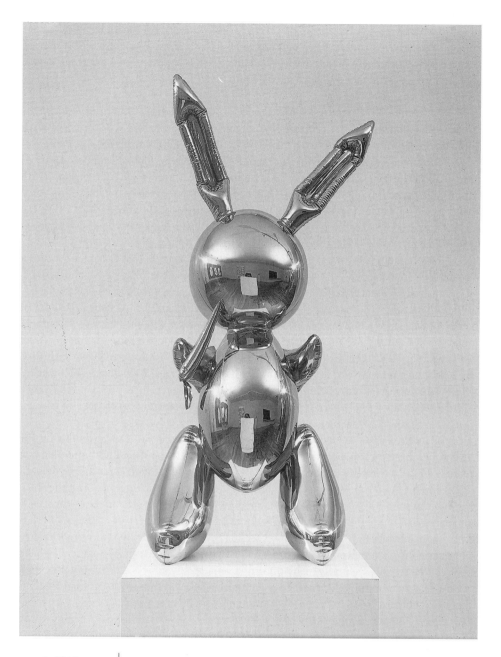

1-4 Jeff Koons | *Rabbit*, **1987**
Stainless steel, 40 15/16 x 18 15/16 x 11 3/4 inches (104 x 48 x 30 cm)
Courtesy of Sonnabend Gallery

of artworks, gained an important means of controlling the sale of video and computer artworks in limited editions to collectors. Of course, DVDs are easily copied, and in spite of copyright protection, bootleg versions of artists' original recordings are now traded and downloaded on the Internet and viewed on sites such as YouTube.

Meanwhile, fast-paced developments in digital video production and editing, holography, light art, and interactive computer sites have spawned new arenas for artistic exploration. These new media have also spilled over into the practice of other media; for example, new media are often incorporated into installation and performance art events.[10]

New technologies produce new paradigms. Today, digital technologies have the potential to alter images dramatically. Paradigms of the nature and structure of perception and conception are shifting. Particularly in the last half of the period this book covers, the availability of desktop computers and the increasing sophistication and ease of using computer graphics programs are bringing about "a transformation in the nature of visuality probably more profound than the break that separates mediaeval imagery from Renaissance perspective," in the words of art historian Jonathan Crary.[11] We are experiencing an epochal shift from an analog world, a world of everyday perception, to a digital world rendered in binary code.

The computer stores vast quantities of detailed information that is digitalized into a binary code. It enables an image of any subject to be manipulated, duplicated, transformed, and transmitted to a degree that is unprecedented in human history. Digital images, of subjects both real and imaginary, can look so convincing that the distinction between the actual and the made-up is almost impossible to detect. At the same time, unlike early viewers of photographs, today's audiences know that images are manipulated and manufactured all the time; they allow themselves to suspend disbelief in order to enjoy the illusion of reality. As a culture embracing and immersed in new media, we appear on the verge of a general willingness to suspend disbelief in the paradigm of a singular reality.

Virtual reality blurs boundaries. The blurring of the boundaries of fact and fabrication is epitomized by the development of *virtual reality* as a field of investigation. The term virtuality refers to "an image or space that is not real but appears to be. In our own time, these include cyberspace, the Internet, the telephone, television and virtual reality."[12] Virtual reality proper generally refers to a simulated, computer-generated environment. A viewer wears special goggles and earphones and interacts with the environment by moving her or his head or manipulating controls. Throughout the 1980s and early 1990s, the promise of virtual reality outstripped the actual achievement, but since then, advances in software and technology have made forays into virtual reality more satisfying for viewer and artist/designer alike. Experiments in virtual reality have been conducted mainly in the realm of computer gaming, but it is only a matter of time before designers/authors of interactive computer games create works in that medium that are embraced by an expanded definition of contemporary art.

Visual culture is duplicated and shared worldwide. In addition to enabling the rapid, radical manipulation of imagery, the computer now makes possible the almost instantaneous dissemination of images and data of all kinds. Since the mid-1990s, the growth of the Internet and World Wide Web has allowed users to transmit and receive images and other information within virtual space instantly all over the world. The digitalization of information is a powerful force in speeding up the sharing of artist-generated images in all media, as well as the appropriation by computer-savvy artists of information streams from other arenas of culture. In our role as viewers, we are no longer dependent on being in a specific place. We can plug into the Web or into our computer's memory anywhere we have access. Acknowledging this trend, the Whitney Museum included Internet art for the first time in its Biennial Exhibition in 2000.[13]

Vast quantities of images and data are flowing from every source imaginable—science, art, advertising, news, entertainment, governments, and, increasingly, ordinary citizens (using personal digital cameras, cell phone cameras, scanners, and webcams). Enormous digital databases are replacing physical archives (the latter ranging from libraries to family photo albums). The creative exploration and manipulation of digital databases, as virtual structures, is now central to the practice of an increasing number of new media artists. The practice of these artists can resemble that of a virtual architect—reconfiguring an existing built structure (the database) to accentuate or reveal new properties and ideas.

In addition to the accelerated exchange of information and images, another significant quality of global visual culture is the uniformity of imagery that is disseminated by the mass media. Through this process, many people share an identical storehouse of mediated experiences. Such high uniformity of memory never occurred prior to the invention of the Internet, television, radio, cinema, and photography. With each new technological breakthrough, the capacity of pop culture to overwhelm the sphere of private experience expands. Today's mass media information culture is channeled into formats that tend to homogenize the presentation of information. Contemporary artists, however, have found ways to counteract this phenomenon. Christian Marclay combined snippets from over a hundred movies to create *Video Quartet* (2003), which is projected simultaneously on four oversized screens, and David Byrne, widely known as a musician, utilizes Microsoft's PowerPoint software to produce imaginative illustrations and animation that are a far cry from the staid sameness of most PowerPoint presentations seen in the business or academic world.[14]

Although the languages of digital media are in their infancy, they are bound to have a radical impact on visual art as the twenty-first century continues to unfold. Artists who are concentrating on this area are pioneers in helping us to confront what it means to live in a world of accelerated information flow from multiple channels and to find ourselves entranced by manufactured virtual worlds. Meanwhile, many of the most interesting critical theories of the twenty-first century—evolving from the emerging disciplines of new media and visual culture studies—take on the expanding varieties and sites of artistic practices as key areas of analysis. Already, the paradigm that advancing technologies produces a heightening of homogenization is challenged: when there were only three primary television stations in the United States, the commonality of television viewing among the population increased. Now, with the exponential increase in television stations, as well as the rise of alternative media, there is less likelihood that any of us is tuned in to the same programming as our neighbors.

A Spectrum of Voices Emerges

In the United States in the period from the late 1960s to the start of the 1980s, the rebellions and successes of the women's movement and civil rights movement impacted art by opening up the stage to more voices. These newly visible participants brought new ideas to the field, as well as expanded ideas about means, media, and techniques for expressing those ideas. Since 1980, the highly visible activism of lesbian, gay, bisexual, and transgendered (LGBT) artists has added more voices to the mix. Although they have yet to achieve full equality, in terms of income, influence, prestige, and recognition, women and minority artists in the West have become empowered and have had a major impact on who makes art, what art is about, and how art is viewed and interpreted. Artists of color, women artists, and LGBT artists have been at the heart of discussions about contemporary art in the 1980s, 1990s, and today. The collective imagination of what is possible in art has opened up to acknowledge diversity.

Over the past thirty years, artists have become more conscious of diversity internationally as well as in their midst. For example, beginning about 1980, the American art world in general turned its attention to artistic developments in Western Europe. Subsequently, as a result of shifts in national borders, regimes, and political and economic structures, artists from all over the world have become widely known in Western Europe and North America, often because they have emigrated, contributing to their visibility.

Artists and audiences outside the West likewise are paying attention to developments both within and far beyond their borders. New collectors and art dealers are emerging all over the world, pulling the focus from Europe and the United States as the centers of gravity. From 1980 onward, with increasing complications, artists in Africa, South America, Asia, and the Pacific have been gaining visibility on a world stage. We live in an internationalized world, where people with different cultural knowledge are meeting, mixing, and negotiating histories, definitions, and boundaries. Artists use visual means to convey positions or paradoxes about where cultures draw boundary lines and what belongs on one side or the other.

To cite just one example of a complicated path followed by a contemporary artist, Cai Guo-Qiang was born in Quanzhou City, China, in 1957 and grew up during the Cultural Revolution. He studied stage design in Shanghai before moving to Japan in 1986. In 1995, he relocated to New York City. His art production includes large-scale drawings, installations, and performance events and has involved gunpowder, fireworks, Chinese herbal medicines, computers, and vending machines among many other materials and means. Cai's elaborate installation *Cultural Melting Bath*, which has been installed in various locations, including the Queens Museum in New York in 1997 [1-5], provides a symbol of the therapeutic cultural mixing that Cai hopes his art fosters. The installation includes a Chinese rock garden, banyan tree roots, and a Western-style hot tub infused with Chinese medicinal herbs, in which a multicultural array of museum visitors are invited to bathe together. A controversial artist in China for many years, today Cai travels frequently back to China to work and served as the art director of visual and special effects for the opening and closing ceremonies for the 2008 Summer Olympics in Beijing. His midcareer survey, which included his dramatic installation *Inopportune: Stage One* [1-1], toured internationally and was at the National Art Museum of China during the Olympics.

Globalization

Awareness of international developments in art has made the art world more dynamic and complex. But internationalism is not an unequivocal good, particularly when art production comes under market pressure from international institutions and corporations that support the production and display of contemporary art. Increasingly, the world is becoming linked by a global economy, a development that is inevitably influencing the production and reception of art. Consumer capitalism, especially the approach developed most aggressively in the United States, made huge strides during

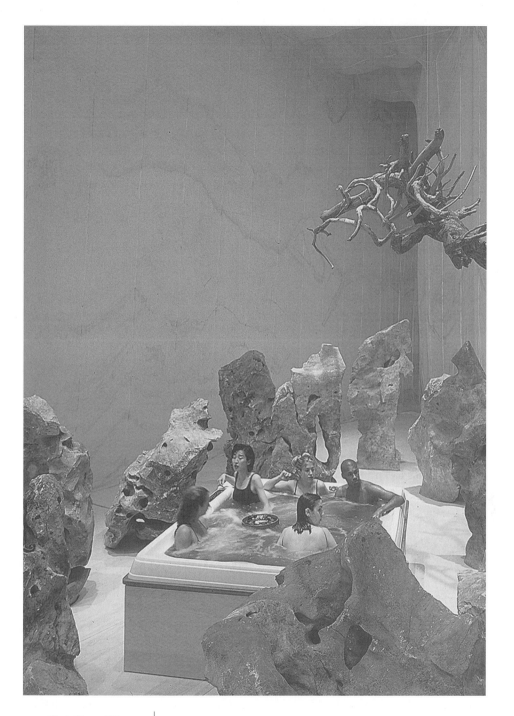

1-5 Cai Guo-Qiang | *Cultural Melting Bath: Projects for the 20th Century,* **1997**

First realized August 1997 at Queens Museum of Art, New York
18 Taihu rocks, hot tub with hydrotherapy jets, bathwater infused with herbs, banyan tree root, translucent fabric, and live birds
Dimensions variable, Various venues, Collection du Musée d'art contemporain de Lyon, Installation view at Queens Museum of Art, 1997
Photo by Hiro Ihara
Courtesy of Cai Studio

the contemporary period in extending its reach to global markets. The collapse of the communist system in the former Soviet Union and the economic rise of countries of the Pacific Rim, especially China with its steps toward a more capitalist-style economy, have opened up portions of the world that had been significantly insulated from capitalist business practices. Meanwhile, multinational corporations and supranational economic institutions, such as the World Bank and World Trade Organization, are engaged in activities that sometimes support and sometimes are in conflict with national interests. Systems of power are now a globalized network that is not centered in any one country (although the United States retains considerable power).

The emergence of a linked global society (linked both technologically and economically) has not resulted in international unity and worldwide equality; indeed, it is questionable whether any institution operating on a global scale can possibly represent the political, cultural, or aesthetic interests of the diverse individuals in all countries. According to Stuart Hall, "you see massive disparities of access, of visibility, huge yawning gaps between who can and can't be represented in any effective way."[15]

The global economy has impacted the entertainment and culture markets. International art fairs and biennial and triennial international contemporary art survey exhibitions have proliferated and are held in numerous cities on every continent (at least eighty-five locations by 2005), to the point where they are nearly impossible to keep up with.[16] Geographic mobility has become important, and artists, gallery dealers, critics, and collectors who have the resources to participate in international events increase their visibility and influence. The directors and curators who select artists and orchestrate the international events have remarkable status and power.

In addition to globalized markets, the emergence of new telecommunications technologies, specifically the continued spread of television throughout the world, and the rapid development of the computer and Internet for both personal and business use, has significantly promoted globalization. At the same time, not every person everywhere has access to a computer and the Internet, and new technologies reinforce privilege and power for those who are well connected to the flow of information.

Besides issues of access and visibility, another issue is the potential for homogenization of culture. One could argue that globalization is dehumanizing people and leveling out differences because it is bringing the same consumer products, images, and information to everyone all over the world. In terms of art, critic Julia A. Fenton asks, "Has the explosion of international art expositions around the world, and the mobility of artists from all cultures (either through the high art market or the internet) served to erase the particular in favor of the general—in style, content and theory? Do formal considerations again become primary when we have obliterated cultural boundaries and posited a new universality?"[17] Critics observe, for instance, that expensive but repetitive video and multimedia installations are ubiquitous in international surveys because they are eye-catching, as well as portable and reproducible.

At the same time, many artists continue to produce art whose materials, techniques, subjects, and forms appear to relate to local histories and identities. Such expressions of cultural difference often are genuine and can serve as a form of resistance to globalization by disrupting standardization. However, some of this kind of art is not sincere, but is a simulation of cultural difference, promoted by international capitalism because it is marketable. Fredric Jameson, an important Marxist theorist, pointed out the many contradictions in globalization, such as this argument about whether globalizing economic forces prefer to market cultural sameness or difference. Jameson further pointed out the irony that nationalism, once seen as driving European colonialism, is espoused today as a model by formerly colonized people who want to resist the forces of globalization.[18] Gilane Tawadros stated, "The idea of nation continues to grip our collective imagination, equally in the art gallery as on the football pitch. Nationality remains an important vehicle for expressing a shared identity, whether real or imagined."[19]

Theory Flexes Its Muscles

Numerous artists and critics active since 1980 have been heavily invested in theory and critical analysis. In the wake of conceptual art, art became increasingly theoretical and idea driven and began to sprout difficult and obscure branches. The direct embrace of theory seemed to crest midway through this period; by the early 1990s, influential art graduate schools in Europe and the United States were advocating the acquisition of theoretical knowledge and teaching analytical and interpretative skills. Discussing master of fine art degree programs in the United States, writer and curator Bennett Simpson maintained, "Employing conceptual, post-minimal, video and performance artists from the sixties and seventies, schools such as CalArts, UCLA, Art Center, Yale and the Whitney Museum's Independent Study Programme tended to privilege intellectual and critical study over the more traditional training in manual skills like drawing, figure painting and sculpture. 'Knowledge work' became detached from its antecedent, technical work."[20] (Although today technical skill and refined production values have become priorities again for many of the best-known artists' creations, often these works are made by assistants working for the artist or his institutional sponsor.)

Concepts from a range of theoretical perspectives, including postmodernism, semiotics, poststructuralism, feminism, and postcolonialism, to name several of the most influential, have shaped the creation and reception of art that has been produced since 1980. The theoretical critique of the period examined many arenas of visual culture, including the structure and biases of art history; the politics and practices of museums, galleries, and festivals; the nature and operation of art-market economics and how reputations are built; the visual means through which the mass media influence ideas and taste; and the representation in visual media of all kinds of identities revolving around gender, race, sexuality, age, religion, and nationality. We discuss theories in more depth as they become relevant in different thematic chapters. Here we just provide a brief overview.

Postmodernism became a catch-all term. The term *postmodernism* cropped up in art criticism in the 1970s, but became more commonly used in the 1980s. Writers and thinkers who engaged with postmodernism include Jean-François Lyotard, Jean Baudrillard, Julia Kristeva, Charles Jencks, and Umberto Eco. The term is vague and open ended, initially implying an opposition to some of the tenets of modernism, including modernists' confidence in social and technological progress; faith that history unfolds in a rational, linear direction; and belief in individual self-determination. Postmodernists are skeptical about progress; tend to be anti-elitist (for example, embracing kitsch as readily as the art of museums); think that the forms of culture are hybrid, eclectic, and heterogeneous, rather than pure and easily defined and contained; and believe that individuals are inevitably molded by culture.[21] Postmodernists believe that we are all prisoners, to some degree, of identities that are constructed for us by the artistic and popular media. Moreover, the contemporary world is becoming increasingly more artificial because secondhand images that are filtered through television, film, and other media now substitute for direct experiences and exert a powerful influence on how we perceive and understand the world. In addition, more and more mediated images and experiences are manufactured illusions with no basis in tangible reality—*simulacra*, to use Baudrillard's term. Baudrillard, according to art historian John Rajchman, "took the words 'simulation' and 'simulacrum' to describe the 'Beaubourg effect'—no longer able to distinguish model from copy, we had lost any sense of reality, leaving us only with 'irony,' hyperrealism, kitsch, quotation, appropriation."[22]

There is no single style associated with postmodernism; instead, any and all styles and visual vocabularies are valid, and pluralism rules. However, appropriation became a frequent strategy used by postmodernists. Most postmodern appropriationists mine the distant and recent past in a nostalgic fashion, usually with little true historical consciousness of what visual representations meant in their own past context. In addition to evoking nostalgia, postmodernists also quote from the past and vernacular culture with an attitude of irony or even parody.

Many artists use appropriation uncritically, simply adopting the approach as a contemporary artistic fashion. But some artists attend to the conceptual implications of the ready-made, using found objects and appropriated styles and images as a means to raise philosophical questions about whether it is possible for artists to be original or express authentic feelings and beliefs. Such artists include German Gerhard Richter, the Russian team Komar and Melamid, and American Cindy Sherman. The most politically motivated appropriationists, including American Sherrie Levine, also challenge as elitist the modernist identification and celebration of a handful of supposedly innovative artists. By appropriating, such artists imply that originality does not matter.

Although influential in the 1980s and 1990s, today the term *postmodernism* has become such a generalized catch-all term for so many different trends and ideas that it has lost nuance and functionality. Moreover, many people disavow the term as dualistic and as keeping Western aesthetics in the center by implying a dialectical relationship with modernism for all countertrends.

Art is understood as a kind of language. Influenced by the ideas of Swiss linguist Ferdinand de Saussure and the American philosopher Charles Sanders Peirce, both active in the late nineteenth century, artists applied complex permutations of *semiotics* (the science of signs) to the visual arts in the late twentieth century. While linguists analyze the structure of (verbal) language, semioticians open up virtually any field of human activity as a potential subject for an analysis of the signs that function within that field. Clothing styles, rules of etiquette, codes of conduct for men and for women—all these and countless other realms of experience can be analyzed in terms of semiotics.

As scholars (and artists) surmised, all the arts also function on the basis of the conventional use of signs, so semiotics is a powerful tool for analyzing the practice of art. Art topics, such as styles of representation, the rules of linear perspective, and the metalanguage of various media (painting, for instance, signals "tradition" in a way that video does not), are ripe for analysis through the magnifying glass of semiotics. For example, Cal Lane developed a process of cutting industrial metal with a welding torch to create lace patterns in automobile fenders, garden shovels [1-6], dumpsters, and other found objects. Lace-making is understood as a feminine textile practice used for domestic purposes, while metal-cutting signals a traditionally masculine skill used to

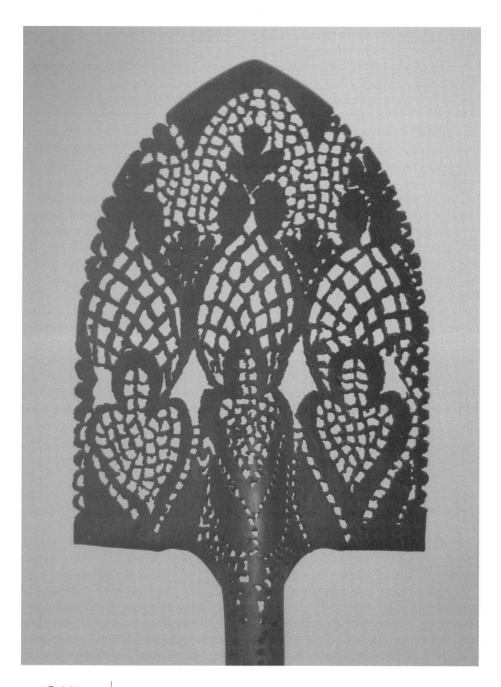

1-6 Cal Lane | *Shovels,* **2005**

Plasma cut steel
Courtesy of Foley Gallery

make tools and machines. Lane, who is female, creates semiotic dissonance by mixing the two.

Theories associated with *poststructuralism* are closely identified with postmodernism and semiotics. What poststructuralism added to the mix was the concept that the underlying structure of a language or any other symbolic system is not fixed and permanent.[23] With individual variations, these poststructuralist thinkers argued that any symbolic system or cultural artifact (such as a language, a work of literature, a painting, or a social system)—what they called a *text*—can be shown to have internal contradictions and hidden ideologies. Poststructuralists use a strategy developed by French philosopher Jacques Derrida, known as *deconstruction*, to analyze visual and verbal texts. Deconstruction looks at a text or symbolic system in terms of the underlying worldview that gave rise to it, exposing contradictions and hidden biases in order to challenge the validity of the worldview as well as the text. Derrida also argued that the meanings of texts are unstable because different readers (or viewers, in the case of visual texts) bring their own worldviews to their reading and looking, which skew interpretation. No text has any single, correct interpretation; meanings change with the reader, the time, and the context.[24]

According to postmodernists and poststructuralists, truth and reality are not as truthful and real as they may seem; in fact, there are many truths and many realities. All truths and realities are relative and contingent, constructed by culture, dependent on context, and subject to negotiation and change; none is inherent in the natural order of things. Moreover, today the contradictions are more apparent because the cultural landscape is filled with texts that express competing worldviews, simultaneously available and bleeding over into each other's domain because of the rapid flow of information from numerous sources constantly bombarding us. These texts interact and compete with one another (creating a condition of *intertextuality*, to use the term favored by Derrida and Roland Barthes, another influential French theorist). Poststructuralist thinkers believe that the onslaught of information in our media-saturated society has made it impossible for any single worldview to dominate. Instead, boundaries and divisions between categories of all kinds are eroding. In particular, the dualities, or binary pairs, that are so common in Western thinking and culture are no longer convincing as polar opposites. Male and female, gay and straight, white and black, public and private, painting and sculpture, high art and low art—distinctions between these and other categories dissolve in a postmodern world, and the elements merge into hybrids.

Feminism and postcolonialism offer bolder, broader perspectives. The perspectives of feminism and postcolonialism have profoundly affected contemporary visual culture. Feminists and postcolonialists challenge artists, art historians, critics, and audiences to consider politics and social issues. Feminists look at experience from the perspective of gender and are particularly concerned to ensure that women have the same rights and opportunities as men. Feminist theoretical critiques analyze hierarchical structures that contribute to male dominance, what feminists call *patriarchy*, that is, the cultural beliefs, rules, and structures that reinforce and sustain masculine values and male power. A key area of feminist analysis in the visual arts is the *gaze*, a term used to refer to how categories of people are stereotyped in visual representations by gender, race, sexuality, and other factors.

Postcolonialists are interested in cultural interactions of all kinds (in politics, economics, religion, the arts, philosophy, the mass media, and so on) among peoples of different nations, regions, and communities. They examine how peoples' histories and identities demonstrate the economic, political, social, and psychological legacy of colonialism in particular locations, which oppressed indigenous peoples and resulted in *hybridity* and *syncretism*, or a mingling of peoples and cultures. They also analyze migrations and displacements of peoples (*diasporas* and *nomadism*, to use two of the current terms) and highlight the diversity of cultures that coexist in contemporary communities. Postcolonialists' attention to the visual cultures of Africa, Asia, the Americas, and the Pacific has helped foster the internationalization of the contemporary art world.

Many different theories have influenced feminism and postcolonialism, and ideas and positions are constantly mutating.[25] The perspectives are usually multidisciplinary, drawing from literature, history, sociology, anthropology, and other disciplines. Since 1980, critics and artists have used deconstructive strategies to analyze, or "decode," how power functions to limit the achievements and potential of women and postcolonial people around the world. Feminists and postcolonialists have applied other theories as well, including Marxism and psychoanalysis, and have contributed theories of their own. Postcolonialists have promoted the use of theoretical models that attempt to understand the visual arts of various cultures on their own terms, rather than in comparison to art traditions in Europe and the United States.[26]

The theories discussed here, as well as others that were not discussed, such as Marxist and psychoanalytic theories, permeate the production, reception, and interpretation of contemporary art. But the explicit embrace of theory has not been universal or constant over the past three decades, and its influence is often diffuse and unacknowledged, rather than systematic. For example, there has been a widespread cultural backlash against feminism; as a result, younger women artists are often reluctant to call themselves feminists, even when their art and ideas support feminist tenets.

Artists didn't seem to pay attention to theory as much after 1990, and the debates of the previous decade over modernism, postmodernism, and poststructuralism died down. According to curator Toby Kamps, in "an ideologically uncertain moment, artistic strategies of the 1980s—appropriation, critiques of commodification, deconstruction—seemed empty or calculating. Instead, artists took up accessibility, communication, humor, and play. As a style, Postmodernism, positing stylistic eclecticism, social criticism, and end-of-history irony, appeared bankrupt; as an attitude, however, it was the definitive zeitgeist. The art of the 1990s, with its interest in complexity, multivalency, and ambiguity, mirrored an uncertain, transitional period."[27]

Although in general over the past fifteen years artists have seemed less committed to strong political positions and not as well versed in academic theories, that does not mean that art has lacked meaningful content. To the contrary, a preoccupation with deep moral and ethical questions and resonant themes, such as political agency, spirituality, beauty, violence, sexuality, transience, extinction, memory, and healing, is a powerful current in the most recent art. The real world is treacherous and volatile. According to Richard Cork, the question posed by Joseph Beuys's 1985 work *The End of the Twentieth Century* still resonates: "Is [our era] about to terminate prematurely in a nuclear apocalypse, or will it be succeeded by an era which asserts a less destructive set of values?"[28] Or as Homi K. Bhabha wrote: "The '80s inaugurated a dream of difference which is now being haunted by horror and doubt: abhorrence of the 'deterritorialized flows' of global terror networks; doubts about the feasibility of global politics with the increase in 'homeland' security and international surveillance; doubts about preemptive strikes; doubts about war; doubts about our rights and responsibilities for the world and ourselves. What happened to the dream?"[29]

We end this section with an extended example in which we unpack some of the complexities of how actual artists have engaged with theory in their creative practice. Our example addresses contemporary artists who knowingly engage with the language of abstract art in a semiotic manner.

Abstraction is intimately associated with the high Modernism of the twentieth century in Western art, which is often a target and devalued in contemporary theory. The "heroic" generation of post–World War II American abstract painters, including Abstract Expressionists, such as Jackson Pollock, believed fervently in art as self-expression and maintained that artists should work intuitively as much as possible, relying on the subconscious to stimulate vital, uncensored gestures and marks. They believed that every artist has a unique, "authentic" touch, as identifiable as a person's handwriting, which will emerge if the artist creates in a free process. They also believed that receptive viewers have a visceral response to the resulting paintings, echoing the passion of their creator. In contrast, many in our current age are skeptical that genuine self-expression is possible and argue that our "individual" expressions and responses are really just reflections of cultural conditioning. Maybe at one time a painter could make a fluid gesture that was truly spontaneous, but today's painters must be self-consciously aware that a gestural style is supposed to be a sign of freedom, and thus they can no longer make gestures in a totally unself-conscious manner.

Artists today who engage with abstraction in a semiotic way may adopt characteristics of the abstract expressionists or minimalists precisely because they know that those devices have become conventions that a knowledgeable audience recognizes. One artist may make obviously contrived gestures to subvert the notion of painting as spontaneous expression; another artist may choose a grid or another convention of geometric abstraction to critique an earlier generation's dreams of social utopia and "encode" a warning about ideological rigidity. For example, American painter Peter Halley has used rectangular motifs that are reminiscent of Piet Mondrian and other painters of geometric abstraction to design images that hint at diagrams for a network of passages, perhaps in a prison ward or underground bunker. American Rachel Lachowitz's lipstick-coated copies of minimalist sculptures mock the supposed "masculine" objectivity and logic encoded in those impersonal, hard-edged structures. Lachowitz's choice of lipstick as an art material signals, in semiotic terms, a conscious application of feminist theory to the arena of art world politics. Her choice is also inflected with humor and irony, a sign that, in the end, she realizes that her action will probably have little consequence.

Is abstract art a worn-out style from the past? Even in the face of skepticism, some contemporary artists choose to work abstractly with heartfelt commitment rather than irony. Those who argue that art is valuable when it provides a focus for perception and contemplation often prefer abstraction. The reductions of abstraction yield a strong contrast to the visual overload of mass-media images. And without recognizable images or narrative to occupy their thoughts, viewers are not distracted from the immediate sensory experience of looking. Today's artists who are sincere about abstraction are not necessarily returning to the abstract expressionists' notion of abstraction as self-expression. As painter Laurie Fendrich wrote, abstraction "is also about ideas—the complex struggle between order and chaos, for example, or how the flux of the organic world modifies the rigor of geometry."[30] Abstract painting can serve as an antidote to our hypermediated society.

Art Meets Contemporary Culture

One of the leitmotifs of art over the past hundred years has been the blurring of distinctions between the realm of art and other categories of culture. In the contemporary period, the dissolution of boundaries between art and life has continued in a number of directions. There continues to be cross-fertilization between high and low art. The use of found objects and the ready-made, along with appropriation and remixing of images and styles, remains significant, frequently involving borrowings from consumer and popular culture. For example, the alternative use of comic-book and cartoon imagery and styles has become a thriving subculture of visual culture as a whole and inflects the art of Raymond Pettibon, Laylah Ali, Glen Baxter, and Christian Schumann, among numerous others. Japanese *anime* (animation films) and *manga* comics, with their supercute, superviolent, and supersexualized imagery done in an insistently flattened style, have exerted a particularly strong influence on the younger generation of Japanese visual artists. The painters Takashi Murakami and Yoshitomo Nara, for instance, are known internationally for their characteristic approach to painting in the "superflat" style (a term coined by Murakami).

Distinctions between art and the larger visual culture are dissolving and even disappearing. Artists bring nonart experiences into the sphere of art; they also introduce art into the larger visual culture. Artists mingle their works with other products of visual culture by choosing not to limit their display opportunities to art venues only. Artists, according to curator Benjamin Weil, "have been exploring approaches akin to an ambient strategy, focusing on ways to insert their projects within the chaos of an overmediated public sphere. Billboards, usually designed to advertise commercial products, have been used by artists such as the late Felix Gonzalez-Torres to 'sell' ideas. Marquees of abandoned theaters are ideal surfaces for the placement of inconspicuous messages; stickers, posters, and other forms of street culture become compelling instruments in the hands of artists."[31]

Popular culture, including television, films, rock music, and video games, has a powerful influence on artists. At the same time, art appears increasingly to be in competition with the bold graphics, seductive objects, and lively stories of commerce and entertainment. Some artists adapt by making art that has become more like entertainment, adopting strategies of display and production from popular culture; installing multimedia spectacles in exhibition sites; crossing over into the domains of film, music, and fashion; and serving professionally as consultants and even entrepreneurs in commercial enterprises, such as restaurants and magazines. Criticizing the trend, photographer Jeff Wall said, "I think a new kind of art has emerged since the '70s, a kind that is easier to appreciate, more like entertainment, more attached to media attitudes.... It's much closer to entertainment and depends on production value and on spectacle in a way that serious art never did before."[32]

The pervasiveness of new information and communication technologies, which have been embraced enthusiastically by young people around the world, is a powerful influence on the production of contemporary art in countries from Korea to Brazil. Not only do we live in a new world of greatly expanded information, but the structure of information has changed dramatically. The decentralized Internet of Google, YouTube, Wikipedia, MySpace, and blogs is vastly different from the world of physical libraries; handwritten diaries; and printed books, newspapers, and encyclopedias. The Internet is bringing us closer to the concept of a universal library or marketplace where one can search for scholarly articles, news, recipes, past acquaintances, maps, weather reports, medical information, pornography, consumer products, and trivia or watch video on almost any subject imaginable, in formats from movies to television programs to live footage from webcams that ordinary people have installed in their "private" living spaces. The creation of knowledge is social because anyone can add to the flow of information. Wikipedia, for instance, the online encyclopedia begun in 2001, now has more than 75,000 active contributors.

The term *rhizome* was used conceptually by French philosophers Gilles Deleuze and Félix Guattari in their book *A Thousand Plateaus: Capitalism and Schizophrenia* to describe nonhierarchical knowledge networks that allow for multiple entry and exit points.[33] They borrowed the term from the botanical rhizome, a category that includes ginger, some species of iris and ferns, and similar plants that send out horizontal stems and shoots from their nodes. Deleuze and Guattari used the term to characterize research and thought that is interconnected but has no beginning and end, has no set pathways through the system, resists rigid organization and dominating ideas, and has the capacity to link together heterogeneous elements. Cartography, which allows you to enter a map from any point, rather than follow a set path, is a long-standing example of a rhizomatic system. Rhizome theory has gained currency in cultural discourse because so many of today's systems of representing and interpreting knowledge are fluid, nonhierarchical, nonlinear, and decentered. Computer-based information technology, notably the World Wide Web, is a prime case of a rhizomatic model of knowledge. Any bit of information exists within an enormous network: anyone can enter the information stream anywhere and move among multiple pathways by links, creating a synthesis of potentially unlike elements; anyone can search, duplicate, manipulate, add to, or transmit information.

British artist Keith Tyson's monumental artwork *Large Field Array*[34] (2006–07) [1-7] is rhizomatic in structure and conception. The sculpture comprises three hundred modular units, most of which were formed from polystrene into implied two-foot cubes; the cubes are arranged into a grid occupying both the floor and walls of a gallery when installed. Each highly crafted unit is unique and references something recognizable from the natural world, science, popular culture, consumer products, art history, or a range of other sources. Individual sculptures include an airborne skateboarder, fungi, stacked cans of beer, a volcano, a model of the Hoover dam, a man spanking a boy with a belt, a square patch of cornfield, a rainbow over a jackpot, and an elaborate house of cards, as well as appropriations from other artists, including Claes Oldenburg, the Chapman Brothers, and Yves Klein. A visitor can move through the cubes on the floor via multiple pathways of one's own choosing: forward, sideways, diagonally. Although Tyson fosters certain associations through his choices for juxtapositions of individual sculptures, each visitor is ultimately responsible for imagining his or her own visual, psychological, and philosophical connections and meanings among the disparate units. A kind of three-dimensional analog version of an online encyclopedia, *Large Field Array* proposes that everything can be linked without the control or singularity of a hierarchical structure. Tyson said that *Large Field Array* is a celebration of our transi-

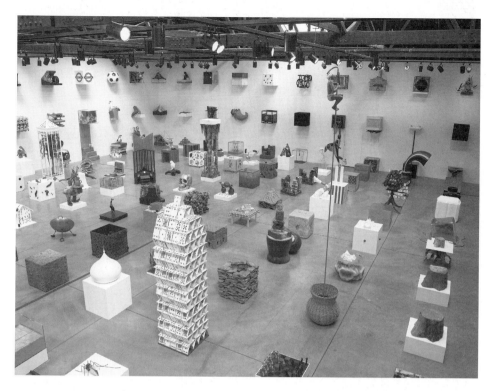

1-7 **Keith Tyson** | Installation view of Keith Tyson: *Large Field Array*, PaceWildenstein, New York
September 7-October 20, 2007
Photo by Ellen Labenski
courtesy of PaceWildenstein, New York

tion from an industrial to an information age. "[We] embrace complexity as a positive force. We can trust the rhizome to look after itself.... The system will take care of itself. And I think we are more capable—this generation is more capable—of trusting the dynamic, than any other generation before us."[35]

New rhizomatic artworks, such as Tyson's, emphasize abrupt juxtapositions, linking, fragmentation, and multiplicity. They require new forms of visual literacy, asking their audiences to cross borders between genres and subjects and to make a leap of faith that connections exist even though the web of knowledge is too large and complex for anyone to master. Tyson's artwork, assembling three hundred sculptures into one cohesive installation, embodies a reconnoitering of reality from the diverse perspectives represented (including pop culture, science, religion, history, politics, sexuality). Tyson's *Large Field Array* implies that no one field of knowledge can provide all the information or answers or frame the most probing questions. In a similar spirit, *Themes of Contemporary Art* is a reconnoitering mission through the past thirty years of art. We end by reasserting this chapter's initial premise: *content matters*, even if the meanings are open ended. It is with this fundamental idea in mind that we turn to an examination of contemporary artworks that embody seven resonating and interlinked themes: identity, the body, time, place, language, science, and spirituality.

Notes

1. We discuss this installation in a profile on Eduardo Kac after chapter 7, Science. For additional information, see Eduardo Kac's website, at www.ekac.org, or the published book about the project: *The Eighth Day: The Transgenic Art of Eduardo Kac* (Tempe: Institute for Studies in the Arts, Arizona State University, 2003).

2. Co-curators for the Wrong Gallery exhibition were curator Massimiliano Gioni and artist Maurizio Cattelan.

3. Erika Doss, *Twentieth-Century American Art* (Oxford, England: Oxford University Press, 2002), p. 203.

4. We discuss an ongoing series of large-scale installations in the Turbine Hall at the Tate Modern in a profile after chapter 5, Place.

5. Stephen Koch, "Andy Warhol, 1928–1987," *Artforum*, April 2003, p. 94.

6. Haim Steinbach, "Haim Steinbach Talks to Tim Griffin," interview by Tim Griffin, *Artforum*, April 2003, p. 230.

7. Neal Benezra and Olga M. Viso, *Distemper: Dissonant Themes in the Art of the 1990s* (Washington, D.C.: Hirshhorn Museum and Sculpture Garden, Smithsonian Institution), p. 10. An exhibition catalog.

8. Doss, *Twentieth-Century American Art*, p. 217.

9. Artists working with appropriation in the 1980s and after include Sigmar Polke in Germany, Jeff Koons, Mike Bidlo, and Louise Lawler in the United States; Carlo Maria Mariani in Italy; and Wang Guangyi in China.

10. Some active practitioners within the expanding field of new media include Rebecca Horn, Jon Kessler, Alan Rath, Laurie Anderson, Margot Lovejoy, Pipilotti Rist, Mariko Mori, Jeffrey Shaw, and Michal Rovner.

11. Quoted in Liz Wells, *Photography: A Critical Introduction* (London and New York: Routledge, 1997), p. 257.

12. Nicholas Mirzoeff, *An Introduction to Visual Culture* (London and New York: Routledge, 1999), p. 91.

13. In the age of mechanical reproduction, such processes as photolithography allowed newspapers and magazines to duplicate and disseminate images. The electronic age, however, is different in degree as well as in kind from preceding eras because imagery is now sent around the world at the speed of light.

14. For descriptions of Byrne's work, see David Byrne, *Envisioning Emotional Epistemological Information* (New York: Steidl and Pace-McGill Gallery, 2003).

15. Quoted in Stuart Hall and Michael Hardt, "Changing States: In the Shadow of Empire," in Gilane Tawadros, ed., *Changing States: Contemporary Art and Ideas in an Era of Globalisation* (London, Institute of International Visual Arts, 2004), p. 133. Much of the preceding discussion is indebted to Hall's arguments.

16. See the map, "Biennial and Triennial International Contemporary Art Surveys Worldwide," in *Universal Experience: Art, Life, and the Tourist's Eye* (Chicago: Museum of Contemporary Art; New York: Distributed Art Publishers, 2005), pp. 204–205.

17. Julia A. Fenton, "World Churning: Globalism and the Return of the Local," *Art Papers* 25, May–June 2001, p. 11.

18. See Fredric Jameson, "Globalization as a Philosophical Issue," in Fredric Jameson and Masao Miyohsi (Durham, N.C.: Duke University Press, 1998), pp. 75–76.

19. Gilane Tawadros, "Nation," in Tawadros. ed., *Changing States*, p. 71

20. Bennett Simpson, "Pushing an Open Door: The Artist as Culture Broker," in *The Americans*: New Art (London: Booth-Clibborn Editions, 2001), p. 296. An exhibition catalog.

21. Prior to postmodernism, various artists, including the Dadaists and many surrealists, were also interested in kitsch.

22. John Rajchman, "Unhappy Returns," *Artforum*, April 2003, p. 61. "Beaubourg" is a nickname for the Centre Georges Pompidou, a cultural center that opened in Paris in 1977.

23. Influential theorists of poststructuralism include the French intellectuals Michel Foucault, Jacques Derrida, Roland Barthes, and Jacques Lacan.

24. See chapter 6, Language, for a further discussion of poststructuralism.

25. The many feminist thinkers who have influenced the visual arts include Julia Kristeva, Luce Irigaray, Hélène Cixous, Gayatri Chakravorty Spivak, Craig Owens, Laura Mulvey, Lucy Lippard, and Griselda Pollock. Thinkers associated with postcolonialism include Homi K. Bhabha, Edward Said, Rasheed Araeen, Paul Gilroy, and Olu Oguibe. Intellectuals involved with both feminism and postcolonialism include bell hooks, Trinh T. Minh-Ha, and Ella Habiba Shohat.

26. See chapter 2, Identity, and chapter 3, The Body, for further discussions of feminism and postcolonialism.

27. Toby Kamps, "Lateral Thinking: Art of the 1990s," in *Lateral Thinking: Art of the 1990s* (La Jolla, Calif.: Museum of Contemporary Art San Diego, 2002), p. 15. An exhibition catalog.

28. Richard Cork, "The End of the Twentieth Century," in *Breaking Down the Barriers: Art in the 1990s*, by Richard Cork (New Haven, Conn.: Yale University Press, 2003), p. 628.

29. Homi K. Bhabha, "Making Difference," *Artforum*, April 2003, p. 76.

30. Laurie Fendrich, *Why Painting Still Matters* (Bloomington, Ind.: Phi Delta Kappa Educational Foundation, 2000), p. 16.

31. Benjamin Weil, "Ambient Art and Our Changing Relationship to the Art Idea," in *010101: Art in Technological Times* (San Francisco: San Francisco Museum of Modern Art, 2001), pp. 58–59. An exhibition catalog.

32. Jeff Wall, "Jeff Wall talks to Bob Nickas," interview by Bob Nickas, *Artforum*, March 2003, p. 87.

33. Gilles Deleuze and Félix Guattari, *A Thousand Plateaus: Capitalism and Schizophrenia*, translated by Brian Massumi (Minneapolis: University of Minnesota Press, 1987).

34. The title of Tyson's artwork, *Large Field Array*, makes reference to the Very Large Array (VLA), an astronomy observatory located in a barren stretch of the New Mexico landscape. VLA's power as a scientific research instrument—an outlook on the cosmos—stems from the holistic gathering of information from the twenty-seven large independent radio antennae (each arm is thirteen miles in length) that are arranged in an enormous Y-shape configuration.

35. Keith Tyson, quoted in an online interview, "Keith Tyson—Large Field Array, Part 2," http://www.tabblo.com/studio/stories/view/255949/?nextnav=favs&navuser=233142 (accessed June 27, 2008).

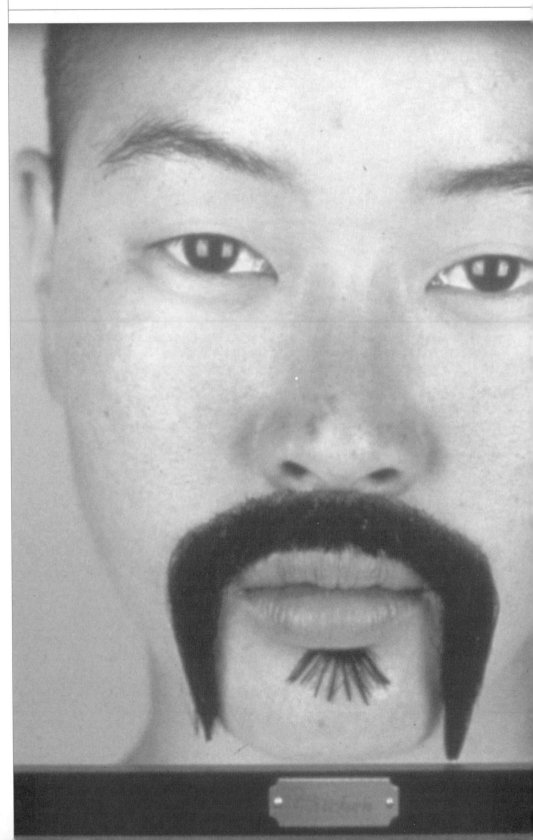

Detail of 2-8

CHAPTER TWO

Identity

Beginning art students often fervently believe that they want to find out who they are as unique individuals and convey this in their art. In our own teaching, we find that many students admire the stance (if not always the art) of the "heroic" generation of abstract expressionist painters, active after World War II, who strove to express their personal feelings and their sense of their own radical individuality. The postwar generation asked questions that philosophers have been asking since ancient times: What is the true nature of the self? What does it mean to be human? For some of these artists, including Jackson Pollock and Mark Rothko, the true self was a self-directed, free individual. Influenced by Jungian psychology and existentialist philosophy, they held up the ideal of an integrated, stable, unique self who acts independently with meaningful intentions and a coherent inner psychology. According to Claire Pajaczkowska, the belief in a true inner self is "liberal humanism," where "answers to the question of what it is to be human [are] phrased in terms of philosophical concepts such as 'self-knowledge,' 'consciousness,' and 'thought,' which emphasize the significance of self rather than the significance of division."[1]

In contrast, artists who want to express who they are sometimes identify themselves in terms of a communal as well as an individual sense of self. James Luna's performance *The Artifact Piece* (1987) [2-1] provides an example. Luna, born in California in 1950, strongly identifies with being Luiseño and has lived on the La Jolla Indian Reservation for more than thirty years. In *The Artifact Piece*, Luna turned himself into a human artifact in an anthropology museum by laying clad only in a breechcloth on a display case in the San Diego Museum of Man, in a section devoted to the Kumeyaay Indians, who once inhabited San Diego County. Labels beside his body explained his physical scars (caused by drunkenness and fights) and hidden emotional scars (caused by life experiences); personal objects, such as favorite books, music cassettes, and family photographs, were displayed nearby. According to writer Linda Weintraub, "The gallery was otherwise given over to relics and dioramas honoring the revered aspects of Native American life. No part of its permanent display addressed the real problems that beset the living representatives of these people. Rather, the museum placed Indian life in the same category as dinosaur skeletons and plant fossils. Luna shattered the impression

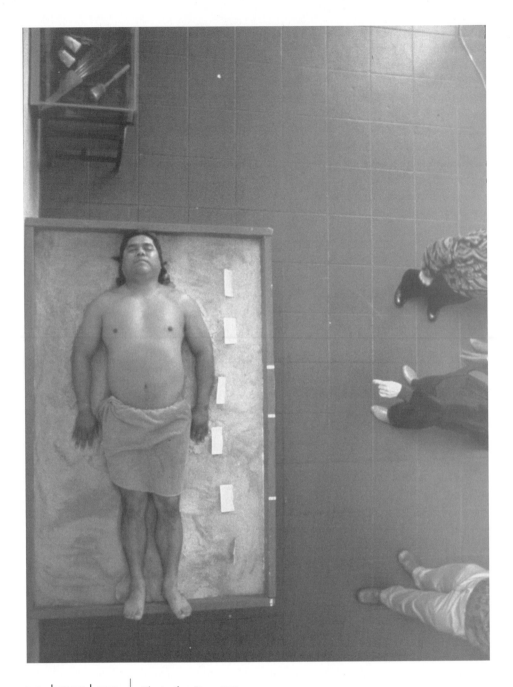

2-1 |ames Luna │ *The Artifact Piece*, **1987**

Mixed media installation and performance, dimensions variable
Courtesy of the artist (from the photo collections of the San Diego Museum of Man)

that Indians are extinct by presenting himself as a breathing artifact."[2] Throughout his
ensuing career, Luna has continued to make art that interweaves autobiography, indigenous cultural histories, and Luiseño traditions and that exposes Westernized stereotypes
about Native Americans.

Luna matured as an artist in the mid-1980s, when identity, defined in terms of communal affiliations, was becoming popular in the art world. Critic Lucy R. Lippard wrote an influential 1990 book, *Mixed Blessings: New Art in a Multicultural America*, in which she brought attention to the vitality of contemporary artists who were representing themselves in communal terms. Lippard argued strongly in support of the artists' desire to connect with their cultures, stating that "an individual 'identity' forged without relation to anyone or anything else hardly deserves the name."[3] She maintained that identity is relational and defined by our similarities and differences with others. Lippard advocated embracing a collective self, expressed through naming oneself as a member of various cultural groups and representing oneself verbally and visually in terms of shared identities. The artists Lippard foregrounded came of age during the feminist and civil rights movements of the 1960s and 1970s. They were proud of their roots and affiliations and readily named themselves members of identity-based groups ("women artists," "black artists," "Chicano artists," "Asian American artists"). They created artworks that represented their communal identities and often at the same time advanced social agendas.

A plethora of exhibitions in the second half of the 1980s and the first half of the 1990s turned a spotlight on identity defined collectively, especially identity defined in terms of race, ethnicity, gender, or sexuality; the exhibitions simultaneously set off a firestorm of debate on the value, ethics, and meaning of art and exhibitions that engage issues of identity. Two high-profile exhibitions were particularly contentious: Magiciens de la Terre (1989) at the Centre Pompidou in Paris, and the 1993 Whitney Biennial (sometimes nicknamed "the Identity Biennial").[4] The former showed contemporary artists from previously colonized cultures in Africa, Oceania, and elsewhere next to artists from the West, trying to treat all artists as equals. The exhibition was criticized for romanticizing artists from cultures outside the West and turning them into exotic "Others" in comparison to supposedly "mainstream" Western artists, and for not recognizing diversity among artists from the same location. The 1993 Whitney Biennial was likewise criticized for creating overly simplified identity categories and for curatorial selections of artworks that were seen as didactic, highly political in tone, and lacking in aesthetic appeal. Both exhibitions also had their defenders, who saw their multicultural worldview as validating and empowering for artists from ethnic, racial, and gender groups who were underrepresented in the mainstream art world.[5]

In this chapter, we provide some historical context about identity as a theme in art and then look at evolving concepts about identity over the past thirty years, discussing shifting terms that go in and out of favor. Although identity is always an implicit factor in the creation and interpretation of art, the use of identity as a highly theorized and often politically charged theme in art is a recent development. Contemporary artists are self-conscious about identity to a degree that was rare in previous periods. The theories, ideas, terms, and definitions surrounding the large topic of identity are numerous and have been morphing constantly in the period that this book covers, and the value of emphasizing identity has generated much debate.

The artists whose works could be discussed under the heading of identity are numerous and diverse. Every kind of art medium is involved, every scale, every type of forum and venue, and many purposes and ideas. The artworks we show in this chapter are varied but only hint at the range of what artists have produced. Many of the images show the human figure (and thus relate to the theme of chapter 3, The Body). Certainly the body carries many signs of identity (hair, skin color, gestures, posture, clothing, and so on), but identity is expressed by other means as well, including by words, symbols, objects, and settings. These may be used alone or in conjunction with figurative imagery. For example, Pepón Osorio's *La Bicicleta* [2-2] is a found bicycle that the artist embellished with plastic streamers and knickknacks. Osorio's sculpture is both a tribute to the vernacular culture of his native Puerto Rico, where ordinary objects are often exuberantly decorated (although rarely to the degree of Osorio's bicycle), and an exploration of his heightened awareness of cultural identity after he moved to New York City as an adult.

Identity in Art History

Within the Western tradition, two genres with enduring histories, the portrait and the self-portrait, are directly linked to the artistic exploration of the theme of identity in art today. Rembrandt, Pablo Picasso, and Frida Kahlo are among those who invested significant energy in recording their own likenesses. Indeed, popular myths that romanticize artists as a special category of people are fed by such representations; think of the dramatic self-portraits of Vincent van Gogh. Closer in time to ourselves, postwar artists of note, including the British painter Francis Bacon and the American pop artist Andy Warhol, produced influential bodies of work that featured a range of portraits and self-portraits. Each artist of talent who took up these genres did so in a way that revitalized the traditions. Bacon, for instance, revealed a startling capacity for retaining an identifiable likeness of a specific person while forcing the painted representation to undergo

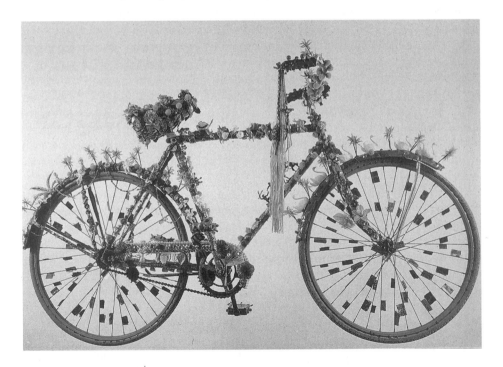

2-2 Pepón Osorio | *La Bicicleta*, 1985
Mixed mediums, approximately 42 x 60 x 24 inches
© Pepón Osorio, courtesy of Ronald Feldman Fine Arts, New York

expressive contortions. Warhol, through a pristine, almost mechanical, application of color, created mass media icons of recognizably famous persons.

In the contemporary period, a number of artists have continued to create images and objects that are anchored in the familiar traditions of portraiture and self-portraiture. Americans Chuck Close, Alex Katz, and Susanna Coffey; British artist Lucian Freud; Italian artist Francisco Clemente; and Chinese artist Zhang Xiaogang, for instance, have each demonstrated how representations of human likeness are manifested through the prism of artistic style.

A deep, implicit connection between art and human identity has existed throughout art history. How the world views you, how you view yourself, how you view others—these fundamental dimensions of human identity have influenced artists' ideas, emotions, and creative expressions in classical Greece, in eighteenth-century sub-Saharan Africa, and during the Tang Dynasty in China. An artwork's subject matter, its formal properties, and the very materials it is created from reflect the identity characteristics, on the individual and broader cultural level, of both the artist and the intended audience.

While a connection between art and identity has existed throughout history, the ways in which humans understand themselves, or conceive of their identity, are constantly changing. In some periods and in some societies (such as the dynastic period of Egypt's Old Kingdom), these changes seem almost glacial in their slowness and subtlety. In other periods, changes have occurred at a cataclysmic pace. For example, the Enlightenment in Europe and North America was marked by profound social, political, and scientific changes that altered how humans understood themselves. Starting with the American Revolution in 1776, a series of conflicts over the right of self-determination produced a new democratic order, in which the individual came to be seen as the agent of his own free will, rather than part of a rigid social structure.

In our own contemporary period, many interweaving forces and events have reshaped concepts of identity on a worldwide basis. Among them have been rapid technological change, the dismantling of the Soviet Union, incremental victories for feminist and civil rights causes, the rising world influence of societies beyond Europe and the United States, the ever-increasing speed of information transfer, the globalizing of economic systems, and the influence of feminist, postmodern, and postcolonial theories on a range of intellectual and cultural arenas. Such changes have not taken place everywhere or equally, of course, but they have occurred in a wide range of societies over the past two and half decades. Think of the expanding economies of the Pacific Rim, the unification of much of Europe within one monetary system, and the dismantling of apartheid in South Africa. Such changes in the fabric of whole societies, even when transformation has been followed by a period of retrenchment or reversal, inevitably influence artists. A new international awareness, a new vision of possibility, produces new understandings of what it means to be human; these understandings, in turn, are embodied in artistic portrayals of human identity that look unlike the art of the past.

The current interest in diverse identities is a rediscovery and reinterpretation of their relevance. Through trade and colonization, Europeans in the nineteenth and early twentieth centuries, for example, were well aware that cultural Others existed elsewhere in the world. While recent and ongoing changes in concepts of identity mirror the dramatic and decisive interactions in other periods (e.g., the deep influence of colonial Spain on the art and identity of the Native peoples of Mexico during the sixteenth century), contemporary artists offer a new spin on the question, What does it mean to be human?

Identity is Communal or Relational

Identity was a key theme in artistic production in the United States and Europe right after World War II. For the immediate postwar generation of artists, identity meant individual identity. Later in the twentieth century, this belief in a consistent, unique inner self and the individual's ability to act independently of society was severely questioned. The challenges came from philosophers, social activists, artists, psychologists, and others who doubted all claims to ultimate truth. Roland Barthes's formulation of the "death of the author" is a famous example of the challenge to individual self-determination and self-expression.[6] In Barthes's view, there is no single, unchanging meaning for any text ("text" would encompass both written and verbal communications, including those we make as individuals in our efforts to express our personality and identity). The originator of the text is not the ultimate authority for its meaning. Each reader (receiver) of the text formulates his or her own interpretation, based on the impression that the language makes on him or her. For many reasons, Barthes and other critical thinkers grew skeptical of the emphasis on singular identity and uniqueness and instead focused on how people are powerfully influenced by forces outside themselves (in addition to whatever unconscious motivations propel behavior).

In contrast to the existential focus on independent individual identity, today when Western artists and writers on art use the term *identity*, they are usually referring to social and cultural identity. A contemporary artist who is interested in the theme of identity is asking not only, Who am I as an individual? but, Who are we as members of groups? An example of an artist working with multifaceted communal identities is provided by Carrie Mae Weems in her *Kitchen Table Series*, a series of twenty untitled photographs, one of which is presented here [2-3]. The same woman protagonist (Weems using herself as the model) appears in all the photographs, sometimes alone and sometimes with various other people, and she is always at the same kitchen table but with different props around her. Any of the photographs viewed singly might be mistaken for a simple portrait. But viewing the entire series, we realize that the woman's identity is shaped by many variables, including her gender, her status as a working-class black American, her relationships with other people, and her social history. This last variable is represented by the photograph of the civil rights leader Malcolm X on the back wall in Figure 2-3.

Although collective identities conceivably could be based on many traits, in art discussions in the West in the 1980s and 1990s, the traits that were most often emphasized fall into the categories of gender, race, ethnicity, and sexual orientation. Other categories of group identity include class, religion, and age. These categories have played a lesser role in contemporary artworks made in the United States. In Europe, where class-consciousness is more pronounced, artworks that reflect class values, or class identity, are more apparent. For example, in 1993 a young British sculptor, Rachel Whiteread, gained great attention by casting as one monolithic sculpture the negative space of a building scheduled for demolition in London's East End. Made by filling the entire interior volume of a row house with concrete, Whiteread's *House* signified the working-class identity of the inhabitants of this typically constricted space. Whiteread's *House* is also an example of how themes of identity and place can intersect. In addition, by filling in the negative space Whiteread switched the focus from the architectural container (the material fabric of the building) to inner spaces—the psychological, social,

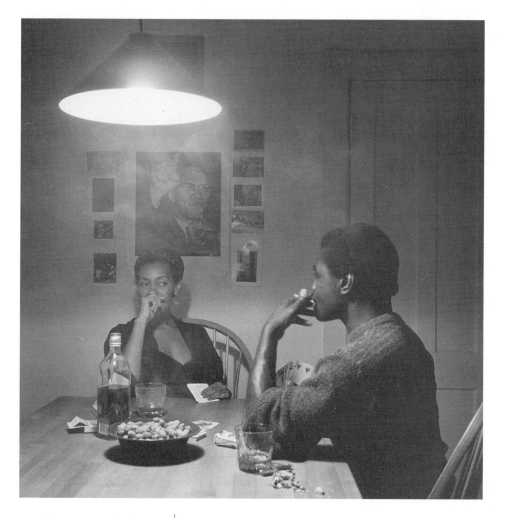

2-3 Carrie Mae Weems | *"Untitled," from the Kitchen Table Series,* **1990**
Gelatin silver print, 28 1/4" x 28 1/4"
Courtesy of the artist and Jack Shainman Gallery

and political zones that the occupants once inhabited. The artwork became an impenetrable monolith sealing in the patterns of living.

Most of the art that we illustrate in this chapter is embedded in concepts of race, ethnicity, gender, and sexuality, reflecting the prominence of these concerns in the "identity art" of the 1980s and 1990s. In chapter 3, we continue a discussion of sexuality and gender within our exploration of the theme of the body, and in chapter 8, we discuss religious identities.

Identity Politics

When artists began to name themselves as part of a group, they at first used general terms such as *women, African Americans,* and *Asian Americans.* This made political sense: however simplistic with respect to the framework of intellectual ideas (people in practice really belong to multiple cohorts), the strategy was functionally savvy. In the art world as in the rest of the world, people have often been stereotyped and discriminated against on the basis of their perceived gender or ethnic identity or class. Discrimination includes unequal access to opportunities for making money in the arts and little or no representation in art exhibitions, gallery shows and sales, art history texts and teaching, art criticism, or any other kind of art discussion and analysis. Economic and institutional discrimination used to be rampant and still occurs. It is one reason why feminists, among others, got so angry about the "white male patriarchy." People observed that a high percentage of the artists who were succeeding in the Western art world in terms of exhibitions and sales were white and male. They started to question why, since they could see for themselves that there are many excellent women artists and artists of color.[7]

Artists responded to the exclusionary politics of the art world in many ways, including picketing, demonstrating, speaking out in public forums, and working for equal opportunities for all artists to participate in art institutions and the public interpretation of art. Some also made art with a political agenda, sometimes called *activist art*. The Guerrilla Girls, for instance, a feminist group working anonymously (since 1985), primarily in New York City, battled the patriarchal power structure of the art world on behalf of women and other underrepresented artists. Still active as provocateurs for social change, none of the Guerrilla Girls is ever named as an individual, but without doubt each is also doing feminist work in other arenas. When any member of the collective appears in public as a Guerrilla Girl, she wears a gorilla mask and costume that conceals part of the torso. One of the group's favorite strategies is to use advertising forms, such as bumper stickers, posters, and ads in magazines, to communicate socially activist visual messages. An example is their 1989 poster with a text that bluntly asks, "Does a woman have to be naked to get into the Metropolitan Museum of Art?" The implication, of course, is that women artists are underrepresented, while the sexualized female form, signified as models in male artists' work, remains ubiquitous in the display of the art historical record.

Identity politics is a term used to refer to the beliefs and activities of those who target racism, sexism, and other forms of prejudice and work for social rights and economic parity. The emphasis on and recognition of cultural differences is also called *multiculturalism*, a term that became widely used to highlight discrimination against people on the basis of gender, race, or sexual orientation. Proponents of multiculturalism advocate cultural differences as desirable and good, rather than as something to be feared and repressed. A multiculturalist may admire the European cultural tradition but does not elevate that tradition above all others.

Identity politics in the art world was a fierce arena in the 1980s and 1990s. Activist art on the theme of identity continues to have some powerful contemporary practitioners and defenders, including Adrian Piper, Barbara Kruger, David Hammons, Daniel Joseph Martinez, William Pope.L, and Hachivi Edgar Heap of Birds. At the same time, other people, both from the art world and the world at large, remain steadfastly critical of art made with an overt political agenda. As in earlier periods, the sanctioned purposes of art are hotly contested in our current age. Nevertheless, it cannot be denied that from the recent era of social activism onward, women artists, queer artists, and artists of color continually surface as voices that matter in the art world.

The focus on issues of identity in art mirrors the influence of these topics in the society at large. Such concerns are not limited to the West, of course. In a statement for a 1998 exhibition of her work at ShanghART, one of the premier private galleries displaying experimental contemporary art in the People's Republic of China, artist Jin Weihong expressed her view of her situation as a young woman in contemporary China with these words: "I am always confronted by such of questions: 'As a woman, how will you deal with this?' . . . But we never hear that some male individuals can be asked this kind of questions." Jin Weihong hypothesizes a world in which all humans would share all possible gender characteristics, or, in her terms, we would be "human beings of obscure sex."[8] Her delicate ink brush paintings, while reflecting Chinese tradition in the choice of medium, explore the poetic possibilities of such a fanciful future world.

Essentialism

In the 1970s and early 1980s, artists who identified with a group tended to play down distinctions among group members in the interest of building a large, cohesive coalition. Artists who identify themselves as belonging to a group have sometimes made art that zeroes in on generalized traits or experiences that members of the group share. Thus an older generation of feminist artists, including Judy Chicago, Carolee Schneemann, and Monica Sjoo, have made art about pregnancy, birth, and menstruation and about domestic tasks that are largely carried out by women, such as housecleaning. Rachel Rosenthal, Mary Beth Edelson, and others have looked back to history for real or mythical heroines they could identify with and incorporated them as subjects. African American artists, such as Raymond Saunders and Jacob Lawrence, likewise have found heroes and role models by researching history and current events in the United States, as well as gazing over the ocean at Africa and examining aspects of their African lineage. Some have made art that emphasizes a shared history of slavery and consciousness of present-day racism.

Kerry James Marshall, a painter now residing in Chicago, has made the present-day culture and activities of African Americans his primary subject matter. He creates complicated narrative and symbolic paintings [5-2] in which virtually all the figures have dark, inky skin. Through the repetition of this one intense tone, Marshall seems to identify that blackness (as a color and as a concept) is fundamental to what it means to be African American. Marshall's stylized exaggeration of skin tone functions ambiguously: at a minimum, the representation of blackness simultaneously registers as an echo of the "darkface" representations of pop culture, a celebration of the color black's distinct formal beauty, and a foregrounding of the significance of the sociological concept of "black" America. Marshall's art appears to reify (and thereby critique) the practice of employing the term *black* to refer to any African American of any skin coloration.

Although such general statements can be powerful and unifying, in awkward hands, generalized interpretations of group identity can be challenged easily. Two issues for an artist claiming a communal identity are How large a group do you identify with? and Who is making visual and verbal claims on behalf of your group? By the late 1980s, people resisted claims that sounded too sweeping. Attributing certain qualities or points of view to "women" or "blacks" seemed simplistic. The term *essentialism* began to be applied to statements and images that conveyed overly generalized or stereotyped notions of identity. In particular, an accusation of essentialism is often made when claims about a group's identity are based on the notion that the shared qualities are natural, or based on biology. If the order of things is "natural," then you have an insurmountable obstacle to overcome if you are on a lower rung of the existing order. The term *essentialist* is usually used negatively, often to resist a claim made about you by someone claiming to speak on your behalf. For example, most feminists today would resist as essentialist any claim that women are "naturally" suited to nurturing roles and thus should bear the major responsibility for child rearing or tending the sick in society.

Diversity

By the 1990s, writers, such as bell hooks, Edward Said, Homi Bhabha, and Gayatri Chakravorty Spivak, were discussing identity in increasingly complex terms. They were theorizing that identities are not formed around and dominated by one central variable like race. Instead, identity is formed within a complex matrix of many variables, including gender, sexuality, ethnicity, class, religion, community, and nation. Moreover, the members of a group are not alike in every way; they have *diversity* within their own commonality. Among the new conceptions today is that those who are interested in diversity recognize internal differences within the context of their own community.

Awareness of diversity contrasts strongly with essentialism. Instead of looking for sameness, one looks for multiple affiliations and characteristics. Groups still exist, but they are smaller, and an individual may identify with different groups in different situations. As Walter Truett Anderson wrote, "The postmodern person is a *multi-community* person, and his or her life as a social being is based on adjusting to shifting contexts and being true to divergent—and occasionally conflicting—commitments."[9]

Lyle Ashton Harris is an American artist who, over the past twenty years, has used self-portrait photography to investigate notions of identity complicated by issues of race, sexual orientation, and gender. Harris, who is black, queer, and male, uses costume, makeup, gesture, and pose to deconstruct and mock simple binary codes: male versus female; homosexual versus heterosexual; black versus white. In some self-portrait photos, he has taken on feminine identities, including ballerina and supermodel, while contradicting the femininity of the poses by revealing his anatomically male torso. Harris's *Memoirs of Hadrian #26* (2002) [2-4] is one of a series of twelve unique 20-by-24-inch Polaroids. The title is borrowed from a 1951 novel by Marguerite Yourcenar, whose text takes the form of a letter written by the aging Roman Emperor Marcus Aurelius to his successor Hadrian following the drowning of his lover, Antinous. In eight of the photos, Harris poses as a bare-chested prizefighter wearing Everlast boxing gloves and a Duke jockstrap. Harris's evocative self-images of an isolated, bloodied, bruised, tormented fighter seem to suggest both Harris's private emotional self and his need to defend his multifaceted public identity. The series may also reference the historical role of boxing in the construction of African American identity. Although an individual sport, boxing provides a culturally constructed image of African American manhood, a display of athletic prowess to the point of injury for a voyeuristic crowd.

The cultural theorist bell hooks embraces the concept of diversity as liberating and politically desirable for people who have been stereotyped by essentialist thinking. Speaking of African Americans, she observed, "Such a critique [of essentialism] allows us to affirm multiple black identities, varied black experience. It also challenges colonial imperialist paradigms of black identity which represent blackness one-dimensionally

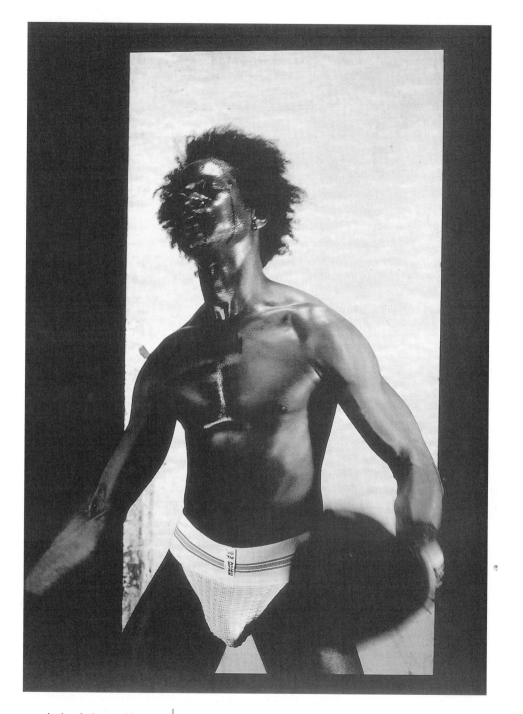

Lyle Ashton Harris | *Memoirs of Hadrian #26,* **2003**
Unique Polaroid, 20 x 24 inches
Courtesy of the artist and CRG Gallery

in ways that reinforce and sustain white supremacy." Although hooks values diversity and is against simplistic generalizing, she argues that it still makes sense to talk about a communal black identity that is cultural and formed by sharing a major stream of history with other African Americans. She advocates that people should pay attention to "the specific history and experience of African-Americans and the unique sensibilities and culture that arise from that experience."[10]

Hybridity

One concept about identity that gained currency in the mid-1990s is *hybridity*, which is related to the notions of multiculturalism and diversity. (The term *syncretism* is used more or less synonymously with hybridity.)[11] A working definition provided by Rohini Malik and Gavin Jantjes defines *hybridity* as "a state of being, arrived at through the innovative mixing and borrowing of ideas, languages and modes of practice."[12] The study of hybridity focuses on the blending and synthesis of different cultures that come into contact with one another. This cultural blending, or syncretism, can be voluntary and seamless or can be the outcome of a painful culture clash, such as the forced imposition of one culture on another as happens in colonization, when inhabitants from one country move into and dominate another people's territory. Forced colonization happened in the Americas, Africa, Australia, and other parts of the world when Europeans displaced or conquered native peoples. Of course, even after the colonial regime is dismantled, the mixture of diverse cultures continues.

In addition to colonization, a great deal of hybridity all over the world is the result of immigration. Indeed, nearly all the people living in the United States have ancestors who were voluntary or involuntary immigrants or are immigrants themselves. Over the centuries, people have moved to the United States from virtually every other place in the world. Hybridity, a blending or fusion of cultural influences, is endemic to being an American.

Hybridity is found in all cultures worldwide; no culture has ever been immune to the ongoing exchanges and adaptations that result from migration, displacement, and contact with other cultures. Even ancient and isolated peoples, such as the Anasazi living in cave dwellings in remote areas of what is now New Mexico, did not live in total isolation. The phenomenon of hybridity has been intensified today, however, because of the rapid spread of information and ideas through international media and commercial forces. The notion of hybridity, or syncretism, qualifies the concept of group identity, suggesting that there is not now nor has there ever been an absolute difference between self and others. As South African artist Gavin Jantjes says, "There are no uncontaminated peripheries full of authentic others."[13]

Numerous artists have expressed concepts of hybridity in their works. One example is Hung Liu, who emigrated to the United States from China in 1984, at the age of thirty-six. Hung Liu built the composition of her painting *Judgment of Paris* [2-5] around her own painted copies of historical images of Chinese and European women. The two Chinese figures, standing in pink at either side, are painted from vintage "photographs of young Chinese prostitutes posed in elaborate Western settings typical of the Victorian era." These constructed images, from around 1900, "had been made by Chinese photographers to promote the services of such women among their countrymen."[14] The two Chinese women flank a central panel with Hung Liu's painting of a late Qing-era porcelain vase. The vase is decorated with a painting of a European-style

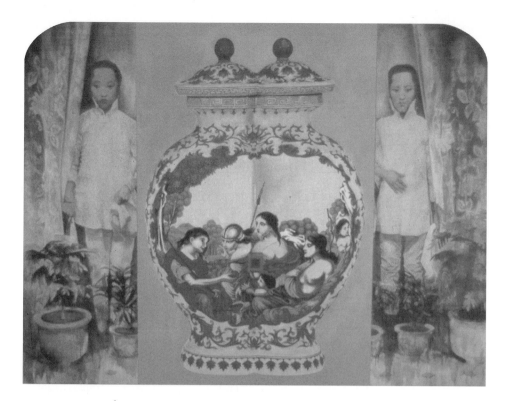

2-5 Hung Liu | *Judgment of Paris*, **1992**
Oil on canvas with lacquered wood, triptych, 72 x 96 x 4 3/4 inches
Courtesy of Bernice Steinbaum Gallery, Miami

mythological scene that includes two goddesses with breasts exposed, one of them in a classic reclining nude pose. Such vases were made in eighteenth-century China to appeal to Western male tastes and were exported to Europe for sale. Hung Liu includes references to eighteenth-, nineteenth-, and twentieth-century cultural clashes and remixing in a work that expresses a feminist point of view. The artist is expressing something about hybridity within Hung Liu, the person, as well. Hung Liu is bicultural at a minimum, fusing worldviews of China and the United States.

Will Wilson, a photographer born in 1969 to a Navajo mother and white father, mixes ethnic motifs, techniques, and content with ideas and formal strategies learned from Western modern and postmodern art. His multimedia installation *Auto Immune Response* (2005) consists of a life-size skeletal metal hogan (a traditional Navajo house) and seven large-scale digitally manipulated photographs, one of which is illustrated [2-6]. The installation reveals Wilson as a hybrid of artistic and cultural influences; for instance, one photograph shows the interior of an actual hogan built with traditional roof timbers, with the artist inside surrounded by cameras and computers that point to his embrace of new media for making his art.

Wilson is deeply interested in expressing the continuing impact of colonization on the identity of Native peoples. He says that he is interested in the impact on Native identity of "holocausts, genocides, and architectures of confinement going back to board-

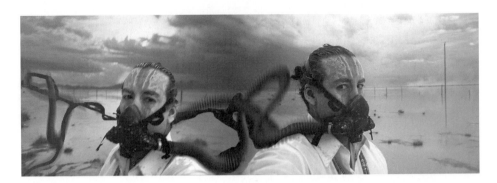

2-6 Will Wilson | *Autoimmune Response #5,* **2005**
Digital inkjet print, 44 x 109 inches
© Will Wilson 2005

ing school on the rez."[15] *Auto Immune Response* subverts the romantic, essentializing images of Native Americans made for tourists that show Natives garbed in exotic costumes posed in natural landscapes, as if nature and "primitives" were bonded and both were untouched by time and history. In Figure 2-6, Wilson depicts himself wearing a Westernized white shirt with his face painted with mud and his hair tied Navajo style, breathing through a gas mask and posed against a flooded, ravaged-looking landscape. Although seemingly postapocalyptic (Wilson as the last Indian standing after a genocide), *Auto Immune Response* also refers to an actual catastrophe—the 1979 bursting of a dam in Church Rock, New Mexico, when radioactive liquid from uranium mining flooded Wilson's reservation; the poisonous effects on residents and the environment continue to this day. Art historian Jennifer Vigil analyzes *Auto Immune Response* as an ironic commentary on "the history of conscious and unconscious germ warfare against Native people," such as the distribution of smallpox-infected blankets by white settlers.[16]

Hybridity can be especially dramatic in the art of recently arrived immigrants or those who live along borders or in places where strong ethnic enclaves exist side by side. Guillermo Gómez-Peña uses the term *border art* to describe his own and other artists' works that blend ideas from cultures in close proximity. Gómez-Peña was born in Mexico in 1955; since the 1980s, he has divided his time between Mexico City and the United States, often working in San Diego, California. In his installations and performances [2-7], the artist asserts a proud hybrid identity even as he portrays the uprootings and disjunctures that are products of colonialism. In his irreverent artworks, Gómez-Peña exudes an aesthetic sensibility and bravado known as *Rasquachismo*, a visual and verbal style associated with the Chicano and Mexican working class. *Rasquachismo* is a defiant, ironic, excessive aesthetic that affirms Mexican identity and resists assimilation into dominant culture within the United States.[17] Although confrontational, Gómez-Peña's art reflects a root optimism—a faith that clashes of cultures and ideologies can fuel a creative synthesis that is ultimately beneficial to many.

Identity is Constructed

An important concept that distinguishes art about identity in the contemporary period is the notion that identity is constructed. The initial formulation of this concept and its

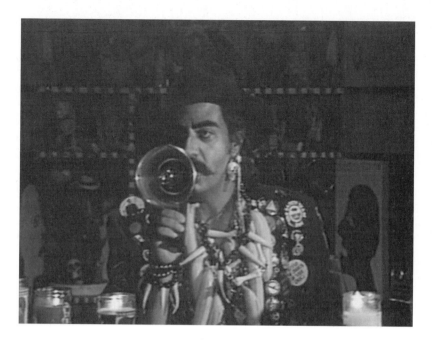

2-7 Guillermo Gomez-Peña | *Border Brujo*, **1989**
Performance art still
Courtesy of the Video Data Bank, www.vdb.org

eventual widespread acceptance in the contemporary art world can be traced back to the writings of intellectuals and academicians who were active in the 1960s and 1970s. Among the most influential was a group of French philosophers, semioticians, and structural anthropologists, including Jacques Derrida and Michel Foucault. Their writings provided key parts of the intellectual scaffolding upon which postmodern theory was built.

These thinkers posited the idea that identity results from a network of interdependent forces that define roles, reward status, govern behavior, and order power relationships for all members of a community. They argued that different identities are formed mainly through social interactions and shared histories; that is, they are learned within certain cultural and political settings, rather than being set at birth. While those in science, religion, and other fields still believed (and argued) that key aspects of identity are biological or spiritual in origin, these points of view were not considered pertinent to the "reading" of most critically championed contemporary art. For those who embrace the concept that identity is constructed, no one is born with a unified, inevitable identity; rather, a person's identity is a product of, and in concert with, human culture, the colored water in the fishbowl in which each of us swims.

Otherness and Representation

In philosophy, an *Other* is someone singled out as different. The body of criticism that developed around the construction of identity delineated the extent to which multicultural awareness has been tainted by binary thinking that constructs the identity of an alleged Other by simplistic comparison of two supposedly mutually exclusive terms:

male/female, black/white, heterosexual/homosexual, Western/non-Western, and so on. Binary thinking maintains Euro-American centrality: inevitably the identity of the Other is defined as a stereotyped contrast to a Westernized mainstream identity, thus hierarchically reinforcing the latter as the norm and the more important and desirable identity. Philosophers also use the term *alterity* for this practice of constructing the identity of cultural Others through negative comparison.

Gender and sexual identities provide examples of the construction of Otherness through binary terms that are simplistic and hierarchical, and that attempt to level out diversity within identity categories. In mainstream Western culture, "male" and "female" are understood as clear opposites, and heterosexuality is viewed as normal in opposition to homosexuality. But in people's actual lives, as well as in the realms of art and theory, gender and sexual identities are more complicated and diverse, more open to change and debate. Philosopher Judith Butler's influential 1990 book *Gender Trouble*,[18] along with the emergence of "queer theory" in the early 1990s, helped make people aware of the heterosexual bias of previous art theory and practice, and brought new visibility to the work of lesbian, gay, bisexual, and transgendered (LGBT) artists.

Artists counter binary thinking by representing their diverse identities from their own perspective, seeking a voice and taking control of their own representation. With sexual identity, for example, artists have increasingly represented the great diversity of sexual identities in our midst, registering desires that cross the old boundaries of age, race, class, disability, nationality, and ethnicity. Harris's *Memoirs of Hadrian #26* [2-4] is one example. Another example is provided by Catherine Opie's photograph *Chicken* (1991) [2-8], from her portraits of lesbians in drag in the series *Being and Having* (1990–91).

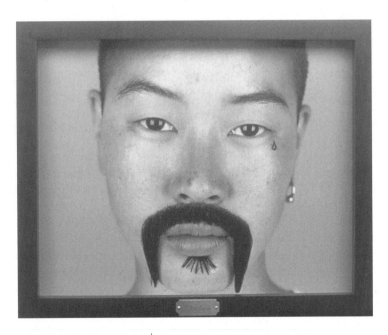

2-8 Catherine Opie | *Chicken (from Being and Having)*, 1991
Chromogenic print, 17 x 22 inches
© Catherine Opie, 1991, courtesy of Gorney Bravin + Lee, New York and Regen Projects, Los Angeles, CA

Deconstructing Difference

In addition to taking control of representing their identity from their own point of view, artists counter Othering by demonstrating that all identities are constructed, even supposedly "normal" mainstream identities; no identity is natural and essential. Kehinde Wiley, a young American painter, appropriates iconography that served to construct codes of masculinity in different periods and cultures, remixing elements from past and present. *Prince Tommaso Francesco of Savoy-Carignano* (2006) [color plate 1], based on an equestrian portrait of a seventeenth-century Italian prince, is from an extensive series of large-scale paintings in which Wiley recasts contemporary African American men as characters from European Old Master portraits. Dressed in a puffy jacket, baggy jeans, designer sneakers, and a flashy chain bracelet and ring, the young man takes the pose of confident mastery on a rearing horse, which in the European grand tradition, indicated the power and control of the white authority figure. The decorative fleurs-de-lis painted in a pattern across the surface make a flat counterpoint to the photo-realistic rendering of man and horse, enhancing the overall impression of artificiality of style.

Wiley's insertions of black men into the world of aristocratic portraiture serve to unmask the Eurocentrism and class privilege that created a visual history of the white, wealthy, and powerful and excluded people of color (a strategy pursued by other artists, including Renée Cox [color plate 3]). Beyond that, though, Wiley appears interested in revealing how masculinity in general is constructed by visual clichés, such as fashion and posing. The worlds of Italian Baroque privilege and urban hip-hop collide but also reveal startling parallels: men of both cultures seem intent on conveying hypermasculinity through posturing and a reveling in the consumer excesses of their day.

Artists have deconstructed ways in which gender and sexual identities are stereotyped by race or national origin. Their critique counters a Eurocentric point of view that has historically pervaded Western representations of sexuality; for example, white women are held up as socially acceptable objects of desire, while women of color (on the rare occasions they are depicted in high art) are portrayed as racially and sexually Other. Although treated as sexually taboo (for the presumed white male viewer), women of color are frequently stereotyped as sexually promiscuous and erotically exotic. Thus, women of color are not only objectified, as white women are, but they endure the added pain and shame of finding themselves the objects of extreme fetishization and pornographic voyeurism. Postcolonial theorists, such as Rasheed Araeen, bell hooks, Trin T. Minh-ha, M. A. Jaimes Guerrero, Ella Habiba Shohat, and Kobena Mercer, have traced these attitudes back to the power dynamics of colonialism, when European conquerors justified slavery, rape, and other forms of oppression and violence by stereotyping their captives as wild, overly physical beings, without any subjectivity of their own, who had to be controlled by extreme measures. Voyeuristic and patriarchal attitudes also permeated Western medicine, anthropology, and ethnography. In the nineteenth century, colonized people were regarded as specimens to be studied and were measured, photographed, and put on actual display in public spectacles to feed the fantasies of Western audiences.[19]

Even well-intentioned Western feminists often direct a Eurocentric gaze at sexual practices and politics elsewhere in the world. Ella Shohat wrote about "Western feminists' imperial fantasies of rescuing clitoridectomized and veiled women,"[20] suggesting that the tendency to see white Western values as universal is not limited to men. For instance, the films and photographs of Shirin Neshat (see the profile), which show Iranian women garbed in the head-to-toe black garment known as the chador, are typically assumed by Western viewers to be unambiguous critiques of the practice of veiling in a Muslim country. Neshat's own view acknowledges the importance of context; the artist recognizes, for instance, that veiling may even serve as a protest against Western hegemonic influence. In contemporary Western culture, it is deemed important to have nothing veiled, including female sexuality, but is that an unequivocally positive social value?

The belief that identity is a cultural construction can be exhilarating or frightening. Some people welcome the idea that identity is constructed because this condition holds the possibility of change. Indeed, the ability to start over, to remake yourself, is part of the mythology of being an American and an attraction to youths in many cultures, who are increasingly exposed to the American mass media. For others, letting go of the idea of a fixed self is unnerving. Perhaps as a defense, irony sometimes characterizes art about postmodern, constructed identity. For example, Paul McCarthy's video performance *Santa Claus* can be interpreted as an ironic riff on the theme of identity. In the performance, McCarthy enacts a demented parody of Santa Claus, a beloved icon of Western culture, turning the benevolent old man who makes toys for Christmas into a caricature of anger and degradation. Among the other themes that McCarthy's performance connects with (popular culture, religion, and fairy tales, among them), *Santa Claus* also seems to reflect on being white, specifically being a white man. McCarthy's alternately abject and violent figure is a parody of a white male authority figure, who appears on the verge of madness at the loss of his former confidence about his position, role in life, and identity.

The Fluidity of Identity

Related closely to the concept that identity is constructed is the concept that identity is not fixed or consistent. Individuals are continually engaged in a process of exchange and adaptation as groups intermingle. The forces that influence the construction of identity are not stable, and thus identity itself is always in flux. Identity is fluid and transformable as the context changes.

The notion of a fluid identity can be hard to grasp. But think about how you behave differently in different situations: in a classroom, at home with your family, on a date, at a job interview, or in a situation in which you are outnumbered by people of a different age or race or nationality or religion. Are you the same person in all those situations, or do you present a somewhat different public image of yourself in each context? A contemporary theorist might say that you are "performing" constructed versions of your identity that work in different contexts; none of these versions is a true self because each identity is transformed or abandoned in other situations.

Motifs of mutating and shifting identity run through the work of numerous artists in the current era. Gender instability is one area of particular interest. Gender differences are encoded visually; we learn to read a person's gender and sexual orientation by noting stereotyped visual clues, such as hairstyle, clothing, pose, and gesture. Artists who want to subvert the social stereotypes of masculinity and femininity employ props, masks, makeup, and costumes to represent bodies of uncertain gender that resist classification by viewers, as Opie does in *Chicken* [2-8]. Opie's photograph may disconcert viewers who are not certain if they are looking at a male or a female. On a fundamental level, such transgressions do more than challenge gender stereotypes; they undermine the whole notion of a stable, consistent gender identity.

Contemporary male artists, including Matthew Barney and Robert Mapplethorpe, have explored gender identity as a flexible continuum of negotiable possibilities. In a memorable scene in his film *Cremaster 3* (2002), Barney, a former star high school quarterback, scales the walls of the spiraling ramp inside New York's Guggenheim Museum. Such a taxing physical feat may be a metaphor for facing the challenges of defining maleness within contemporary culture. Interpretations of Barney's work are as varied as the range of images in the films, but some see Barney's gymnastics as a symbolic search for a new balance—a third sex, so to speak.

Photography, performance art, and video are especially popular practices among artists who are interested in constructed, unfixed identities. Cindy Sherman, who became well known, starting in the 1980s, for using herself as a model in staged photographs exploring female identity, has made many series that deconstruct stereotyped images that are presented in the fashion world, advertising, movies, pornography, and other mass-media sources. Sherman is never an unchanging, unchangeable self in her photographs; she assumes a different identity in each one, reinforcing the idea that identity is artificially constructed and transformable. In her series *Historical Portraits* (1989), Sherman posed in female and male costumes and used makeup and fake body parts to parody the figures in historical paintings. The series demonstrates how photographs, like other images, offer compelling role models for building identity, but models that do not apply in all times and places. Identity is always transformable.

Japanese photographer and video artist Yasumasa Morimura has made work depicting transvestism and other behaviors that blur binary gender boundaries. Morimura like Sherman appears in all his works of art. He is himself and, simultaneously, he becomes a range of famous historical art-world personalities. We see Morimura in a still from a video sequence [2-9] in which the artist accompanies himself on an electronic keyboard instrument while he appears, then disappears, then appears, over and over, dressed as the Mexican artist Frida Kahlo as she appears in her own painted self-portraits, which capture her multiple identities.

Beyond the fluidity of identities defined around race, gender, ethnicity, and sexuality, the mixing and mutating of humans, animals, and machines in various combinations are topics of increasing fascination in art (as well as in culture more broadly). An early experimenter in this realm is Nancy Burson, who, since the early 1980s, has created many images that are composites of several photographic portraits scanned into a computer and combined into one face, including images that mix human and other animals [2-10]. The taxonomic identity and moral standing of such creatures are ambiguous matters. Barney's cheetah-woman in *Cremaster 3* [3-7] is a fully sentient, physically and mentally impressive creature who draws our fascinated gaze. Patricia Piccinini's humanoid sculptures [7-14 and color plate 16], the seeming product of genetic engineering, raise many issues about the moral implications of new scientific research, a topic we return to in chapter 7, Science.

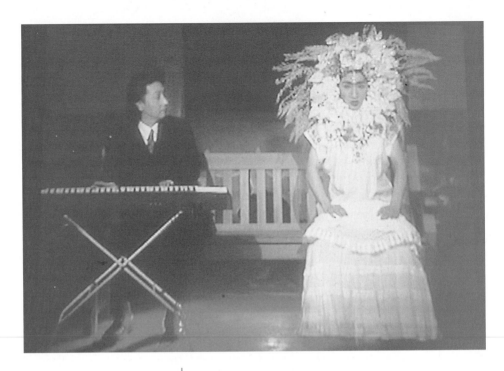

2-9 Yasumasa Morimura │ *Still from Dialogue with Myself (Encounter),* **2001**
DVD projection, one-hour loop
Courtesy of the artist and Luhring Augustine, NY

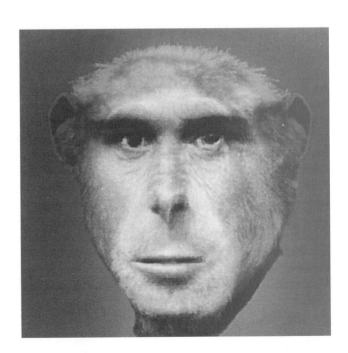

2-10 Nancy Burson │ *Evolution II*
(Chimpanzee and Man), **1984**
Computer composite, 11 x 14 in
Courtesy of the artist

Post Identity

There is evidence that interest in identity defined around race, ethnicity, gender, and sexuality is waning in the mainstream art world. Although social and economic parity is still a distant dream for too many all over the world, the political need for art that self-consciously promotes identity may appear less pressing where some real societal advances have been made. Moreover, even if political activism is needed, the increasing diversity and fragmentation of identities, while adding to the rich variety of art we enjoy in the current scene, make it harder to build coalitions around shared interests and needs.

Art-world fashions and theories change; already the terms *multiculturalism* and *identity* sound dated and even misguided.[21] With different motives, many people began to view multiculturalism as a form of political correctness. Even proponents of identity politics increasingly believe that multiculturalism has become an institutionalized strategy that has led to the assimilation of diverse populations within parameters that pretend to value race, ethnicity, and other markers of identity but instead actually homogenize meaningful differences and mask pervasive racism, sexism, and homophobia.

Meanwhile, a younger generation, born after the political struggles of the 1960s–80s, wants to move beyond identity labels and make art about a wide variety of themes. Many express little interest in being spokespersons for racial, ethnic, or gender identity and prefer to focus on their individual projects. With playful seriousness, curator Thelma Golden used the evocative term *post-black* to characterize the art and ideas of artists she included in the 2001 exhibition Freestyle. These are artists who emerged at the end of the 1990s "who were adamant about not being labeled as 'black' artists, though their work was steeped, in fact, deeply interested, in redefining complex notions of blackness." Golden explained that post-black artists "emerged empowered" by the multicultural debates and identity politics of the previous decade: as a result, they have the confidence to develop in individual directions. But theirs is not the self-contained individualism of a pre-multicultural generation. They are embracing multiple histories and influences, and are reinventing identities for the twenty-first century.[22]

Similar arguments have been made for other artists who would have been categorized mainly by gender, race, or ethnicity in a previous generation. The term *post-feminist* describes a range of art by women who feel empowered by earlier feminist struggles but for various reasons want to distance themselves from being identified as feminist artists. Similarly, Susette S. Min, one of three curators of the 2006 exhibition, One Way or Another: Asian American Art Now, gave her catalog essay the title, "The Last Asian American Exhibition in the Whole Entire World, " ironically suggesting a postidentity world for Asian Americans. (Min actually argues in the essay that the need for identity politics in a market-driven art economy is not over, although the strategies need to be reconceived.)[23] In the same catalog, curator Margo Machida says that even though they are justifiably wary of being forced "into racialized or ideologically driven straitjackets," postidentity artists build on "what is now a well established and highly elaborated body of critique surrounding the construction of identity, 'othering,' and the politics of representation."[24]

What new theories, political ideas, technological developments, and historical events will influence how identity is defined and represented in art as the twenty-first century continues to unfold? Many developments are possible. There is a growing interest in creating invented virtual identities, a direction supported by new digital technologies. In everyday interactions on the computer, many people are now creating artificial identities that they use to interact in cyberspace. In the fine arts, artists use digital media to create sophisticated manipulated images of people.

Another factor that will continue to impact identity as an artistic theme is globalization. Indeed, some of the current ideological resistance to multiculturalism is a response to the perceived manipulation of identity by global capitalism. In this view, global market forces encourage artists to make art that looks ethnic in order to have exotic commodities from far-flung corners of the world to sell. The artists once again become Others without real freedom to express themselves on their own terms.

Identity remains an acute issue for artists who were raised in one culture and now live and work somewhere else. For artists who operate regularly on an international stage, especially if they live and work in more than one location, the collapsing boundaries of local and national communities make the establishment of a coherent identity more complicated. Even artists who remain rooted in one place are shaped by interchanges with people, ideas, images, and products from elsewhere.

One example of an artist who lives an international nomadic existence is sculptor Do Ho Suh, who was born in Seoul, Korea, in 1963, studied art in Korea and the United States, and now divides his time between New York and Korea. To the extent that identity is tied to place (for anyone who feels a powerful cultural and emotional connection to a particular locale and geography), the kind of displacement that Suh experiences every time he changes locations works against a stable sense of identity. Some of Suh's floor sculptures are composed of thousands of miniature human figures cast in plastic and tightly packed with little personal space. Critics have debated whether Suh is giving a positive or negative view of a collective. Is he celebrating workers joining forces for a common goal, or is he showing how individuality becomes lost in a crowd? According to curator Susan Sollins, "Whether addressing the dynamic of personal space versus public space, or exploring the fine line between strength in numbers or homogeneity, Do Ho Suh's sculptures continually question the identity of the individual in today's increasingly transnational, global society."[25]

Suh's sculpture *Karma* (2003) [2-11] places miniature figures in two swarms below the feet of a pair of colossal legs clad in suit pants and men's black dress shoes; the giant appears on the verge of crushing the figures, who are breaking formation and beginning to run. *Karma* could be interpreted as symbolizing some giant of privilege crushing the masses: either the force of global capitalism crushing individual identities by homogenizing cultures worldwide or, alternatively, a totalitarian regime repressing its citizens. On the other hand, looking closely, we see that Suh's small figures are not really all the same but are differentiated by dress and other details into different genders and "types;" we miss these distinctions when we glance quickly at a crowd. Suh seems to suggest that it is our responsibility to continue to distinguish differences among identities, even in an era of globalization.

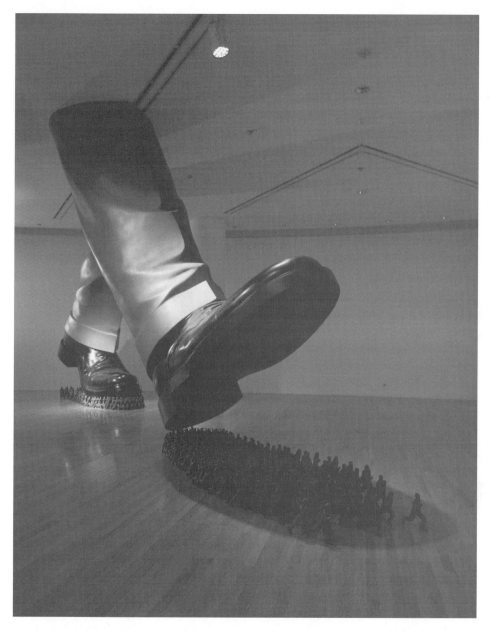

2-11 DO HO SUH | *Karma (Installation at Artsonje Center in Seoul, Korea)*, **2003**
Urethane paint on fiberglass/resin
153.94 x 118 x 291 inches (391 x 299.7 x 739.1 cm)
Courtesy of the artist and Lehmann Maupin Gallery, NY

How do we react when physical characteristics mix across gender or race or species? In a series of computer-generated composite portraits made in the 1980s, photographer Nancy Burson envisioned mixtures that ask us to consider the philosophical, ethical, and emotional effects of morphing identities. To make *Androgyny (6 Men and 6 Women)* (1982), Burson digitally layered photographic portraits of actual men and women (six each, adjusted to a standard size) to create a composite face that discomfits precisely because we cannot decide its gender. For *Mankind (Oriental, Caucasian, and Black, weighted according to current population statistics)* (1983–85) [2-12], Burson combined photographs of three real male faces, each one's features shown according to the percentage of his "race" counted in world population statistics in the early 1980s; the resulting "typical" human looks more Chinese than anything else. In *Evolution II (Chimpanzee and Man)* (1984) [2-10], Burson imagined what a face might look like if evolution had taken a different route, one that created a single species evenly merging primate and human ancestors; Burson's hybrid has the self-aware gaze of a human peering from eyes in a furry face with a cranium shaped like that of a monkey.

Although today software that enables morphing and digital recombination of photographs is readily available, Burson was a pioneer when she first used computers to alter photographs, collaborating with computer scientists and engineers as early as 1976 to develop digital morphing technologies, generating composite faces using those technologies.[26] Her concepts for the hypothetical composites were in line with then emerging philosophical ideas about "Otherness," difference, and cultural stereotyping, as well as simulation and virtual reality, and presaged later artistic preoccupations with themes of DNA recombination and genetic engineering.

Burson's first success occurred when she and her collaborators developed "aging" software that generated images of how people would look as they age, adding wrinkles and softened muscles to adult faces and, for children, stretching their faces and overlaying features from parents to turn a young person into a credible version of an older self. In 1981 Burson patented this software, which in addition to its artistic novelty, has been used practically by the FBI to help locate missing children and adults. Burson next collaborated with David Kramlich, a computer scientist, to refine the system and produced aged portraits of celebrities that were published in *People* magazine, bringing Burson considerable attention. The pair also created an interactive "aging machine" that allowed anyone to sit in a booth and see his or her own face scanned and encoded into a computer and then aged. She continued working with Kramlich on realizing additional concepts for composites, including "beauty" composites that melded faces of movie stars from the 1950s and compared them to composites of stars' faces from the 1980s, composite portraits of leaders of countries owning nuclear arsenals with their features statistically weighted by the number of weapons each leader controlled, composites of human faces with features from dolls and mannequins, and composites of human faces and artists' renderings of space aliens. Some of the concepts also

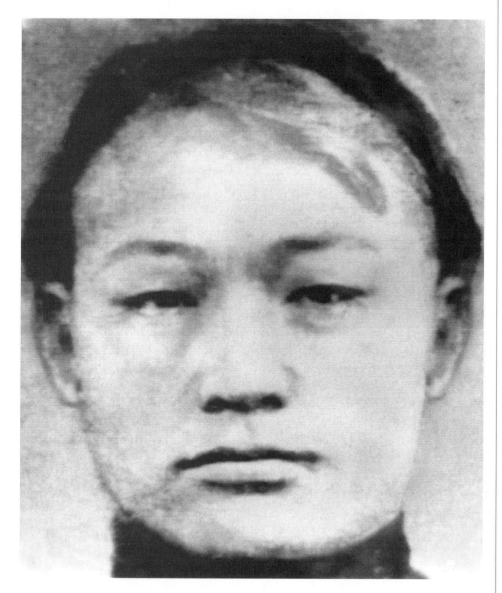

2-12 Nancy Burson | *Mankind (Oriental, Caucasian, and Black, weighted according to current population statistics)*, **1983–1985**
Gelatin silver print
© Nancy Burson, courtesy of ClampArt Gallery

became interactive installations akin to the aging machine, including a machine allowing viewers to meld their features with those of celebrities and a couples' machine that enabled two people to merge their faces.

The general presentation of Burson's composite portraits as still photographs is similar. Each image shows a disembodied head in tightly cropped close-up, facing frontally, with a dark or neutral background. Although generated by a digital process,

Burson has usually turned the completed composite into an analog photograph shot from the computer screen, either a gelatin silver print or, later, a large-format color Polaroid. The resulting photographs look seamless and preserve a documentary aura even though we know they have been computer altered. The effect is unsettling because we are able to read the new face as animate and as a representation of an actual hybrid being. In discussing Burson's composites, curator Chris Bruce pointed to philosopher Jean Baudrillard's theory that simulations are subsuming reality in contemporary society. According to Baudrillard, we live in a world where images are ubiquitous and have become more compelling than reality. Moreover, images increasingly are simulacra that appear real but are actually constructions without any tangible counterpart in reality. Following up on this idea, Bruce argued that Burson's composite illustrated in 2-12 "may be more universally representative of our world—as a piece of information, as the photograph you might send into space—than any single image of a real person. The fascination it engenders is based on broad conceptual questions of 'the real,' a term which now seems forever destined to live in quotes."[27] Although convincing, Burson's composites often have a blurry quality unlike the crispness normally expected of documentary photographic portraiture. For Bruce, the fuzziness is part of the fascination of Burson's composites and encapsulates the conceptual transition in the 1980s from documentary to constructed photography and from analog to computer technology. "What I like most about Burson's piece is its fugitive shimmer, its uncertain state, unlike more recent computer-generated images which can reek of perfect illusion. *Three Major Races* seems to exist between virtual reality and traditional image, an awkward pause in the conversation between the two forms and technological states."[28] As discussed in chapter 2, the long tradition of portraiture is bound up with the exploration and expression of identity. We learn to read identity in the morphology of a human face—the shape, structure, coloring, and other outward physical qualities of a head and visage—and we make determinations about gender, age, race, social class, beauty, and other qualities based on our perceptions. Such judgments are largely socially determined (certain hairstyles signal "female," rather than "male," for instance). Outward appearance doesn't tell us much, if anything, about underlying physiological human functions (how brains work has nothing to do with the size of a nose, for instance). Nevertheless we persist in categorizing and judging individuals on the basis of physical appearance. Burson's computer composites examine classifications made on the basis of morphology, unraveling the limitations of information about identity we "read" into a human face. *Evolution II* [2-10], for example, can be interpreted as a wry send-up of the now debunked field of study known as phrenology, which tried to establish links between physical appearance and intelligence.

In the 1990s Burson moved back to more traditional (undoctored) photographic portraiture of real individuals. Her interests continued to include themes of identity and issues of human difference and cultural stereotyping. One large body of work comprises portraits of individuals with progeria (premature aging) or with facial deformities caused by disease or genetic anomalies. Burson's romantic lighting and soft focus seem designed to cause empathy with the Other along with a reconsideration of physical standards used to determine normalcy.

Burson's *He/She* series (1996–97), from which we illustrate one image [2-13], are analog counterparts to her earlier composite *Androgyny*. The series comprises

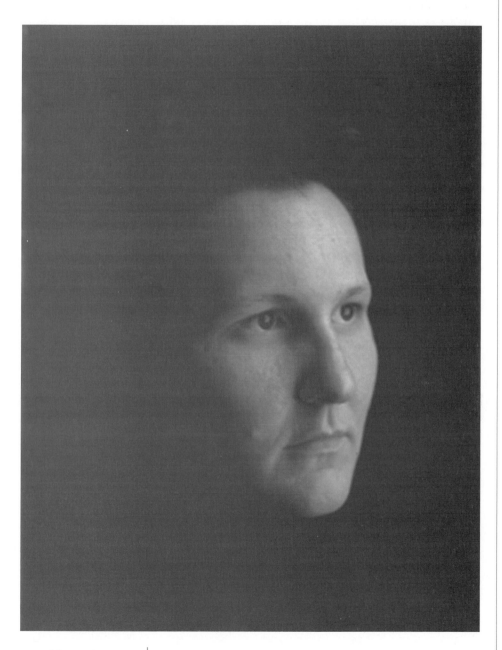

2-13 Nancy Burson | *"Untitled" from the He/She Series,* **1997**
Polaroid
© Nancy Burson, courtesy of ClampArt Gallery

formal color portraits that challenge perceptions about gender based on features of the human face. Each dramatically lit portrait shows an actual person whose features are on the edge of male and female. According to Michael Sand, "The *He/She* series, like so much of Burson's work, asks viewers to stop and wonder at the latent potential for mutability in everyone."[29]

Another series, *Guys Who Look Like Jesus* (2000–01), presents portraits of eight men who cultivate a Jesus look by growing their hair and beard, including one black, one Hispanic, and one Japanese American. (Burson took out an ad in the *Village Voice* to find the men.) In addition to the individual portraits, Burson also made one digital composite fusing all the photographs and a second composite melding painted representations of Christ in European art. The former composite appears closer to Christ's identity as a Middle Eastern Jew than the pale-skinned, light-haired ideal of Northern European whiteness. According to Maurice Berger, "*Guys Who Look Like Jesus* questions deeply rooted cultural associations between whiteness and all things pure, good, and sacred."[30] Burson is an idealist who believes fervently in our common humanness. Her popular interactive project, *The Human Race Machine* (1999 to the present), invites viewers to enter a booth and select features of different racial types (such as Caucasian, Asian, and African American) to morph onto their own face. Burson's ambitious intention is to alter perceptions about race and diversity. The artist explained, "*The Human Race Machine* is an opportunity to move beyond our differences and arrive at sameness. The more we recognize ourselves in others, the more we can connect the human race. . . . Genetically, we are 99.9% the same. There are groups of genes that make up various characteristics, but there is no gene for 'race.' The concept of race is purely political and social."[31] *The Human Race Machine*, like many of Burson's intriguing artworks, gains traction at that key theoretical juncture where the appearance and purpose of the indexical documentary photograph (created from a subject that "really" exists outside the frame) crosses paths with the constructed digitalized image (created from a perspective that exposes the political agency at the heart of all representation).

Nancy Burson was born in 1948 in St. Louis, Missouri. She studied painting for two years at Colorado Women's College before moving in 1968 to New York, where she continues to live and work.

PROFILE: Shirin Neshat

Shirin Neshat, known for her work in film, video, and photography, undertakes multilevel projects that we could examine through the lens of most themes in this book, particularly time, place, identity, the body, language, and spirituality. Here we discuss Neshat's work primarily in terms of identity, an especially rich theme for this artist, who has explored her multiple identities as artist, woman, Iranian (and Persian), immigrant, and foreigner.

Born in Iran in 1957, Neshat moved to the United States in 1973 to study art in Los Angeles. When she was growing up, her homeland was under the leadership of the shah, who supported a liberalization of social behavior and economic changes modeled after the West. In 1979, however, while Neshat was still in America, Iran underwent a cataclysmic transformation: an Islamic revolution overthrew the shah, and in its aftermath the new regime of the fundamentalist Ayatollah Khomeini reasserted control over public and private behavior. Under his rule, even minute details of dress were dictated by sacred strictures. (A similar return to fundamentalism occurred in many Islamic nations in the Middle East and northern Africa in the latter part of the twentieth century.)

Returning for a visit to Iran in 1990 after a twelve-year absence, Neshat was stunned by the magnitude of the change, which left her own cultural identity in a state of limbo: She had not adopted a fully westernized identity, yet she no longer felt anchored to the culture of her homeland. The shock inspired her to try to understand and express through art what had happened to Iranian national identity, particularly as it concerned women. Through her art, she also began to explore gender roles, conflicts between tradition and modernity, and the psychological pressures felt by dislocated people who come to feel like perpetual outsiders.

One of the most visible changes that Neshat saw in Iran was that women everywhere now wore the head-to-toe black chador, the loose robe and veil traditionally worn by women in Iran, which had been abolished in 1936. Women in chadors became an iconic presence in Neshat's art. In her first mature body of work, a provocative series of photographs called *Women of Allah* (1993–97), Neshat explores the ideology of Iranian women who are caught up in the revolution, even to the point of being willing to die as martyrs. Within each photograph [2-14], Neshat layers Farsi (modern Persian) calligraphy, the image of a gun, and the black veil, challenging "the western stereotype of the eastern Muslim woman as weak and subordinate."[32] The writing adorns those specific female body parts that remain visible in a fundamentalist Islamic land: the eyes, face, hands, and feet. The failure of cross-cultural communication is embodied in Neshat's use of writing that is illegible to most Western readers. Westerners recognize the beauty of the calligraphy but don't recognize it as poetry that is considered radical in Iran because individual poems offer different views on the value of wearing the chador. Whatever quick judgments that cultural outsiders may make when they look at the female figure and the gun, the presence of the writing implies that true understanding requires deeper learning.

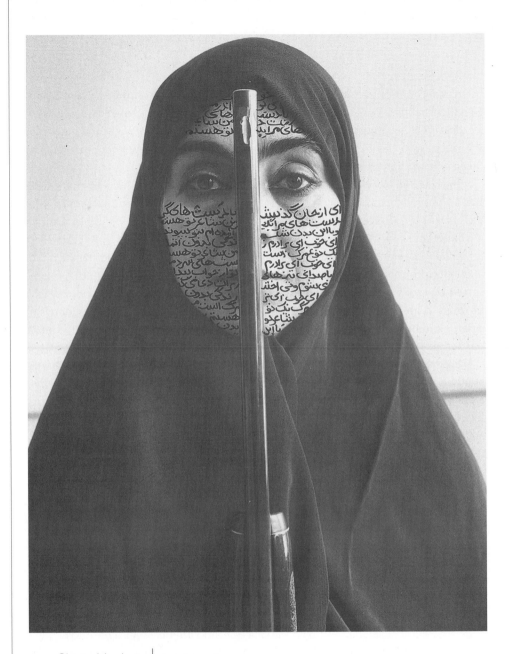

2-14 Shirin Neshat | *Rebellious Silence*, 1994
B & W RC print & ink, 11 x 14 inches
Photo by Cynthia Preston
© Shirin Neshat

While many in the West expressed dismay and disdain at Iran's return to fundamentalism (charging, for instance, that fundamentalism totally subjugates women),
Neshat's artistic responses have been nuanced and full of ambiguity. Old and new
stereotypes about the "Orient," the Islamic world, gender roles, religious fanati-

cism, and violence meet and mix in Neshat's work, without any resolution. In interviews, the artist acknowledges her awareness of the contradictions that are inherent in her use of loaded imagery.

Neshat's rise to international prominence stems primarily from the acclaim that greeted a trilogy of films: *Turbulent* (1998), *Rapture* (1999), and *Fervor* (2000). Shot dramatically in black and white, these films examine a mythic existence in an imaginary version of Iran stripped down to its poetic essentials. The Iranians (played in her first films by Moroccan actors), like people everywhere, struggle for individual freedom while simultaneously seeking meaning in shared values and traditions. The tension between these tendencies turns Neshat's staged tableaus into tragic sagas.

In *Turbulent*, a male singer performs a traditional song of lost love. He sings facing the camera, with his back to a small audience of men dressed in matching dark pants and white shirts. After his performance, a woman, perhaps the subject of the man's song, begins her own song. The contrast is stunning: the woman's singing is personal, intuitive, emotional, a sort of musical scream. While the man's performance is locked within tradition—a tradition that, however beautiful, inhibits his expression—the woman's performance appears without precedent and without boundaries. The woman's singing rivets us, as well as the male singer, who watches and listens to the woman from the other wall. What makes the film especially poignant is knowing that in present-day Iran, it is forbidden for a woman to sing in public.

In the films of the trilogy, as well as many subsequent film installations, Neshat projects paired narratives on opposite walls. Typically, the dual projections show men and women separated into different spheres. This format allows Neshat to present dichotomies—masculine and feminine, culture and nature, tradition and change, public and private, control and freedom. As the audience, we occupy the void between the two streams of moving images; unable to see the entire artwork at one time, we must choose which side to watch and which to miss. The inability of the audience to see things fully is a leitmotif in Neshat's work. The layered meanings of her art thus remain a partly veiled mystery, glimpsed but never fully fathomed.

In the second work in the trilogy, *Rapture*, two twelve-and-a-half-minute videos are projected simultaneously. In one, a throng of more than a hundred men, again clad in uniform dark pants and white shirts, march through a town, eventually making their way to an ancient fortress. There the men undertake ritualistic activities; they climb ladders, practice drills, wash their hands, unroll carpets, and wrestle. They seem to be working, perhaps preparing for an attack on the worn fortress. Yet the men seem as much to be prisoners of the fortress, a symbol of their "man-made," tradition-bound society. On the facing screen, a similar number of women appear on a barren desert. Each wears the all-engulfing chador that hides her individual identity, her figure a sculptural presence against the landscape. The women look across to the other filmed image, observe the men, and begin in unison to make a traditional wailing sound that in the Middle East serves as either a warning or a congratulatory acknowledgment. The movement of the women is breathtakingly beautiful. As if blown by the wind, they gather at a shoreline where a half dozen of the women, assisted by the others, shove off to sea in a small, fragile-looking wooden boat, choosing escape, however dangerous. On the facing wall, the projection shows the men saluting from their fortress in the direction of the women.

While Neshat's films have the look of realistic documentaries, in fact they are carefully staged and choreographed. Neshat simulates the behavior of veiled women and then makes us aware of the constructed and fluid meanings of veiling, showing us different meanings in different contexts. Within her work, the chador serves multiple purposes: it shrouds the female body in mystery, it protects the body, and it gives women some power by allowing them to conceal aspects of their multilayered identities. Above all, being veiled in Neshat's world does not equate with being bound, blinded, or silenced. Neshat shows us women actively navigating landscapes, gazing at others, and giving voice to their feelings in song and cries. The women are powerful agents. At the same time, Neshat probes the challenges and costs for both men and women of separating the sexes. In the final film in her trilogy, *Fervor*, a tale of sexual desire, the physical division of masculine and feminine space sometimes is evident in one stark, monumental image [2-15].

The main audiences for Neshat's works to date have been in Europe and the United States. Hence, whatever the artist's intentions, her images of women wearing veils evoke associations with the veiled, eroticized figure of the Muslim harem girl, a fantasy figure of Western colonialism, which continues to connote sexual allure. The historic Western fantasy of the veiled and cloistered Muslim woman also embraced the notion of a repressed woman who is too passive and fatalistic to attempt to resist her oppression and needs to be rescued by the West; this view of the veil as a symbol of a repressive society helped justify colonialism.

Looking at images of veiled women in Islamic societies, the current-day viewer in the West may feel superior, imagining the freedom of Western women. In contrast to this view, Neshat observes: "In the West where you can talk specifically about the body and sexuality, things are so extroverted that in the end there is no mystery, there is no boundary."[33] Neshat describes her own identity as that of an outsider who is caught between two worlds. "I always think of myself as an outcast, whether I'm among Iranians or Westerners." She relates her own experience as an exile to the characters in her films. "When I look back at my work retrospectively, I find it ironic that all my female characters are also 'outcasts' within their social realms whether due to sexual, cultural or political factors. There is a constant tension between the 'individual' versus the 'community,' and often the impossibility of their integration."[34] Shirin Neshat was born in 1957 in Qazvin, Iran and moved to the United States in 1973. She received a master of fine arts degree at the University of California–Berkeley. She currently lives in New York City.

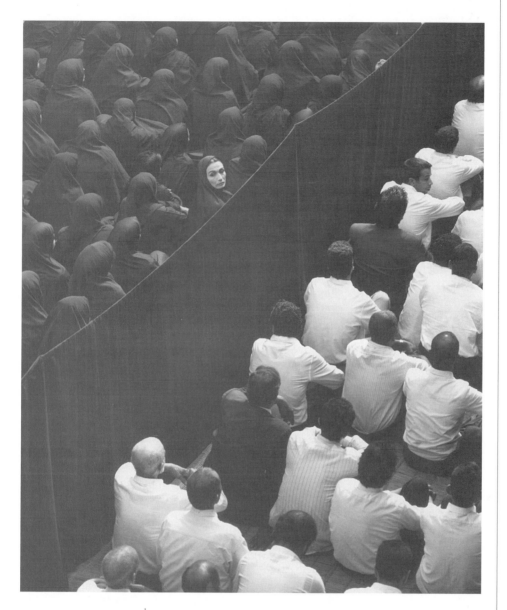

2-15 Shirin Neshat | *Fervor,* 2000

Production still
Photo by Larry Barns
© Shirin Neshat

Notes

1. Claire Pajaczkowska, "Issues in Feminist Visual Culture," in Fiona Carson and Claire Pajaczkowska, eds., *Feminist Visual Culture* (New York: Routledge, 2000), p. 8.

2. Linda Weintraub, *Art on the Edge and Over: Searching for Art's Meaning in Contemporary Society 1970s–1990s* (Litchfield, Conn: Art Insights, 1996), p. 99.

3. Lucy R. Lippard, *Mixed Blessings: New Art in a Multicultural America* (New York: Pantheon Books, 1990), p. 21.

4. Looking at just one city—New York—additional influential (and controversial) shows about identity that were held in the 1990s included these: The Decade Show: Frameworks of Identity in the 1980s, which was held simultaneously in New York in 1990 at the Studio Museum in Harlem, the New Museum of Contemporary Art, and the Museum of Contemporary Hispanic Art; Asia/America: Identities in Contemporary Asian American Art at the Asia Society Galleries (1994); Black Male: Representations of Masculinity in Contemporary American Art at the Whitney Museum (1994); Bad Girls at the New Museum of Contemporary Art (1994); and Too Jewish? Challenging Traditional Identities at the Jewish Museum (1996).

5. For a more nuanced consideration of these two exhibitions and others of the previous fifteen years organized around identity themes, see a set of essays developed from a 2004 College Art Association panel organized by curator Norman L. Kleeblatt, "Identity Roller Coaster," *Art Journal* 64 (Spring 2005): pp. 61–94.

6. See Roland Barthes, "The Death of the Author," in *Image, Music, Text*, trans. and ed. Stephen Heath (New York: Noonday Press, 1977), pp. 142–148.

7. For a comprehensive discussion of feminist activism vis-à-vis the arts in the United States beginning in the 1970s, see Norma Broude and Mary D. Garrard, eds., *The Power of Feminist Art: The American Movement of the 1970s, History and Impact* (New York: Harry N. Abrams, 1994).

8. Jin Weihong, "A Theme of Me—Woman," in *Jin Weihong* (Shanghai: ShanghART, 1998), p. 3. An exhibition catalog.

9. Walter Truett Anderson, ed., *The Truth about the Truth: De-confusing and Re-constructing the Postmodern World* (New York: Putnam, 1995), p. 128.

10. bell hooks, "Postmodern Blackness," in *The Truth about the Truth*, p. 122.

11. Homi K. Bhabha, Edward Said, Olu Oguibe, Trin T. Minh-ha, and Sarat Maharaj are among the many writers who have contributed to discussions of hybridity and syncretism.

12. Rohini Malik and Gavin Jantjes, *A Fruitful Incoherence: Dialogues with Artists on Internationalism* (London: Institute of International Visual Arts, 1998), S.V. "hybridity" (in the glossary).

13. Gavin Jantjes, Introduction to *A Fruitful Incoherence*, p. 16.

14. Margo Machida, "Out of Asia: Negotiating Asian Identities in America," in *Asia/America: Identities in Contemporary Asian American Art* (New York: Asia Society Galleries and New Press, 1994), p. 107. An exhibition catalog.

15. Quoted in Jennifer Vigil, "Will Wilson," in James H. Nottage, ed., *Diversity and Dialogue: The Eiteljorg Fellowship for Native American Fine Art* (Indianapolis: Eiteljorg Museum of American Indians and Native American Art, 2007), p. 98. An exhibition catalog.

16. Vigil, "Will Wilson," in *Diversity and Dialogue*, p. 104.

17. For an introduction to two of the major scholars of *Rasquachismo* and a discussion of the misunderstanding of the term in the United States, see Holly Barnet-Sanchez, "Tomás Ybarra-Frausto and Amalia Mesa-Bains: A Critical Discourse from Within," in *Art Journal* 64 (Winter 2005): pp. 91–93.

18. Judith Butler, *Gender Trouble: Feminism and the Subversion of Identity* (London and New York: Routledge, 1993).

19. Some of these concepts are discussed in the profile about Renée Cox following chapter 3, The Body.

20. Ella Shohat, introduction to *Talking Visions: Multicultural Feminism in a Transnational Age*, ed. Shohat (New York: New Museum of Contemporary Art; Cambridge: MIT Press, 1998), p. 12.

21. Gavin Jantjes told artist Marlene Dumas that he prefers the term *new internationalism* to *multiculturalism*. He explained, "I have been using the term internationalism as an open ended term. I have not used multiculturalism because I think that certain associations, both

historical and cultural, make it a discourse of the past. I speak of internationalism because it allows me to understand what is happening in the world on the back of those historical notions of multiculturalism." Gavin Jantjes, "Marlene Dumas," in *A Fruitful Incoherence*, p. 55.

22. Thelma Golden, Introduction to *Freestyle* (New York: Studio Museum in Harlem, 2001), p. 15. An exhibition catalog.

23. Susette S. Min, "The Last Asian American Exhibition in the Whole Entire World," in Melissa Chiu, Karin Higa, and Susette S. Min, eds., *One Way or Another: Asian American Art Now* (New York: Asia Society; New Haven, Conn.: Yale University Press, 2006), pp. 34–41.

24. Margo Machida, "Reframing Asian American," in *One Way or Another*, pp. 17, 16. Machida also makes a compelling argument that the complex currents in today's art by Asian Americans are more of a continuum than a rupture with identity art of the 1980s and 1990s; that the latter was more heterogeneous than those looking back always recognize.

25. Susan Sollins, *Art 21: Art in the Twenty-First Century 2* (New York: Harry N. Abrams, 2003), p. 213.

26. Composite photos were made prior to the advent of computers in the history of photography, previously involving darkroom processes for layering analog negatives.

27. Chris Bruce, "Navigating in the Hall of Mirrors," in Chris Bruce and Andy Grundberg, *After Art: Rethinking 150 Years of Photography* (Seattle: Henry Art Gallery and University of Washington Press, 1994), p. 23. An exhibition catalog.

28. Ibid. Although he uses a different title, Bruce is referring to the photograph illustrated in Figure 2-12.

29. Michael L. Sand, "Nancy Burson and the Art of Seeing," in Christopher French, ed., *Seeing and Believing: The Art of Nancy Burson* (Santa Fe: Twin Palms Publishers, 2002), p. 19. An exhibition catalog.

30. Maurice Berger, "White Purity: Nancy Burson," in Maurice Berger, ed., *White: White and Race in Contemporary Art* (Baltimore: Center for Art and Visual Culture, University of Maryland Baltimore County; New York: Distributed Art Publishers, 2004), p. 52.

31. Nancy Burson, "Seeing and Believing: The Art of Nancy Burson: Interview with Lynn Gumpert and Terrie Sultan," in *Seeing and Believing*, p. 153.

32. Tina Sherwell, "Bodies in Representation: Contemporary Arab Women Artists," in Fran Lloyd, ed., *Contemporary Arab Women's Art* (London: Women's Art Library, 1999), p. 65.

33. As quoted in Marine Van Hoof, "Shirin Neshat: Veils in the Wind," *Art Press* 279 (May 2002): p. 38.

34. As quoted in Helena Kontova, "Marina Abramovic, Vanessa Beecroft, Shirin Neshat: Modern Nomads," *Flash Art* 40 (July–September 2007): p. 103.

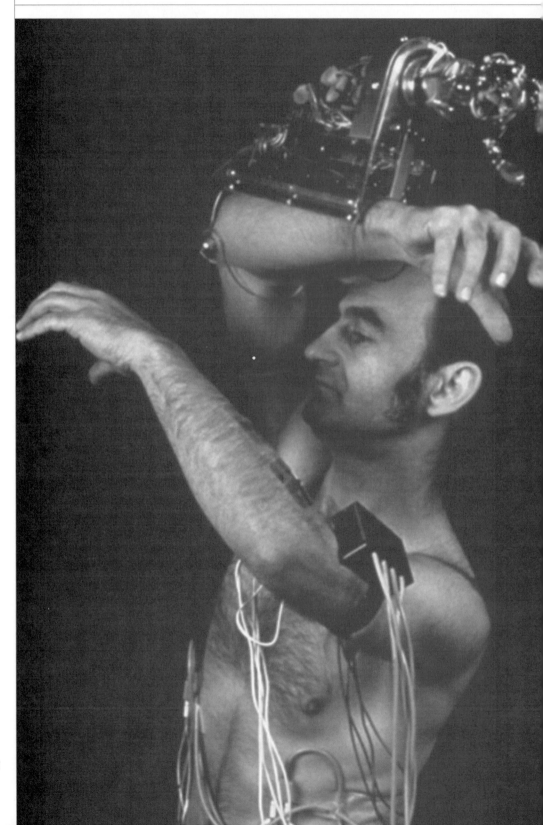

Detail of 3-11

CHAPTER THREE

The Body

What are we to make of Paul McCarthy's *Mutant* (1994) [3-1], which features an armless grinning figure perched cross-legged on a museum display pedestal, with a head that is freakishly oversized in proportion to its body? Created by combining a rubber "Indian" mask with a child-sized mannequin, the sculpture presents a hybrid body that seems to draw from cartoons, children's playrooms, theme parks, science fiction, surrealism, and science laboratories. The title—*Mutant*—insinuates that the creature before us could be any of the following: the purposeful product of human intervention through biotechnology, the result of a scientific experiment gone awry (some weird equivalent of a Frankenstein scenario), or the result of a bizarre mutation (a freak of nature). *Mutant* is very much a physical specimen (the armless nude torso provokes a heightened awareness of its body) and an agent of culture (its shiny black shoes and feather headdress signal conscious choices of cultural signification, although of what remains a mystery). Together, the corporeal and cultural qualities demand our vigilant interpretation: Who is this? What does it want from us?

Until recently, when experiments in science and bioengineering have raised the possibility of creating transgenic creatures that meld human bodies with those of other creatures, the bodies we inhabit have distinguished humans from all other species on the planet. After a million years or more of evolution, our shared human physiology of flesh and bone and blood and muscle (including our unique hands with opposable thumbs), the structure of our sensory apparatus, and the complex network of synapses in our brain shape our physical being and our sense of our own humanity. Our body functions like a prism through which we perceive the world.

According to many religions (and the worldviews of societies that are permeated by those religions), the body is also the earthly home for the soul. This idea has had a paramount influence on past Western art. As art historian and critic Thomas McEvilley noted, "Traditional Western sculpture of the figure, from Pheidias to Michelangelo to Rodin, attempted to portray the soul in the body—or rather, the body ensouled. . . . The soul was the essential truth of human nature and the sculptor was engaged in the portrayal—ultimately the embodiment—of that essence."[1]

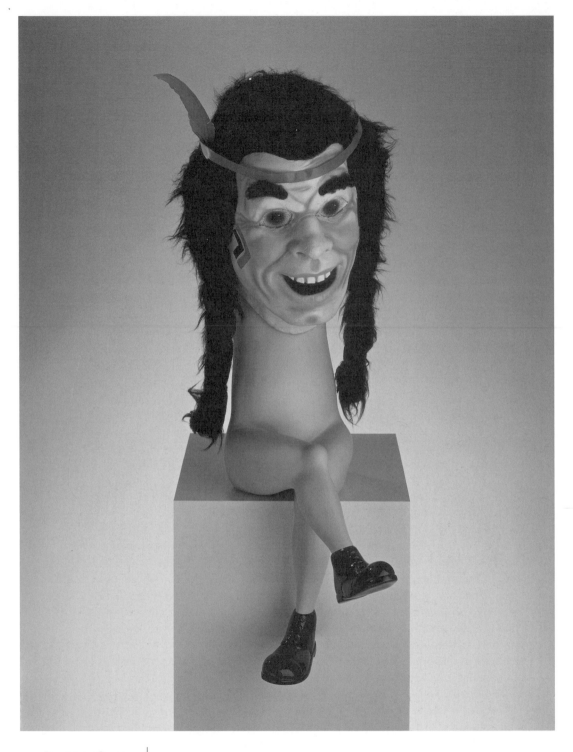

3-1 Paul McCarthy | *Mutant, 1993*
Acrylic fur, metal, paint, foam rubber, fiberglass
Collection of the Vancouver Art Gallery, Vancouver/CA

In the postmodern outlook, in contrast, there is no soul but only the body. We are bodies alone. Postmodern art of the figure deals with this condition, according to McEvilley, by portraying the body as an empty vessel. The figurative works of Juan Muñoz, Mike Kelley, Jeff Koons, and James Croak [3-2], among others, are examples that McEvilley believes show "the human figure as empty in itself or emptied out, gutted, by experience."[2] Croak, for instance, has made skinlike suits of cast latex that

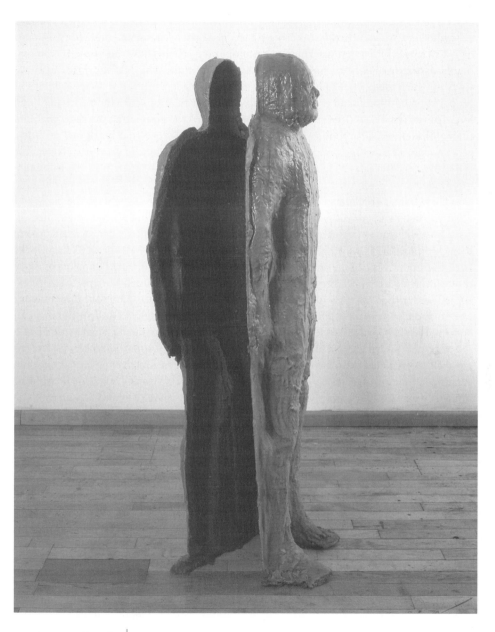

3-2 James Croak | *Decentered Skin,* 1995
Mixed media
Courtesy of James Croak

appear hollow, as if emptied of any essence or soul. McCarthy's cartoon composites, such as *Mutant*, also point in their own way to an unmooring of humanness from the body, as well as body-boundary confusion between the human and everything-not-human.

Is the body a biological organism or a cultural artifact? Bodily experiences are complex. Certainly many characteristics of the body are intrinsically physical. Men and women have different reproductive organs, people age, and physical disabilities and diseases are real conditions, no matter what their causes and consequences. Other aspects of the body are affected by social and cultural factors, such as whether a person in a wheelchair has difficulty entering a building or whether someone with gray hair or AIDS is welcomed in a workplace. Contemporary artists show the human form as a material, corporeal entity, a tissue of flesh and bodily fluids; they also explore the many ways in which the body, like identity, is a cultural artifact, reflecting a society's views of proper behavior, social and economic roles, and power relationships. Indeed, as explored by artists of the 1980s, 1990s, and today, the theme of the body often overlaps with the theme of identity. The body carries many of the visual signs that mark our own and others' identity as to age, gender, race, and so on. Thus, artists who want to make visible the enormous diversity of identities in our midst and to renegotiate how we value different identities often turn to body imagery.

This chapter considers contemporary art that is focused directly on the body and what the body means. As we look at this art, keep in mind that theme and subject in an artwork are not synonymous, even though they do, of course, bear a relationship to each other. The two often, but not always, overlap; while the majority of artworks with the body as a theme include figurative imagery, the reverse is not necessarily the case. Many artworks showing a human form (or parts thereof) are primarily concerned with other themes, such as time, spirituality, and place. Moreover, an artwork can be about the body without depicting the human form directly. For instance, an artist may use an article of clothing or a piece of domestic furniture, such as a bed, as a metaphorical substitute for the body. Maureen Connor's *Thinner Than You* [3-3] uses a tightly stretched dress form as a metaphor for the pressure that American women are under today to strive for extreme thinness. Connor's empty dress also could be interpreted as an instance of the postmodern "empty vessel," a body drained of the illusion of a soul.

Past Figurative Art

The human figure is one of the oldest and most significant motifs in the art of most cultures, other than a few cultures that have prohibited figurative imagery in art used for religious worship. (Both Islam and Judaism are notable as religions that limit figurative imagery in religious art.) In the West, the vast majority of sculptures were figurative forms until artists began experimenting with nonobjective art in the twentieth century. In the European academic tradition, paintings showing the human figure were considered a greater accomplishment than paintings showing a landscape, still life, or other nonfigurative motif, and painters who aspired to fame devoted years to learning how to render figures. From its invention in 1839, photography took the human figure as a major motif. Even in twentieth-century modernism, after figurative art had lost its dominance, significant artists continued to take up the challenge of the figure. Among these were renowned artists, such as Pablo Picasso, Henri Matisse, Käthe

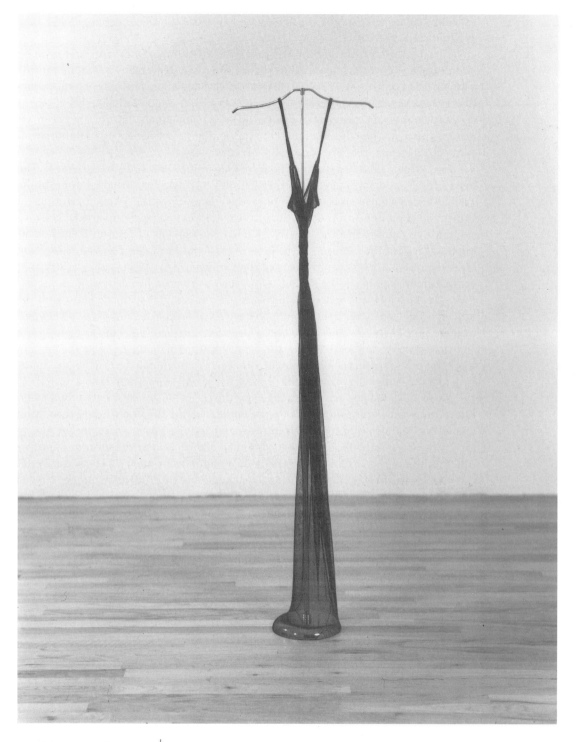

3-3 Maureen Connor | *Thinner Than You,* 1990
Stainless steel and cloth, 60 x 15 x 7.5 in
Courtesy of the artist

Kollwitz, Henry Moore, Alberto Giacometti, Salvador Dali, Diego Rivera, Frida Kahlo, and Romare Bearden.

Through history, the figure has provided artists with both form and content. Human figures are challenging, versatile forms that can strike many poses and provide a multitude of contrasting, complex shapes and visual relationships. As content, human figures have served to express deeply cherished cultural values, including beliefs about religion, politics, and personal and social identity. Sometimes but not always in art history, the figure has also been used to represent ideas about the body as a corporeal entity, for instance, ideas about sexuality and mortality.

Figurative art has had a tumultuous history in the West since World War II. The most critically acclaimed new art in the 1950s was nonobjective (although some of the abstract expressionists also made figurative works, such as the *Women* paintings of Willem de Kooning). At the same time, much attention was given to artists' gestures and creative process; think of the well-known photographs of Jackson Pollock making his drip paintings. Artists' self-consciousness about their own physical actions and creative process helped open the way to the various live-art forms—the performance art that flourished in the 1960s and 1970s, such as Happenings, Fluxus, Actions, and Body Art. Body art, a subset of performance art consisting of art made on or with the human body—where the artist's body literally serves as the medium—has an obvious connection to themes of the body. There have been forms of body art in many times and places, such as tattoos, body piercing, and scarification. Body art as a movement in contemporary art includes works ranging from self-mutilation to feats of bodily endurance to more benign demonstrations of the artist's body as a form in space.

Meanwhile, the pop art that emerged by the early 1960s reintroduced the human figure into avant-garde painting. Pop representations were clearly artificial, secondhand images appropriated from popular entertainment and mass-media advertising. Also in the 1960s, abstract, nonfigurative art continued and evolved in the form of minimalism. Starting in the 1970s in Europe and booming in the United States in the 1980s, neo-expressionism moved figurative painting and sculpture to center stage. Buoyed by a frenzy of interest from well-heeled collectors, prominent German, Italian, and American neo-expressionist artists, such as Jörg Immendorff, Georg Baselitz, Sandro Chia, Mimmo Paladino, and Julian Schnabel, turned art's brightest lights back on the figure and, not coincidentally, back on painting. Neo-expressionism, with its emphasis on the physicality of the creative process and the tactility of the materials used, proved an attention-getting vehicle. Neo-expressionist figurative art, however, was often about history, personal psychology, or mythology and literature, rather than about issues of the body per se.

A New Spin on the Body

Art that focused directly on issues of the body as a theme surfaced overtly and dramatically in the late 1960s and 1970s in art by women artists that was inspired by the consciousness-raising and activism of the political movement for women's rights.[3] Pioneering feminist artists claimed women's experiences, emotions, dreams, and goals as legitimate subject matter for art. Female sexual desire was a major topic they addressed from the outset, along with many others, such as women's history; women's spirituality; and activist issues of equal access to education, jobs, and income. Early feminist artists explored a liberated sexuality through a range of media, from painting and sculpture to photography, video, installation, and performance.

Because women's sexual side had been repressed and unacknowledged for so long, artists at the outset used a sort of shock therapy to claim female sexuality as a theme. Women artists often breached the boundaries of the hitherto private realm of the female libido with sensational public displays. In some cases, women artists of the 1960s and 1970s, including Carolee Schneemann and Hannah Wilke, flaunted their own hyper-sexualized bodies in erotic performances that celebrated their newfound sexual power. These works have been characterized as narcissistic and exhibitionist by some critics, but the approach was effective in asserting women's active sexual agency.

A famous, widely publicized achievement of the early 1970s was the exhibition Womanhouse, organized by Judy Chicago and Miriam Schapiro and created by them and their students in the pioneering Feminist Art Program at the California Institute of the Arts.[4] Working in a house in Los Angeles, the women created installations that exuberantly displayed tampons, underwear, and other items that referred directly to biological functions of female bodies, including menstruation and childbirth. Various sections of the exhibition and accompanying performances raised issues of sexual violence, the psychic confinement of traditional women's roles, and restrictive social standards of feminine beauty.

Judy Chicago's collaborative installation *The Dinner Party* (1974–79) was another landmark. Besides recovering women of distinction from the dustbins of history, the iconography of *The Dinner Party*, particularly the use of vulva designs on the plates, was a clarion call to rescue the female body from Western male stereotypes. Indeed, the use of "cunt imagery" (to use Chicago's terminology) from the 1970s on has been a recurring strategy for resisting male voyeurism and asserting a female sexuality centered on female perception.

In the 1980s, feminists along with many minority and queer artists, continued to engage with politicized issues pertaining directly to the body. Cindy Sherman, Barbara Kruger, Mary Kelly, Helen Chadwick, Adrian Piper, and Lorna Simpson, to name a few, deconstructed the ideological meanings of objectified and stereotyped representations of the body from the past and present. Ideas from the theoretical discourses of post-Freudian psychology, Marxism, poststructuralism, and postmodernism, articulated by writers and theorists, such as Hélène Cixous, Julia Kristeva, Luce Irigary, Griselda Pollock, Craig Owens, Lisa Tickner, and Kate Linker, exerted a strong influence on artists engaged with the politics of the body.

In the 1990s and early 2000s artists have reinvigorated and reinvented figurative art, emphasizing the physical and the tactile. To a greater degree than ever before, such art has not only shown the figure, but has been about the body. Artists have given visual form to previously taboo aspects of sexuality; they have explored the impact on the body of developments in computer technology, medicine, and the life sciences; and they have vigorously expressed what it feels like and what it means to inhabit a mortal, physically changing, and vulnerable body.

In exploring the theme of the body, contemporary artists have utilized a range of strategies and motifs. Artists have dealt with the body in unusual ways—by multiplying it, by fragmenting it, by isolating body parts, by using hair or bodily fluids like blood as stand-ins, and by showing organs and other elements of the body's interior. Moreover, a great deal of art evokes the body without presenting any human image or including an actual person. Clothing has served as a metaphor for the body, as have household furnishings, such as beds, which are in intimate contact with the body. Negative spaces in sculptures record imprints made by the body. Installations resemble empty stage sets, waiting for a human presence. At the same time, contemporary artists have continued to use the body as an artistic medium in both live events and recorded performances.[5]

The Body Is a Battleground

"Your body is a battleground," proclaims a text in a 1989 artwork by Barbara Kruger. Kruger was referring specifically to the pro-choice movement and women's struggle for reproductive rights, but the slogan more generally encapsulates the notion that the body, including its expression in sexuality, "is one of the great political arenas of our times," as Thomas Laqueur put it.[6] Cultural battles over bodies are waged in the mass media, in the streets, in halls of government, and in sleeping quarters the world over. Controversies address the following issues and more: conventions regarding the most socially preferred size, shape, age, and color of bodies; taboos against specific forms of sexual expression; attitudes toward what constitutes mental and physical well-being; moral and legal ramifications of medical decisions affecting the sick and dying; and rules governing the treatment of prisoners, patients, and other institutionalized people. Battles over bodies generally boil down to the question: Who should be in control? Who is in charge of how we see a body, when we see it, why we see it, and what it means to us when we see it?

Artistic explorations of the body in contemporary art reflect attitudes about the body in the culture at large, but attitudes about the body are seldom clear-cut and totally one-sided. Fundamentalist churches exercise a considerable degree of power in the United States, for instance, by spending money to buy advertising to communicate messages about the moral need to abstain from premarital sex; at the same time, this message competes with the forceful message that runs through much of pop culture, that sexual desire and its fulfillment are highly pleasurable and a natural and healthy expression of youth. This is a battle over the control of aspects of sexual expression. Similar contests for the attitudes that citizens hold regarding the appearance and display of the body are waged in societies all over the world. Think, for instance, of the mid-1990s Taliban law in Afghanistan decreeing that each woman's body and face must be hidden by a burka.

The "culture wars" in the United States over the past two decades have turned frequently over issues of control of bodies, particularly as artistic representations challenge mainstream commercial representations. Much of the widely debated art of the period—such as Robert Mapplethorpe's photographs of homosexual subcultures and Karen Finley's performance pieces in which she sometimes smeared food on herself (chocolate, eggs, kidney beans) to present herself metaphorically as an abused woman—confronts the viewer with the often shrouded but everyday occurrence of bodily processes and physical desires. The culture wars were concerned with protests against sexually explicit art, as well as politically activist protest art and art that some deemed religiously offensive. The distinction in types of content can be blurred. For instance, sexually explicit art, especially if it is homoerotic, came under attack because religious fundamentalists often viewed such depictions as immoral on religious grounds. As artists transgressed taboos, controversies erupted and attempts at censorship reached courtrooms and the halls of the U.S. Congress, primarily through attempts to pressure politicians to cut off public funding for art exhibitions.

The Body Is a Sign

The body has value, and its value is often measured relative to the value of other bodies. In contemporary Western society, for example, thinness is a prized characteristic of female bodies. Size and strength are highly valued characteristics of male bodies. These values are communicated by the preponderance of messages in the mass media linking thin female bodies and strong male bodies with other qualities that are valued. For example, a study conducted by researchers at Michigan State University showed that thin female characters in television shows are far more likely to be involved in romantic relationships than are their heavier counterparts.[7] This linkage of values involves viewers in the interpretation of the body as a sign; when a thin female body is seen, we are trained to read sexual potential into it. The body is a sign in a language of social meaning. Connor's sculpture, *Thinner Than You* [3-3], exaggerates the quality of thinness to such an extreme that its positive value is called into question. The thinness is so excessive that it no longer functions as a sign of sexual appeal but, according to Alison Ferris, refers "directly to the extreme consequences of the current fitness and slimming mania—anorexia and bulimia."[8]

Identification of a person by gender is a key area in which we rely on bodily signs to name someone as "male" and "female." In chapter 2, we discussed the fluidity of identity as understood by contemporary theorists and artists. In terms of gender, this perspective suggests that gender identities, such as masculinity and femininity, are roles influenced by culture. Hence, gender roles are open to challenge, negotiation, and redefinition. The fluidity of gender and sexual identity is one theme of Collier Schorr's posed photographs taken in Germany of young models. In Schorr's photo *In the Garden (Karin in Grass)* (1996) [3-4], the body of the model is displayed as

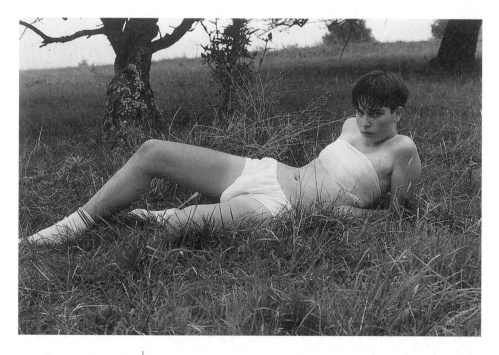

3-4 Collier Schorr | *In the Garden (Karin in Grass)*, **1996**
C-print, 9 x 13 1/4 inches
Courtesy of 303 Gallery, New York

an erotic object, while the model's gender is ambiguous. The model lies in a reclining pose that is part of Western male artists' conventions for depicting the female. The model wears makeup and a gauzy bra bound tightly across the chest, yet displays signs of "maleness," such as a short haircut, hairy legs, and underwear bunched at the crotch in a phallic shape. Reactions to Schorr's photographs also reveal national differences; for instance, German viewers do not automatically see unshaven legs as male.

The practice of using the body symbolically in visual art is long standing. For example, in ancient Egyptian sculptures and paintings, the pharaoh is often shown much larger than ordinary mortals, to emphasize his higher status; moreover, he stands in an erect, stiff posture that signifies his unyielding majesty and authority. Artists utilize a range of symbol-making strategies. For instance, art dealing with the body may employ a *metonym*, a part that symbolizes the whole. The dress shape in *Thinner Than You* [3-3] is an article of clothing that stands for the whole, a clothed female body.

The use of a partial body or body parts is a decidedly anticlassical strategy in contemporary art. While related to such historic masterworks as the Venus de Milo (a well-known classical Greek statue with missing arms), contemporary fragmented figures are deliberate, not the result of accidental breakage.[9] For example, British artist Marc Quinn created life-size figurative sculptures carved in marble, whose pristine white surfaces at first glance evoke classical statues that have lost limbs or exist only as fragments. A closer look reveals that the sculptures are portraits of actual people who are missing one or more limbs. Quinn's sculptures "challenge and displace the classical ideal of 'beauty' and the category of the heroic and perfected nude," an effect that was accentuated in a 2001 installation of his sculptures in a hall of Neoclassical statues at the Victoria and Albert Museum in London.[10]

Sculptures by artists like Bruce Nauman, Kiki Smith, and Dinos and Jake Chapman have featured dismembered body parts (such as heads rotating on a carousel-like contraption by Nauman). Rona Pondick has made sculptures in which anthropomorphic pieces of furniture or articles of clothing serve as substitutes for the body and as sexual fetishes. Pondick's *Baby Fat* (1991) [3-5] shows just the lower half of an anatomically grotesque body wearing little-girl shoes (a sign of gender and age). The "baby fat" sags around the girl's ankles, implying her lack of control over her body. Pondick's figure conveys the powerlessness and psychic stresses of childhood. It also can be interpreted as a metaphor for child abuse; in this way, Pondick's art is an effort to make public a type of bodily and psychological harm that is usually hidden.

According to Helaine Posner, who curated Corporal Politics, an important exhibition of art showing fragmented bodies held in 1992 at the MIT List Visual Arts Center, "The dismemberment of the body in late-twentieth-century art is no accident. It is the result of living in a world in which violence, oppression, social injustice, and physical and psychological stress predominate. We may long for the secure ideals of beauty and wholeness embraced by past generations, but experience tells us that this worldview is obsolete."[11]

Performing Bodies

We experience the world through our body. Our body's sensory apparatus allows us to gain knowledge about the world and to seek pleasure and feel pain. People are tactile, physical, visceral beings. Artists have focused on this fact with great intensity, using

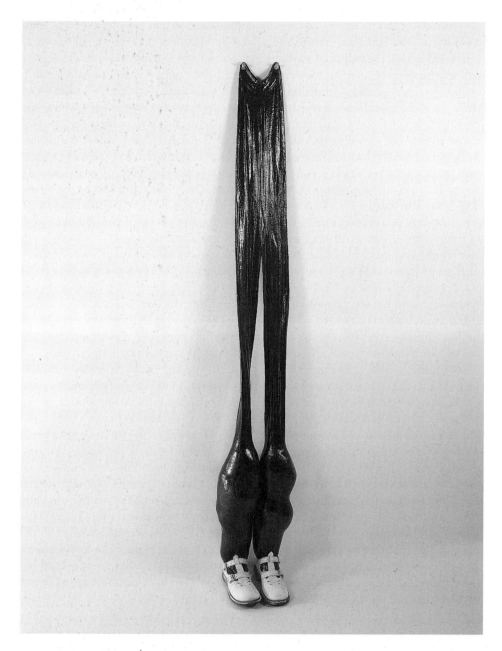

3-5 Rona Pondick | *Baby Fat,* **1991**
Tights, polyester stuffing, shoes, and acrylic resin
Courtesy of Sonnabend Gallery

actual bodies as tools or body materials as art media. For example, Anne Wilson created a series of artworks by embroidering human hair into remnants of antique table linens, and Adrian Piper, in her work-in-progress *What Will Become of Me?* presents in honey jars the artist's own hair, nails, and skin saved since 1985.

Janine Antoni, an artist who grew up in the Bahamas and now lives in New York, has become well known for works she creates by using her body as a tool. Antoni is interested in how the body and its physical processes can manipulate and mark objects and what meanings different viewers infer when they perceive the residue of bodily actions. In *Gnaw* (1992) Antoni created a pair of sculptures by biting enormous cubes of lard and chocolate, leaving the imprint of her teeth on the blocks. To make *Eureka* (1993), she had herself lowered into a bathtub filled with lard then exhibited the tub with the imprint of her now-absent body. In 2003 at the Luhring Augustine Gallery in New York, Antoni performed *To Draw a Line* [3-6], a work for which she spent equal time over an extended preparatory period disciplining her body to learn to tightrope walk and to fall safely. During the performance, Antoni walked the tightrope as long as she could maintain balance on a structure she had painstakingly crafted of handmade rope stretched between one-ton spools. Inevitably she finally fell, descending into a mound of soft raw hemp. The structure of tightrope and spools and the mound of billowy hemp bearing the imprint of her fall remained on view for several weeks as relics of Antoni's walk and fall. Antoni's tightrope walk, during which she had constantly to adjust her body position to maintain balance, seemed to suggest that moments of balance (in life and in art) occur but are fleeting; no possibility of permanent stasis exists. The fall itself was a wonderful unique event in the arc of the performance, wherein the artist relinquished conscious control over her body in the confidence that her kinesthetic memory, achieved through months of rehearsal, would bring her to a safe landing.

Why have many contemporary artists focused on the body? In some cases, this focus is a result of an activist stance toward art making, in which the personal becomes political. In an essay analyzing the formation of the feminist art movement in the United States, artist Suzanne Lacy provides a list of key ideas that helped propel the work that feminist artists were making in the 1970s and into the 1980s. Among these ideas, she noted that the body became a primary site for works of art. Lacy explained: "Not only was the body a site, it was an important source of information. Much of women's social status was seen as based in the body, so issues like violence, birthing, sexuality and beauty were frequent subjects."[12] In other cases, artists using the body have made an aggressive decision to blur the boundaries between art and life. Linda Montano, discussing a work of performance art in which she was tied by rope to the artist Tehching Hsieh for one continuous year (1983–84), explained the consequences of viewing all their bodily actions as forms of art "because I believe that everything we do is art—fighting, eating, sleeping—then even the negativities are raised to the dignity of art."[13]

The Body Beautiful

Although the human body is a perennial theme in art, not all body images are equally valued; in any culture, some images have high status, while others are despised and even censored. Western concepts and images of the human body owe much to the ancient Greeks, who believed that the gods took human form and that the most physically perfect humans reflected the ideal beauty of the gods. Greek figurative art typically showed an intact, young, healthy body with proportions that the culture considered most desirable—a model of the perfection they believed humans should aspire to. From the Renaissance onward, classical Greek ideals of physical beauty pervaded European

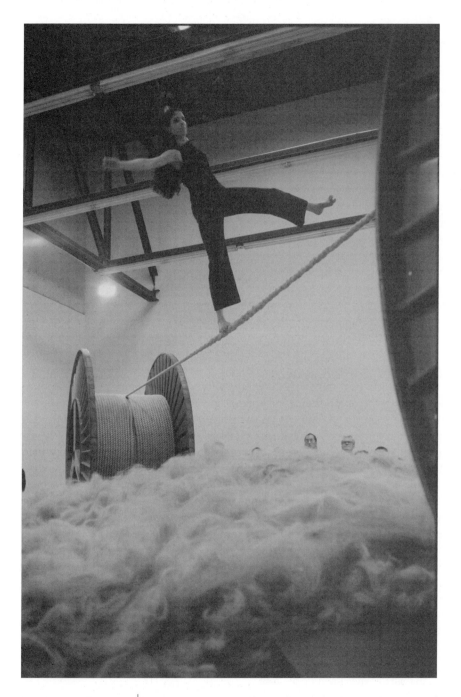

3-6 |anine Antoni | *To Draw a Line,* **2003**

Performance, tightrope stretched between one-ton spools
September 5th, 2003, Luhring Augustine Gallery, New York
4000 lbs. of raw hemp fiber, 120 feet of handmade hemp rope spliced into 1200 feet of
machine-made hemp rope
Photo by Paula Court
Courtesy of the artist and Luhring Augustine, New York

art. Even today, some artists, including sculptor Robert Graham, photographer Jock Sturges, and painters Mel Ramos and Carlo Maria Mariani, continue to produce variations on the classic image of the young beautiful body.

While the specific Greek ideal of a young, classically proportioned body has been influential, alternate ideals of physical beauty can be found in many cultures. For example, although contemporary Americans make a fetish of the slim female body and well-toned male body, in sixteenth- and seventeenth-century Europe, an ample body was most admired as evidence of a person's wealth and power. Cultural ideals dominate the representation of bodies in art even though few real bodies resemble the images. Whatever the culture's dominant body ideals, people see so many images of the preferred body types that they may think these types are common and innately superior and that other kinds of bodies are lesser and defective. But a look at history destroys the illusion of the natural superiority of any one culture's ideals of what is beautiful.

Every culture constructs images of attractiveness. Certain body types are presented as the ideal objects of desire, and they dominate advertising, movies, and other areas of visual culture, while other body types are denigrated and characterized as undesirable. In Western culture today, for example, the beauty ideal for women is defined within incredibly narrow parameters—they must be young, thin, and fit—and there is enormous pressure on women to strive for this ideal, however unrealistic. As Ynestra King wrote, discussing disabled women in particular, "It is no longer enough to be thin; one must have ubiquitous muscle definition, nothing loose, flabby, or ill defined, no fuzzy boundaries. And of course, there's the importance of control. Control over aging, bodily processes, weight, fertility, muscle tone, skin quality, and movement. Disabled women, regardless of how thin, are without full bodily control."[14]

Various artists, including Martha Wilson and Maureen Connor, explore the psychic stresses that accompany eating disorders, excessive plastic surgeries, restrictive clothing, and other self-punishing attempts at conforming to the social ideal. Some artists, including Lorna Simpson and Barbara Kruger, strive to "lay bare the ideological underpinnings (including sexism, ageism, and racism) of ideals of beauty."[15]

One strategy that is popular today is the use of humor, parody, or excessiveness to subvert stereotypes of the ideal body. Drawing on the work and terminology of the Russian literary critic Mikhail Bahktin, writers and artists use notions of *carnival* and *the grotesque body* to discuss works that borrow "tropes from the traditions of the carnivalesque, the tradition of licensed subversion in which hierarchical rank and prohibitions are suspended via vulgar humour, profanities, and costumes and masks."[16] For example, Nancy Davidson takes inflated giant weather balloons and molds them with fetishistic props, such as fishnets, corsets, and G-strings, into camp versions of voluptuous female buttocks and breasts. According to Davidson, "I am interested in humor, excess and the gigantic woman. It comes from being a longtime feminist and being aware as a woman, feeling powerful. When you feel in control, you can take a risk. You can play the part of the clown or the fool."[17]

In contemporary consumer culture—in advertising and popular media, such as television and films (especially in so-called action films)—narrowly defined ideals of physical beauty continue to dominate. In art, in contrast, the human body appears in great variety. Not only do artists represent bodies of all types, some expose the narrowness and artificiality of having an ideal of physical beauty in the first place. For her 1998 performance *Show* at the Guggenheim Museum in New York, Italian-born Vanessa

Beecroft posed fashion models (a few in the nude, most wearing black bikini underwear) in a triangular formation. Her tableau presented living, breathing women, yet the models were so similar in their tall thin proportions that en masse they appeared bizarrely dehumanized, lacking in the individuality we expect to see in crowds. Although there are differences of opinion about the meaning of this and other similar performance works orchestrated by Beecroft, *Show* can be read as a deconstruction of the artificial ideal of the female body promoted by consumer culture.

Artistic challenges to normative views of beauty are seen in works that display body types of all sizes and shapes and that question what terms such as *wholeness, beauty,* and *health* mean and who has the power to define them. Over and over, we find artists making works that critique the narrow standards of beauty and sexual attractiveness. Some artists, among them Hannah Wilke, Joanna Frueh, John Coplans, Laura Aguilar, Jo Spence, Jenny Saville, and Matthew Barney, challenge the assumption that the "perfect" body found in media images is the only attractive one by representing people who are old, physically large, disabled, or scarred who are also brimming with erotic energy. These artists seem to be asking: Why can't age, like youth, be considered beautiful or erotic? Who decided that a disability or a scar or a missing breast or limb are abnormal and must be masked? Of course a wound to the body or a disability causes unavoidable hardships, but societal assumptions and value judgments add unnecessary pain.

Saville deviates from the classical ideal in paintings in which she reveals her own and other nude bodies in gargantuan proportions. Barney's film *Cremaster 3* features an actress, Aimee Mullins, who has a prosthetic leg [3-7], and who exudes a confident sexuality. (The film cycle itself is titled after a muscle in the male body, the cremaster, which raises and lowers the testicles.) Such bodies provide a spectacular contrast to the sanitized, frozen-in-time images found in the world of fashion and advertising.

Sexual Bodies

Sexuality has been expressed in artistic renditions of the body from early times, although it has been denied or repressed in some times and places. For example, early Hindu figurative art was often sensual to the point of being erotic, while early Christian art hid the sensuality of the body under stiff, stylized garments. When figures were depicted in sexualized poses in Christian art before the Renaissance, their purpose was to portray sinful behavior that could lead to damnation. (Later Christian art, especially in the baroque period, became more openly sensual and accepting of sexuality.)

The contemporary period in the West includes many examples of figurative art in which bodies are explicitly sexualized. Sometimes art showing sexualized bodies simply celebrates the pleasures of the flesh; at other times, sexualized bodies serve as a means for investigating concerns about sexism, racism, gender roles, sexual identity, homophobia, reproductive rights, sexual violence, and the boundary between pornography and erotica. For example, lesbian, gay, bisexual, and transgendered (LGBT) artists in the late twentieth century and today have fought for the visibility of their sexual identities by openly representing homosexual desire and same-sex relationships in artworks.

Sexualized bodies represented in the art of the 1980s, 1990s, and early 2000s are often excessive in the desire or eroticism they convey. Robert Colescott, a famous expressionist painter who emerged in the mid-1970s, has painted many such figures.

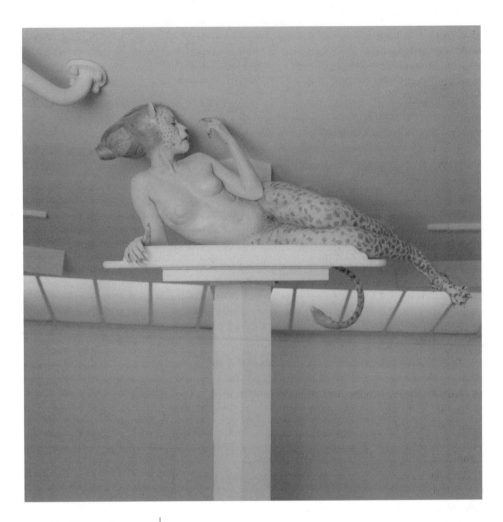

3-7 Matthew Barney | *Cremaster 3*, **2002**
Production still
Photo by Chris Winget
© 2002 Matthew Berney, courtesy of Barbara Gladstone

His painting *Knowledge of the Past Is the Key to the Future (Love Makes the World Go Round)* (1985) is on one level an over-the-top image of voracious sexual attraction; it depicts mutual lust between a man and a woman. But the painting's reception is also complicated by the fact that the male is black and the female white. As Colescott knows, race is an area in which sexuality has been highly charged throughout American history. Lucy R. Lippard noted that in this painting, the naked figures "are shackled together, slaves to passion, as well as to historical precedent and taboo."[18] Colescott uses broad exaggeration to force viewers to acknowledge the violent history of racial mixing in America and our present conflicted attitudes toward eroticism and race.

One of the startling developments in contemporary visual art is the unparalleled rise in artistic representations of sexual pleasure and desire by women artists. Instead of appearing as passive, eroticized objects, women who are represented in art by women frankly register sexual needs and desires of their own. As with other sexual themes, the representation of eroticism has evolved over time. At first, emancipated women artists expressed conventional forms of heterosexual eroticism; their breakthrough was in asserting a female libido and in frankly showing their desire for men. Gradually, women artists gained the confidence to enter the forbidden territory of representing same-gender or cross-racial desire.

In the 1980s, artists and critics increasingly focused on how sexuality is socially and psychologically manifested, rather than on its biological expression. There was a move away from personal, vernacular work based on autobiography toward more conceptual pieces. Some women artists rejected any display of the fleshy, needy, organic female body, preferring to examine the social, political, and psychic systems that shape or constrict female sexuality. As Fiona Carson explained, "The physicality of the female body began to disappear under the weight of its own history in the early 1980s, becoming almost a taboo subject for image-makers because one would add to the overwhelming pile of objectified and stereotyped representations in the dominant culture. As its physical representation became increasingly problematic, the female body dissolved into a flux of shifting signifiers and tangential references. . . . What mattered was to deconstruct its ideological meanings, the interrogation of signs across its surface."[19]

The 1990s and today have seen a renewed emphasis on physical displays of female potency in art. Younger women artists are highly transgressive, giving visual form to multiple, complex aspects of sexual pleasure and lust, in works that may refer to voyeurism, fetishism, and erotomania. For example, Annie Sprinkle, a former worker in the sex industry, achieved notoriety in the 1990s for performances in which she invited audience members to examine her cervix through a speculum. In a series begun in the mid-1990s, Ghada Amer took images from sex magazines of women masturbating and remade them in embroidery thread adhered to painted canvases, her signature technique. Marlene Dumas likewise has used pornographic images as source material. The now routine depictions of explicit sexual acts in films and other forms of popular visual culture may be forcing women artists to up the shock value of their works as they try to get viewers to recognize female perspectives on sexual issues.

Artists and writers about art have also examined the ways in which erotic responses, like other aspects of sexuality, are culturally constructed. For example, Laura Letinsky photographs staged intimate encounters between real heterosexual couples that highlight, in their everyday details and awkward poses, the discrepancy between actual sexual encounters and our romantic expectations for them based on Hollywood images.

Not surprisingly, the expression of female eroticism in visual art is highly controversial. Some feminists, including the artist and writer Mary Kelly, are wary of pleasurable representations of female sexuality, particularly displays of an erogenous female body. Their reasoning is that because mass-media versions of the female body, which reinforce the view of women as sexual objects, are so pervasive, they compromise, and even predetermine how viewers see images of female eroticism in a fine-art context.

Many contemporary feminists recognize that if an artist wants to articulate fully what it means to inhabit a female body, she should not repress her own sexual desires. As Amer said about her attraction to pornography, "At first I lied to myself because I was worried about my family's reaction. I thought I was using sewing because it is a submissive act, and the women showing their bodies in the magazine is a submissive act, so the work was about double submission. Instead, in my work there is an indication of women's pleasure. I think women like to show their bodies and men like to look at them. There is an allusion to masturbation for women, to pleasure."[20]

Women artists who strive to reclaim subjectivity in sexual expression and representation seek two often competing goals: how to advance freedom of sexual expression and how to repel the voyeuristic, controlling scrutiny of male viewers. One strategy is to embrace ambiguity. For instance, Patty Chang has made videos that convey mixed messages about sexual pleasure and erotic response. In *Untitled (Eels)* (2001), she sits dressed in schoolgirl attire, contorting her face and body as something writhes under her white blouse leaving wet spots; as Chang squirms, we glimpse her panties beneath a short black skirt. In fact, unseen by us, large live eels are moving around inside the artist's blouse. The scene is creepy and erotically charged; the expressions on Chang's face do not tell us clearly if she is experiencing erotic arousal or disgust.

Artists who represent female eroticism in ways that are simultaneously attractive and alienating, arousing and anxiety producing, may deliberately reflect the confusion about sexuality in contemporary culture. These artists, working within a society in which women's sexuality is a Pandora's box, may feel they are damned if they open it and damned if they don't.

The Gaze

A useful concept for thinking about sexual bodies in art is *the gaze*, a term that reflects the intertwining of visual control and power structures in society. In the West, we tend to privilege the sense of sight as we interpret the world. This reliance on visual perception means that how we look and how we are looked at influence who we are as social beings. Those who hold the most power in society exercise some control over others by dominating the visual representations of people who lack power. This process of controlling vision (who gets looked at and how they get looked at) is what is meant by *the gaze*. The powerful want to gaze at images that give them pleasure and that reinforce their worldview. Those with less power often feel they must conform to prevalent images or risk being marginalized or ignored.

According to theories of the gaze advanced by John Berger, Michel Foucault, and others, looking is never neutral. Visual representations are not addressed to a neutral, universal audience, but instead assume that viewers are of a certain gender, class, race, and age. The concept of the gaze was given a feminist elaboration by film theorist Laura Mulvey, who argued that the gaze is gendered and who helped promote the argument that in the West the gaze addressed by most imagery historically has been male, heterosexual, white, and economically well-to-do, reflecting a patriarchal power structure built on gender, race, and class.[21] According to Mulvey, Western visual representations of females typically assume a male spectator gazing at the female as a passive object. Furthermore, the gaze is voyeuristic when the female is seen as a pleasurable sexual object.

Representations of female sexuality have occurred throughout the history of Western art, but until recently, they were almost invariably produced by male artists. The female nude was a long-standing artistic subject but not one permitted to women artists. Typical depictions by male artists of sexualized females were objectified, the women rendered in a state of total passivity as objects to be exploited for male sexual gratification (and as sources of energy to be absorbed by the turned-on male). Female sexual desire, when it was shown at all by male artists, tended to be debased, as in the figure of the fallen woman, a temptress associated with carnal sin who led men astray, such as Eve or Salome.

Writings and artworks that analyze the gaze have considered many types of viewers and images. For example, various artists, including video artist Julia Scher, have examined the gaze of surveillance cameras that watch us in stores and other public places [5-10]. In terms of sexuality, up to now the most frequently considered topic pertaining to the gaze has been the voyeuristic gaze of men looking at representations of women as erotic objects. In European and Euro-American visual culture, most representations of sexual bodies are female stereotypes, depicted completely or partially naked, that appeal to the male heterosexual imagination. Women appear as passive and sexually desirable according to a narrowly defined ideal, which is often hypereroticized.

Artists who have made explicit the voyeuristic male gaze abound in recent decades. In their sculptural tableau *The Rhinestone Beaver Peep Show* (1980), Ed and Nancy Reddin Kienholz present an intense scenario pairing power and lust, in which someone with sufficient money can pay to spy on a female stranger's naked flesh. More recently, John Currin has combined meticulous craftsmanship with dry wit in painted scenes that include sexualized caricatures, such as large-breasted young women in tight sweaters. Lisa Yuskavage plays with the notion of the male gaze in many of her paintings by endowing her female figures with strangely shaped breasts and buttocks, simultaneously riveting and repelling the gaze on parts of women's bodies that are often fetishized [color plate 2]. (It is debatable whether Currin and Yuskavage subvert or pander to the male gaze.)

The concept of the gaze has provided a key area of analysis for women artists who are feminists. Feminist artists have resisted the male gaze by asserting the presence of a female consciousness and answering with a gaze of their own. Moreover, since the 1980s, a great deal of effort has gone into revealing masculinist values embedded in the process of looking, as artists have deconstructed stereotyped images in art history and visual culture generally.

In an openly feminist deconstruction of the hidden sexism in historical images addressed to the male gaze, Zoe Leonard juxtaposed her own unambiguous photographs of women's crotches with seventeenth-century portraits of women, all painted by men, in an installation *(Untitled)* at the Neue Galerie in Kassel, Germany, in 1992. Helen McDonald described one juxtaposition: "a hand masturbates a vulva, while in the adjacent painting a seventeenth-century lady fondles her hair and veil in such a way as to reveal her naked breast and shoulder. Thus the frankness of the photograph shows up techniques of erotic titillation in the history of painting."[22]

Mona Hatoum, a Palestinian artist from Lebanon who now lives in London, has represented her own body from the inside out. She employed specialist medical echographic technology to record the sounds of her body and endoscopic and colonoscopic technology to create a visual scan of her body's exterior and interior surfaces. The close-up imagery is presented as one sweeping continuous video image projected on the floor inside a white enclosure [3-8] in her installation *Corps étranger* (meaning "foreign body"). In watching the video, accompanied by recorded sounds of Hatoum's heartbeat and breathing, viewers follow as the camera pans the body, eventually penetrating the interior of the stomach, intestines, and vagina through various orifices. The meanings and politics of *Corps étranger* are ambiguous. On one level, Hatoum appears to

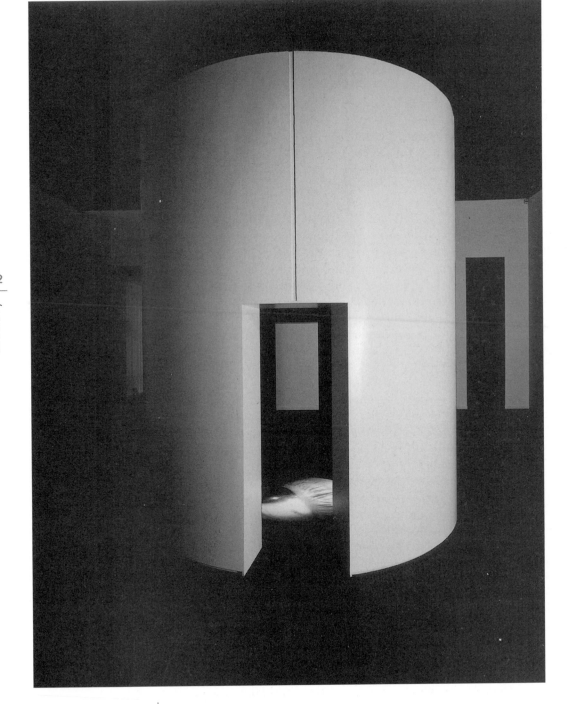

be examining the increasing power and voyeurism of the clinical medical gaze, which now can invade the internal spaces of the body; at the same time, the artist resists and destabilizes the customary male gaze by presenting views that are not erotic. As Amelia Jones wrote: "Here the naked female body is all *vagina dentata*, all *hole*, with nothing phallic/fetishistic left to palliate the male gaze."[23]

Multiculturalists and postcolonial writers have employed the idea of the gaze to analyze how Europeans and Euro-Americans dominated and objectified those they subjugated or enslaved. In the past, when Western artists, such as the French painter Paul Gauguin, represented people of color, they often portrayed their subjects as primitive, exotic, and sexually promiscuous.[24] Lorna Simpson, Coco Fusco, Sonia Boyce, Michele Wallace, and Renée Cox (see the profile) are among the artists who have struggled to make visible issues of racial difference that affect the politics of the gaze and to claim control over their bodies, including how and by whom they are depicted.

Finally, contemporary Western culture has begun to objectify the male body. The trim, sculpted "hard body" of the male that is found in mass-media images has become an object of intense longing and desire; in American teen parlance in the early 2000s, a man, as well as a woman, can merit being called "hot." It will be interesting to see how this development influences future revisions of the theory of the gaze.

Sex and Violence

The sexual politics of the past few decades have included a growing analysis of sexual violence, including rape, incest, and domestic abuse. An examination of art history reveals that eroticized images of women are often presented within a context of male violence. Poussin's painting *Rape of the Sabine Women* (c. 1636–37) and Peter Paul Rubens's *Rape of the Daughters of Leucippus* (c. 1616–17) are famous examples from the baroque period in European art. This tendency is found in visual art up to the present day. The widely popular use of titillating imagery in violent narratives in virtually all forms of mass media, including movies, television programs, music videos, and video games, has impacted cultures across the globe with increasing force over the past thirty years.

In contrast to this torrent of eroticized images, many artists have represented violent sexual experiences as painful. They have created works that reveal and examine the relationship between sexuality and violence, depicting the physical and psychological trauma that women and men experience from rape, battery, murder, and sexual harassment, and, in some instances, critiquing social practices and attitudes that ignore or hide sexual abuse. The history of such artworks by women can be traced back at least as far as Artemisia Gentileschi, who was active as a painter in seventeenth-century Italy, but such historic examples are rare indeed. Feminist activism in the 1960s brought a dramatic surge in art about violence toward women. In the early 1960s, for example, Yoko Ono performed her *Cut Piece*, inviting audience members to come up on stage and cut off pieces of her clothing. The performance revealed viewers' willingness to watch and even participate in a ritualistic violation of a woman's body.

Exploration of (and outrage over) the pairing of sexuality and the cult of violence continues in contemporary art. Sue Coe's painting *New Bedford Rape* (1983), based on an actual rape in Massachusetts, shows a woman pinned on a pool table while men line up to take their turn. Barbara Kruger has made many works since the early 1980s that spotlight ways in which language reinforces stereotypes that facilitate violence against women as well as LGBTs, blacks, and other racial and ethnic minorities. Sue Williams's painting *A Funny Thing Happened* (1992) expresses rage about sexual violence using a cartoonish technique. In a startling reversal of the power dynamics of most sex crimes, Nicole Eisenman made several paintings in the 1990s depicting women castrating men.

For feminists, violence against women and girls has everything to do with the social and political structures that normalize, and even naturalize, male assumptions about women. In patriarchal society, females have conventionally been viewed as helpers, followers, and servants of men, and this inequality opened the door to exploitation, mistreatment, and abuse. Women's art about sexual violence often functions as a kind of visual consciousness-raising, demonstrating the prevalence of abuse and suggesting causes and solutions. Still, women artists face an uphill climb in their efforts to represent the grim reality of sexual violence because of the weird (and wildly profitable) fusing of violence and glamour in the mass media. Western popular culture is obsessed with violence and with depicting victims of violence as young, glamorous, and sensual. In contrast, the victims of violence in artworks by women are neither glamorous nor erotic; they are vulnerable and diverse, in pain and angry.

Mortal Bodies

Numerous contemporary artists believe that in order to understand fully the human condition, we need to perceive the body in its raw physicality and in all its changing shapes and states. In particular, conditions that remind us of mortality—aging, disability, pain, illness, and death—must not be hidden. John Coplans, for example, revealed his own aging body in a series of large-scale photographic self-portraits (first exhibited in 1986 and continued until the artist's death in 2003) that provide close-ups of wrinkles and sagging flesh. Especially since the advent of AIDS in the 1980s, art has increasingly presented the human body as fragile, diseased, wounded, or dying. David Wojnarowicz and Felix Gonzales-Torres were well-known artists who dealt with AIDS as a theme in the 1980s and 1990s, respectively. (Both artists died as a result of contracting the virus.) Diamanda Galás and Ron Athey are artists today who continue to make art that refers to AIDS.

The large color photographs in Andres Serrano's series *The Morgue* (1992) show close-ups of corpses of people who died violently, their heads, hands, and feet bearing stab wounds, surgical incisions, burns, and cuts, or their flesh bloated from drowning or discolored by poisons. Lucinda Devlin shows no actual bodies, although the gloom of unnatural death also permeates her ongoing series, *The Omega Suites*. For more than ten years, Devlin has been photographing the death chambers and instruments of death (gallows, gas chambers, lethal injection apparatus) in penitentiaries all over the United States. The antiseptic sterility of these strange rooms makes the places themselves stand-ins for the chilling finality of death.

Numerous artists have made art about illnesses and dying, including Hannah Wilke, Nancy Fried, and Hollis Sigler about breast cancer and Bob Flanagan about cystic fibrosis. When she was dying of lymphoma in 1993, Wilke made a series of life-size color photographs of her nude body swollen from cancer treatments. Fried, who made a series of sculptures about her own mastectomy, said, "I wonder if this society will ever break the tradition of the idealized female figure and create a new norm that looks at every woman's beauty with pride and acceptance no matter what shape her body is in? Will we ever get over the assumption that only flawless bodies are deserving of public display, approval and sexual expression?"[25]

In recent art, body images and forms in which the figure has lost control over bodily processes, muscle tone, weight, and mobility are prevalent. Bodies sag, bleed, ooze, and drip; they sprout hair in odd places; limbs are wrenched off; surfaces are broken open to show blood and viscera below the skin. These nonconformist and anarchic bodies are another form of the "grotesque"; they defy the classical image of unchanging perfection. According to critic Sally Banes, who writes about dance and performance: "the classical body is smooth, finished, closed, and complete, in contrast to the grotesque body, which is rough, uneven, unfinished, open, and full of apertures."[26]

The grotesque body is marked by time and life events. Although disagreeable, embarrassing, and even offensive to some, grotesque bodies assert the corporeal existence of the body and its mortality. Moreover, by transgressing acceptable boundaries of appearance and behavior, grotesque bodies subvert and resist social practices that tend to suppress individual differences or constrain freedom of expression. Furthermore, grotesque bodies can reveal suffering, violence, and abuse experienced by real people.

Many artists have produced works that include images of transgressive bodies. Joel-Peter Witkin constructs and photographs surreal tableaus using dismembered corpses or living models who have missing limbs or ambiguous sexual organs. Kiki Smith has made sculptures of figures losing control of bodily processes, oozing blood or trailing feces behind them. Dinos and Jake Chapman, brothers who work collaboratively, have made sculptures using plastic and fiberglass mannequins (sometimes fused together) with grotesque anatomical features. Robert Gober has created wax sculptures showing grotesque, fragmented anatomy, including hairy men's legs emerging from gallery walls, a sagging male torso [3-9], and a human torso that is half male and half female.

Representations of mortal, suffering, wounded, grotesque bodies provoke repulsion among viewers, a reaction one could characterize as *abject*, using a concept first formulated by Julia Kristeva, a French philosopher and psychoanalyst. Abjection refers to the heightened horror and vulnerability one feels when confronted with a dismembered limb or blood, semen, hair, vomit, and excrement outside the body, and hence no longer part of a whole. Traumatically reminded of our own materiality, we react with repulsion.[27] At the same time, grotesque artworks serve a valuable purpose in making us focus on our own corporeality and fragile existence in a world in constant flux. Visual culture theorist Francesca Alfano Miglietti wrote, "This sort of 'impurity' of the body terrorises and frightens, almost appears as a threat, as a demonstration of the precariousness of our own body. A wound obliges us to an almost primitive confrontation and relationship in an era in which we often claim that the image has lost all power."[28]

Posthuman Bodies

Imagine a future not far from now, when you no longer have a cell phone because a miniature implant near your ear, equipped with wireless technology, allows you to communicate at any time to any continent via the Internet. You have a new heart transplanted from a pig. You own a puppy who is a clone of your former deceased dog. You are awaiting the birth of your child, whose height, hair and skin color, athletic prowess, sexual orientation, and intelligence have been preselected by you after screening available embryos.

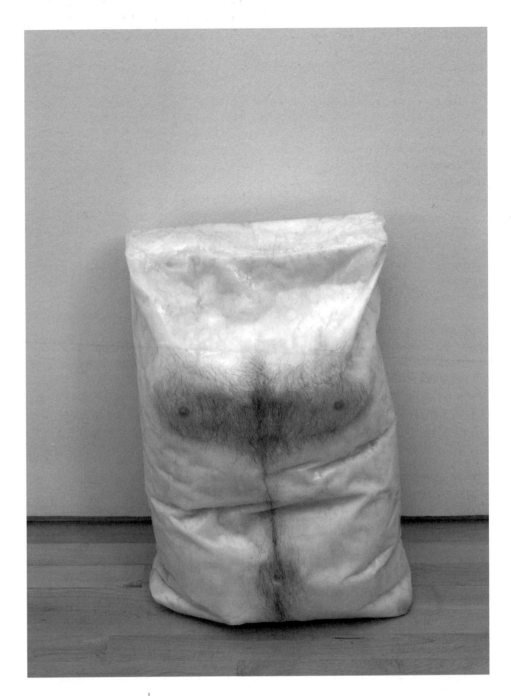

3-9 Robert Gober | *Untitled,* **1990**

Beeswax, pigment, and human hair
23 3/4 in. x 17 1/2 in. x 11 1/4 in. (60.33 cm x 44.45 cm x 28.58 cm)
San Francisco Museum of Modern Art
Purchased through a gift of Rita and Toby Schreiber, by exchange, various donors, the Members Accessions Fund, the
Lenore and Ira Gershwin Fund, and the Accessions Committee Fund: gift of Carla Emil and Rich Silberstein, Lisa and
John Miller, Helen and Charles Schwab, Norah and Norman Stone, Danielle and Brooks Walker, Jr., and Robin Wright.
© Robert Gober

Even stranger changes appear increasingly likely. Indeed, at the dawn of the twenty-first century, we already have been witness to extraordinary developments connected with the body: routine plastic surgery for cosmetic purposes, artificial organs and prosthetic limbs, the wide acceptance of behavior-altering drugs like Prozac and Ritalin, and the successful cloning of mammals. Sophisticated tools, such as mechanical arms, replicate and even surpass human functions. Computers with the superhuman capacity to perform complex calculations and other mental functions as well as to communicate across the globe are used daily even by toddlers. Drugs, prosthetics, bionics, cybernetics, cross-species organ transplants, artificial intelligence, and genetic engineering have made it possible to manipulate the body and its processes in ways that are pushing the boundaries of what it means to be a living organism with a body.

The term *posthuman* has been used by Jeffrey Deitch, among others, to suggest that humans are entering a new phase of evolution in which biotechnology and computer science will give us the power to reconstruct and extend human bodies in artificial ways that take us far beyond biological evolution.[29] The future is near: in 2002 worldwide news media reported that, in a scientific experiment, a British professor was implanted with technology "enabling his nervous system to be linked to a computer . . . effectively [making] him the world's first cyborg—part human, part machine."[30]

The human organism is not entirely organic anymore. Where can and should we draw any line between human, animal, and machine? A posthuman world will inevitably produce new social behaviors and structures. Some people find the prospects of such a world enormously seductive, while others are repelled. Many people are ambivalent about the interface of human bodies with technology. We may feel alienated by technology or fear our dependence on it, yet we also are fascinated by it and always hungry for the latest developments.

Here we give an introduction to how biotechnology, robotics, and computer science are inspiring art about the human body. (In chapter 7, we discuss a range of additional topics related to new discoveries in science that are intersecting with contemporary art.) Of course, the concept of bodies that combine human and nonhuman elements is not new. Images of mutated, transformed, and hybridized bodies—combinations of humans with animals, insects, minerals, or machines—long predate recent biotechnologies and appear throughout the history of art and literature. Satyrs, centaurs, chimeras, griffins, sphinxes, vampires, werewolves, mermaids, and cyborgs are a few of the many instances. In the annals of art, one could think of the strange denizens of Hieronymous Bosch's triptych, *The Garden of Earthly Delights* (c. 1504). More recent examples include the fusions of the human and the mechanical conceived by the futurists in early twentieth-century Europe and the admixtures of humans, insects, and machines found in surrealist art.

Robots and automata, machines that perform human functions, appeared with increasing frequency in Western art and popular culture after the Industrial Revolution made machinery and machine-made objects common in everyday life. Such contraptions are found in contemporary art as well. Alan Rath, who has a degree in electrical engineering from the Massachusetts Institute of Technology, makes mechanical sculptures that embed human features in machine bodies. In *Infoglut* (1996) [3-10], a moving mouth and signaling hands convey messages on video screens that rest on a "neck" and "arms" made of industrial components, suggesting that human communication is dependent on technology. In some artists' works, machines even take the place of the artist. Rebecca Horn's

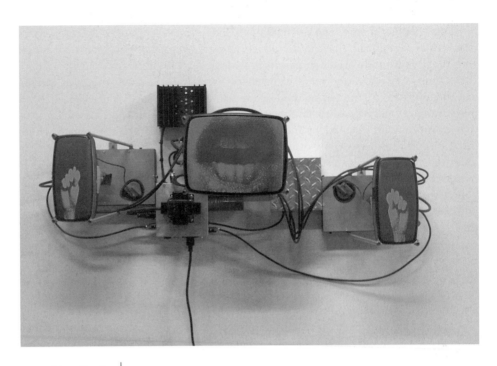

3-10 Alan Rath | *Infoglut*, **1996**

Aluminum, electronics, cathode ray tubes, 22 x 46 x 15 in
© Alan Rath, courtesy of the artist

Painting Machine (1988) and Roxy Paine's *SCUMAK* (1998), a computer-driven machine programmed by the artist to produce one abstract sculpture each day, are two examples.

Belgian artist Wim Delvoye's *Cloaca*, begun in 2000, is a conceptual parody both of efforts to duplicate human functions with machines and of consumerism. The project includes a series of large-scale installations created with the help of biologists, chemists, and engineers that mechanically replicate the human digestive system. Real food is fed into one end of a structure made of glass and metal; then proceeds through tubes where the food is swallowed, ground, and digested by machine organs; and is finally defecated at the other end in an organic form similar to actual human feces. The project includes drawings, models, photographs, and videos, as well as a website where you can order vacuum-sealed feces and various Cloaca merchandise.[31]

Today's new world of bodily transformations produced through plastic surgeries, prosthetics, drugs, and bioengineering provides a powerful stimulus to the imagination of artists. A controversial example is provided by French artist Orlan, who gradually transformed her appearance through nine plastic surgeries from 1990 to 1993 that she describes as art performances and that were filmed and broadcast live to galleries throughout the world. Each surgery altered a specific facial feature based on a prototype selected by Orlan from art history, including the forehead of Leonardo da Vinci's *Mona Lisa* and the chin of Sandro Botticelli's Venus. Orlan's gory, brutal images of her surgeries and her altered physiognomy engendered debates about whether she is making art; the relationship between sculpture and plastic surgery; and the connections among identity, physical appearance, body modifications, and beauty.

Artists are concerned not just with how genetically, surgically, and mechanically altered bodies may look, but with what they mean. In photographs, Margi Geerlinks plays with the visual oddities and conceptual perplexity that can result from the quest for eternal youth by depicting elderly women whose wrinkles were digitally erased. Her images crystallize the miscalculations about age that are occurring as cosmetic surgeries and Botox injections become increasingly commonplace in disguising the aging process. Anthony Aziz and Sammy Cucher, a collaborative team, have created sculptures and photographs that examine anxieties produced by the blurring of traditional boundaries between the organic and the artificial. *Dystopia* (1994–95) is their series of digitally manipulated photographs that imagine mutated people with bizarre skin growths that seal their eyes and mouths, preventing communication. The series *Chimeras* (1998) consists of images of uncanny biotechnological forms that appear to be mutant organs without any body to belong to.

The cyborg, a hybrid creature that is part organism, part machine, has propelled work by Australian artist Stelarc, who has experimented with technologically sophisticated prosthetics and implants attached to his own body. Stelarc has performed with a robotic hand and arm attached as a third appendage to his body; the arm is capable of independent motion, activated by signals from the artist's abdominal and leg muscles. Stelarc also has developed a computer program that allows the third hand to be activated from a library of gesture icons available on a touch-screen interface; meanwhile electrodes attached to his actual limbs stimulate countermovements [3-11]. Other cyborglike modifications that Stelarc has explored include wiring his body for sound, implanting cells cultivated in the shape of his own ear beneath the skin of his left forearm, and exploring the inside of his body with microminiaturized nanotechnologies.

Stelarc is fascinated by the potential obsolescence of the body. He proposes building a stronger, less vulnerable body with synthetic skin, greater brain capacity, fewer organs, and microcircuits that enhance hearing, sight, and other senses. Stelarc maintains that technological redesign of the body is not just an exciting experiment, but is necessary for human survival. Miglietti wrote, "The body, according to Stelarc, is no longer capable of adequately confronting a reality that is evolving at uncontrollable velocities: the technologies and their use in systems of social organization imposed and implemented by the economic strategies of the last century have modified the environment in a radical manner that is dangerous to the human body, rendering the habitat unfriendly to man and provoking the need to make use of artificial 'cures' for the safeguarding of individuals. Stelarc believes that human 'salvation' is linked to the possibility of beginning to conceive of a body that is capable of competing with various new technologies and that is capable of absorbing and redeveloping the highly information-based reality in which it exists."[32]

Today the fascination with links between the body and technology has extended into the digital realm for artists and nonartists alike. Stelarc, for example, has used the Web to create virtual surrogates for the human body. On the Web, we can interface in virtual reality with people we cannot see in person. We can invent new identities for ourselves; we can even inhabit new physical bodies in the form of "avatars," beings who visibly move through cyberspace as substitutes for the person sitting in front of the screen. What does all this imply for how we think about and value humans as organisms? Has digital technology enabled us to transcend the limitations of our own bodies? Will we someday prefer the company of avatars to flesh-and-blood humans?

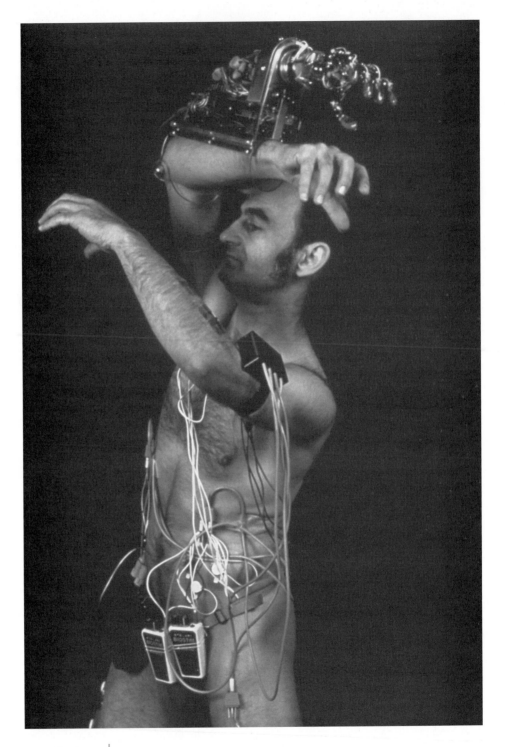

3-11 Stelarc | *The Third Hand,* 1980

Tokyo, Yokohama, Nagoya
Photo by Simon Hunter
Courtesy of the artist

Deciphering and influencing the patterns of a posthuman world is one of the greatest challenges that contemporary artists face. With increasing acceleration, our species appears headed for a voyage in which scientific and technological advancements will release us from our genetically imprinted, biological bodies. In cyberspace, our virtual egos are already inserted into a new construct of post-body-ness. We are creating realities in which material bodies do not exist. In following this path, we seem to be discovering pathways that mystics glimpsed in earlier eras: as we acquire the capacity to extend, alter, and magnify our bodies to a degree that appears almost supernatural and that allows us to inhabit astrallike projections. This state of post-body human-ness may turn the relationship of art to life inside out; in the future, life may be a subset of art, not the other way around.

The gaze in Western societies has long fastened on the black female body as an object of voyeuristic fascination.[33] An infamous example is Saartje Baartman, a Khoisan woman from South Africa, who was exhibited as a sideshow attraction in London and Paris for five years early in the nineteenth century. Advertised under the name Hottentot Venus ("Hottentot" was a derogatory term for the Khoi people), Baartman drew crowds who paid to see her naked body, which had large buttocks and elongated genitalia. For an extra fee, visitors could touch her buttocks. After Baartman died at around age 25 in 1815 (either of smallpox or pneumonia), her body was dissected in the name of science, and her skeleton and preserved genitals and brain were put on display in the Musée de l'Homme in Paris. Nearly two hundred years later, after an eight-year legal battle initiated by then South African president Nelson Mandela, her remains were returned to her native land in 2002 for burial. An icon of the colonial exploitation of women of color, Baartman has inspired works of fiction, visual art, and film, as well as scholarly studies. Her outrageous treatment raises issues of power, colonialism, racism, ideal beauty, and taboo sexuality.[34]

Multimedia artist Renée Cox recast herself as Baartman in her black-and-white photograph *Hott-En-Tot* (1994) [3-12].[35] The artist attached oversized fake breasts and buttocks to her nude body, thus emphasizing parts of the anatomy that are repeatedly fetishized in visual representations of black women. The cartoonish prostheses mock the pseudoscientific strategy that was once used to argue for the social inferiority of black people on the basis of physical differences; Cox is critiquing how past displays directed the gaze to anatomical features, such as large buttocks, that contradict the idealized norms found in classical Western nudes.[36] Moreover, Cox stands in the profile pose that, along with frontal views of bare-breasted women, was supposed to display certain human "types" in nineteenth-century illustrations objectively. The poses are associated with a pseudo-anthropology that attempted to link desirable and undesirable social characteristics to physical features. Cox's flagrant parody of racist visual clichés is intended to show their inherent manipulation and falseness. Cox, with beautifully coiffed dreadlocks, makeup, and manicured nails, gazes back directly out of the frame, affirming her pride in possessing a black female body.

The humiliating display and accompanying ridicule of Baartman's physical attributes were typical of colonial European representations of indigenous people, including black African women, who were viewed as inferior and sexually deviant.[37] Representations of black Africans in artistic, cultural, and scientific contexts were intended to maintain racial boundaries by establishing their Otherness in comparison to white Europeans. Their physical attributes were stereotyped and exaggerated and then interpreted as proof of European superiority in morals and civilization.

High art in the West from the ancient Greeks forward has perpetuated and reinforced standards of beauty that are associated with idealized European body types, that is, whiteness and a limited range of proportions and other physical

3-12 Renée Cox │ *Hott-En-Tot,* 1994

Gelatin silver print
Courtesy of the artist

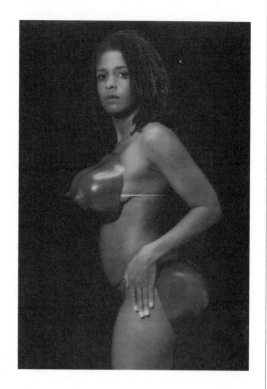

attributes; black women whose bodies did not fit these standards were made to seem abnormal and inferior. At the same time, black women in nude depictions were seen as sexually promiscuous and erotically available, a fantasy reinforced by the association of nudity with sin; thus images of nude black women paradoxically evoked desire in European viewers who craved the exotic. As Lisa E. Farrington asserted, "The white male attribute that was projected upon the black women was uncontrollable sexual desire. Although there is little doubt that the sexual aggressors in interactions between women of color and white men were males, women were nonetheless classified as the wanton and licentious ones."[38]

Since the early 1990s, Cox has photographed her own voluptuous body, often nude, in staged scenes that address historical stereotypes, the paucity of images of blacks in Western art, motherhood and family roles, and female sexual pleasure. She uses her own body in an attempt to reverse the objectification of black women and claim self-empowered subjectivity by freely presenting her own body in any pose for any purpose she wishes.

Historically, representations of black women in fine art made by Western artists have been uncommon. When black women appear, it has generally been in the stereotyped roles of servant, slave, prostitute, or exotic savage. (Representations in popular visual culture, especially after the invention of photography, have been more numerous but equally demeaning.) With the aim of exposing the scarcity of black subjects in Western high art, Cox has made large-format color photographs that show herself, family members, and friends inserted into famous works of art.

In several of these photographs, she takes on the ultimate representation of the idealized, eroticized white female in Western art—the reclining nude—replacing the white model in the original with her own image and substituting new accessories. For instance, in *Baby Back* (2001 Cox poses as the nude in Ingres's famous *Grande Odalisque* (1814), wearing red high heels and holding a whip in place of the phallic feather fan in the painting [color plate 3]. In *Olympia's Boyz* (2001), Cox puts herself in the pose of Manet's *Olympia* (1863) with her two adolescent sons standing behind her in place of the black maid in the painting. In these startling, bold images, the artist gazes back assertively at the camera, challenging assumptions about whiteness as an ideal of beauty.

Cox has developed alter egos who appear in some of her staged photos. Rajé is a superhero attired in a costume of red, gold, green, and black, the colors of the Jamaican and Rastafarian flags. In a series of campy digitally manipulated photographs, Rajé battles racial prejudice, for example, by rescuing sexy young versions of Aunt Jemima and Uncle Ben from their package labels and halting taxicabs that are ignoring African Americans. Another character, Yo Mama, is a sensual and empowered black mother, far removed from the asexual Mammy figure prominent in the mythology of the antebellum American South.

Cox's works have been controversial among critics, who variously have called her work exhibitionist, narcissistic, and even obscene. In a 2001 interview, Cox said in response, "The Met is full of naked Greek statues and no one is upset about that."[39] Particularly controversial are explicitly erotic photographs in which Cox assumes provocative poses wearing fetishistic attire, such as a black leather corset, lacy garter belt, and furry thong, often framing her torso and crotch in close-ups without the rest of her body; other photographs juxtapose full-body erotic self-portraits next to vintage photographs of her mother, other family members, and her adolescent self wearing a Catholic school uniform. Cox's erotic photographs express female-directed fantasy and desire and challenge taboos about proper behavior for a wife and mother.

B. E. Meyers argued that despite the power of Cox's images and her political intentions, Cox like other female artists of color has a daunting task to try to overcome the conditioning of viewers. Meyers claimed that "part of what makes Black women's audiences unable to recognize them as fully human is the fact that their dark bodies are over-determined. The bodies themselves signify too greatly because they are heavy with history, and audiences come to understand these historical memories through at least two voices: through a scientifically-laden analytical lexicon; as well as through the wordless and very neurotic push of desire."[40] Cox aims to offer images of a self-empowered woman in control of the display of her own body. Yet the question remains, Can a representation of a nude black woman—in some viewers' eyes—ever transcend race or sexual desire?

Renée Cox was born in Jamaica in 1960 and raised in New York. She worked as a fashion photographer for more than ten years before returning to school to earn a master of fine arts degree from the School of Visual Arts, New York.

In the period that this book addresses, mainland China has gone through a rapid economic and social transformation, becoming a major player in the global economy and more receptive to external cultural influences as well as internal social pressures for modernization. Zhang Huan emerged as an artist in China during the tumultuous 1990s, joining other rebellious artists who challenged the forces of tradition despite the repressive climate after the Tiananmen Square student uprising in June 1989. Zhang moved from Henan Province to Beijing in 1991, and in 1993 established the "Beijing East Village" with a small group of avant-garde artists in a poor, garbage-filled district on the outskirts of the capital. Several of these artists were among the few in China to work in performance art in the 1990s, when such practices were largely underground to avoid official censoring.

Zhang first became recognized for works for which he used his own body as his artistic material, notably projects involving nudity (a taboo in China) and feats of endurance and masochism. For instance, in *12 Square Meters* (1994) he sat upright and immobile for an hour on a toilet in a filthy, fly-infested public latrine (the title indicates the dimensions of the latrine floor), with fish oil and honey coating his naked body and his head shaved punk style. In *65 Kilograms* (1994), the artist hung naked suspended from chains from the ceiling of his squalid studio while blood dripped from cuts on his neck onto a hot plate below him. In *25mm Threading Steel* (1995), Zhang lay near where workers were grinding steel tubes at a skyscraper construction site, allowing flying sparks to land on his nude body. Performed in private before small audiences, these and other works brought Zhang international attention through their photographic documentation.

Commentators have compared Zhang's performances of this type to Western body art performances of the late 1960s and 1970s—by Chris Burden, Stuart Brisley, Gina Pane, and others—that likewise offered an iconography of pain and presented the artist as a living embodiment of self-control in situations of mortification, suffering, and humiliation. As with Western body art, Zhang's performances seemed to use the body enduring pain as a metaphor for individual singularity and resistance in the face of pressures for social and political conformity. But Zhang's performances have other interpretations that reflect his biography along with a specifically Chinese context. According to art historian Gao Minglu, "Zhang Huan is concerned with the general living situations of ordinary people as refracted through his own individual experience."[41] The squalid village latrine in *12 Square Meters*, for instance, was the one Zhang actually used along with peasants in the Beijing East Village; his performance symbolized the wretched living conditions of the Chinese poor as well as his own destitute situation as a marginalized artist.

In a 1999 interview, Zhang suggested an undercurrent of Buddhism in his endurance works, specifically the Buddhist notion that the mind and body are melded and inseparable. He explained, "It is only in such conditions that I am able to experience the relationship between the body and the spirit. In performance, I try to let my mind leave my body and forget the surrounding conditions. At that moment, I cannot feel any pain. Yet, the mind cannot really leave the body. Instead, it keeps going back to the body. And when the mind returns to the body, there comes an ever stronger feeling of the body's real situation. . . . But it is not the physical pain in the physical body, but rather the spiritual uneasiness. The shift between the mind and the body is what I prefer to experience."[42]

In the late 1990s, after Zhang came to the United States, his focus shifted to the public sphere, as he staged performances in museums and outdoor public locations. For *Pilgrimage—Wind and Water in New York* (1998), performed in the courtyard at the P.S.1 Contemporary Art Center, Zhang lay on a mattress of ice resting on a Chinese Ming-style bed with seven dogs tied to its frame; after ten minutes, the intense cold forced him to rise. Critic Eleanor Heartney wrote, "The work was a commentary on his uncertain place in his new home: instead of warming the ice with his body heat, Zhang Huan came close to freezing, raising questions about the kind of impact an immigrant may hope to have on his new environment. The dogs were meant to refer to the coexistence of races (and species) in his new home, but they also added an uneasy undercurrent, blurring the line between their status as predators and as pets."[43]

The strangeness of the West as perceived by the Chinese artist provided artistic fodder for other works. For *My New York (Worker)* (2002) [color plate 4], one of a series of staged events responding to different places in the United States and elsewhere, Zhang strode through the streets of New York wearing a heavy suit constructed from pieces of raw beef to make him look like a body builder and periodically releasing white doves (a symbol of peace). In an artist's statement, he compared the status of the United States as a superpower to his observations of people in New York engaged in extreme bodybuilding. "Something may appear to be formidable, but I will question whether or not it truly is so powerful. Sometimes such things may be extremely fragile, like body builders who take drugs and push themselves beyond the limits of their training on a long-term basis, until their heart cannot possibly bear such enormous stress."[44] In the anxious political climate of the post–9/11 world, the image of powerful flesh encasing the slight figure of the artist can be read as a symbol of the vulnerability of even the most powerful nation on earth.

Zhang's eight years in New York heightened his self-consciousness about his enduring Chinese identity and his interest in Chinese history and culture. His work evolved from a focus on performance to an ambitious exploration of painting, sculpture, and printmaking. These works maintain a strong focus on the body while embracing the broader themes of cultural identity and spirituality, themes he has continued to explore since his return to China in 2006. Since 2003, references to Buddhism have proliferated in his art, including hollow-copper sculptures that depict greatly enlarged fragments of body parts—fingers, feet, hands, legs—adapted from Buddha statues that were broken during China's Cultural Revolution. Zhang has also used the image of his own body in sculptures that incorporate Buddhist iconography. In a few works, he juxtaposed bronze casts of his body with

3-13 **Zhang Huan** | *Giant No. 3,* **2008**

Cowskin, steel, wood and polystyrene foam
15' 1" x 32' 10" x 13' 9" (4.6 m x 10 m x 4.2 m)
Photo by Gordon R. Christmas
© Zhang Huan Studio, courtesy of PaceWildenstein,
New York

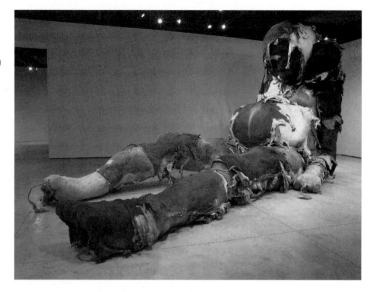

large bells based on Tibetan temple bells; in others, he has made monumental self-portrait heads with features of the Buddha, such as long earlobes, which are covered in the ash residue from incense burned in temples.

In the twenty-first century, Zhang is firmly part of the global art network, exhibiting internationally and acting as an artist-impresario who oversees the production of ambitious artworks that involve many hours of human labor carried out by skilled artisans at a factory-like workshop that Zhang established outside Shanghai. Zhang's recent works include colossal figurative sculptures, such as *Giant No. 3* (2008) [3-13], which depicts a fifteen-foot pregnant beggar with a child clinging to one shoulder; the figures are swathed in ragged garments made from a vast quantity of cowhides stapled together, their hooves and tails still attached. Getting bigger brings no protection against adversity, the artist seems to say; the body is always vulnerable.

Zhang Huan was born in 1965 in Anyang, Henan Province, China. He studied traditional painting as a graduate student at the Central Academy of Fine Arts in Beijing. Zhang relocated to New York City in 1998, where he lived for eight years before moving back to China in 2006 and settling in Shanghai.

Notes

1. Thomas McEvilley, *Sculpture in the Age of Doubt* (New York: Allworth Press, 1999), 384.
2. Ibid., p. 386.
3. Several sections in this chapter, beginning here, appeared in a previous form in Jean Robertson, "Artistic Behavior in the Human Female," in Betsy Stirratt and Catherine Johnson, eds., *Feminine Persuasion: Art and Essays on Sexuality* (Bloomington: Indiana University Press, 2003), pp. 23–38. Passages of that earlier essay have been revised and inserted at appropriate points in the remainder of this chapter, with the permission of Indiana University Press.

4. For a history of the Feminist Art Program written by one of the key participants, see Faith Wilding, "The Feminist Art Programs at Fresno and CalArts, 1970–75," in Norma Broude and Mary D. Garrard, eds., *The Power of Feminist Art: The American Movement of the 1970s, History and Impact* (New York: Harry N. Abrams, 1994), pp. 32–47. For a discussion of Womanhouse in particular, see Arlene Raven, "Womanhouse," in the same volume.

5. Performance artists who have worked with issues pertaining to the body in the past few decades include Bob Flanagan, Marina Abramovic, Linda Montano, Karin Finley, Tim Miller, and Franko B, among numerous others. In addition to live events, performances about body issues recorded by still and video cameras became increasingly prevalent after 1980, as seen in works by Hannah Wilke, Paul McCarthy, Matthew Barney, and Orlan.

6. Thomas Laqueur, "Clio Looks at Corporal Politics," in Donald Hall, *Corporal Politics* (Cambridge: MIT List Visual Arts Center; Boston: Beacon Press, 1992), p. 14. An exhibition catalog.

7. The Michigan State University study was reported by Nanci Hellmich, in "Obese Characters Are Stereotyped," writing for *USA Today*, reprinted in *Indianapolis Star, TV Week*, Sunday, January 6, 2002, p. 11.

8. Alison Ferris, "Discursive Dress," in *Discursive Dress* (Sheboyan, Wis.: John Michael Kohler Arts Center, 1994), p. 11. An exhibition catalog.

9. The Venus de Milo, with its arms missing, was discovered on a beach in Greece in 1821. Interpretations of its meaning and explanations of its appeal to viewers have not been homogeneous. In an essay first published in 1980, Peter Fuller argues that among the reasons for the appeal of the Venus de Milo to modern viewers is, in fact, its fragmented form. A concise analysis of Fuller's argument is offered in Jonathan Harris, *The New Art History: A Critical Introduction* (London: Routledge, 2001), pp. 140–142.

10. *Give & Take* (London: Serpentine Gallery and Victoria and Albert Museum, 2001), p. 33. The actual carving of the figures was done by stonemasons in Italy. An exhibition catalog.

11. Helaine Posner, "Separation Anxiety," in Hall, *Corporal Politics*, p. 30.

12. Suzanne Lacy, "The Name of the Game," *Art Journal* 50, no. 2 (Summer 1991), reprinted in Kristine Stiles and Peter Selz, eds., *Theories and Documents of Contemporary Art: A Sourcebook of Artists' Writings* (Berkeley: University of California Press, 1996), p. 784.

13. Linda Montano and Tehching Hsieh, "One Year Art/Life Performance: Alex and Allyson Grey Ask Questions About the Year of the Rope," *High Performance* 27 (1984), reprinted in Stiles and Selz, eds., *Theories and Documents of Contemporary Art*, p. 780.

14. Ynestra King, "The Other Body: Reflections on Difference, Disability, and Identity Politics," *Ms.*, March–April 1993, p. 74.

15. Amelia Jones, ed., *Sexual Politics: Judy Chicago's "Dinner Party" in Feminist Art History* (Los Angeles: UCLA/Armand Hammer Museum of Art and Cultural Center, in association with University of California Press, 1996), p. 257. An exhibition catalog.

16. Jessica Evans, "Photography," in Fiona Carson and Claire Pajaczkowska, eds., *Feminist Visual Culture* (New York: Routledge, 2001), p. 114.

17. Quoted in Lauren Parker, "Inflated Desire," *Smock* 2, no. 1 (Winter 2002): p. 75.

18. Lucy R. Lippard, *Mixed Blessings: New Art in a Multicultural America* (New York: Pantheon Books, 1990), Plate 38 sidebar.

19. Fiona Carson, "Sculpture and Installation," in *Feminist Visual Culture*, p. 62.

20. Ghada Amer, "Interview with Ghada Amer," by Marilu Knode, *New Art Examiner* 27, no. 4 (December–January 1999/2000): p. 38.

21. Mulvey's seminal essay presenting her argument that the gaze is gendered and is distinctly male is "Visual Pleasure and Narrative Cinema," *Screen* 16 no. 3 (Autumn 1975): pp. 6–18, and reprinted in Mulvey, *Visual and Other Pleasures* (Basingstroke, United Kingdom: Macmillan, 1989).

22. Helen McDonald, *Erotic Ambiguities: The Female Nude in Art* (London and New York: Routledge, 2001), p. 94.

23. Amelia Jones, "Survey," in Tracey Warr, ed., *The Artist's Body* (London: Phaidon Press, 2000), p. 43.

24. A groundbreaking analysis of Gauguin's stereotyped view of native bodies is the essay by Abigail Solomon-Godeau, "Going Native: Paul Gauguin and the Invention of Primitivist Modernism," *Art in America* 77 (July 1989): 118–129, and reprinted in Norma Broude and Mary D. Garrard, eds., *The Expanding Discourse: Feminism and Art History* (New York: HarperCollins, 1992), pp. 313–329.

25. Cited in Matuschka, "Got to Get This Off My Chest," *On the Issues* 25 (Winter 1992): p. 33.

26. Sally Banes, "'A New Kind of Beauty': From Classicism to Karole Armitage's Early Ballets," in *Beauty Matters*, ed. Peg Zeglin Brand (Bloomington: Indiana University Press, 2000), p. 271.

27. Julia Kristeva, *Powers of Horror: An Essay on Abjection* (New York: Columbia University Press, 1982).

28. Francesca Alfano Miglietti, *Extreme Bodies: The Use and Abuse of the Body in Art* (Milan: Skira, 2003), p. 35.

29. Deitch curated a groundbreaking exhibition on this theme. See the exhibition catalog, Jeffrey Deitch, *Post Human* (Pully and Lausanne: FAE Musée d"art Contemporain; New York: Distributed Art Publishers, 1992). An exhibition catalog.

30. The story, from CNN.com, was carried on the World Wide Web, http://cnn.netscape.cnn.com/news/March 22, 2002.

31. See the Cloaca website, which parodies online consumer shopping sites: http://www.cloaca.be/.

32. Miglietti, *Extreme Bodies*, p. 194.

33. See the discussion of the gaze in chapter 3, "The Body."

34. The history and enduring legacy of Saartje Baartman are explored in Janell Hobson, *Venus in the Dark: Blackness and Beauty in Popular Culture* (New York: Routledge, 2005), a cultural history of black female beauty.

35. *Venus Hottentot 2000* (1995) is a second version of this image, with Cox posing as Baartman for a color photograph taken by the photographer Lyle Ashton Harris.

36. Janell Hobson provides a fascinating discussion of African and African-based cultures, including Jamaica (Cox's country of origin), that celebrate the female derrière as an aspect of physical beauty, in her chapter, "The 'Batty' Politic: Toward an Aesthetic of the Black Female Body," in *Venus in the Dark*, pp. 87–112.

37. Examples of these historical representations, along with scholarly essays investigating them, are presented in Barbara Thompson, ed., *Black Womanhood: Images, Icons, and Ideologies of the African Body* (Hanover, New Hampshire: Hood Museum of Art, Dartmouth College; Seattle: In association with University of Washington Press, 2008). An exhibition catalog.

38. Lisa E. Farrington, "Reinventing Herself: The Black Female Nude," *Women's Art Journal* 24 (Fall 2003–Winter 2004): p. 17.

39. Karen Croft, 22 February 2001, "Using Her Body," p. 2, http://archive.salon.com/sex/feature/2001/02/22/renee_cox/index.html (accessed June 8, 2008).

40. B. E. Myers, "What Is My Legacy? Transient Consciousness and the 'Fixed' Subject in the Photography of Renée Cox," in Salah M. Hassan, ed., *Gendered Visions: The Art of Contemporary Africana Women Artists* (Trenton, N.J. and Asmara, Eritrea: Africa World Press, 1997), p. 32.

41. Gao Minglu, "From Elite to Small Man: The Many Faces of a Transitional Avant-Garde in Mainland China," in Gao Minglu, ed., *Inside Out: New Chinese Art* (Berkeley and Los Angeles: University of California Press, 1998), p. 164. An exhibition catalog.

42. Qian Zhijian, "Performing Bodies: Zhang Huan, Ma Liuming, and Performance Art in China," *Art Journal* 58 (Summer 1999): p. 68.

43. Eleanor Heartney, "Zhang Huan: Becoming the Body," in Melissa Chiu, ed., *Zhang Huan: Altered States* (New York: Asia Society, 2007), p. 43. An exhibition catalog.

44. As quoted in Britta Erickson, *On the Edge: Contemporary Chinese Artists Encounter the West* (Stanford, Calif.: Iris & B. Gerald Cantor Center for Visual Arts, 2005), p. 69. An exhibition catalog.

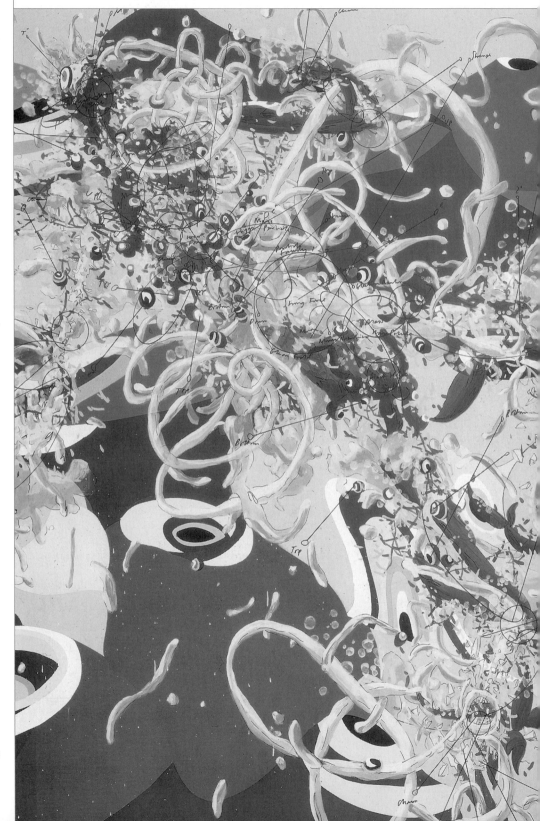

Detail of 4-6

CHAPTER FOUR

Time

Time is a vital topic in contemporary art, addressed in a rich range of works that involve a variety of media, approaches, and concepts. In this chapter, we look at the prevalence of the theme of time in art after 1980, as well as some definitions, historical contexts, artistic strategies, and subthemes that begin to map aspects of this far-reaching topic.

To begin exploring the complexity and variety of artists' reflections on matters of time, let's look at two works of art: a film by a team of Swiss artists, Peter Fischli and David Weiss, and a sculpture by American Heide Fasnacht. In Fischli and Weiss's entertaining thirty-minute film, *Der Lauf der Dinge (The Way Things Go)* (1985–87) [4-1], the camera pans the long floor of a warehouse, along which are arrayed makeshift conglomerations of simple props, such as buckets of water, rubber tires, Styrofoam cups, string, and balloons. Through the action of fire, gravity, chemicals, and gunpowder, each object spills, falls, rotates, ignites, or explodes in turn. Each object's demise triggers what happens to the next object in line. The chain reaction embodies time in its absurd kinetics: one thing is engineered to lead to the next in what appears to be a continuous thirty-minute sequence in real time. (In fact, though, Fischli and Weiss had to film some of the micro-events separately and splice segments of film together to achieve the appearance of a seamless chain of events.) Fischli and Weiss do not structure time as a narrative in this film: there is no plot with a beginning, middle, and end, and the chain reaction has no ultimate goal or final outcome. Rather, their approach to time favors sequencing without narrative. In the view of curator Amy Cappellazzo, "Since the objects are set up to have a domino effect but rely on time, rather than a story line, to dictate their next move, the entire work can be viewed as a kind of time-piece or clock."[1]

Besides coming close to representing a real-life experience of time, *The Way Things Go* may also have a moral subtext. Fischli and Weiss devoted months of tinkering to achieve their house-of-cards effects. The implication is that there is value in time spent making something essentially useless that exists only for a short time, simply for the joy of seeing an idea come to life. This devotion to time spent in creative play generally contradicts how time is valued in day-to-day life in industrial societies.

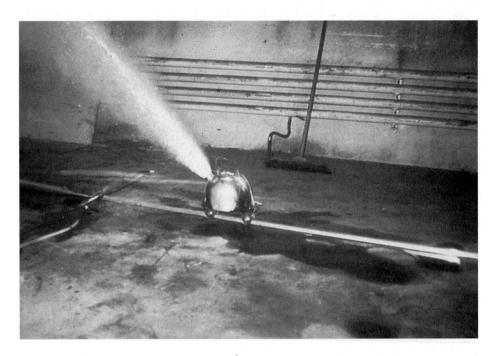

4-1 Peter Fischli and David Weiss │ *still from Der Lauf der Dinge (The Way Things Go),*
1985–1987

16mm film
© Peter Fischli David Weiss, courtesy of Matthew Marks Gallery, New York

Heide Fasnacht's sculpture *Demo* (2000) [4-2] conveys a sense of time that is more instantaneous yet paradoxically more permanent than the sequence of time expressed in Fischli and Weiss's film. In a highly unusual approach to sculpture, *Demo* freezes a split second in time, suspending the explosion of a building in midair (much like in a stop-action photograph). To create *Demo*, Fasnacht referred to black-and-white photographs that were made during the detonation of an actual building. Working at a scale slightly larger than a standing human and using nontraditional materials (Styrofoam and neoprene), Fasnacht suspended the myriad shards of an exploding building flying outward into space. What would normally occur in the blink of an eye is frozen for us to peruse at our leisure, unlike the constantly changing mini-events in Fishli and Weiss's film. A key difference between these works is that Fischli and Weiss's film *embodies* time, whereas Fasnacht's sculpture *represents* the explosion of a building as a suspended moment in time.

Demo is one in a series of stop-action sculptures that Fasnacht began in 1997, when she first introduced a human sneeze as a subject. Since then, in numerous drawings and sculptures, the artist has represented a range of eccentric events—including sneezes, geysers, fires, and military explosions—which, according to Nancy Princenthal, "fall at the threshold of visibility, in the realm of things that, while not imperceptible, are more or less impossible to visualize in any stable, conventional way."[2]

Intriguingly, *Demo* manipulates the dimension of time on multiple levels. First, there is the (rapidly moving) time of the actual explosion; second, the (stopped) time of the artwork's depiction; and third, the (much slower but still moving) time of the

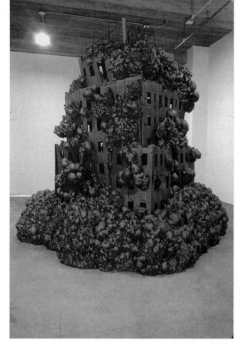

4-2 Heide Fasnacht | *Demo,* **2000**
Neoprene, styrofoam, pigment, approximately 9 1/2 x 10 1/2 x 10 feet
Courtesy of the artist and Kent Gallery, NY

viewer's experience walking around and looking at the artwork. In addition, the subject of the artwork provides a fourth, metaphoric level of meaning. The sculptural simulation of an explosion, with its unreal quality of suspended animation, expresses the futility of any belief that we can control time. Moreover, the sculpture, made in 2000, has taken on another, prophetic meaning. After the September 11, 2001, terrorist attacks on the World Trade Center towers, Fasnacht's fellow Americans can regard *Demo* as a metaphor for the traumatic attack and a cautionary symbol of a possible future apocalypse.

Time and Art History

Concepts of time vary from culture to culture, from the cyclical philosophies of time taught in Hinduism, Buddhism, and many other traditional Asian philosophies to the linear view of time that the Judeo-Christian tradition of the West teaches to the ideas of relativity and simultaneity that modern science proposes and modern culture with its new technologies fosters. Thus, the sense of time that different works of art express can vary widely.

The means that visual artists use to make time visible are also varied. Historically, visual artworks were most commonly static forms—paintings, sculptures, tapestries, ceramics, and the like—physical objects that were not intended to move or change. (Among the exceptions were artworks designed for use in performances and rituals; these artworks generally did not change in form, but performers moved the objects about.) Artists making static works who aimed to express concepts of time could only represent time through symbolization and suggestion. For example, a Hindu artist holding a cyclical philosophy of time might incorporate a wheel in his art as a symbol for the cycle of birth, death, and reincarnation. A Christian artist with a linear view of time might paint three different scenes from a biblical story to imply a progression forward through time.

Alternatively, time can manifest itself in visual artworks through the use of actual movement, since our experience of time often depends on our movement in space. A *kinetic* (moving) sculpture shows time through the motion of its parts. The modern visual media of performance art, film, and video likewise rely on motion as a major element. Change (which relates closely to movement) is also a condition that reveals time. We become aware of the passage of time if a work of art changes perceptibly as we observe it. Of course, the process of change affects all works of art, even when unwanted. For example, we read time and aging into the cracks and darkened varnish of an old master painting, even though the process of decay is so slow that we do not see it happening at any given moment. Artists who want to make time an intentional element in their works might build observable physical change into their works by using fragile or volatile materials, such as cut flowers, snow, or melting wax as art materials.

In the next two sections, we look at some ways in which static forms of art represent time and then consider how moving and changing forms embody time. As we show, some works of art are hybrids that both represent and embody time. Imagine, for example, an installation that juxtaposes a painting of a clock and an actual clock.

Representing Time

What do we mean when we say that time is represented in a work of art? Representation is the symbolic process by which an artwork refers to a subject beyond itself. For example, a painting or drawing that includes an image of an hourglass in the composition is representing time through an obvious symbol. Similarly, a depiction of a sunset signals the ending of a day. The passage of time is also implied by depicting an arrested motion or showing a series of actions in a temporal sequence. Artists who want to represent time must deal with an inherent contradiction: while many visual artworks are static (paintings and sculptures don't usually move), time is measured and made manifest by change.

Many ideas about time and strategies for representing it in art can be traced back through the history of art. We can never be certain of the exact meaning of the prehistoric animal images painted on the walls of caves or the specific purpose of ancient fertility figures, of which the Venus of Willendorf is a famous example. But on the basis of present-day knowledge, anthropologists theorize that these visual symbols may have represented ritualistic moments or attempts to control the future. Perhaps, the cave paintings were a way to ensure success in a hunt and the Venus a way to ensure a successful pregnancy.

One of the main reasons that artists throughout history have engaged time in their works is the desire to record and recount events. These events may have been ones within the artist's lifetime, but more often the events came from mythology, religion, legend, and literature. In some cases, the visual record of an event acknowledges the event without depicting it directly, as in a monument with dates and inscriptions. The monument itself is usually a figurative or abstract sculpture that interprets an event in an allegorical way. In other cases, artists depict an event in a *narrative* form; that is, they visualize a story by representing a key moment or moments in an event as it is unfolding. Today, artists who are interested in narrative may choose to work in a moving form, especially film or video. But artists working in a static medium, such as painting or carved sculpture, need devices other than actual movement to mirror the passage of time in a story.

A *multi-episodic* format is one ancient method used in narrative visual art. A multi-episodic narrative represents two or more scenes from the same story. For example, wall reliefs and paintings from ancient Egypt depict a succession of scenes from a story in a sequence of vignettes running in outlined bands across and down a wall. Court painters in ancient China, who produced hand scrolls with images of imperial processions, also employed a kind of multi-episodic format. As a scroll is unrolled, the progress of the emperor on horseback or by boat is revealed in successive scenes. (The scenes are not framed separately but flow into one another.) Multi-episodic formats in Christian art range from two-panel diptychs and three-panel triptychs to artworks with numerous individual panels that are displayed below religious altarpieces.

The multi-episodic forms that are seen most frequently today are comic books and comic strips, which use single static drawings framed and arranged in a sequence to represent a narrative. The sequencing of events may not be strictly chronological; flashbacks can occur, and the main storyline can split into more than one subplot. In the art world, the use of multi-episodic imagery influenced by cartoons is thriving as well. In the 1980s, American painter Ida Applebroog began to make large multicanvas works that often include sequences of cartoonlike figurative images to suggest fragmented stories with a powerful feminist edge. Emerging more recently, Americans Laylah Ali and Kojo Griffin quote the graphic style and often the multi-episodic format of comic books to suggest narratives that are parables of contemporary human behaviors, including unsettling acts of xenophobia and hate crimes.

In contrast to the multi-episodic approach, most Western painting since the perfection of linear perspective during the Renaissance has represented a narrative within the unified pictorial space of one composition. Artists are able to imply a narrative by rendering figures and objects engaged in a variety of actions that appear coherent within the convincing illusory space, "leading the viewer to perceive a narrative sequence when, in fact, all events depicted are present on the picture plane at the same time. The here-and-now of the image [thus encompasses] the past and the future."[3] Sometimes artists combined different episodes from one story in a single composition. A well-known example is *The Tribute Money* (c. 1427) by the early Italian Renaissance painter Masaccio, which includes within one composition three episodes from an event involving Saint Peter.

More often, however, artists have used linear perspective to render a single important scene within a story, in which the characters are frozen at a dramatic moment. In this convention, the tableau implies what preceded and what will follow. (Or, alternatively, the artist relies on the viewer's preexisting knowledge of the storyline to place the event depicted within a context of past and future events.) Since 1980, numerous artists have continued to represent illusionistic space in order to heighten the drama of a suspended moment in time.[4]

Implying a narrative through a single dramatic scene became the favored format in *history painting*. This grand style of figure painting illustrating important events from ancient history, religion, or literature was promoted as the highest form of art by European art academies in the seventeenth and eighteenth centuries. Strongly indebted to Italian Renaissance art, academic history painting blended an illusionistic pictorial style and idealized subject matter, often glorifying dramatic events performed by gods, heroes, and leaders. In the nineteenth century, artists introduced a more realistic approach by painting historic genre scenes in addition to grand events; some artists also took the then unusual step of painting current events. After a long period in the twentieth century when narrative art fell out of critical favor, interest in representing time as narrative revived in the early and mid-1980s, notably in the work of the neo-expressionists, who were creating contemporary versions of history paintings. Other artists working with narrative structures were interested in recovering the neglected or forgotten histories of women, ethnic minorities, and other marginalized groups. The radical revision of history in contemporary art, and the process of deciding which events of the past are to be valued, is explored in greater detail later.

Of course, narrative is not the only way that artists engage with time. Artists working in static media may want to imply movement and change without being interested in telling a story. Any work of art that appears to halt movement at a dynamic moment creates an impression of arrested time. We find this device in all periods of art. A few examples are *Discobolus (The Discus Thrower)* (c. 450 B.C.), a Greek sculpture by Myron showing an athlete who has just brought his arm back and is poised momentarily before swinging the discus forward, Edgar Degas's nineteenth-century sculptures of ballet dancers poised on one leg, and the twentieth-century high-speed photographs by Harold Edgerton that show bullets and other rapidly moving objects "stopped" in midflight. (Edgerton was an engineer, not an artist, but his unusual photographs are often included today in art books.)

Indeed, from the mid-nineteenth century on, motion and speed are increasingly important aspects of the representation of time in art. J. M. W. Turner's dynamic painting of an oncoming steam-engine locomotive, *Rain, Steam and Speed* (1844), is an early example of the representation of speed as an emblem of the modern age, which equated speed with progress. Later in the nineteenth century, the ability to render the momentary effects on color and form of the rapidly changing conditions of light was central to the achievements of the impressionists. Claude Monet's series showing haystacks and the façade of Rouen Cathedral are remarkable efforts to represent changing light conditions at different times of day.

Photography, an invention of the Industrial Revolution, has a special capability for using motion and speed to represent time. By recording the exposure of a light-sensitive surface to the pattern of light at a specific moment, the photograph records the actual appearance of the subject, from the viewpoint of the camera's lens at the time the shutter was open. As photographic technology advanced, that moment became shorter and shorter; cameras achieved exposure times of less than a second in the 1870s, and today exposures can be measured in milliseconds. A photograph can represent the accelerated pace of modern life by recording in sharp, frozen detail a minute slice of a movement that is far too quick for the human eye to perceive.

Photography suited the modern era's preoccupation with time measured through movement, which was more valued the more rapid it was. (People today who drum their fingers impatiently when a Web page takes more than a few seconds to appear on a computer screen are valuing time in terms of speed.) The use of still photography to record rapid movement led to the invention of cinematography, or moving pictures, the temporal medium par excellence of the twentieth century. First, photographers (notably Eadweard Muybridge and Etienne-Jules Marey) began taking sequences of still photographs to study movement in space. Next, inventors figured out how to project sequences of still images in rapid succession, so that the eye was fooled into thinking the sequence of frames reproduced real motion. By the turn of the twentieth century, film was attracting practitioners in the arts and popular culture.

The experiments in sequential still photography and in film, which linked the perception of time with movement in space, paralleled new concepts of time that emerged early in the twentieth century, as seen in the physics of Albert Einstein, the psychology of Sigmund Freud, the philosophy of Henri Bergson, and the literature of James Joyce and Marcel Proust. Meanwhile, artists who were involved in cubism and futurism tried to represent the new, more complex concepts of time in static forms, particularly painting. The cubists fractured time by melding different views of a subject, seen at different times and from different angles, into one static composition. In contrast, the futurists painted a sequence of movements sweeping across a single composition, with the various phases of movement linked by geometric color structures. They believed that the past did not hold any value or importance for those in the present, and their imagery evoked the speeded-up tempo of urban life in the young twentieth century, made possible by new inventions, such as the automobile and airplane.

In contrast to the futurists, the surrealists slowed time down. They often depicted time standing still with images of frozen clocks signifying a dream state or creating a dreamlike ambience. A frozen clock watches over the plaza of Giorgio de Chirico's *The Soothsayer's Recompense* (1913), and in Salvador Dali's famous painting *The Persistence of Memory* (1931), limp pocket watches, their hands useless, are draped within an eerie landscape, hinting at the futility of culture. The representation of a time-made-strange occurs repeatedly in surrealist art. In René Magritte's *The Empire of Lights* (1954), an ordinary afternoon sky floats above an evening scene of a house nestled in dark trees. This simple juxtaposition of daytime and nighttime produces a mystery that resists explanation, while knowledgeable viewers recognize that the unexpected juxtaposition of elements is a prototypical surrealist strategy.

A dreamlike surrealistic approach to representing time, which conflates past and present or the mythic and the prosaic, occurs in contemporary art as well, as seen in the paintings of Neo Rauch of Germany [1-2] and Chatchai Puipia of Thailand, to name just two examples. Moreover, the surrealists' bag of temporal tricks—speeding time up, slowing it down, stopping it, making it double back on itself—can be seen, in altered fashion and for different aesthetic reasons, in contemporary works that embody time, such as the videos of Bill Viola (see the profile in chapter 8, Spirituality).

One final strategy that artists employ to represent past time is to appropriate and recycle found materials in their art. *Found objects, ready-mades, appropriations, relics, collections, archives*—these related terms are part of the vocabulary and conceptual apparatus of modern and contemporary art. Julian Schnabel's incorporation of broken crockery into the surfaces of his epic-scaled paintings in the early 1980s, which caused a sensation in the New York art world, evoked powerful emotions (violence, rage) and signified the passage of time (decay). Schnabel's creative process relied to a great extent on using used things as large-scale collage material.

Found materials do not really have to be old to evoke time. For example, the use of dolls and toys, even new ones, makes viewers think about the time of childhood. In the 1990s, American artist Mike Kelley produced a series of sculptures combining tattered stuffed animals to represent childhood, a distressing time of life in Kelley's vision. But recycled materials that are truly old are tied to the past in a direct way. They are a form of relic, an actual piece of a thing made and used for some purpose in the past, and thus these materials have strong associations with a specific historical time (and embody that time in their physical presence). Relics have the power to evoke memories and temporal reflections. American Whitfield Lovell, for instance, combines charcoal portraits (based on vintage photographs of African Americans from the early years of the twentieth century) with found historical objects. Lovell draws the portraits [4-3] on worn wood planks, similar to the floorboards or wallboards found in older homes. The artist "wants the viewer to connect with a phenomenon of time past being time present. . . . We can, he suggests, consider these people either as ciphers in a large historical continuum or as individuals who have attained fulfillment with honor and grace."[5]

Lovell's art exemplifies a curious feature of much art that uses aged materials to represent the passage of time. Using distressed wood with peeling paint as a support for the artist's drawn portraits reproduces the frayed and faded look of an antique photograph, but these qualities of wear were not present in the objects when they were seen by people in the past. Originally, the wood was smooth and freshly painted, and the photograph was in mint condition. The worn qualities we see now signify the distance separating our time from the bygone era. A time traveler to today would say, "Look at how these objects and photos have aged. I hardly recognize them."

The representation of time through used and worn materials is an example of a symbol or semiotic sign, known specifically as an *index*. To function as an index, a symbol requires more than an abstract or arbitrary relationship to that which it signifies. (Smoke, for example, is an index of fire; the English word *fire*, on the other hand, is not an index of an actual blaze.) Such an indexical embodiment of time relates to (overlaps with) the embodiment of time discussed in the following section.

Embodying Time

A static art form can represent time by containing physical evidence of the protracted length of time that was required to make it. Examples would be a work of installation art that is created through a process of slow accumulation or a work of embroidery with tens of thousands of tiny stitches. Other forms of art embody time; that is, time itself is an integral component of the work. In these cases, artists manipulate time much as they manipulate any other malleable material (such as wood, paint, or bronze) and give it form (including texture, color, mass, and shape). Indeed, the term *time arts* is commonly used today to refer to art forms in which temporality is central, such as performance art and video art. Of course, works that manipulate time as an integral element do not necessarily otherwise address time as a theme. A video can be about the body or language or any number of other themes, for example. We are particularly interested here in the subset of works that embody time and express additional thematic ideas about time.

Although much less common than static visual artworks, works of visual art that embody time have occurred throughout history. Two examples are the large wooden masks made by Native Americans of the Northwest Coast, which were crafted with hinges and strings so that one mask opened to reveal another mask, and the Navajo sand paintings of the American Southwest, which were ritually destroyed after completion. But the embodiment of time has become increasingly significant over the past one hundred years, because of philosophical and scientific changes in how time is

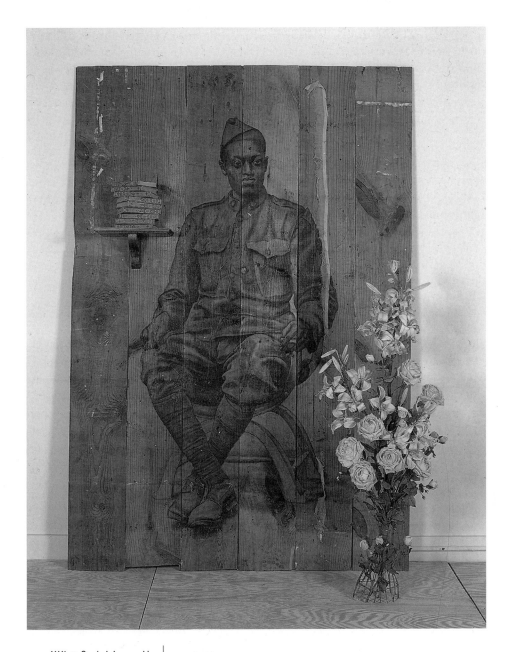

4-3 Whitfield Lovell | *Epoch*, **2001**

Charcoal on wood, found objects, 77 1/2 x 55 x 17 1/2 inches
Collection: Flint Institute of Arts, Michigan
Photo courtesy DC Moore Gallery, NYC
Courtesy of DC Moore Gallery, NYC

understood and because of the invention of new technologies (film, then video, then digital media) that enable artists to produce images that viewers perceive as moving. In this section, we look at materials, techniques, and forms that artists use to embody time as an element. Generally speaking, there are three basic ways of embodying time:

the artwork actually moves, the artwork uses media that create the illusion of movement, or the artwork is one in which the creative process counts for more than a finished object, and materials and forms are intentionally in flux during the life of the artwork.

Kinetic art, art that contains moving parts, and *performance art,* live art activities that encompass elements of theater and visual art, are two types of art that actually move. Versions of kinetic art and performance art have existed in some form in many cultures. The masks used by Northwest Coast peoples were both kinetic and used for ceremonial performances. It is recorded that Leonardo da Vinci designed and fabricated elaborate kinetic pieces to entertain guests at a patron's festivals. Modern precursors of today's performance art include the dada and futurist events of the early twentieth century and the happenings and Fluxus activities of the 1960s. Forerunners of contemporary kinetic art include the constructivist machines of Naum Gabo and Laszlo Moholy-Nagy, the mobiles of Alexander Calder, the kinetic sculptures of George Rickey and Jean Tinguely, and the collaborations between artists and engineers at the Center for Advanced Visual Studies (CAVS) at the Massachusetts Institute of Technology, which were ongoing after CAVS was founded by Gyorgy Kepes in 1967.

A fundamental concept underlying performance and kinetic art was that one had to be there in person to watch the work unfold in "live" time to get the full effect. In their embrace of real time, such artworks resembled works of music or theater. However, the "live" idea is sometimes modified today; hybrid temporal approaches have evolved that combine real-time elements with other elements, for example, live performances on a stage that include projections of videos in the background. In addition, performance and kinetic art pieces are routinely filmed today and hence have a recorded life beyond their real-time existence.

Nevertheless, live art continues to be made. In a 2002 performance, *The House with the Ocean View,* Serbian Marina Abramovic lived for twelve days on a balcony-like structure at New York's Sean Kelly Gallery in full view of a gallery audience, without eating, speaking, or engaging in any mental activities, such as reading or writing; a metronome ticked off the passage of time in seconds. The real time of life and the time of art coincided exactly. Other contemporary artists who are involved in performance projects that involve life in real time include Tehching Hsieh, Linda Montano, and Gilbert and George. (The proliferation and popularity today of "reality shows" on television, which supposedly show ordinary people doing things in real time, have made the art-life efforts of visual artists seem less unusual.)

Contemporary instances of kinetic art include the sculptures of German Rebecca Horn. Her *Concert for Anarchy* (1990) features a grand piano suspended upside-down in the air, whose lid opens and closes by means of hidden electronics, with an accompanying crash of dissonant noise that is far from the harmonic progressions of classical music. American Roxy Paine's artistic inventions include computer-driven machines, such as *Painter Dipper* (1997) and *SCUMAK (Auto Sculpture Maker)* (1998) that mechanically produce unique artworks in assembly-line fashion. Jonathan Borofsky, Tim Hawkinson, Tom Sachs, and Arthur Ganson are a few of the other artists who are making kinetic sculptures today.

Kinetic and performance art projects have become more complicated since 1980 because of new technologies, particularly advances in robotics and computer-based interactivity (although some artists continue to embrace a low-tech approach). For example, for the past thirty years, San Francisco-based Mark Pauline and his Survival Research Laboratory (SRL) have been creating remote-controlled, self-propelled machines and robots that run amok and destroy one another in loud performance spectacles that satirize modern technology and military exercises. Since 1997, SRL has added new information technologies to its toolbox. During performances, devices for operating the machines are available on the Internet for anonymous, remote controllers to activate, and live, wireless, streaming video of SRL shows is broadcast over the Web.

Timepieces designed by artists comprise a subgroup of kinetic artworks that deal explicitly with the theme of time. Contemporary American woodworkers, including Wendell Castle and Tommy Simpson [4-4], produce clever, beautifully crafted, functional variations on the traditional grandfather clock. Other artists have produced various clocks that serve as social metaphors. A well-known example by Cuban-born Felix Gonzales-Torres, *Untitled (Perfect Lovers)* (1987–90), consists of two clocks that appear to keep time in perfect synchronicity. The pairing offers a metaphor of same-sex romance. Only upon careful scrutiny does the viewer realize that the two clocks are not exactly the same.

Time can also be embodied in a work of art through optical illusions of movement. With the invention of cinema in the late nineteenth century, artists finally had the capability to produce a convincing illusion of moving images. (Flipbooks and lantern slide shows existed earlier than film, but were much more limited and far less convincing in their portrayal of movement.) In films and other media showing moving images, time appears to flow as it does in the actual world of the viewer. As Irene Netta explained, "In motion pictures the individual moment dissolves in a continuous narrative, whereas the narrative in a fixed image emerges from the individual moment depicted."[6]

Film, like its precursor, still photography, is one of the most popular art forms. It is used for both mass entertainment and for visual art efforts with a more limited audience. The same is true for video; the medium encompasses works made for popular consumption (particularly for television and Internet websites) and for the world of art museums and galleries. In 1965, Sony Corporation started to sell the first portable videotape recorder, making video technology affordable and accessible. With this tool, artists, such as Korean-born Nam June Paik, began to use video as an art form. Today video is ubiquitous in the art world (relying on digital rather than analog equipment).

Cinema and television became the dominant means for creating visual narratives for mass audiences over the past century. Although the plots in commercial films tend to be conventional, the way stories are told visually is extremely sophisticated because of the development of editing and montage techniques that can carefully shape a story shot by shot. We also have witnessed the proliferation of a highly condensed visual narrative form that Vicki Goldberg characterized as "the stroboscopic story, told in a flash," evidenced in movie trailers, music videos, and television commercials.[7] Today videos made for YouTube and other online sites can be added to the list.

Fine artists, too, use film and video to create narratives, although their stories are far from conventional. To create their narratives, artists sometimes choose the simplest technique of using a single camera and filming a continuous event in one take; in other instances, they use editing and montage techniques from commercial films and advertising to create narrative complexity. Visual artists also use film and video technologies to create temporal works that are nonnarrative, such as the plotless perpetual-motion

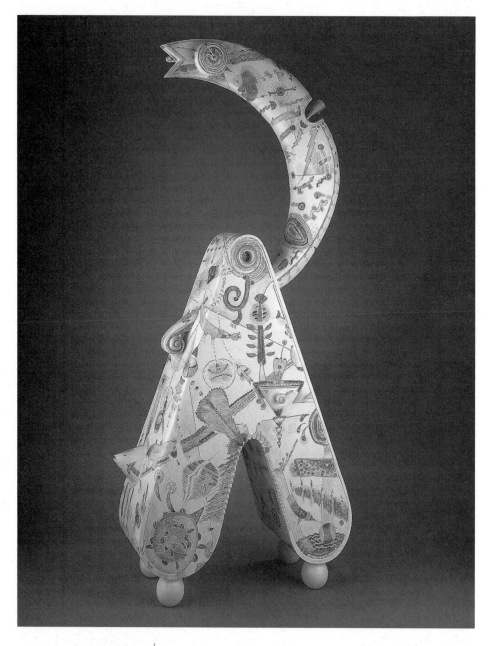

4-4 Tommy Simpson | *Boy with Fish,* **1994**
Carved and painted wooden clock and cabinet, 73 x 32 x 11 inches
Courtesy of the artist

sequence captured in Fischli and Weiss's video [4-1], discussed earlier. American Andrea Bowers takes a different but also nonnarrative strategy in her video *Waiting* (1999), which shows a young figure skater kneeling on the ice, perfectly still until she suddenly lifts her cold hands off the ice; the 45-second segment replays over and over in a continuous loop. The audience waits for a narrative that never begins, and so little changes that it is almost as if the video is a painting rather than a moving image.

A third approach to embodying time in visual art is encompassed in works that we can loosely characterize as *process art*. The term was first used in the late 1960s to refer to art made from mutable materials, such as asphalt, wax, plants, felt, latex, ice, and water, that took form as a result of processes or forces like gravity, weight, flexibility, expansion, warming, cooling, and pressure. A wide range of artists active after 1980 continued to discover creative possibilities in working with ephemeral materials and natural processes. Such art does not have a fixed form but bends, flows, melts, decays, and changes in other ways over time. Observing the materials in flux is the heart of the artistic experience. Indeed, if the materials are truly perishable, over time the work of art ceases to exist. The work's existence is temporary. For example, American Ann Hamilton chooses mutable (often organic) materials, such as leaves, insects, cornhusks, soybeans, moth larvae, and dried algae, to make installations that embody time by incorporating processes of decay. In her piece, *Dominion* (1990), created at the Wexner Center in Columbus, Ohio, thousands of moths went through their entire life cycle in an enclosed space. *Offerings*, her installation at the 1991 Carnegie International Exhibition in Pittsburgh [4-5], included a vitrine filled with hollow wax heads slowly melting through the bottom. German Sigmar Polke also experimented with a latter-day conception of process art when he made some paintings in the 1990s that mixed synthetic paints with minerals in a chemical combination that is changing the imagery unpredictably over time.

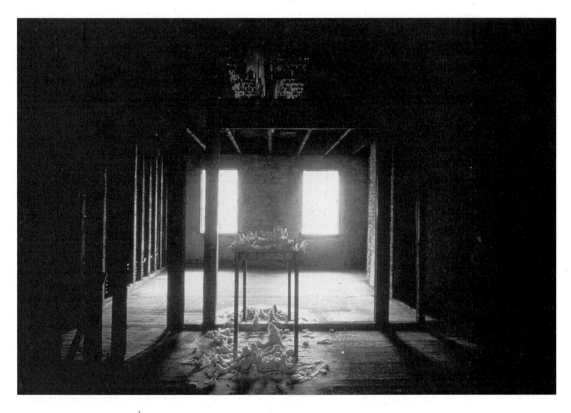

4-5 Ann Hamilton | *Offerings*, 1991
Installation
Courtesy of the artist and Sean Kelly Gallery, New York

Works of art that include time as a theme may be hybrids that both represent and embody time. The films of South African William Kentridge are a case in point. In a series begun in 1989 chronicling the life of a fictional character, Soho Eckstein, Kentridge employs a unique form of stop-action animation that combines drawing and film. For each film, Kentridge makes around twenty drawings, erasing and redrawing parts of each drawing repeatedly, and photographing each alteration. The photos become the frames of an animated sequence, "resulting in dreamlike images merging from one into another, with traces of previous forms and configurations lingering in the background. . . . His technique metaphorically parallels the acts of effacement and remembrance that characterize South Africa's postapartheid state—a nation erasing, drafting, and redrawing itself."[8]

Changing Views of Time

Transience, permanence, change, moment, now, then, duration, pause, minute, hour, year, past, present, future, eternity. These are just a few of the multitude of words related to time that occur in everyday speech. These words identify some of the concepts we use as we think about time. Within the syntax of language, the tense of verbs is another concept that is part of people's general understanding of time. In fact, markers of tense, which distinguish events in the past, present, and future, are universal features of all known languages. While some of our ideas about time seem stable, social and technological changes, as well as changes in our understanding of the physical and psychological universes we inhabit, are reshaping the ways we perceive and conceive of time. In addition, conceptions of time in other places and in earlier eras contrast markedly with our own beliefs.

In its most common cultural manifestations, time is conceived as cyclical, linear, or simultaneous, and time may be predictable or unpredictable. The recurring seasons and other natural cycles (such as the rise and fall of the moon) produce experiences of cyclical time. In contrast, linear time flows in one direction. With the invention of mechanical devices, such as the metronome, clock, and wristwatch, linear time became regulated, or marked off in standard increments. Linear time provides a view of history as a progression and an improvement over the past. (This view was characteristic of modern art, whose theorists and historians described art as progressing forward, with one style evolving out of and finally supplanting its immediate predecessor.) Simultaneous time is both the oldest and the newest conception of time; simultaneity encompasses all that happens in the durationless present. This idea encompasses the time of primal myths (e.g., the *Dreamtime* stories of the Australian Aboriginals) and the time of the Internet, when the flow of information is everywhere and nowhere, all at once.

Other conceptions of time, of course, are available. Take the metaphor of a bicycle wheel; its spin combines cyclical (recurring) time within the context of linear time as the bicycle moves forward through time and space. In this conception, the cyclical pattern of the seasons occurs simultaneously with the forward flow of years. Alternative conceptions of time (often referred to as the fourth dimension) can be found in the imaginary worlds of artists who envision the far-off future, parallel universes, the deepest reaches of the past, mythic times, and the strange alterations of time in science fiction. British-born Matthew Ritchie's ongoing project is a cycle of interrelated paintings and graphics involving complex diagrams of an entire universe of his own invention

[4-6]. Some charted events that Ritchie imagines occurred at the dawn of time. Other artists and writers on art posit that time does not exist outside our own world of history. Rosalind Krauss commented, "The Imaginary is the realm of fantasy, specified as a-temporal, because disengaged from the conditions of history."[9]

No matter what shape time appears to take—cyclical, linear, simultaneous, or some other form—the pace at which time moves within its structure can seem to fluctuate subtly or dramatically. For a child anticipating a major holiday, days can drag on one after the other at a snail's pace, while the holiday itself may pass in a flash. However, not all our emotional feelings are linked directly to our consciousness of time. We may, for example, be so swept up in joy or anger that we are not aware of the passage of time. Living in the moment, paradoxically, may mean that we lose track of our awareness of time. But whenever our experience of duration is linked to our awareness of our feelings, we experience time as having an emotional quality. When we are in suspense, our emotional life is bound up with an acute sensitivity to the passage of time (When will it happen? Soon?). Time is also linked to emotion when we feel nostalgia or regret, emotions that focus on events or qualities that we sense are far away from us in time. When an emotion persists over time, the emotion becomes a mood, meaning a recognizably consistent coloring of our perceptions ("He was in a funk.").

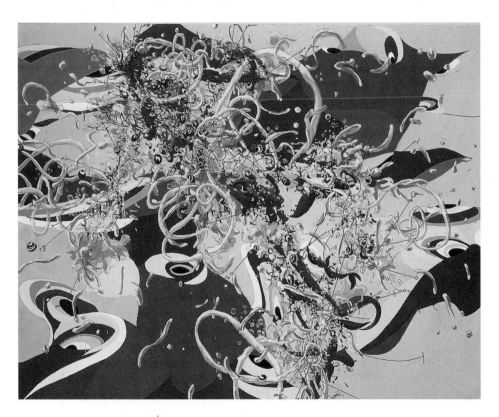

4-6 Matthew Ritchie | *Self-Portrait in 2064,* 2001
Oil and marker on canvas, 80 x 100 inches
Photo by Oren Slor
Courtesy of Andrea Rosen Gallery, New York, © Matthew Ritchie

The specific passage of time represented or embodied in an artwork may refer to a different subject than what is actually shown. For example, in a still life painting, the representation of change (the decaying fruit) may symbolize the inevitable frailty and aging of human beings. Such a painting, called a *memento mori*, imbues time with metaphorical meaning. The sequence of changes that we see in Fischli and Weiss's video [4-1], discussed earlier, changes that appear purposeless, can be interpreted as a metaphor for the directionless course that, to some observers, Western civilization seems to be taking. American Gary Simmons draws in chalk on a black surface, half erasing the drawings so they are on the verge of disappearing. His images reflect the concept that the experiences of African Americans in the United States are in danger of erasure when they are not written in a permanent form in historical records. The drawings can also be interpreted as a metaphor for the fleeting, evasive character of memories in general, which are so easily lost or altered.

Our notions of time keep changing. In *The Special Theory of Relativity* (1905), Albert Einstein dramatically challenged long-standing Western paradigms of physical science, including some basic notions of temporality. In Einstein's scheme, "man cannot assume that his subjective sense of 'now' applies to all parts of the universe. For, Einstein points out, 'every reference body . . . has its own particular time; unless we are told the reference body to which the statement of time refers, there is no meaning in a statement of the time of an event.'" In one of his famous "thought experiments," Einstein proved what seems counterintuitive to the ordinary (thunderstruck) reader: "Lightning flashes which are simultaneous relative to the stationary observer are *not* simultaneous relative to the observer on [a moving] train."[10]

Einstein's theory that our universe is a time-space continuum, that it makes no sense to dissociate time from the dimensions of space, exerted a wide influence. Today, we realize that time's flow is not a fixed constant, and because of the relativity of time, we always face a decision of what frame of reference to use. According to artist Victor Burgin, "Locations . . . are fixed by definition, but the actual spaces to which they refer are in continual flux and so impossible to separate from time."[11]

Since 1980, our concepts of time have been greatly influenced by emerging networks that offer instantaneous information (cell phones and text messaging, cable news programs, the World Wide Web). Arguably, we are losing our ability to put events in any temporal or historical context. Curator Douglas Fogle commented, "It is by now almost a cliché to state that the current generation has no sense of memory whatsoever. Subject almost from birth to the ahistorical temporality of cathode ray transmissions, ours has been labeled an amnesiac culture. . . . In effect, one could argue that we are caught up in a crisis of memory and an epidemic of forgetting."[12]

Exploring the Structure of Time

Time has structure; among its chief elements are duration, speed, rhythm, and direction. In this section, we examine some of the ways that a number of contemporary artists are controlling, altering, fracturing, and dissolving the structure of time in their work and why. While artists working in a range of media have dealt with this theme, video artists have explored the structure of time most intensively in the contemporary period.

A significant way in which artists manipulate time is by breaking down a chronological sequence. Instead of clearly distinguishing past, present, and future events and mapping them in a linear or cyclical fashion, artists may present moments out of chronological order. This approach goes beyond the flashbacks and flash-forwards that are a staple of commercial films. Contemporary visual artists often depict fragments of time coexisting in a state of collision or confusion. Conceptually, this approach is associated with the deflation of the modernist view that history is progressive and has a coherent, knowable shape. Moreover, today's artists show temporal fragments in collision, an approach that provides a metaphor for how our high-tech age presents information and events. Vast quantities of information are stored in electronic databases and can be accessed rapidly at any moment in any order using digital technologies, but this synchronicity and continual overload of information can make it nearly impossible to piece together coherent explanations of cause and effect. The fracturing of time can also be an artistic tool for metaphorically conveying the processes of memory and dreams, where the temporal structure is perpetually breaking down and meanings are fleeting and transient.

Fracturing Time

In painting, photography, and installation art, artists often create temporal dislocations by juxtaposing or layering images, objects, and styles from different contexts without setting up a logical flow or relationship among them. German Sigmar Polke and American David Salle are two painters who became closely identified with postmodernism in the 1980s for this strategy. The Mexican painter Julio Galán also fractures temporal structure; in his case, the layering achieves "the hallucinatory precision of involuntary acts of memory. . . . [Galán] assembles complex rebuses with no solution, their elements drawn from sources as diverse as his personal past (and even future), children's illustrations, Catholic icons, and pre-Columbian creation myths."[13]

Artists working in video have an array of tools at their disposal to alter the structure of time. They have built on strategies pioneered by photographers and filmmakers in the late nineteenth and early twentieth century—flashback, jump cut, fade-in and fade-out, and speeded-up time—which are now readily recognized by most viewers. While the earliest films were shot in real time and remained that way in the finished product, it wasn't long before editing allowed the narrative structure to be shaped.

Due, in part, to a desire to distinguish their work from Hollywood and mainstream television, many video artists have avoided any attempt to tell traditional narratives in linear time. Single-channel videos dominated most of the work done in the 1960s and 1970s, but by the 1980s, multichannel videos gained favor, partly because the technology for such projects had become more available and affordable. Making use of multiple projections and sophisticated equipment and editing software, video artists began to use techniques, such as synchronization, slowing down the speed of movement, reversing the flow, and fracturing and multiplying sequences. For example, Mary Lucier's *Wilderness*, from the mid-1980s, incorporates three synchronized videotapes that are interwoven as they are projected on seven large television monitors. Like other works by Lucier, *Wilderness* is an investigation of how historical time conflicts with mythic time. The forward march of American progress stands in conflict with the dream of an untrammeled wilderness. The conflict is embodied implicitly in the contrasting images that are shown simultaneously.

Real Time

Ironically, one way that artists manipulate the experience of time is by creating works that *appear* to unfold in real time; the audience experiences the work as if the events shown are happening in the present without any editing or restructuring. Fischli and Weiss's video *The Way Things Go* [4-1] has the quality of a real-time sequence, although the artists actually achieved this seamless effect through deceptive editing. Marina Abramovic's twelve-day performance, described earlier, was an attempt to merge real time and the time of an artwork's duration. Various artists are working with real-time live video projections on monitors or on the Internet (so-called streaming video), an approach pioneered by Nam June Paik early in his career. For example, Spanish-born Inigo Manglano-Ovalle's *Nocturne (tulipa obscura)* (2002) is a night-vision-enhanced real-time video projection relayed from a camera filming an Afghan tulip. American Julia Scher [5-10] works with standard security-industry equipment to spy on gallery goers in real time; her work is a critique of the increasing surveillance of our public lives by means of security cameras.

The interest in real time is partly a reaction to the artificial time structures we have become accustomed to as a result of watching commercial films and television. According to critic Amy Cappellazzo, "television and movies have trained modern viewers to expect life in condensed narratives, with scenes of heightened action and sound accompaniments that echo our emotions."[14] Paradoxically, part of the appeal of the "reality shows" that have sprung up over the recent past on television can be attributed to the unexpected difference in temporal rhythm and pace that such shows have compared to the packed plotlines of typical television dramas and comedies. Unlike either fictional stories on television or reality TV, everyday experiences of time are more likely to be taken up with nonevents, meandering activities that have no obvious drama or tidy conclusion.

Contemporary artists have approached the recording and representation of our experience of real time in many unexpected and novel ways, including using the static arts of painting and still photography. Japanese conceptual artist On Kawara, for example, marks time one day at a time in his ongoing production of "date" paintings. Each consists of a flat background and carefully painted text stating the date on which the painting was executed (e.g., August 24, 1988). On Kawara keeps to a rigorous set of rules: each painting must be made entirely within the twenty-four-hour period of the day named on the painting itself. The artist adds newspaper clippings from that particular day to complete the artwork.

British artist David Hockney pioneered an approach to photography in which multiple individual snapshots are arranged together into one artwork, producing a representation of the subject that, according to the artist, more closely parallels the way we really see. In Hockney's *The Scrabble Game* (1983), several dozen snapshots (some butting and some slightly overlapping) show various gestures that players made during the slice of time that Hockney photographed. In analyzing his achievement, Hockney recalled that one of the subjects declared *The Scrabble Game* is "better than a movie." Hockney explained that "a movie must traffic in literal time and can only go forward. Even when it pretends to go back, the spool is moving forward, forcing us to keep to an established, dictated pace. There's no time for looking, as there always is in the world. . . . I've been trying to figure out ways of telling stories in which the viewer can set his own pace, moving forward and back, in and out, at his own discretion."[15]

Many artists who work with real time emphasize the element of duration (an interval of time) rather than narrative (storytelling and drama). In this, they follow the experiments in musical composition made by the American John Cage, who from the

1950s maintained that duration is the most fundamental structuring idea in music, as opposed to the concept of harmony, which has dominated musical composition, especially in the West, since the time of Bach. Andy Warhol was another important precursor of today's artists who explore time as duration. In the 1960s, Warhol made several films in which he recorded static (nonnarrative) imagery over an extended time. His famous film *Empire* (1964) recorded from a distant, stationary view eight hours and five minutes in the "life" of the Empire State Building. Not much happens except that lights occasionally go on and off and the sky changes color. The length of these films challenges any viewer's patience. American Bruce Nauman and Tacita Dean of England are two artists who have worked more recently in filming scenes of protracted duration in real time. The length and slowness of their videos make viewers exceptionally aware of the passage of time, both the time portrayed in the videos and the time needed to watch them.

Building on Warhol's work, Scottish artist Douglas Gordon videotaped the movement of people coming and going as Warhol's *Empire* was being shown in a gallery. Gordon's resulting two-hour video, *Bootleg (Empire)* (1997), thus appropriates Warhol's film and wittily highlights the problem of its length and static content. Because we have been conditioned by the rapid-fire cadence of television, pop music, and action films, a filmed work of art that fails to compress experience to a similar degree is bound to try our viewing patience. This tension can be felt strongly even in the case of viewing a painting; because no optimal time of viewing is specified or mandated, viewers tend to give paintings short shrift.

Changing Rhythm

Another way that artists in the "time arts" alter the structure of time is by speeding up or slowing down the tempo of a program. English artist Sam Taylor-Wood used time-lapse photography to film *Still Life* (2001) at an accelerated pace. The resulting film shows an elegant bowl of fruit decaying before our eyes, ending in a mass of rotten fragments infested with maggots. More than speed, however, artists are interested in exploring slowness, perhaps as a contrast to the frenzied pace of contemporary society. "Why has pleasure in slowness disappeared?" asked Czech novelist Milan Kundera. Probing the degree to which our sense of time has accelerated from previous generations, philosopher Walter Benjamin once noted that some strollers in the shopping arcades of nineteenth-century cities walked with a tortoise on a lead.[16] When tempo is radically slowed down, the resulting conflict with a viewer's inner clock is palpable. By altering the clocklike rhythm of time, an artist explores time much as a composer explores rhythm in music.

Over the past fifteen years, the slowed-down video has become something of a genre all its own, with an exceptional variety of aesthetic results. Well-known practitioners include Douglas Gordon and American Bill Viola. These artists work from the assumption that slowness can be an intensification of experience. Our attention as viewers becomes so focused that even the slightest movement or change in a facial expression appears to have momentous significance. Watching events happen in extreme slow motion, we are caught up entirely in the present moment and lose track of any overall cohesive structure. In *24 Hour Psycho* (1993) [4-7], Gordon replays a video copy of Alfred Hitchcock's 1960 thriller at one-thirteenth of its original speed. Even the dramatic stabbing scene in the shower is slowed down to the point that the

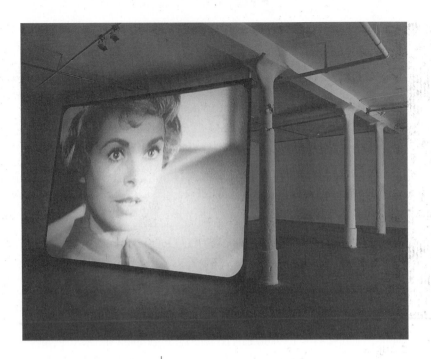

4-7 Douglas Gordon | *24 Hour Psycho*, **1993**
Video installation, single screen 300 x 400 cm; duration 24 hours
Private Collection, London and Kunstmuseum Wolfsburg
Photo by Heidi Kosaniuk (trannie in board)
Photo by Unknown (print and trannie)
Courtesy of Douglas Gordon Archive

mystery of the plot drains out of the scene; a new mystery—the mystery of time made palpable—takes over.

Continuing his interest in altering and partially dissolving the narrative structure of existing film footage, in *Déjà vu* (2000) [4-8], Gordon simultaneously projects three video copies of *D.O.A.*, a 1950 Hollywood film noir directed by Rudolph Matee. From left to right, the three projections play at one frame per second faster than normal, at normal speed, and at one frame per second slower than normal. Thus, the three identical narratives diverge over time, inducing feelings of disorientation in spectators as scenes repeat and soundtracks overlap.

In discussing Gordon's slow-motion videos, one writer explained that the moment "is allowed to flourish in extravagant excess."[17] The point is just as pertinent in looking at some rear-projection color video installations by Bill Viola. The videos are projected in such extreme slow motion that encountering one in a museum, an unsuspecting viewer momentarily may believe the image is static, like some form of electronic painting. For example, in *The Quintet of the Silent* (2001) an action that was filmed in one minute is presented over a fifteen-minute period. (Unlike Gordon, Viola works not with appropriated footage, but with a scene he staged and filmed himself.) Part of the attraction of the work stems from gradually being let in on the secret as we see how time almost imperceptibly unfolds, and we become absorbed in watching the subtly changing facial expressions and hand gestures.

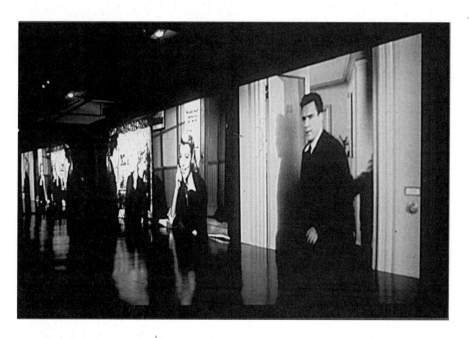

4-8 Douglas Gordon | *Déjà vu*, **2000**
Video installation, dimensions variable
Courtesy of Lisson Gallery and the artist

Exploring Endlessness

Finally, contemporary artists sometimes deal with a concept that, at first glance, may appear to involve the infinite but that, in fact, is significantly different: endlessness. This quality occurs in sculptures that repeat a certain movement over and over, such as Charles Ray's *Rotating Circle* (1988), and in paintings that depict a subject with inherent repetitiveness, such as Guillermo Kuitca's painting, *Terminal* (2000), which shows one of the familiar rotating carousels found in the baggage-claim area of a modern airport. Spanish artist Santiago Sierra has arranged many performances (documented in black-and-white videos) in which he pays hired hands to perform meaningless actions. For example, in 2002 day laborers in Morocco were paid a minimum wage to dig holes in an empty lot with shovels; in 2000 a person earned $10 an hour to remain secluded for 360 continuous hours behind a brick wall erected at P.S.1 Contemporary Art in New York. Sierra's works of this type connect time, labor, and humiliating social control. The endlessness found in such works has nothing to do with the transcendent infinity of the universe contemplated by the spiritually awakened; this is an endlessness founded in extreme boredom, in the dull repetition of meaningless details in contemporary (post-spiritual) life. This is the endlessness of the treadmill or of a neurotic obsession.

In investigating the concept of endlessness, some artists have used the strategy of looping a video or film so that a fragment of it continuously repeats. Typically, the beginning and end meld seamlessly together, so that there is no starting or stopping. Rodney Graham's *Vexation Island* (1997), for example, presents, in an endless loop, a nine-minute scene in which a character (the artist in a pirate's costume) is out cold under a palm tree. He wakes up, only to have a coconut fall on his head, which knocks him back into unconsciousness. Ironically, while repetition often serves to fix an event in memory, in this case the falling of the coconut knocks the incident out of the poor pirate's head, and when he wakes up again, it's as if it were the first time. A similar strategy of looping action in a way that frustrates any sense of forward progress can be seen in Irish artist Willy Doherty's *At the End of the Day* (1994). In this video, we see from a passenger's viewpoint as a car follows a series of roads; on each road the car is stymied by a barricade. The repetition of roadblocks brings to mind the conflicts that for so long prevented any way out of the troubles in Northern Ireland, as the cycle of blame and retaliation in Ireland's troubled history continued.

Revisiting the Past

Art exploring the theme of time includes art about history and memory. Visual representations of history have changed dramatically, reflecting profound shifts in how the past is remembered and interpreted. Today it is widely recognized that the choices of where and whose actions we select to focus on are open to constant negotiation. The history of the West, for example, is not the history of everyone or of everywhere. Likewise, interpretations of actions are not neutral; a historical event that one society celebrates may register as a tragedy somewhere else. At the same time, even the simplest statement of historical fact requires documentary and physical evidence to support it. For anyone who is engaged in writing, telling, or visually representing history, the search for a convincing "why" seems the most problematic because motives are always subject to question and doubt.

Our views of the past have changed, in part, because mental attitudes about the *present* have changed, in ways that reflect attitudinal shifts in the culture at large. Throughout the modern period in the West, an allegiance to the idea of historical truth remained paramount. Historians, politicians, the public, and artists may have lacked the data needed to confirm historical truth, but there was a tacit agreement that if sufficient information were available, the truth about history could be established. Today a singular truth of history is no longer assumed.

The factors contributing to the dismantling of the idea of a "grand narrative" are numerous. Certainly the influence of minorities, who felt that their stories were not accounted for in mainstream history, led to recognition that historians needed to expand their scope dramatically. Henceforth, not one history but multiple histories demanded exploration and expression. French historian Michel Foucault, who strongly influenced postmodernist thinking in the 1970s and 1980s, theorized a condition of multiple histories. According to Foucault, legitimate "official" histories existed alongside the excluded histories of those who lacked sufficient power to control the formation of knowledge. It was also recognized that history as a discipline used symbols that reflected power relationships in the wider social structure.

Art that looks back in time to the historical past or remembered events has been common in the period this book covers. In the 1980s, neo-expressionists, such as Anselm Kiefer in Germany and Mimmo Paladino in Italy, focused on their respective national histories and cultural origins, referring to history, literature, mythology, landscape, and religion in their heavily symbolic paintings. The former artist team of Vitaly Komar and Alexander Melamid (who emigrated to the United States from Russia) appropriated the old-fashioned official style of socialist realism to satirize the glorification of Stalin and Soviet history.

Other contemporary artists who look to the past seek to understand the nature of history—who and what is remembered and how and why. They scrutinize the content and approaches of historical study and remembrance.

Recovering History

Contemporary artists want to tell the stories of people who for centuries were left out of history books and the visual record, particularly if they themselves belong to a disenfranchised group. Foucault coined the term *counter memory* to describe this recovery of lost history. According to curator Douglas Fogle, the term describes "a new kind of historiography where the marginal and the everyday take precedence over world historical figures."[18] Judy Baca's mural project *The Great Wall of Los Angeles* (1976–83) was a monumental effort in this inclusive vein. More than thirteen feet high and almost a half-mile long, the mural depicts a multiethnic history of the Los Angeles area from prehistory until after World War II. Baca's subjects include women's suffrage, the Japanese internment camps, and the Zoot Suit Riots. To complete the mural, Baca and her collaborators interviewed hundreds of residents and academics about the history of Los Angeles, and four hundred fifty inner-city youths and forty community artists executed the designs. Baca explained, "Murals embody certain qualities of visual storytelling. First, there is the difference between public voice and private voice. Murals are pulpits: what you say in the pulpit is different from what you say to an intimate. Next, you must consider their scale. Scale is about amplifying the voice, about making it the voice of people who were excluded from history."[19]

Besides recovering lost histories, many artists are interested in deconstructing the principles and methodologies used to record and shape historical events. For example, Brazilian artist Adriana Varejão makes constant references in her work to the iconography of the seventeenth-century baroque, which was the leading artistic style in the European countries that conquered South America (Portugal, in the case of Brazil). Her motives include the (postcolonial) desire to challenge a history of Brazil that suggests that European culture subsumed and replaced indigenous culture, exemplified by the prevalence in Brazilian art and material culture of baroque-inflected designs and motifs. Varejão believes that Brazilians were able to absorb and transform the colonizers' culture without completely losing their own history and identity. The process was not without struggle and wounds, hence the violent, visceral imagery in much of her work. One series of relief paintings depicts writhing masses of bloody, fleshlike forms erupting from beneath floors tiled in *azulejo*, the terracotta tile used widely in Portuguese national art and in Portugal's former colonies, including Brazil [color plate 5]. Like a range of other Brazilian theorists and artists, Varejão uses cannibalism as a metaphor and sometimes includes images of humans consuming one another in her paintings. According to Rina Carvajal, the artist's use of cannibalism as a cultural allegory "suggests the swallowing, the critical absorption of foreign influences; of the discourse of 'the other,' and its re-making in Brazilian terms."[20]

Historical memory is dependent on the forms in which historical material is conveyed: history books, historical novels, painting, sculpture, photography, and, increasingly, film and video. These various media structure the content and perception of history. Various artists have deconstructed how the popular understanding of history is shaped by fictional treatments of the past. For example, Piotr Uklanski, who was born in Poland, created *The Nazis* (1998), an installation of 166 publicity photographs showing famous movie actors in costume as Nazi officers, from Ronald Reagan to Ralph Fiennes. In presenting images of Nazis from popular culture, Uklanski demonstrates that stars with alluring faces have repeatedly been selected to play these roles, thus fetishizing the perception of Nazis. American Kara Walker is concerned with how the history of the Civil War-era South is romanticized and sugarcoated in popular portrayals, such as the novel *Gone With the Wind*. Initially trained as a painter, Walker makes cutout black-paper silhouettes, a craft technique previously associated with genteel portraits and sentimental genre scenes. Walker's large wall-mounted works, such as *Camptown Ladies* (1998) [4-9], are parodies of historical romances that undermine any nostalgic expectations that the silhouette technique might imply. In her dramatic vignettes, blacks and whites alike enact sadomasochistic behaviors, as figures morph into one another. Her strategy is to inflate and reverse stereotypes so that they unravel into kitsch parodies of racist imagery. Walker's works are controversial among viewers of all races and have provoked debate about how to represent the history of slavery and the South in the United States.

Reshuffling the Past

Why, in recent decades, has there been a revival of period styles and a rush to appropriate elements from the past? With the rise of postmodernism in the 1980s, an increased

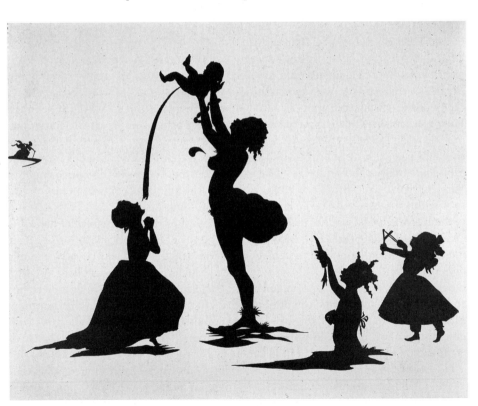

4-9 Kara Walker │ *Detail of Camptown Ladies*, **1998**
Cut paper and adhesive on wall, 9 x 67 feet
Collection: Rubell Family
Courtesy of Brent Sikkema NYC

interest in using art historical styles and images dovetailed with the trend of increasingly rapid-style changes in popular culture, where, for example, styles of cars and clothing change every year. Of course, a rapid change of styles results in a heterogeneous mixture, since the examples of past styles are not eliminated entirely but continue to exist in a mix with more recent versions. The utilization of a pastiche of past images (or forms) became a recognized hallmark of postmodern art. Following the belief that "there is nothing new under the sun," numerous artists, from David Salle in the 1980s to Christian Schumann more recently, have forged their own individual styles by the characteristic manner in which they recycle the past. These artists work in ways that tend to destabilize the present; for them, the present is conceived as a reshuffling of mementos from the past.

If an artist "quotes" earlier works of art or imagery from visual culture, the viewer who recognizes the quotation interprets the new work of art, in part, as an exploration of the theme of memory or history. For example, British brothers Jake and Dinos Chapman borrowed the gory tableau of mangled bodies in their sculpture *Great Deeds Against the Dead* (1994) from an early nineteenth-century etching in Francisco Goya's *Disasters of War* series. Knowledgeable viewers find themselves weighing the bad taste of the Chapmans' macabre scene against the genuine despair of Goya's firsthand witnessing of the real horrors of the Napoleonic wars. American comic-book artist Alex Ross, who has a cult following among devotees of the genre, appropriated famous characters (Superman, Captain America) and imagined them in middle age in one of his comic books. The conceptual subtlety of Ross's work depends on his audience's knowledge of the past exploits and foibles of his superheroes in their younger incarnations.

Reframing the Present

Underlying the work of Kara Walker [4-9] and many contemporary artists who revisit history is a determination to change how we understand the present. When we revisit history, time collapses; what was once present and is now past becomes vividly present once again. The present appears in a new context, and it becomes possible to see the present more critically through the past. Walker, for example, wants viewers to consider how representations of history affect race relations today. Atul Dodiya, a contemporary painter in India, has made paintings on the corrugated metal exteriors of roll-up doors that detached from actual shops. The exterior paintings celebrate India's history by depicting historical figures, such as Gandhi and the Nobel Laureate Rabindranath Tagore. The doors raise to reveal more surreal painted versions of events underneath. Critic John Brunetti remarked, "These hidden images are stark portrayals of an India very different from that presented by Gandhi's non-violent resistance."[21] Dodiya shows how celebratory versions of history prevent India from taking a hard look at present problems and anxieties.

A number of contemporary artists, including American Allison Smith and Israeli-born, Berlin-based Omer Fast, have made works that examine historical reenactments. Smith's *The Muster* (2005) was a public art project that mixed the aesthetic vernacular of the Civil War reenactment community with idiosyncratic contemporary artistic expressions. Smith invited fifty individuals and collaborative groups to build campsites at Fort Jay on Governor's Island in New York City, making costumes, banners, flags, and installations intended to celebrate whatever anyone was fighting for. Fast's two-channel video projection *Godville* (2005) shows segments from interviews that the artist conducted with eighteenth-century character interpreters who live and work in Colonial Williamsburg, a living history museum in Virginia. The interpreters speak both in the voices of their eighteenth-century characters and as themselves, in the present. Fast edited and collaged the interviews into a temporally dissonant narrative: actual historical events, the theme park world of the living history museum, and the individuals' current lives meld in unsettling ways. One person, for example, did a tour of duty in Iraq and portrays a militia member as a Williamsburg interpreter; it becomes strangely murky which war his rambling, often ranting, remarks apply to.

In many cases, the history that artists review is the recent past or even very recent events—a history that is still alive in the memories of firsthand witnesses. Willie Doherty is concerned with recent political events in Northern Ireland. Well aware of the power of television in controlling what and how the public perceives events in Ireland, Doherty purposely uses the tools of the news media: video and language. As Douglas Fogle commented, "Calling into question our reliance upon the truth value of the news broadcast or newspaper report to make sense of the world, Doherty at the same time stresses the power of mediated language in constituting our own collective memory."[22]

Artists revisiting history have also turned their attention to their own personal and family histories. For example, English artist Tracey Emin's installation, *Everyone I Have Ever Slept With 1963–1995* (1995), was a tent embroidered with the names of all the people Emin had shared a bed with over the prior three decades.[23] Roger Shimomura, an American of Japanese descent, was inspired by his grandmother's diaries, as well as his own childhood memories, to create prints and paintings depicting life in the Minidoka internment camp in Idaho during World War II [4-10].

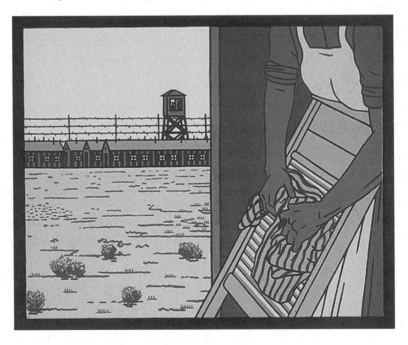

4-10 Roger Shimomura | *American Diary: October 16, 1942 (Minidoka),* 1997
Acrylic, 11 x 14 inches
Courtesy of Bernice Steinbaum Gallery

Autobiography and social history are not distinct realms and cannot be wholly separated. Many works about personal history, such as Shimomura's, also highlight the profound impact of culture. What is significant in an artist's own life is tied to larger public events, as well as to historically based social concepts that are often charged with emotion.

Commemorating the Past

Since 1980, there has been a resurgent interest in creating *memorials*, which pay tribute to the dead, and *monuments*, which pay tribute to the past. This interest stems from a number of factors: the need to reassess the past (seen, for example, in monuments dedicated to the civil rights movement in the United States and the Holocaust in Europe), a desire to mark recent tragic events (exemplified by the Vietnam Veterans Memorial), and a desire to legitimate the right of a government and social structure to continue into the future (in reverse fashion, the world watched the toppling of statues of dictators in the former Soviet Union and Iraq as a dramatic way of signaling the demise of a government).

While people in previous eras also felt the need to remember past events and people in some tangible and permanent form, we may feel a unique pressure to do so today because of the impact that the information age, and information overload in particular, has had on the process of remembering. Andreas Huyssen, a historian of contemporary culture, observed that "the more memory is stored on data banks and image tracks, the less our culture is willing and able to remember." Increasingly we abdicate our power to remember as individuals and as communities in favor of the artificial, and mediated, memory banks supplied by technology. Every snippet of coded knowledge about the past, present, and future is available almost instantaneously to anyone with a computer and high-speed Internet access. The result? What Huyssen termed a "synchronicity of the archive" that dissolves time and confuses memory. In analyzing Huyssen's contributions to our understanding of the "tenuous place of history and memory in our time," curators Neal Benezra and Olga Viso explained, "[Huyssen] sees society's current assertion of memory as a struggle for history and a form of 'temporal anchoring' against high-tech amnesia."[24] Artists creating memorials and monuments offer forms that slow down the looking of viewers, providing time for contemplation and counteracting our collective forgetfulness.

Of course, our relationship to the past is never free of emotional baggage, politics, and value-laden ideologies. In designing memorials and monuments, contemporary artists find they are (willingly or not) tiptoeing through minefields of public opinion. The Vietnam Veterans Memorial, dedicated in 1982 on the Mall in Washington, D.C., provoked widespread debate when its design was first announced. Maya Lin, then a senior at Yale University, won the design competition with a plan that proposed a pair of elegant black granite walls, dug into the earth, and gaining height as the viewer descends to the place where the two walls meet at an open angle of about 125 degrees. Lin proposed carving into the wall surface the names of the more than fifty-five thousand Americans who lost their lives during the conflict or remained missing in action at the war's close. Looking at a section of the wall, viewers would see a dim, ghostlike reflection of themselves, appearing behind the wall. Opponents felt the design should be more conventionally heroic, featuring figures in uniform, as is typical of most war memorials.

The Vietnam Veterans Memorial is now the most visited monument in Washington, D.C. Its focus on time occurs on several distinct levels. The entire sculpture commemorates U.S. involvement in the war as a chapter in national history. Indeed, the shape of the sculpture seems to echo the shape of a book opening, thereby hinting at additional chapters yet to be written. The individual names of the dead and missing in action are arranged in chronological order. Time is marked on the wall by the names.[25] Time is also central to the experience of viewers. As Lin explained, "I think of all my works not as static objects, but strictly in terms of a personal journey or experience of it. A crucial element to this work is my reliance on time."[26] Older visitors bring their own sense of time to the experience as they reflect on what they were doing in the 1960s when all those listed were making the "ultimate sacrifice." Seeing the dates, we inevitably think of how much time has passed since these deaths occurred. Analyzing the form and meaning of the memorial, philosopher Charles Griswold called the work "fundamentally interrogative": Americans as a whole must ask themselves, were these deaths worth it?[27] Griswold noted that the Vietnam Veterans Memorial, like any war memorial, "seeks to instruct posterity about the past . . . [the memorial is the result of] a decision about what is worth recovering."[28]

In contrast to memorials created from a material that will endure permanently, artists' projects may commemorate events in ephemeral or temporary forms. For example, Krzysztof Wodiczko's *Hiroshima Project* (1999) lasted for only two nights. The work consisted of a sequence of large-scale photographic images of Japanese survivors' hands projected along the waterfront in Hiroshima while the survivors' recorded testimonies were amplified. The hand gestures represented anguish and grief. The short-lived and dematerialized nature of the event transformed the survivors into ethereal presences, as if ghosts from the atomic blast had returned to recount their experiences.

One trend in public art today is the production of *antimonuments*, works that deconstruct traditional forms of public monuments or commemorate unexpected events and memories. For example, American sculptor Chris Burden pursued a challenging alternative vision in creating the *Other Vietnam Memorial* (1991), which symbolically names the 3 million dead Vietnamese in the war. German Thomas Schütte questions traditional forms of commemoration by making groupings of figures whose scales are mismatched in relation to one another. Neal Benezra and Olga Vigo remarked, "Addressing the significance of public monuments in a post-Cold War world, Schütte questions the ability of traditional forms of commemoration to serve as effective carriers of memory and meaning in our time."[29] In the 2002 Whitney Biennial in New York, American Keith Edmier exhibited in Central Park two three-quarters-life-size bronze sculptures of men in uniform; the two were not the usual "great men" of commemorative statuary but represented Edmier's two grandfathers, who played modest roles in World War II.

In creating a memorial or monument, an artist faces a range of complicated issues. Because the work will be seen in a public setting, the various emotional and political attitudes of a multitude of viewers must be addressed (or ignored at a considerable risk). In addition, people who live in the future will eventually view the public monuments we erect today; for them, the same symbols may not carry the same meanings. One of the poignant debates in the aftermath of the terrorist attacks on the World Trade Center focused on what kind of monument should be erected on the site to commemorate the magnitude of events that occurred on September 11, 2001.

Over time, works of art may gain unintended elegiac and memorial resonance for viewers. For example, Joel Meyerowitz, starting in 1981, created a series of photographs showing the southern view of Manhattan out his studio window [color plates 6 and 7]. Echoing Claude Monet's series of paintings of haystacks and the Rouen Cathedral at different times of day and in different weather conditions, Meyerowitz's photographs show the changing pattern of color and light in the sky and the expanse of buildings. A key focal point in each photograph is the double towers of the World Trade Center, looming deep in the background. The sense of time, and of tragedy, is invoked in these images now in ways that the artist could not have contemplated as he was creating them.

Finally, although we have been discussing memorials and monuments in terms of the theme of time, we note that the topic can also tie into the theme of place, the topic of our next chapter, notably when a memorial or monument commemorates an event associated with its site. Wodiczko's *Hiroshima Project* is a case in point. Various themes can intersect.

PROFILE: Brian Tolle

The past keeps surfacing into the present—this is a leitmotif in much of Brian Tolle's art. We can see this perspective embodied in *The Philadelphia* (1995), a sculptural installation featuring the artist's version of an eighteenth-century gunship's rotting hull, still half submerged, rising from the depths (the water's surface represented by the colored floor of the gallery). Tolle's artwork re-creates an actual event: the *Philadelphia*, a Revolutionary War gunship that sank fighting the British, was raised in 1935. To accomplish the salvage operation, the ship's cannonballs were brought up first. Tolle references this process by filling the gallery floor with cannonballs carved out of Styrofoam. In the actual event, freed of the dead weight, the ship floated up to the surface; in Tolle's reimagining, the process of remembering history is never complete; our collective recall is partial.

While in Tolle's artistic vision, the sense of history is fragmentary, it is also the case that partial echoes of the past keep surfacing in surprising ways, inserting themselves into the present, but with their original shapes and meanings distorted by time. For example, in *Declaration of Independence Desk: Thomas Jefferson* (1994), Tolle replicated not one but a whole series of versions of Thomas Jefferson's portable writing desk. Jefferson's original desk, left to an heir, had taken on the status of a national relic, famous as the surface on which the founding document was written. Over the decades, knock-offs of the original desk were carefully crafted to satisfy the demand of luminaries (Henry Ford and President Lyndon Johnson, for instance) who wanted to own a distinctive reference to American history. Tolle took the process a step further, fabricating a simulation of the original desk by Jefferson, as well as simulations of the earlier knock-offs, each with its own idiosyncratic details that identify the owner. Tolle's simulations of other people's simulations of Jefferson's desk place us in a peculiar position, two steps removed from Jefferson's original version. The viewer may feel a sense of vertigo, as the process of creating new simulations seems capable of expanding endlessly. Tolle's project, in terms of the infinite reduplication of culture (as if culture has taken on the condition of fecund nature), epitomizes what Jean Baudrillard termed *hyperrealism*: "the meticulous reduplication of the real, preferably through another, reproductive medium. . .[reduplication] becomes reality for its own sake, the fetishism of the lost object"[30]

Tolle's most widely known project is the *Irish Hunger Memorial* (2002) [color plate 8 and 4-11], located in Battery Park City, New York. This artwork focuses on the Great Hunger of 1845–52, when the population of Ireland decreased from 8 million to 5 million. Approximately 1 million people died as a result of a widespread blight of Ireland's potato crop over a period of several years, a condition that, many historians believe, was worsened by mismanagement of the crisis. Another 1.5 million Irish emigrated, fleeing the famine. Many of them entered America through Ellis Island in New York's harbor, a site that is visible from the upper portions of Tolle's memorial.

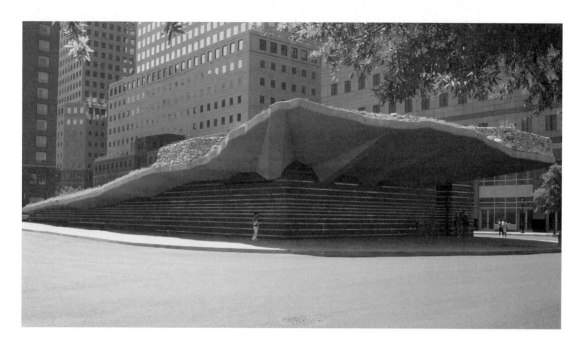

4-11 Brian Tolle │ *Irish Hunger Memorial*, installed Battery Park, NYC, **2002**
Stone, landscaping, glass, illumination, audio, and concrete, 96 x 170 feet
Photo by Stan Ries
Courtesy of the artist

To symbolize the suffering and loss and the flight by many to America, Tolle replicated a chunk of harsh Irish countryside on a half-acre site. The site is nestled among the tall buildings of lower Manhattan. The plants and shrubs that are incorporated into the artwork are native to County Mayo. There's even a stone cottage like those inhabited by Irish farming families during the early 1800s. The cottage is roofless, a vivid reminder of a tragic fact: to "prove" their poverty, and therefore be eligible for government aid, many farmers tore the roofs off their dwellings. The half-acre duplicates the maximum-size plot that farmers were allowed to own to qualify for famine relief.

The artwork is elevated (twenty-five feet above ground level at its highest point), and cantilevers out from a base of stone and glass. These structural features emphasize that *Irish Hunger Memorial* is a sculptural object, not a nature retreat or a theme park. Climbing over the path that leads past the abandoned cottage and fallow potato field, viewers are catapulted backward in time, while responding to the present conceptual and tactile qualities of Tolle's work. Indeed, Tolle places primary emphasis on contemporary visitors' experience of the artwork itself, rather than asserting that we focus on the Irish back in time. "I'm not interested in situations where there's an empathetic other. When you're dealing with history, it's too easy to say, 'This is about them, then.' It's about the experience that you're having right now. It's about you."[31] Along the base below the sod [4-11], printed lines of text recount memories by the Irish victims of the Great Hunger, while other interspersed passages reference recurring instances of famine worldwide.

The cottage is a memorial within the memorial, and it is also the real thing—an actual farmhouse. Relatives (still living in Ireland) of Brian Clyne, Tolle's partner, donated the cottage for the project. The farmhouse was shipped over and rebuilt, rock by rock. According to Tolle, the use of the dwelling in the artwork is appropriate: "to be able to have an actual place that has a history and not feel anxious about taking something from where it belonged, because the house was in fact a gift between families and between nations and had a history and a history as part of my extended family."[32]

Tolle's art transforms our view of history and historic architecture, calling into question the reliability of any view of the world we thought we knew. With *Eureka* (2000), Tolle transformed the front facade of a seventeenth-century home facing a canal in Ghent, Belgium. For this project, the artist collaborated with computer specialists who helped digitally map the appearance of wave patterns, complete with the wakes of passing boats, on top of the building's actual exterior. The model was output using a computer-operated milling machine. The result—a false front of carved and painted Styrofoam that re-creates the building's reflection in the canal—was installed on the front of the original facade of the building. The structure itself appears to reflect the reflection in the canal; Tolle refers to the result as "liquid architecture."

For an exhibit entitled *Alice and Job* at Shoshana Wayne gallery in New York in 2000, Tolle installed two enormous stone hearths [4-12], representative of what little remains today of Llano del Rio, a socialist community, founded in the early 1900s in Southern California. Each hearth bears an initial, "A" and "J": "A" signifies Alice Austin, architect for Llano del Rio's city plan, and "J" is for Job Harriman, visionary leader of the community. The two hearths are stand-ins for Alice and Job.

As symbols for minor historical figures, people who pursued a dream of creating a utopian society, the hearths operate on multiple levels. Individually, the hearths can be seen as memorials to the two individuals whose initials they bear (like large gravestone markers). Together, the hearths and the pristine room they are in constitute an exhibition that serves as a monument to a failed utopia. At first, viewers may see the hearths as authentic artifacts of a bygone lifestyle. On closer examination, it becomes apparent that the artist fabricated the fireplaces; they are meant to look like clever fakes. Furthermore, the mystery of the large, faux-stone sculptures deepens as viewers realize that they are moving slowly around the room. At a rate of approximately a foot per minute, the hearths' motions seem robotic, or alive, but functioning much slower than humans today. In writing about Tolle's exhibit, critic Josh Blackwell observed, "Modernism and the twentieth century heralded the arrival of speed and efficiency. . . . Time became a precious commodity, something to be saved and not wasted. . . . Consequently, slowness became a demonized notion, and wonder and reverie were transformed into anxiety and distraction."[33]Viewers with a sophisticated knowledge of the theoretical appara-

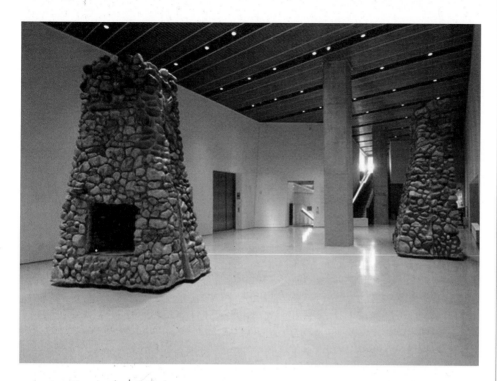

4-12 Brian Tolle | *Job and Alice*, Contemporary Arts Center, Cincinnati, OH, **2006**
Hand carved styrofoam, robotics, acrylic paint; 14 ½' x 10' x 6' each
Photo by Tony Walsh
Courtesy of the artist

tus surrounding the reception of contemporary art may understand Tolle's art as employing a strategy by which the past becomes a text we interpret within the context of our own present perspective. Theoretically inclined viewers may "read" his sculptural forms—the Styrofoam cannonballs of *The Philadelphia*, the simulations of Thomas Jefferson's desk, and the stone hearths *Alice* and *Job* meandering endlessly—as indications of how the past is retraced by the present in allegorical terms. In an influential essay first published in 1980, the late critic and theorist Craig Owens outlined how a vital quality of allegory is its "capacity to rescue from historical oblivion that which threatens to disappear."[34] It would be a fascinating project in critical interpretation to analyze Tolle's art in terms of Owens's essay, which outlines the impulse to "supplant" an original meaning, in danger of being "foreclosed" in the distance of time, by a fresh, fabricated overlay. Indeed, many of the key qualities that Owens identified as facets and strategies of the contemporary impulse for allegory in the visual arts—including appropriation, hybridization, pastiche, site-specificity, and the referencing of the past in fragmentary terms, as well as the representation of the past in ruins—are arguably central to Tolle's work.

Looking at examples of Tolle's body of work, our perspective on history, time, and perception keeps shifting. In fact, many qualities in Tolle's art conspire to disorient the visitor: if the present is the culmination of the past, but the past keeps shifting, then where are we now, how can we take our bearings? In the face of temporal disorientation, Tolle's work requires that we pay attention and refuse to take the present for granted.

Brian Tolle was born in 1964, the son of a mechanical engineer and a real estate agent. He was raised on Long Island and studied at the Parsons School of Design and Yale University School of Art. He now lives in New York, working in a studio in Williamsburg, Brooklyn.

PROFILE: Cornelia Parker

Found objects that are recycled in artworks generally impart a sense of time to the degree that the objects' past history and identity remain evident. In a wide-ranging body of work, British artist Cornelia Parker has used found materials in inventive, often startling, ways that complicate their connection to both past and present and ask us to recognize the relentlessness of change in the meaning and form of everything over time. For example, *The Maybe* (1995) was a wall installation displaying a truly surprising array of found and borrowed objects, each with a factual relationship to history. Among the borrowed items in this bravura work were psychoanalyst Sigmund Freud's pillow and blanket from his couch, a quill pen used by novelist Charles Dickens, and a rosary owned by Napoleon. *The Maybe* asked larger questions about these mementos than how they were used by their famous owners. Why *do* we keep relics around? Do they tell us something about the past or about the present? Can, and should, an artist transform relics into art materials, thereby giving them new life and meaning in the present? By altering the meaning of an artifact, is the artist somehow also altering the meaning of the past?

Other artworks by Parker explore time in nuanced variations on the same basic themes found in *The Maybe*—the complicated, ambiguous relationship of past and present, and the tricks and transformations wrought by time. For instance, to create *Shared Fate* (1998), Parker managed to borrow the actual guillotine that beheaded Marie Antoinette in 1793, which she then used as a tool to cleave apart all kinds of things from everyday items, such as bread and a necktie, to eccentric collectibles. As art historian Geoffrey Batchen put it, "These otherwise ordinary objects now share a fate with one of the great historical figures of the French Revolution, cut as much by the weight of that knowledge as by a metal blade."[35] One object that Parker guillotined was a doll based on a fictional character, the protagonist in Charles Dickens's novel *Oliver Twist*. The Oliver doll was designed so he appears to wince, an allusion to an episode in the novel in which Oliver's ear is twisted. The wince acquired a new layer of emotion when the artist used her historically freighted tool to slice Oliver in half at the waist! In Parker's wickedly humorous artwork, a fictional character's story becomes linked with the life of a real person from history. The cleaved Oliver doll confronts us with some mysterious questions: Can truth and fiction coalesce over time? Is some aspect of the historical person Marie Antoinette now invested in the doll because the very same blade sliced them both? Does the guillotine's association with past horrors invest the artwork with the power to rattle us?

As we described in the previous profile, Brian Tolle created simulations of historic relics when he replicated Thomas Jefferson's writing desk and some of its copies. Parker, in contrast, has incorporated actual relics in her artworks. Both artists explore how time can be manifested in the physical as well as the conceptual changes that material objects undergo. Time becomes palpable when experienced through physical objects whose form and meaning are constantly and unstoppably changing.

Parker has made several installations in which she creates an illusion of stasis—by displaying a halted action—but also undercuts that illusion by using recycled materials that show how completely and rapidly one thing can change into another. Parker's installation *Cold Dark Matter: An Exploded View* (1991) suspends the remnants of a destroyed building from the gallery ceiling on thin strands and other support mechanisms. The hovering shards coalesce (as a visual gestalt) into a facsimile of the original structure, a ten-foot-wide garden shed whose demolition was deliberately arranged by the artist (the shed was blown up with the help of the British Army). Before the explosion, Parker crammed the shed with used objects she had acquired at yard sales (such as garden tools, books, and toys), the remains of which are scattered throughout the installation. To make the related installations *Mass (Colder Darker Matter)* (1997) and *Anti-Mass* (2005) [4-13], Parker obtained the remnants of two small wooden churches: *Mass* had burned after being struck by lighting in Texas, while *Anti-Mass* was destroyed by arsonists in Kentucky. In each case, her installation suspends the charred fragments into a cube about the size of the small church prior to its destruction. Not coincidentally, the titles of these installations refer to fundamental physical properties and the Big Bang, the cosmic explosion that many scientists believe gave birth to our universe. Parker, who was raised as a Catholic, has also suggested a religious subtext to her artwork, stating, "The whole notion of transubstantiation, the changing of one substance into another, has clearly influenced the way I think as an artist."[36]

It is interesting to compare Parker's partial reassemblages of architectural fragments to Heide Fasnacht's sculpture *Demo* (2000) [4-2], which represents a building frozen in the middle of imploding, with the entire mass about to tumble down. Despite an affinity in subject matter (the destruction of man-made structures), the works measure time differently. Fasnacht's *Demo* freezes a split second of linear time; time seems to stand still as in a tableau from a play or a stop-action photograph. The sense of time in Parker's *Mass (Colder Darker Matter)* and *Anti-Mass* is more ambiguous and more expansive. The charred fragments hover in a transitional state; they are no longer part of a whole, but they resist the pull of gravity. Or perhaps Parker's sculptures hint of an afterlife; the parts have risen, Lazarus-like, to become a ghost or a memory of a former self.

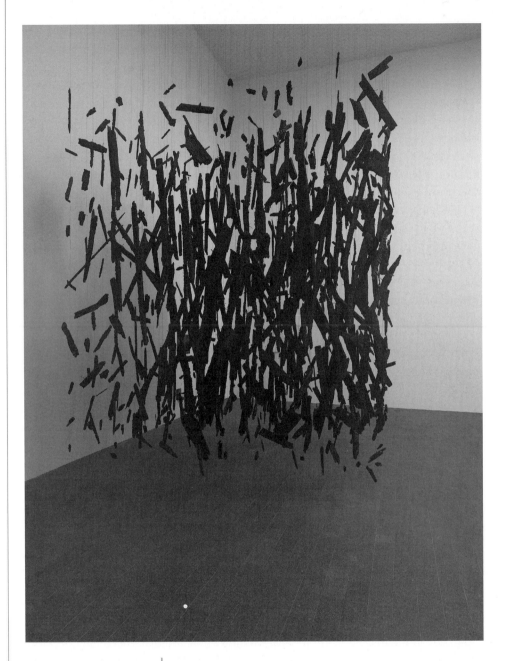

4-13 Cornelia Parker | *Anti-Mass,* **2005**

Charcoal retrieved from a church burned by arson; nails, and wire
396.2 x 335.3 x 342.9 cm (156 x 132 x 135 in.)
Fine Arts Museums of San Francisco, Museum Purchase, Friends of New Art and
American Art Trust Fund in honor of Harry S. Parker III and Steven A. Nash, 2006.2

What sets Parker's art apart is how she reveals the path of time to be anything but linear and straightforward. History, memory, emotion, and new events overlay new meanings on people, places, and objects. To create *Inhaled Cliffs* (1996), the artist starched bedsheets with chalk from the White Cliffs of Dover, the geological formation bordering the sea channel that separates England from the European continent. In British history, the cliffs at Dover have become a symbol of standing strong against outside invaders. What can it mean that an artist has inserted physical traces from that special place into an artwork? Parker appears to situate meaning on an ambiguous border between optimism, with England continuing to be a proud, strong force on the world stage, and pessimism, the sheets suggesting a shroud burdened with the dust of a civilization that is falling into the sea. In terms of geologic time, the White Cliffs of Dover are in a process of continual transformation from erosion; however substantial they look, they are a transitory entity masquerading as the eternal. Eventually and inevitably, the cliffs will disappear into the waves.

As a metaphor for the passage of time, Parker's art frequently involves physical as well as conceptual transformations of found objects; objects from the past are changed in both appearance and meaning. For example, to create *The Measure of a Man* (2004), the artist melted down a silver war medal and attempted to draw the material into a long thin wire. In doing so, she returned the medal to an earlier physical state (raw metal), but the wire is in a tangled shape, as if to demonstrate that time, or hindsight, changes and confuses everything. In another work, *The Negative of Whispers* (1997), Parker fashioned a pair of earplugs from dust created by visitors to the dome of London's Saint Paul's Cathedral, where the curved ceiling easily carries sound from wall to wall.

To make *Breathless* (2001) [4-14], a permanent grand installation in an atrium of the vast Victoria and Albert Museum, Parker first squashed more than two dozen silver-plated brass band instruments under the weight of the hydraulic lifting mechanisms from London's Tower Bridge. She then suspended the flattened instruments in a circular pattern in the open expanse surrounded by floors of galleries devoted to British art and design from 1500 to 1900. The objects in these galleries were made by working-class people for the upper classes. *Breathless* refers to the working-class bands that were once fixtures of British life when miners, unions, and the Salvation Army had bands. These bands, and by implication the customs and even existence of the groups that maintained them, have almost disappeared. The band instruments in their flattened state serve as a metaphor for cultural traditions that are no longer relevant or vital; they may also refer to hopes that have been squashed or abandoned. Suspended in between floors in a museum that serves as England's collective attic, a national treasure trove of objects with histories, *Breathless* relates to our current chapter's theme, time, while pointing toward the theme of our next chapter, place.

Born in 1956 in Cheshire, England, Parker received a master of fine arts degree from Reading University. She lives and works in London.

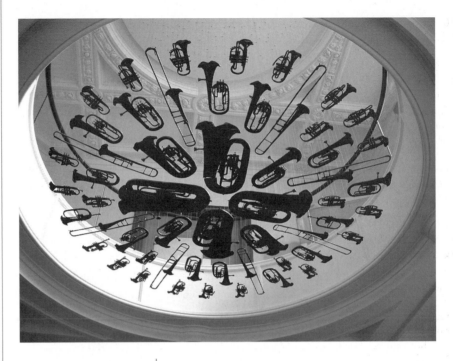

4-14 Cornelia Parker | Breathless, 2001

Brass musical crushed in an industrial press
55 x 500 x 6 cm
Collection by V&A, London
Courtesy of the artist and Frith Street Gallery, London

Notes

1. Amy Cappellazzo, "Fischli/Weiss," in *Making Time: Considering Time as a Material in Contemporary Video and Film* (Lake Worth, Fla.: Palm Beach Institute of Contemporary Art, 2000), p. 41. An exhibition catalog.

2. Nancy Princenthal, "Heide Fasnacht: Exploded View," *Art in America*, February 2001, p. 125.

3. Irene Netta, "Time in the Work of Jan Vermeer and Bill Viola," in Helmut Friedel, ed., *Moments in Time: On Narration and Slowness* (Stuttgart, Germany: Hatje Cantz; New York: Distributed Art Publishers, 1999), p. 157.

4. Contemporary artists working with illusionistic space and the drama of a moment suspended in time include the painters Paula Rego, Odd Nerdrum, and Vincent Desiderio and the photographers Jeff Wall, Tina Barney, and Philip-Lorca DiCorcia.

5. Dominique Nahas, "Enkindled Memories: The Art of Whitfield Lovell," in *Whitfield Lovell: Embers* (New York: DC Moore Gallery, 2002), unpaginated. An exhibition catalog.

6. Netta, "Time," pp. 160–161.

7. Vicki Goldberg, "The Artist Becomes a Storyteller Again," *New York Times*, November 9, 1997, p. 25.

8. *Lateral Thinking: Art of the 1990s* (La Jolla: Museum of Contemporary Art San Diego, 2002), p. 70. An exhibition catalog.

9. Rosalind Krauss, "Notes on the Index, Part 1," reprinted in Charles Harrison and Paul Wood, eds., *Art in Theory: 1900–2000: An Anthology of Changing Ideas*, second ed. (Malden, Mass.: Blackwell Publishing, 2003), p. 996.

10. Lincoln Barnett, *The Universe and Dr. Einstein*, rev. ed. (New York: Bantam Books, 1957), p. 53.

11. Victor Burgin, "Situational Aesthetics," reprinted in Harrison and Wood, eds., *Art in Theory*, p. 896.

12. Douglas Fogle, "Volatile Memories," in *No Place (Like Home)* (Minneapolis: Walker Art Center, 1997), p. 116. An exhibition catalog.

13. Lynne Cook, Bice Curiger and Greg Hilty, "Notes on the Artists and Biographies," in *Doubletake: Collective Memory and Current Art* (London: South Bank Centre and Parkett Publishers, 1992), p. 221. An exhibition catalog.

14. Amy Cappellazzo, "Making Time: Considering Time as a Material in Contemporary Video and Film," in *Making Time: Considering Time as a Material in Contemporary Video and Film* (Lake Worth, Fla.: Palm Beach Institute of Contemporary Art, 2000), p. 16. An exhibition catalog.

15. David Hockney, *Cameraworks* (New York: Alfred A. Knopf, 1984), p. 33.

16. Kundera's and Benjamin's observations are both described in Helmut Friedel, "why has pleasure in slowness disappeared," in *Moments in Time*, p. 11.

17. Seth McCormick, "Artists' Biographies," in Friedel, ed., *Making Time*, p. 90.

18. Fogle, "Volatile Memories," p. 117.

19. Quoted in Barbara Tannenbaum, "Where Miles of Murals Preach a People's Gospel," *New York Times*," May 26, 2002, p. 29.

20. Rina Carvajal, "Travel Chronicles: The Work of Adriana Varejão," in Lia Gangitano and Steven Nelson, eds., *New Histories* (Boston: Institute of Contemporary Art, 1996), p. 171. An exhibition catalog.

21. John Brunetti, "E.T. and Others," in *Dialogue*, January–February 2003, p. 44.

22. Fogle, "Volatile Memories," p. 117.

23. In 2004 Emin's tent artwork was destroyed in a warehouse fire, thus becoming only a historical memory itself.

24. Neal Benezra and Olga M. Viso, *Distemper: Dissonant Themes in the Art of the 1990s* (Washington, D.C.: Hirshhorn Museum and Sculpture Garden, Smithsonian Institution, 1996), p. 12. An exhibition catalog.

25. The name of the first American casualty (in 1959) is listed in the center where the two walls meet, from where the list extends outward on the right wall. The list continues from the far left of the other wall and ends back in the center, with the name of the last casualty (in 1975).

26. Maya Lin, *Maya Lin, Between Art and Architecture* (New York: Cooper Union, 2000), p. 15. Transcript of a slide lecture.

27. Charles L. Griswold, "The Vietnam Veterans Memorial and the Washington Mall: Philosophical Thoughts on Political Iconography," in Harriet F. Senie and Sally Webster, eds., *Critical Issues in Public Art: Content, Context, and Controversy* (New York: HarperCollins Publishers, 1992), p. 91.

28. Ibid., pp. 71–73.

29. Benezra and Vigo, *Distemper*, p. 12.

30. Jean Baudrillard, "The Hyper-realism of Simulation," a selection reprinted in Charles Harrison and Paul Wood, eds., *Art in Theory: 1900–2000: An Anthology of Changing Ideas*, 2nd ed. (Malden, Mass.: Blackwell Publishing, 2003), p. 1018.

31. William Kaizen, "Brian Tolle," in *Bomb* 77 (Summer 2001), p. 60.

32. As quoted in Lynda Richardson, "Like Potato Fields, His Memorial Lies Fallow," *New York Times*, May 14, 2003, p. B2.

33. Josh Blackwell, "Brian Tolle at Shoshana Wayne," *Art Issues* 63 (Summer 2000), p. 49.

34. See Craig Owens, "The Allegorical Impulse: Towards a Theory of Postmodernism," extracts reprinted in Harrison and Wood, eds., *Art in Theory*, p. 1026.

35. Geoffrey Batchen, "Carnal Knowledge," *Art Journal* 60 (Spring 2001): p. 21.

36. As quoted in Jonathan Goodman, "Cornelia Parker," *Parachute* 92 (October–December 1998): p. 62.

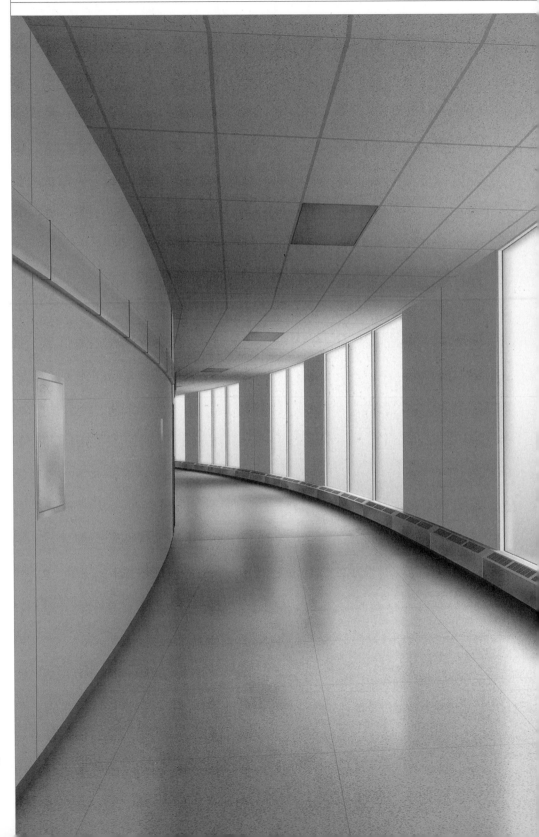

Detail of 5-9

CHAPTER FIVE

Place

Where you hail from and where you now reside are two of the most significant facts about anyone. Place can be a central facet of someone's identity. The place or places where one has lived, with their attendant physical, historical, and cultural attributes, condition what one knows and how one sees. Certainly an artist's geographic history affects the appearance and meaning of his or her art. But beyond this, a conscious awareness of place informs the work of a wide range of contemporary artists. In this chapter, we examine how and why place is an enduring theme in art, with powerful relevance for artists today.

Many contemporary artists who make art that fits the theme of place are responding to specific scenes in front of them or are trying to capture the appearance or feeling of places they remember. More abstractly, some artists are grappling with ideas of place in a conceptual way. For example, they may symbolize or represent what it means to come from a certain geographic location (such as Nigeria or China or a large city or a rural hamlet), or they may try to convey the cultural and emotional qualities of a certain kind of place, such as a wilderness, a city square, a mental institution, or a bedroom. Artists also invent imaginary places. For example, British artist Paul Noble spent eight years on a monumental project depicting a fictional city called Nobstown Newton. His wall-sized drawings, one of which is illustrated [5-1], give aerial views of imaginary architecture.

Many artists of place are responding to broad trends and developments that are changing where and how people live. The map of the world has been redrawn many times in the past thirty years, and we likely will see new maps in the years ahead, affecting how people define identities and structure political power in geographic terms. Moreover, the development of a globalized economy and the worldwide flow of information through cyberspace are connecting once-distant places. At the level of everyday experience, the increasing encroachment of humans on the natural environment and the artificiality of the places in which we live and work mean that many of us have to make a conscious effort to experience wild places firsthand. No wonder artists are making works that express changing ideas about place.

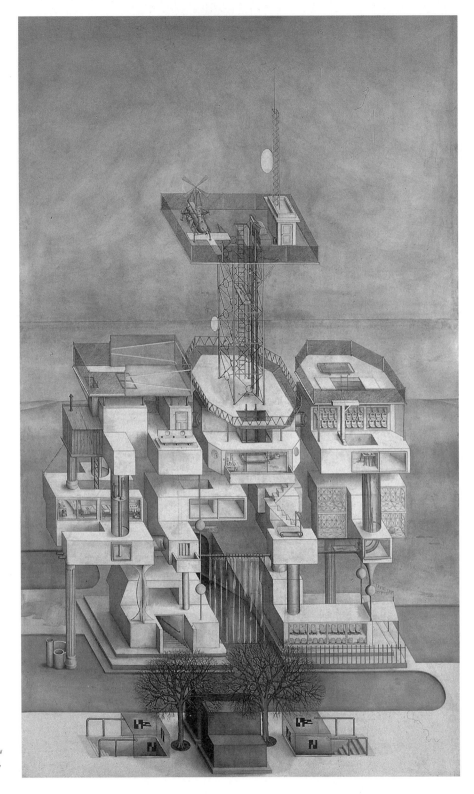

5-1 Paul Noble

Nobspital, **1997–98**

Pencil on paper, 98.5 x 59
inches (250 x 150 cm)
Courtesy of Gorney Bravin + Lee, New
York and Maureen Paley / Interim Art,
London

Places Have Meanings

What is a place beyond a point on a map? Time and space coalesce in a place. Places contain metaphoric or symbolic meanings that go deeper than the surface appearance of a particular landscape or architectural style. Societies transform places, imbuing them with memories, histories, and symbolic significance; they also change them physically. Seen through the lens of culture, a place is a setting for human behavior, an environment infused with a particular spirit. Places come to signify and mirror the viewpoints of inhabitants as well as others. A forest traversed by an indigenous tribe is psychically a much different forest than the one that a band of tourists floats through on boats. Places may have particular meanings that are widely known, or they may have hidden meanings known only to intimates of the place.

The theme of place intersects with the theme of time, especially the subthemes of memory and history. A place is an event as well as a collection of tangible materials, for places inevitably undergo change, however slowly this may occur (only the conception of an idealized place, or *utopia*, remains fixed and static). As events unfold in a specific place, they invest the location with historical significance. The meaning of a place may be charged by events that transpired there (think of the beach at Normandy, where the D-Day invasion took place). A place may be overlaid with multiple histories (think of Jerusalem). Places that are steeped in historical significance may become part of a nation's identity and collective memory (think of the Nazi concentration camps). One artist who has dealt with this last aspect of place is German painter Anselm Kiefer. Beginning in the 1980s, Kiefer created a widely exhibited series of paintings showing charred fields and cavernous rooms with flaming ovens, to call attention to Germany's troubled past. Magdalena Jetelová, born in the former Czechoslovakia, is another artist who has looked at connections between place and time in reference to German history. Jetelová's photographic project *Atlantic Wall* (1995) examines how enormous concrete bunkers erected by the Nazis along the Atlantic Coast from Norway to Spain during World War II have been reduced to crumbling ruins by fifty years of powerful ocean tides. Before photographing, she projected lasers onto the structures to form texts from French philosopher Paul Virilio's book *Bunker Archaeology*, encapsulating his views on the significance of the Atlantic Wall fortifications in relation to the history of military technology and space and the use of images and information to affect perceptions in wartime.

Creating a poignant disjuncture between the present and past identity of a place, California artist Fritz Haeg reminded visitors to the 2008 Whitney Biennial that the valuable real estate that is now New York City used to be a wilderness home for animals. Haeg transformed the courtyard of the museum into *Animal Estates*, an installation of habitats for twelve indigenous species that were displaced by human settlement, including a beaver lodge and an eagle's nest.

In this chapter, we consider contemporary artists who are investigating the political, social, cultural, philosophical, poetic, and psychological implications of place. Many disciplines are engaged in studying the physical features and cognitive meanings of place, including history, geography, cartography, geology, anthropology, literature, architecture, and theater. Visual artists have drawn on insights, information, and theories from all these disciplines and more as they navigate the theme of place.

But before we look at place in contemporary art, it is useful to consider how we use the word *place* in ordinary discourse. A place is a location. A place can be as large as Africa or as small as a closet. A place can be real or imagined. A place is a site of possibility, hypothesis, and fantasy—a somewhere where something may occur. Today, a place can even be a nonplace, perhaps in cyberspace. People interpret places just as they interpret other cultural images, objects, or texts. Place is a function of both perception and cognition.

People in all societies pose similar questions about place: What features define this place? Where are we? Who belongs here? Whose place is this? These questions address description, orientation, identity, and ownership. The ability to navigate places is of vital importance to human survival; nomadic tribes must be concerned with recognizing locations as must civilizations with long histories anchored in specific locales.

Catchphrases and figures of speech hint at how our worldview is saturated with concepts of place. It is common, for instance, to observe that an event "took place." Saying this, we lay bare a bedrock assumption: something doesn't happen unless it happens somewhere. Similarly, when we speak of things being "in place" or "out of place," we imply that having a defined location is valuable and normal. Some cultures have rules for the ideal placements of objects, such as *feng shui* in the Chinese tradition, or the layout of architectural spaces. The post-Enlightenment notion that something cannot be in two places at once remains a powerful idea about the nature of the physical universe (although this assumption is now challenged for the location of light quanta in the world of quantum mechanics).

Places Have Value

Places have literal value; they may contain natural resources, such as timber, oil, or abundant water, or they may contain a large investment in infrastructure, including roads, bridges, and public buildings. Places also have symbolic value. Terrorists targeted the World Trade Center in New York City in 2001 not only because the twin towers represented valuable property and contained thousands of human beings, but because these particular buildings symbolized the enormous prestige and global power of the United States and international capitalism. The World Trade Center and many other places, such as Jerusalem and Belfast, have different symbolic value to different people.

The symbolic value of a place reflects an accumulation of psychic meanings. Some theorists of culture have adopted the term *space* to refer to the social and psychological attributes of a place.[1] The psychic dimensions of a place are changeable and subject to redefinition as new inhabitants occupy a place. Multiple psychic spaces may exist in the same place at the same time. Just as places can be physically transformed, as older buildings are demolished and new ones are erected on the same site, for instance, they can also be transformed culturally, as new psychic spaces open up to replace or coexist with older ones. For example, suppose a women's college became coeducational. The buildings and campus grounds would basically remain the same, but a new, psychic space for the voices and viewpoints of male students would open up.

Some kinds of places can trigger intense physical or emotional responses, such as vertigo, claustrophobia, or disorientation. Some adults experience a fear of heights on tall buildings or bridges or a fear of public places (agoraphobia), and many children are fearful of the place under the bed.

Because places have material and symbolic value, disputes over the ownership, use, development, and naming of places are common. The history of the world is a complicated lineage of shifting borders and changing place names. The maps that we studied as children are not the ones we use today, nor are today's maps likely to remain accurate in the future. Just since 1980, the world has witnessed the breakup of the former Soviet Union into numerous smaller states; the fracturing of Yugoslavia into many countries, including Serbia, Croatia, Kosovo, and Bosnia and Herzegovina; the unification of East and West Germany; and the incorporation of Hong Kong into the People's Republic of China. Throughout history, changes in dominion have often been accompanied by horrendous bloodshed and destruction. Today we still witness confrontations over territory, such as those between Israelis and Palestinians in the Middle East and between India and Pakistan over Kashmir.

Contemporary artists have explored how changes in a geographic location may impact how people value the social landscape. For example, artists in South Africa in the 1990s created works in a range of media that explore memories of an integrated community (District Six) that once stood in the heart of Cape Town. District Six was bulldozed from 1966 to 1981 to clear the way for the more structured and regimented space, divided along racial lines, ordered by the apartheid government then in power. A once-vibrant community became a barren landscape. The contrast is made clear in *Shop/Site/Shrine* (1997), an artwork by South African artist Nadja Daehnke. Composed of a map of the former thriving locale imprinted on a sheet of glass, *Shop/Site/Shrine* functions as a kind of time machine: by looking through the glass in front of the current landscape, the viewer becomes a witness to a symbolic representation of all that is now missing.

History's Influence

Fifty years ago, if you opened a chapter in a book about how artists treat the theme of place, you would read about paintings and photographs of landscapes and cityscapes, perhaps read about how a certain sculpture was sited in its natural or architectural setting, and—if the scope of the book was wide—you might read about the designs of gardens, parks, and city plazas. Today artistic treatments of place go beyond paintings, photographs, and sculptures in traditional media. Contemporary art about place is made using a wide array of materials and styles for an equally diverse range of artistic goals.

In spite of changes in our conceptions of place and the strategies of artists who explore this topic, much contemporary art about place remains anchored in (or at least related to) traditions and ideas that would be recognizable to earlier generations. For starters, the tradition of landscape painting remains vital. Every adult who has grown up in a Western culture knows what a landscape painting looks like. Vast numbers of these paintings were produced over the past several centuries, and many professional and amateur artists today favor landscapes.

The Western tradition of landscape painting can be traced back over two thousand years to wall paintings in Roman villas that included natural scenery. The motif fell out of favor in Europe, however, until it was revived in the sixteenth century, and landscape became an independent genre. In contrast, landscape painting in China, where the tradition of monumental landscape painting is referred to as *shanshui* ("mountain and water"), has maintained great vigor since the tenth century. In nineteenth-century Europe, the realists and impressionists elevated landscapes and cityscapes as they rejected academic history painting. Indeed, many of the great achievements at the beginning of modernism happened in landscape painting. In the United States, landscape painting likewise thrived in the nineteenth century, led by artists of the Hudson River School and artists who represented explorations of the American West. Landscape as a motif continued throughout the twentieth century in Europe and America, serving in avant-garde art as a means to explore formal issues and express personal emotions and visions.[2]

While much has been written about the theme of place in art history,[3] here we will limit ourselves to examining some of the concepts and strategies developed and utilized by earlier artists that recur in contemporary art, with new twists.

(Most) Places Exist in Space

An actual place exists in space, the three-dimensional field of everyday experience. A working artist, however, has a range of options for representing or incorporating space. Even for artists who use three-dimensional media (sculpture and installation art), no single approach to the representation or manipulation of space dominates: spaces can be naturalistic (as in the tableaus using found objects and furniture by Ed and Nancy Kienholz), space can be flattened (as in bas-reliefs), scale can be shifted in an accordion-like arrangement of flat planes (as in the constructions of Red Grooms), and mass can become void and void mass (as in sculptural treatments that build on cubism). The space of a place may be interpenetrated by video, slide, and light projections, and sounds and smells can permeate and fill space.

Artists working in two-dimensional media represent the space of places on a spectrum ranging from illusionistic treatments (including photorealism, magic realism, and naturalistic realism) to diagrammatic treatments (such as the case of an artist utilizing architectural blueprints) to the flattened or collapsed spatial treatments that are frequently found in abstraction.

Each culture invents and manipulates its own archetypal ways of representing space artistically. In the West, for some five hundred years, from the fifteenth century until the late nineteenth century, visual artists working on flat surfaces (in paintings, drawings, and prints) depicted physical space by employing the conventions of linear and atmospheric perspective. The resulting illusionary images show how a scene would appear to a stationary observer from one specific viewpoint. The systems of linear and atmospheric perspective continue to underpin many artistic representations of place. For example, most camera equipment utilizes a lens system that is based on the principles of linear perspective.[4] Contemporary artists who explore a surrealistic aesthetic, creating images of heightened sexuality, sci-fi imagery, or computer gaming, often rely on the contrast between the successful illusion of three dimensionality and the incredibility of the subject to heighten the work's aesthetic impact.

Over the course of the twentieth century, alternative spatial systems attracted many visual artists working in two-dimensional media. Two such strategies remain particularly relevant for contemporary artists. The first is the use of a disjunctive representation of physical space within one artwork. In contrast to portraying a single cohesive space (like that represented in an ordinary photograph or painting with linear perspective), a disjunctive representation shows multiple spaces coexisting or multiple views of a space. For example, Kerry James Marshall made a series of paintings of Chicago housing projects [5-2] whose compositions fuse naturalistic images, flat forms, decorative patterning, and collage elements. Ethiopian-born artist Julie Mehretu

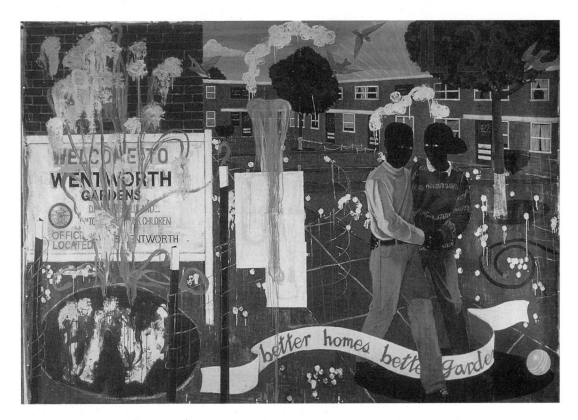

5-2 Kerry James Marshall | *Better Homes Better Gardens*, **1994**
Acrylic and collage on canvas, 100 x 144 inches
Courtesy of the artist and Jack Shainman Gallery, New York

overlays depicted fragments of built environments drawn from varied sources, such as airport plans, weather maps, stadium seating charts, and architectural diagrams of new and ancient buildings. Working with multiple layers of ink and colored pencil on architect's vellum or mylar, Mehretu constructs (and deconstructs) the visually dense, heterogeneous character of urban space.

The second strategy that is widely used by artists to represent space is to adopt or adapt techniques, concepts, and images from cartography. Mapping allows for the layering of information and for documenting a place without committing to a single unchanging vantage point. All locations exist simultaneously; the viewer hovers theoretically at an equal distance above all points on the map. In addition to mapping, artists have employed various forms of diagramming as a way to visualize a subject without resorting to Cartesian perspective. Some artists utilize sophisticated new technologies, such as global positioning systems (GPS), which make it possible to track locations and movements on the earth by satellite. Artists may also combine mapping and diagramming with other systems of spatial representation in the same work, as Mehretu does.[5]

Some of the more intriguing map-based artworks explore the political and emotional aspects of place. Palestinian artist Mona Hatoum created an installation in a gallery in Jerusalem, *Present Tense* (1996), in which she used soap blocks and red beads to reproduce maps pertaining to the division and control of lands on the West Bank, which were accompanied by photographs of local shopping and cooking activities. The maps abstract the Arab-Israeli struggle over territory, while the everyday images and evocative scent of the soap ground the conflict in local habitats and customs. Kathy Prendergast, an artist from Ireland, alters maps to tantalize viewers with alternative readings of geographic identities. According to curator Mel Watkin, for a digital print entitled *Lost* (1999), Prendergast took a "straightforward map of the United States. . . . The map is dotted with hundreds of towns all of which bear the same name: Lost. These are all real towns (Lost River, Lost Gulch, etc.) Every other city in the country, however, has been systematically deleted from the map. What does this imply? Are we lost? Are they lost? Or is she?"[6]

Artists working in three-dimensional media (sculptors, installation artists, and so on) can explore the spatial treatment of place with an even wider spectrum of options. American sculptor Richard Serra, for instance, invites the viewer to walk around and through his huge twisted forms. The viewer is immersed in a warp of space as the sculptor orchestrates how space flows around enormous, curving iron plates. No single vantage point is privileged, in contrast to the frontal viewpoint that is constantly dominant when viewing a painting or a relief sculpture.

The Work of Art Exists in a Place

Art exists in a place. This fact has been an integral part of the aesthetic impact of countless projects through history. Moreover, because in the past much art was permanently located in one place, the connection between art and its context seemed conceptually (sometimes literally) indissoluble. Paleolithic wall paintings positioned deep in caves at Altamira in Spain, carved sculptures attached to Chartres Cathedral in France, and Michelangelo's frescoes adorning the ceiling in the Sistine Chapel in Rome are three unforgettable examples. In fact, in the West, from ancient Greece to seventeenth-century Europe, a large proportion of the most significant examples of art were attached directly to a work of architecture.

It didn't change overnight, but ultimately the strong link between art and its original location weakened. Eventually, a total separation occurred for most works. One aspect of this separation was physical. While there had always been small-scale art objects that could be moved from place to place, such as decorative vases, the arts of painting and sculpture were primarily place bound. But when easel painting was popularized as a practice in Europe some five hundred years ago, the number of painted images that were portable increased exponentially. Even though projects linked to specific architectural sites were still widely undertaken, including murals and sculptures designed for specific buildings and stained-glass windows executed for particular churches, it became commonplace to plan and execute a work of art independent of its setting. This change in the physical nature of art influenced (and was, in turn, affected by) shifts in aesthetic theory and art production alike. Equally important, the invention of photography (in the nineteenth century) and the ability of photography to reproduce artworks with detailed accuracy had a profound impact on changing our notion of art's attachment to place. People now had ready access to reproductions of works of art without seeing their original settings.

The separation of art from its location also involved a mental or cognitive shift. This, too, occurred gradually but took a striking turn during the modern period. Modernists who were formalists believed that the meaning of an artwork should remain consistent regardless of where the artwork is displayed. Archetypal examples of modern art, such as the color-field paintings of the mid-1950s to late 1960s in the United States, which emphasized formal aspects and were designed to be portable, were expected to make the same visual impression on viewers in any exhibition site. Underscoring the de-emphasis on site, modernist artists and curators at the time favored pared-down gallery spaces—white walls, even lighting, no windows—that appear neutral and do not call attention to themselves.

The formalist faith in the self-contained artwork with a consistent meaning did not endure. Beginning in the mid-1960s, the importance of the place where an artwork is displayed was recognized once again. Works sited outdoors obviously interact with the surrounding landscape or architecture, but every gallery, even the modernist "white cube," has its own particular architecture that becomes part of the visual experience of any artwork it contains.[7] By the 1980s, postmodernists, feminists, and multiculturalists all agreed that no art is seen or understood independently of its exhibition context, nor is it entirely free of the cultural connotations of the place in which the art originated.

Acknowledging that the viewing context has an influence on meaning, a wide range of contemporary artists have made *site-specific* artworks, in which the work takes part of its meaning and form from the particular location where it is installed.[8] For example, for the 2002 Whitney Biennial, Roxy Paine made a life-size sculpture of a tree out of shining sheets of aluminum. The artist designed his tree to be placed in Central Park, rather than inside the museum's building on Madison Avenue. Viewed in situ, Paine's simulacrum transformed the surrounding park from what it had been, an island of designed nature within the sea of architecture that is Manhattan, to a zone of skepticism: What is natural? What is constructed? Who or what controls which is which? Nicolas De Oliveira, Nicola Oxley, and Michael Petry offered an expanded definition of site-specificity:

> Site-specificity implies neither simply that a work is to be found in a particular place, nor, quite, that it is that place. It means, rather, that what the work looks like and what it means is dependent in large part on the configuration of the space in which it is realized. . . . What is important about a space can be any one of a number of things: its dimensions . . . , its general character, the materials from which it is constructed, the use to which it has previously been put . . . , the part it played in an event of historical or political significance, and so on.[9]

Earth art or *land art* is one form of site-specific art that emerged in the mid-1960s and continues to be practiced today by such artists as Nancy Holt, Michael Singer, Alan Sonfist, Gabriel Orozco, David Nash, and Meg Webster. Earth artists work in nature, using aspects of the landscape as part of their artistic materials. The artwork may be built directly out of the organic materials in the surrounding environment. British artist Andy Goldsworthy, for example, lays stones, flowers, or leaves in a particular pattern at the outdoor place where he finds the materials. In other instances, manufactured materials are formed and placed in a specific setting, as in the case of the public art projects by Christo and Jeanne-Claude. For example, for *Surrounded Islands* (1983), a series of islands in Biscayne Bay, Florida, were wrapped temporarily in 6.5 million square feet of bright pink, woven polypropylene fabric.

Installation art is often site specific. As an ensemble of elements that are intended to be experienced as a single artwork, an installation is site specific when created especially for a particular location. The viewer is not expected to see a site-specific installation as a self-contained tableau, independent of the place where it is displayed. In the case of a site-specific installation in a gallery or museum, the art melds with the surrounding architecture; the building's walls and spaces become part of the art. American video artist Diana Thater, for instance, projects her large-scale video installations onto columns, windows, ceilings, walls, and floors, thereby accentuating the architectural structure that is the context of our viewing [color plate 9]. (Paradoxically, by casting video projections onto the structure, Thater partly dematerializes the structure's physical presence.)

Contemporary artists who have made installations that specifically address themes of place include Thater, Ann Hamilton, Robert Irwin, Fred Wilson, Sarah Sze, Ilya and Emilia Kabakov, Daniel Buren, and Tadashi Kawamata. Of course, many installations focus on themes other than place; nevertheless, an installation exists as a constructed environment that situates and involves viewers. An installation provides an intensified version of our encounters with actual places in the world. It transforms an entire setting into a work of art. An installation offers a physical experience that can be emotionally and intellectually involving, as if viewers had walked into a stage set (with certain props, scenery, lighting, and sound effects) and found they were called upon to imagine unknown performances.

The concept of site specificity has remained significant throughout the contemporary period, even as its definition and practice continue to evolve.[10] One direction that relates to site-specific installation, as well as to architecture and landscape architecture, is the construction of functional structures by visual artists. Contemporary artists, including Vito Acconci, Dennis Adams, Athena Tacha, and Mary Miss, to name a few, have taken on projects or worked in a team with architects to design structures for specific sites that are used by the people who live or work there. Acconci, who became widely known as an iconoclastic artist in the 1970s with his performances and installations, founded Acconci Studio in 1988, combining his talents and vision with a team of architects, engineers, and other artists. *Courtyard in the Wind* (1997–2000), for example, was constructed for the Administration Building of the Buildings Department in Munich, Germany. The courtyard consists of a ring-shaped portion of landscape that revolves on a large turntable hidden below the ground. The circle of landscape moves as the wind powers a turbine located on a nearby tower. According to the artist's poetic description, "As the wind blows, the ground moves slowly under your feet making it impossible to walk in a straight line. The revolving ring displaces the landscape; grass separates from grass and walkway from walkway . . . two trees become dislodged from a grove."[11]

Looking at Places

Within the theme of place, many contemporary artists have created works that represent the physical and emotional particularities of specific locales, such as the Grand Canyon, Tokyo, the local diner, or the artist's studio. In such works, the tactile and the psychological qualities of places rub off on each other.

In comparison to their nineteenth-century precursors, today's artists are more likely to be conscious that their looking at places is filtered through social concepts. As critic Liz Wells explained, "Land is a natural phenomenon. . . . 'Landscape' is a cultural construct."[12] Places exist out there, external and independent of our thinking about them, but the concepts we use to organize and interpret places are inventions and interventions of human thought.

Since 1980, painters and photographers, such as Neil Welliver, Robert Berlind, Jane Freilicher, Mark Innerst, Joel Meyerowitz [color plates 6 and 7], and William Eggleston, have continued the tradition of working from their own direct observations of specific places. For these artists, aspects like weather and lighting conditions may serve as symbols for human feelings projected onto the landscape. Some artists, including British painter Peter Doig and Americans David Bates and Joan Snyder, create images of remembered places, underscoring the power of places to evoke personal memories and buried feelings. Still others, notably Gerhard Richter in Germany and Vija Celmins in the United States, explore how we relate to particular places whose appearance has been altered by the medium of photography or other technology. In Richter's and Celmins's photo-based paintings, a specific locale, such as an alpine landscape (Richter) or a wave-encrusted ocean (Celmins), is twice removed from the viewer. Although their works are based on photographs of specific scenes, their true subject is less the actual place existing in the real world than the visual information (and style of representation) evident in the photograph.

The practice of rendering local landscapes remains popular in the United States in certain scenic locations, notably Santa Fe and Taos, New Mexico; Provincetown, Massachusetts; and the coast of Maine. These regions support a thriving commercial gallery system that attracts many collectors who seek images of scenic grace, grandeur, or at least charm. A similar emphasis on landscape motifs can be found in other parts of the world. Along the Li River in southern China, for instance, painters continue to depict the steep, rounded mountains that distinguish the region.

Of course, two-dimensional media are not the only ones that contemporary artists have used to represent a specific locale. Numerous artists represent places using other approaches to working with materials. For example, U.S. artist Roxy Paine's *Crop* (1997–98) [I-2] is a life-size and lifelike sculptural representation of a patch of earth with poppies. Robert Lobe pounds sheets of aluminum around large boulders and tree trunks; the result is displayed as a direct cast from nature. British artist Rachel Whiteread has become well known for her casts of negative spaces, such as the empty space under a bed or a desk, the interior of a room, or a stairwell, that preserve, in reverse, specific details, such as the location and design of windows, moldings, and wall plugs.

Within contemporary art, representations of built places are more prevalent than representations of natural places. This fact mirrors a general shift in living patterns worldwide as people inhabit increasingly populated places and become distanced, and sometimes estranged, from nature. The range of built places explored by artists is diverse. Artists are interested not only in how urban environments look, but in how they feel, sound, smell, and impact residents and visitors. They are interested in how cities work and what they mean. In exploring cities and other segments of the built environment, artists address many of the same issues that can provoke strong opinions among city dwellers in general—crowdedness, vulnerability, the economic disparity between rich and poor—as well as those qualities that make cities exciting places to live, such as the dazzling sensory impressions one encounters both night and day.

Wayne Thiebaud's paintings from the early 1980s are highly recognizable for the way in which they exaggerate San Francisco's earthquake-prone topography: depicting buildings and streets perched on steep hills, the images conflate the physical precariousness and emotional pizzazz of the city by the bay. More recently, Chinese sculptor Zhan Wang used stainless steel cookware imported from China to create *San Francisco*

Cityscape (2008), a twenty-two-foot-long installation that is a surprisingly accurate representation of San Francisco, including buildings, the waterfront, and the Golden Gate Bridge. *San Francisco Cityscape* is one of several sculptures in which Wang examines the interlocked histories of impoverished Chinese immigrants and other cultural groups who collectively built northern California. Wang is also known for the many re-creations in stainless steel he has made of Chinese scholars' rocks—rocks placed as representations of mountains in urban gardens in China that serve as idealized evocations of natural places and as sites for seeking tranquility. According to writer Aimee Le Duc, Wang's gleaming simulacra of scholars' rocks challenge "our need to use meditative tools to escape the urban cultures that we so rapidly create, destroy, and build again."[13]

For some artists, a place is defined by the patterns of behavior that are found there. In the early 1980s, Denis Wood created a series of maps that locate idiosyncratic details of his neighborhood. Wood's art charts patterns, such as sidewalk graffiti, traffic and road signage [5-3], and the location of pumpkins in the neighborhood on Halloween night. By graphically documenting a category of details located in a specific place, each of these maps reveals a holistic pattern of social meaning.

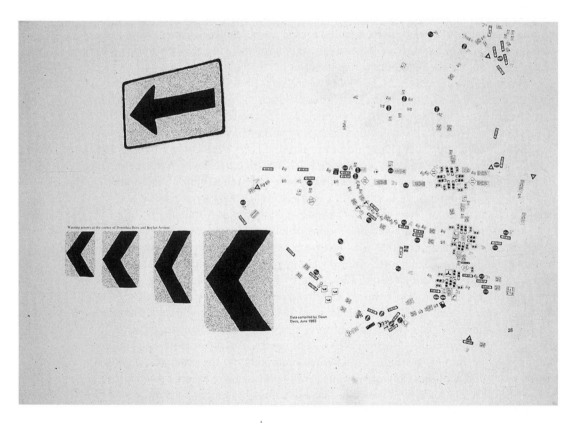

5-3 Denis Wood and Carter Crawford │ *A drawing from Denis Wood's Dancing and Singing: A Narrative Atlas of Boylan Heights: street signs,* **1982**
(map by Carter Crawford and Denis Wood)
Courtesy of the artist

Today, the city serves as the primary stage for human action. In large-scale panoramic photographs, German Andreas Gursky provides breathtaking bird's-eye views of people crowded together in huge places: "International stock-exchange trading floors, vast factories, office buildings, parliaments, libraries, Olympic events, and other subjects produce the same jaw-dropping awe to which Romantic landscape painting once aspired."[14] Gursky's images present visual evidence that places are defined by the people who congregate in them, just as people mirror the places they inhabit. Gursky's photos appeal to our fascination with watching the spectacle of other people. They also capture the huge quantity of visual details that city dwellers must process.

In the twenty-first century, artists increasingly are exploring the aural dimensions of places. Video, performance, and installation artists have helped us to listen to as well as look at the places we inhabit. In addition, contemporary visual art exhibitions often include works by composers and sound artists, such as Maryanne Amacher, who construct forms of aural architecture that immerse the audience in an experience of place that melds sights, sounds, and feelings. In Amacher's works, extremely loud sounds and extremely subtle ones create unique echoes within the body. As we sit within one of these sound art works, our experience of place shifts from one that emphasizes the static and the visual to one that emphasizes the temporal flow of sounds. Sounds engulf us, rising and falling in pitch and volume, changing in tonality.

Looking Out for Places

Why are some places so valuable that artists would devote their art-making efforts to calling for their protection? A number of factors are at work. In the case of attempts to protect natural places, some artists subscribe to a pantheistic view of nature, a belief in wilderness as a source of spiritual energy. For them, a desert is not merely a place of little rainfall, and a mountain is not simply a place of extreme elevation. Rather, a desert may be a site for inducing mystic awareness, and a mountain may be cherished as a place of spiritual birth or rebirth. The idea of nature as a site of sacred significance is exemplified by Native American Truman Lowe's *Red Banks* (1992) [5-4], a twenty-foot-long sculpture created out of wood, purchased from a building supply store, that is adorned with natural branches. The work portrays the riverbank that tribal beliefs mark as the site where the ancestors of the Ho Chunk people first stepped into being. Various artists in other cultures, including in Germany, Japan, Australia, and China, have likewise connected natural sites with the origin of their culture or society. In creation stories around the globe, the explanation of humankind's origin often begins with the place of the gods (or God), from whence flow forces that create the place of earthly life.

The wilderness myth that underlies America's image of itself, "the image of America as a pristine land divinely favored,"[15] has long exerted a pull on artists in the United States, although contemporary artists usually view the myth with nostalgia or irony. For example, in 1994–95, Frank Moore made three large paintings of Niagara Falls that showed the awesome splendor of the falls but also the industrialization that is destroying their scenic beauty. (For example, because water is diverted to supply hydroelectric power, the flow is often reduced to 40 percent of its former force). Critic Faye Hirsch wrote that "all three paintings are framed by copper pipes with faucets at the

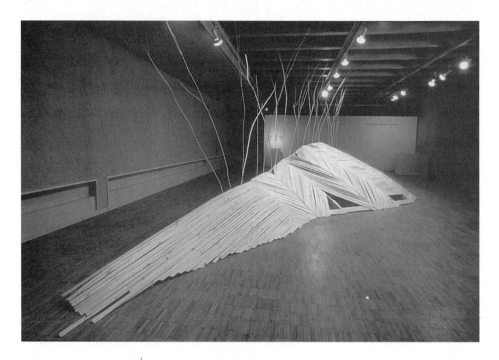

5-4 **Truman Lowe** | *Red Banks,* 1992
Wood, 36 x 144 x 96 inches
Courtesy of the artist

top, and floating through the mists are delicately rendered, screenprinted symbols of the toxic chemicals found in the waters. . . . The thundering torrent, once the paradigm of sublime nature, has here become the emblem of its demise."[16]

Throughout the past three decades, artists have expressed the alarm felt by many people over the increasingly imperiled ecology of the earth. Rather than offer artistic laments about the environment in general, numerous artists have focused on conditions that are specific to one site or region or reveal the interconnections between places. For example, Richard Misrach's photos of deserts in the American West examine the disturbing discrepancy between natural splendor and traces of human incursion [I-1], such as evidence of nuclear bomb tests. Helen and Newton Harrison solidified their reputations as artists who are social activists by identifying ecological problems in various places around the world, researching scientifically feasible solutions, and engaging a community in a dialogue about restoring certain environmental areas to a natural condition. In a project in the former Yugoslavia (1988–91), the Harrisons proposed a reclamation project for the Sava River. Another project (initiated in the late 1970s) involved creating a series of maps that offer potential ways to answer the question, Who owns the sea? The Harrisons view the process of collaborating with community residents as an integral part of their creative process. According to Eleanor Heartney, "they see themselves as catalysts whose outsider status allows them to offer insight or reformulations (to improve an ecological problem area) that might be impossible for those who are more technically trained or more closely tied to local politics. Solutions, the Harrisons believe, will evolve from conversations among all concerned."[17]

The Harrisons are not alone in their willingness to tackle real-world problems. In 1982, Patricia Johanson completed a project in Dallas that restored the ecosystem of a lagoon and created paths, bridges, and benches that buttress the shoreline and allow visitors to enjoy the place. Mel Chin has turned polluted fields into art, reviving them by using plants that leach toxins out of the soil. Betsy Damon designed *Living Water Garden* (1998), an organic system for water purification that now serves the city of Chengdu in mainland China [5-5]. Damon's project is notable because she is a Western artist venturing into a Communist country to propose art as a viable response to serious environmental problems.

Other artists with deeply felt concerns about ecology have opted for less pragmatic, more metaphoric approaches. For example, German-born Justen Ladda's sculpture *Romeo and Juliet* (1988) shows a structure shaped like an automobile engine and constructed from plastic models of buildings that dominates an idyllic landscape. The title, according to one interpretation, refers, in part, to "our troubled romance with nature: we simultaneously idealize it even as we develop and destroy it."[18] Maya Lin is addressing environmental issues by translating geological features, such as underground rivers, hills, and undersea formations, into large-scale installations of aluminum tubing that visitors can walk under and through, with the goal of enhancing their sensitivity to the natural world.

It is not only wild places with imperiled ecosystems that have captured artists' attention; inhabited places have also gained advocates. Beginning in 1989, Alfredo Jaar,

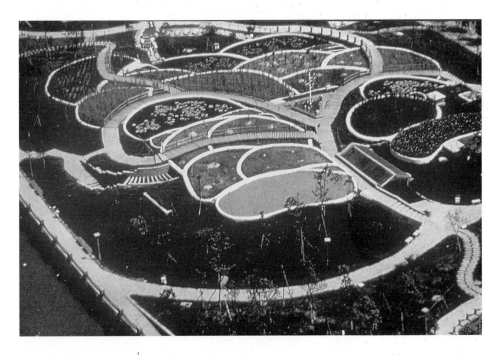

5-5 **Betsy Damon** | *The Living Water Garden,* 1998
Chengdu, China
Aerial image of the constructed wetlands
Courtesy of the artist and Keepers of the Water

an artist born in Chile who resides in New York City, created a series of artworks under the general title *Geography = War*. These artworks take complex forms, layering information so that the ideas presented are elusive to a viewer who gives a cursory look. Upon careful examination, Jaar's overriding concern becomes apparent: he calls into question the moral equation in which developed industrial nations gain power and profit as they manipulate processes that involve economically disadvantaged nations.

In his art, Jaar expands the definition of place. Instead of defining a place solely in terms of its geographic location and physical appearance, Jaar shows how a place is more fully defined in terms of its economic, political, and cultural relationships to other places. For a 1990 installation of *Geography = War*, Jaar embodied his concepts in three primary materials: large maps installed in light boxes, metal barrels, and photographic images of residents [5-6]. Together, these materials reveal the links between a place in Italy where barrels of petroleum from Nigeria are shipped and Koko, a village in Nigeria where toxic waste from Italy is returned in the same barrels and dumped. The economic efficiency is obvious: tankers carry a full cargo in both directions. The maps graphically represent the geographic distance separating Nigeria and Italy. The photographic images show the human faces of the residents in Koko who retrieve the toxic

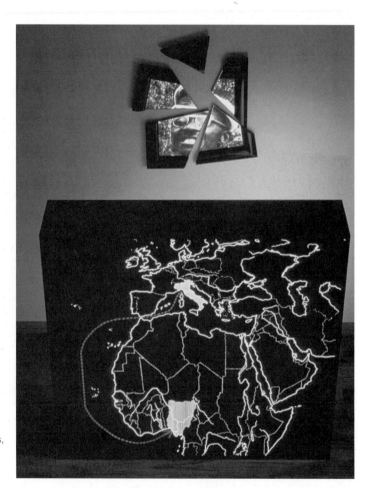

5-6 Alfredo Jaar

Geography=War, **1990**

Double-sided light box with color transparencies,
framed mirror broken in five pieces,
overall dimensions: 50 x 40 x 28 inches
Courtesy of the artist

barrels and reuse them for storage. For better and for worse, an African and a European country are interconnected.

Other approaches to protecting inhabited places examine the appearance and meaning of streets, buildings, parks, and other structures that make up the fabric of cities. In 1988, Japanese sculptor Tadashi Kawamata made *Favela in Battery Park City: Inside/Outside*, a temporary installation in which he attached a crude structure derived from South American slum dwellings (*favelas*) to the World Trade Center in New York City, contrasting urban poverty and corporate wealth as embodied in buildings. Although Kawamata was using the World Trade Center as a symbol of economic stability and power, the destruction of the twin towers thirteen years later shows the provisional nature of all human structures, even the most apparently substantial.

Real and Simulated Places

Some artworks that address the theme of place represent and interpret artificial, fictional, and simulated places. These places include synthetic environments that actually exist (such as Disney World, Las Vegas, Hollywood sets, zoos, and habitat displays in natural history museums) and fantasy environments concocted by artists from their own imagination, which may blend the fictional and the real. In this section, we consider how artists are charting and challenging the false dichotomies that separate real from fictive places and nature from culture or exploring the intermingling of these realms.

One artist who combines the real and the artificial is American Liza Lou, who has created full-scale archetypal Middle American environments, including a kitchen, a suburban backyard, and the interior of a 1949 Spartan Mobile Mansion trailer, using papier maché forms, crystal, and beads. The environments evoke real places through their accurate details, including, in *Kitchen* (1991–95) [5-7], elements such as boxes of food and cleaning products bearing familiar brand names, but the encrustations of brilliantly colored beads transform the places into fantasies. The glittery surfaces of the products can also be read as a comment on the seductive advertising that promotes the excesses of consumerism.

According to curators Jeffrey Deitch and Dan Friedman, all artistic representations of places, even natural landscapes, inevitably have conceptual overtones that are based on social constructs. "Even the generations of artists who strove to depict absolute truth in their renderings of nature tended to spiritualize it, romanticize, or intellectualize it." Artists today are even more prone to see places through the lens of culture because (like the rest of us) the places they experience most of the time are far removed from wilderness. "The Post-Modern artist now confronts a Post-Natural nature," Deitch and Friedman wrote.[19]

As the twenty-first century unfolds, humans are increasingly removed from the natural world. Natural sites are bulldozed to make way for development; we visit the outdoors in the designed environments of parks and playgrounds; we learn about wilderness through the filter of television, video, and film; geneticists are turning animals and plants into constructs of human desires; and we obtain our food already processed and packaged. Artists are responding to the artificial environments made by designers, corporate developers, genetic engineers, computer programmers, museum curators, and others for a variety of social and economic purposes.

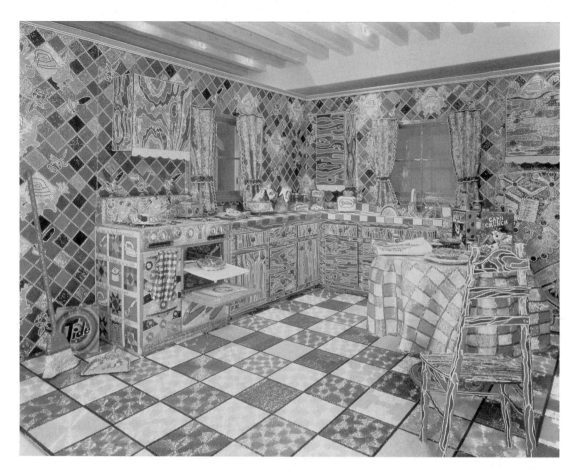

5-7 Liza Lou | *Kitchen*, 1991-95
Mixed media and beads, 8 x 11 x 24 feet
Courtesy of Deitch Projects

One type of synthetic environment that has inspired a subset of artists is *dioramas*. Dioramas include both models, such as architectural models, model train displays, and dollhouses, and full-scale dioramas in museums that are intended to simulate scenes from the past. Dioramas may appear empty like a stage set, or they may be peopled with wax or plastic figures. The artistic roots of contemporary artists' dioramas go back at least to the creation of alternative worlds in the surrealist tradition (for example, the intimate shadow boxes of American artist Joseph Cornell).

Curator Toby Kamps noted that most dioramas "present idealized, concentrated views" and that the simulations "engage our sense of depth perception and, with it, a bodily awareness of space, which encourages us to make the imaginative leap into their constructs."[20] In their uncanny amount of detail, dioramas are precursors of today's virtual reality environments, but according to Ralph Rugoff, a diorama's "antiquated virtual technology has long since ceased to dazzle us," and thus viewers understand that a diorama is a metaphor. An artist can use the obvious artificiality of a diorama-like format to make a distilled statement about some aspect of existence.[21] For instance,

California-born artist Liz Craft presents a comic interpretation of how artificial our home environments have become in her large-scale, diorama-like installation *Living Edge* (1997–98). Using Astroturf, vinyl, and foam, Craft created a synthetic miniature environment complete with artificial flowers and lawn statues of deer. In concocting this fantasy version of a suburban Los Angeles backyard, Craft was influenced more by Walt Disney Studios and Home Depot than by nature itself.

Hiroshi Sugimoto, Mark Dion, and Alexis Rockman are three artists who have responded to the typical habitat display used in natural history museums, a type of diorama that emerged in the nineteenth century. Sugimoto, a Japanese photographer, has made a series of images of actual museum habitat displays that simulate early environments, such as a prehistoric landscape during the Permian era [5-8]. The perfect linear perspective view produced by the camera's lens heightens the weird hyperreality of the museum simulation. Rockman and Dion, both Americans, create diorama-like constructions that ironically subvert the sanitized, idealized view of nature offered in museum displays. For example, an installation by Dion shows animals scavenging through a trash dump, and Rockman has made assemblages depicting ecological horror stories.

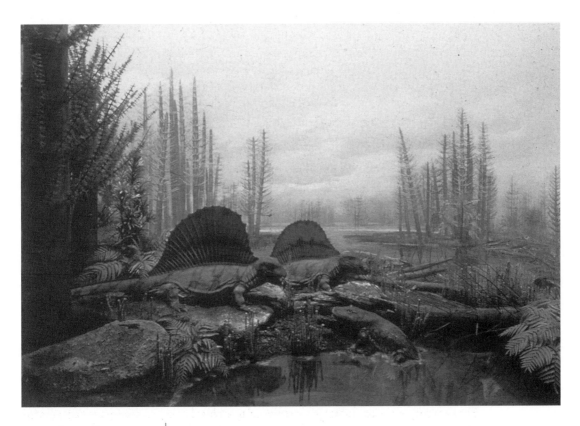

5-8 Hiroshi Sugimoto | *Permian Land*, **1992**
Black and white photograph, 16 x 20 inches
Courtesy of Sonnabend Gallery

One way that artists engage with the constructed nature of place is to invent settings of their own. There is a long history of artists who have depicted their own invented dream scenarios and fantasy places (often concocted from observed elements as well as imagination), including Hieronymous Bosch, Caspar David Friedrich, J. M. W. Turner, and Yves Tanguy. Contemporary artists continue to invent fictional places, working in both two- and three-dimensional media; some also incorporate the dimension of time. In the 1980s, Piero Gilardi, an Italian, started creating what he refers to as *tappeti-natura* ("nature carpets"). These soft-textured bas-reliefs simulate in painstaking detail a single section of the earth's surface, about the size of a small rug. Featuring a tree made from polyurethane foam, *Inverosimile* (1990) is kinetic: branches dance and the sounds of bird calls are heard when viewers squeeze the leaves. The movements are controlled by hidden electronics.

Contemporary artists have combined two- and three-dimensional approaches by building a tableau that they then paint or photograph (perhaps further manipulating the image on a computer). They ultimately destroy the model and display the photograph. American Sandy Skoglund and German Thomas Demand are two among the many who fabricate and then photograph constructed tableaus that are particularly evocative of a sense of place.

In creating a simulated place, an artist is engaged in an unusual quest: to create an alternative world (or a detail of one) that evokes the real one and yet retains its identity as a world apart. Rather than representing or symbolizing an actual place, a simulation offers an intense substitute. Typically, the viewer remains keenly conscious that the simulation is an artifice. Nevertheless, the skilled craftsmanship and involved conception that went into producing the simulation yield an uncanny effect: as viewers we feel ourselves transported into another realm brought magically to life within the borders of art. The Swiss team of Peter Fischli and David Weiss provoke our curiosity with *Room at the Hardturmstrasse* (1990–92), in which all the furniture, tools, and other objects in a workroom were crafted anew in trompe l'oeil fashion from polyurethane and paint. When the conceit is recognized, the ordinary becomes extraordinary, leaving the viewer to wonder why and how such an exacting clone of a place was created.

Recent advances in digital imagery (both still and video) have allowed artists to blend the factual and the fictive dramatically, to warp space and fold time, and to find openings to new dimensions. The ability to create convincing illusions with computer software has given artists a powerful new tool for simulating places, real and imagined. Yoshio Itagaki, for example, in *Tourists on the Moon #2* [1-3] wittily inserted portraits of people into a startling moonscape. His art, although dependent on digital-editing software, still references the history of photography; the images he creates echo nineteenth-century hand-colored prints, and in "Tourists," he picks up on the popular custom of taking snapshots to document a vacation in a foreign place.

Unlike the virtual-reality environments favored in video games, the fictional architectures and topographies created by visual artists do not necessarily aspire to hyperrealism. For example, Paris-based Thomas Hirschhorn used cardboard, packing tape, aluminum foil, and other throwaway materials to produce his installation *Cavemanman* in a gallery in New York in 2002. No viewer was likely to mistake the flimsy, obviously artificial environment for a real place. (*Cavemanman*, supposedly the labyrinthine dwelling of a fictional hermit, also included books, mannequins, and video footage of the cave paintings at Lascaux, France, and seemed to represent the interior of the hermit's mind as well as his physical habitation.)

Shirley Tse, originally from Hong Kong, is another artist who emphasizes the artificiality of her constructed places. Tse, who is fascinated by the proliferation of plastic packaging in the world economy, carved shapes into the surfaces of sections of sheets of polystyrene to make *Polymathicstyrene* (2000), a landscape on shelving that follows the walls of a gallery. Visitors look down on a morphing array of sky-blue "stairs, mazes, buildings, arenas, reservoirs, rivers, pyramids, hills, rock formations. Each section is inspired by different elements of our culture—some are aligned with technology and include forms resembling computer monitors, data chips, and control panels; others are otherworldly, like the surface of another planet or a spaceship launching pad."[22]

The exploration of invented environments can include those that exist only in the shared imaginations of the audience. While the set for a television show, for example, truly exists at a specific location (on a lot in Hollywood, perhaps), the environment it represents is somewhere else, a somewhere that may not be anywhere really. American artist Mark Bennet creates detailed floor plans of the living spaces of fictional television families and groups—the home of the Ricardos from *I Love Lucy*, *Gilligan's Island*, and so forth. In looking at one of Bennet's drawings, we see the architectural context in which the television shows of the fifties, sixties, and seventies were staged. We are touched by the fact that life, even fictional life, can take place in such narrow confines. Bennet's work probes how these domiciles in television-land mirror our own homes, then and now. What does it say about us that a make-believe space (Ralph and Alice's apartment in *The Honeymooners*, for example) can seem more real to us, because we know it in more intimate detail, than our neighbor's house, an interior we may never have been invited into?

Placeless Spaces

Visual artists are increasingly responding to transformations brought on by rapidly evolving technologies, such as the Internet, cell phones, E-mail, electronic banking, and surveillance cameras. The heightened flow of information through vast media networks has accelerated the creation of a world in which multiple media spaces can exist in any physical place and the same media space can exist in multiple physical places. The real and the virtual interpenetrate to such a degree that we have witnessed "a profound cultural shift, permanently altering the way we experience and represent space . . . marked by speed of mobility through space, the viewing of multiple perspectives simultaneously, . . . the breakdown of physical boundaries and temporalities."[23] More and more, we traverse a network of placeless spaces, or spaces that have no fixed geographic location. David Toop poses the change like a riddle, "Where . . . does the music exist if it can be accessed only through the Internet? Or in which space is it created if no physical space (other than a computer screen) or conventional sound-generating tools are used in its construction?"[24]

Responding to and representing the digitizing of information, contemporary artists may investigate places that are not tangible but exist only as virtual spaces. Craig Kalpakjian's *Corridor* (1995) [5-9], for example, is a digital video representation of the view we would experience moving through an environment that was created "entirely on the computer. Every detail of *Corridor*, from the texture of the paint to the slight reflections on each surface, is the result of programming, not the hammering of nails."[25]

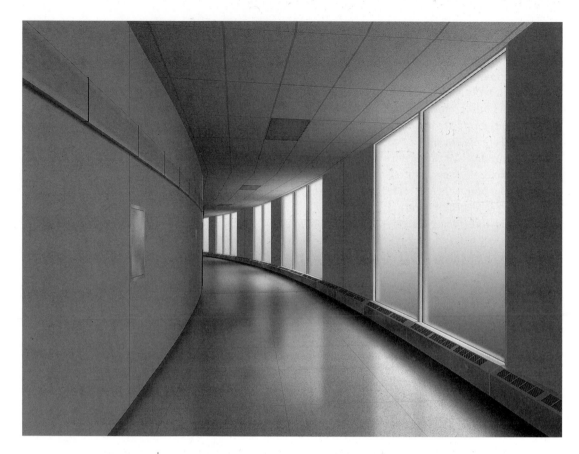

5-9 Craig Kalpakjian | *Corridor,* **1997**

Cibachrome mounted on aluminum, 29 1/2 x 39 1/2 inches
Courtesy of Andrea Rosen Gallery, New York, © Craig Kalpakjian

Cyberspace and other new realms of virtual reality have spawned new conceptions of structure, such as *liquid architecture*, a term that refers to structures that mutate or expand into multiple, seemingly non-Euclidean, dimensions. Another important arena of experimentation, for artists and scientific researchers alike, is virtual immersion environments that are created by three-dimensional (3-D) imaging technology. While some of these environments attempt to mimic the actual world, others present fantastic realms that are strictly computer generated. A participant may enter these worlds, like Alice going down the rabbit hole, by donning goggles (for viewing) and a wired glove or chest device (for navigating).

Artists who are exploring the new terrain of fictional immersion environments include Scandinavian Sven Pahlsson, who creates 3-D computer animations on a computer monitor that allows the viewer to swoop and careen above the landscape, then zoom in for periodic close-up views. Japanese artist Mariko Mori has created nirvana-like dreamscapes, some of which exist only as a computer simulation viewed through 3-D glasses and an advanced 3-D video system, which is projected into a specially designed structure.

Immersive environments are not always computer generated. To create *AUTO-SCOPE* (1996–97), Heike Baranowsky made four copies of a video documenting an actual car trip around Paris. Two of these copies were then flipped, to make a mirror reversal of the original image, and projected flush with the original video. The final four-channel video projection, shown on the gallery wall, takes the viewer on a ride around the City of Lights, but the unusual perspective created by the mirror images funneling together at the center creates a space that does not exist anywhere else on earth. Surely the creative exploration of such placeless spaces will continue at an increased pace as the new century continues.

What's Public? What's Private?

Just as the zone between the real and the artificial is eroding, the borders between public and private are rapidly blurring. Anyone who follows the news knows that differences of opinion concerning the social, legal, psychological, and moral boundaries between the public and the private have crystallized into positions that are hotly debated in political arenas, schools, churches, and households. To name just a few issues: Does the state have the authority to make laws concerning private sexual acts performed between consenting adults in a bedroom? Are the images that you see alone in a room, looking at a computer screen, private or public? Should governments regulate cyberspace? To maintain a competitive edge, is it acceptable for businesses to engage in corporate espionage and attempt to steal one another's secrets? Does an employer have the right to screen employees' E-mail messages and Internet use? Should military and civil authorities watch people on hidden cameras in case some of them are engaged in criminal behavior? Public and private no longer function as absolute terms (if they ever did). The bedroom is more public than a grocery store if it can be viewed on the Internet 24/7; a person talking on a cell phone loudly enough for all to hear in a grocery store mixes a private and a public space.

Communications media have penetrated so many aspects of life that almost no place is free of the possibility of public display or contact with others. Artists responding to this trend have explored the practice of voyeurism, the fear of a political power watching over one's actions (e.g., Big Brother), and the feeling of losing a sense of control over one's personal space. Bruce Nauman, for example, conceived an artwork in which he spied on his own place, which turned into a series of four seven-channel video recordings made in 2000 and 2001 of his New Mexico studio at night. Entitled *Mapping the Studio (Fat Chance John Cage)*, the series "is a portrait of the private life of the artist, made, for the most part, in his absence" that gives audiences "the opportunity to enter the studio of an artist as famously reclusive as Andy Warhol was sociable."[26]

Issues of privacy and who is watching whom in various spheres are not unique to the present age. Architectural historian Witold Rybczynksi explained that in Europe, the concept of privacy in the home began in seventeenth-century Dutch society (from where the concept spread) as the home became separated from the place of work. In consequence, the home became more intimate, less public.[27] Taking a broader view, historian Philippe Aries also identified the growing importance of the public-private divide from the seventeenth century onward. Aries noted that with the rise of large cities, a distinction arose between the private sphere (of one's home and place of work) and the larger public world in which everyone was anonymous. Prior to this period, most people mainly saw other people they knew as they lived out their lives in smaller, rural communities. The cities of nineteenth-century Europe gave rise to the concept of the *flaneur*, a person who freely watches the crowd because he is unknown to them.

Life in contemporary society has created even greater anonymity as well as more opportunities for voyeurism, since there are many more people now and people are more mobile (both in their careers and places of habitation). Yet as cities grow more crowded, the upper and middle classes are retreating to the fortress environments of gated residential communities. Meanwhile, new technologies, such as electronic surveillance equipment, tracking devices, and remote sensors, and changing views about what should be private and public are impacting the places we occupy and how we behave.

Artists exploring the dimensions of public and private space wrestle with a range of serious questions: Who holds the power to control activity within a place? Who is watching whom? Who determines the conventions of behavior in private domestic settings (bedroom, bathroom, kitchen, living room) and in public settings? These questions have also engaged philosophers, such as Michel Foucault, who wrote about the socialization of space, as well as sociologists, such as Erving Goffman, who studied the layered behaviors that allow public and private actions to coexist.

Foucault wrote about mechanisms of social control in institutions, such as prisons, hospitals, schools, factories, and asylums, arguing that those who can be watched can be controlled. Foucault used the model of the *panopticon*, a place where all occupants (prisoners, patients, workers) can be observed from a central point and thus controlled without numerous guards, supervisors, or other personnel. To succeed, this power of surveillance has to be constant, omnipresent, and invisible to those being watched. Building on Foucault's theories, scholars like John Tagg have analyzed the use and meaning of technologies of surveillance in institutions and other settings. From early in its history, photography has been used for surveillance. Since 1980, with the development of video cameras, satellites, and other sophisticated surveillance technologies, we have reached a point where the entire world is "becoming encapsulated by whole networks of orbital devices whose eyes, ears, and silicon brains gather information in endless streams."[28]

Not coincidentally, many of the artists who are preoccupied with issues of surveillance in both institutional and public places are working with camera-based technologies. New York artist Julia Scher has been making work since the mid-1980s about the intrusion of security cameras and other devices that monitor people's movements in public places. In *Security by Julia II*, an installation presented in different places and configurations over the past twenty years, visitors can watch images of themselves and others on a bank of monitors linked to standard security-industry cameras placed throughout the building housing the exhibition [5-10]. The installation reveals and exaggerates the feeling of being watched by mechanical eyes.

While a contemporary city contains multiple worlds, an institution is a place unto itself. Some artists who are making art about institutional places are concerned with the dynamics of how the private world inside an institution contrasts with the public world outside. British-born artist Sue Coe, for example, has made biting drawings of factory slaughterhouses that make public what meat-industry insiders and much of the public would prefer to keep private. She peels back innocuous exteriors to reveal hellish interiors in dark shadows punctured by gleaming lights, where terrified animals are subjected to mechanical cruelties and human workers perform robotically.

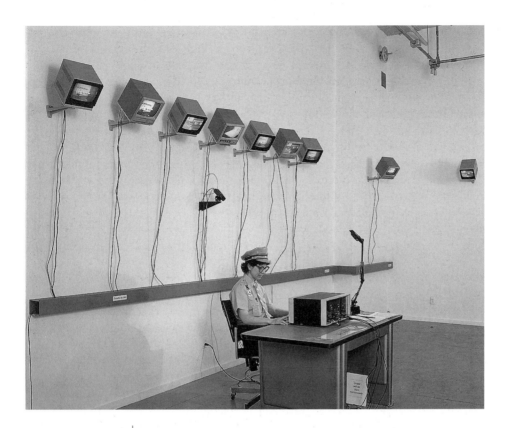

5-10 |Julia Scher | *Security by Julia II,* **1989**

Mixed media, dimensions variable
Installation view at Artists Space, New York, "Dark Rooms," Mar. 2 - Apr. 1, 1989
Courtesy of Andrea Rosen Gallery, New York, © Julia Scher

The home may seem like the paradigmatic private place. But this privacy has both positive and negative connotations. A home can provide security and safety, but it can also be a place of confinement or be bounded by rules and shut off from opportunities and possibilities outside. For example, children in American culture are sometimes punished by being grounded or made to stay indoors, separate from other places and people.

Throughout the 1950s and 1960s in the West, especially in the mass media, the home was portrayed as a special province separate from the "real world" of politics and commerce. From today's perspective, many family shows from the golden age of television seem quaint; now the home is subject to a constant influx of information from electronic communications devices. Nevertheless, the value of preserving the privacy of the home is not clear-cut. Feminists and others have called for breaching the privacy of homes to expose domestic violence and sexual abuse. Ida Applebroog is an artist who has undercut illusions of the safety and comfort of being at home by making art that reveals hidden domestic violence.

Jim Campbell's *Untitled (for Heisenberg)* (1994–95) is an example of art that focuses on the privacy of that seemingly most private of places in the home, the bedroom. Entering the gallery where Campbell's interactive video installation is displayed, a viewer sees what appears to be a double bed with a projected image of naked figures coupling. As the viewer approaches the bed to get a closer look, the video becomes more unfocused and grainier. The viewer's voyeurism is thwarted as hidden electronics control the artwork's focus relative to the viewer's position. The work is one big tease.[29]

Guillermo Kuitca, from Argentina, also alludes to the bed, that private, intimate place for the body, in his well-known series of maps painted onto mattresses. In *San Juan de la Cruz* (1991), Kuitca repeats the Argentinian city's name on a painted map of a region of Poland, and the mattress buttons mark the city's multiple locations. The rivers and roads painted in blue and red evoke the circulatory patterns of veins and arteries. The private place of the human body implied by the mattress serves as the foundation for the artist's mysterious linking of two geographic locations—Argentina and Poland—that are distant from one another.

In-between Places

The flip side of place, locale, home, habitation is placelessness, dislocation, homelessness, journeying. Many people in the world do not live in the place they were born. Many of us move several times in our lives. In America, people change where they live frequently, whether they are moving to a nearby neighborhood or clear across the country. Indeed, the idea of displacement is stitched into the fabric of the national consciousness; America is a land of immigrants and their descendants, and the vision of moving to a new place to seek a better life still drives many Americans.

Some people positively embrace a condition of rootlessness; they yearn to travel and escape from familiar places. During the heyday of European modernism in the first half of the twentieth century, the expatriate artist (for example, Pablo Picasso or Marcel Duchamp) was a romantic, even heroic, figure who voluntarily chose to leave behind his place of origin for the adventure of living and working in a foreign land. The displaced artists of today are more ambiguous figures: many see themselves as exiles, refugees, or nomads. An emotionally shaded reaction to leaving home is expressed in the work of Cuban artist Kcho (Alexis Leyva Machado), who creates boat forms out of found materials. Although his vessels are readily interpreted as evocations of refugees' struggles to escape Cuba and reach the United States, Kcho says his work more generally addresses the experience of living on an island and wanting to overcome the barrier of the ocean [5-11]. According to Deepali Dewan, Kcho's forms "reflect the tension between rootedness and travel, the attachment to home and the desire for the next horizon."[30]

At any given moment, many people on the globe are in transit. Many of them are international business travelers and tourists. Such travelers spend inordinate amounts of time in bland nonplaces, such as airport lounges, hotel rooms, train stations, and highways. According to German photographer Uta Barth, these places of transit echo each other and are "out of place" with the architecture of their various locales: "Anonymous and self-sufficient, these and similar 'non-places' appear across different countries bringing with them an uncanny sense of familiarity while hardly showing a trace of local specificity or exoticism."[31]

More profound than the temporary dislocations of tourists and business travelers are the experiences of those whose understanding of place is fragmented as a result of moving far away from their homeland. Changing geographic locations, once or repeatedly, may involve radical changes in political, cultural, and social milieus. While some of

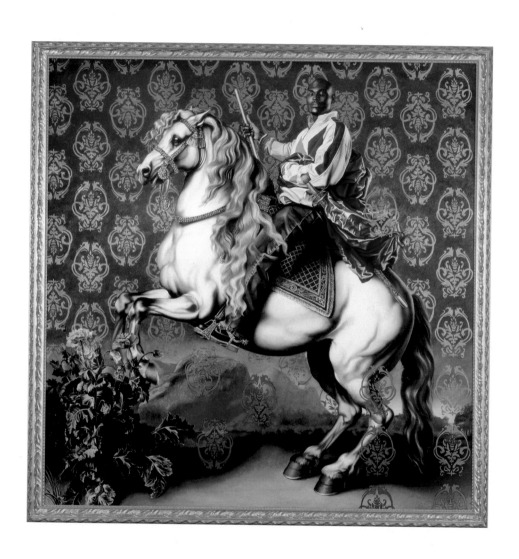

1 Kehinde Wiley | *Prince Tommaso Francesco of Savoy-Carignano,* **2006**
Oil on canvas, 108 x 108 inches
© 2006 Kehinde Wiley

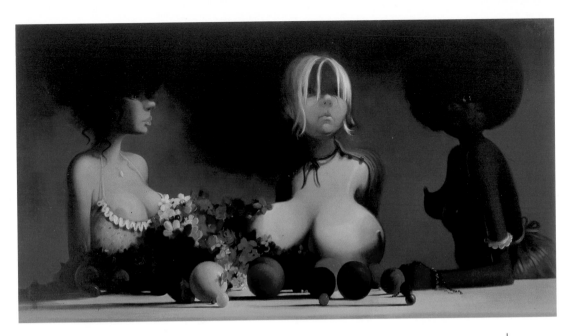

2 Lisa Yuskavage | *XLP*, **1999**
Oil on linen, 40 x 75 inches
Courtesy of Marianne Boesky Gallery

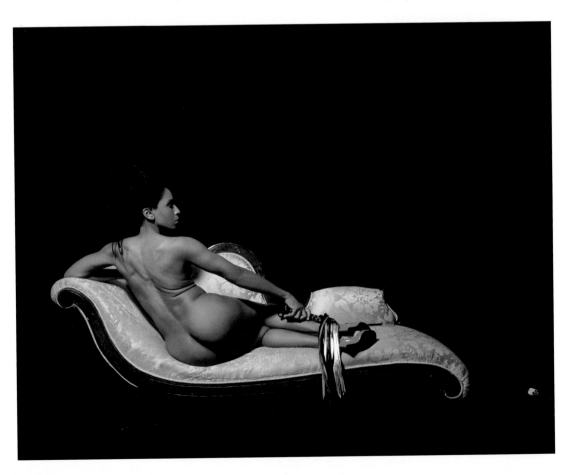

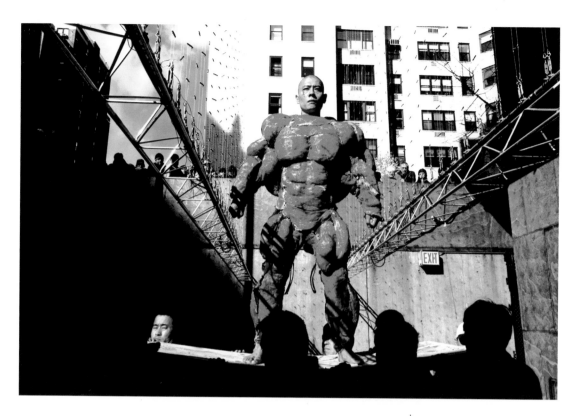

4 Zhang Huan | *My New York (Worker)*, **2002**
Chromogenic color print, 40 x 60 inches (101.6 cm x 152.4 cm)
Edition of 2 Aps
Photo courtesy of PaceWildenstein, New York
© Zhang Huan Studio

3 Renée Cox | *Baby Back*, **2001**
Archival digital c-print mounted on aluminum, 115 x 144 inches
Courtesy of the artist

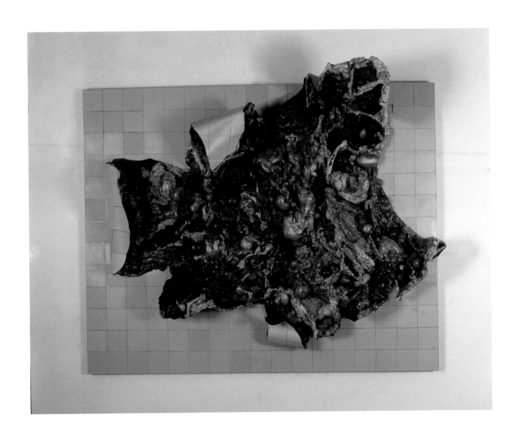

5 Adriana Varejão | *Folds,* **2000–2001**

Oil, foam, aluminum, wood, and canvas
76.77 x 98.43 x 25.98 inches (195 x 250 x 66 cm)
Private Collection, New York
Courtesy of the artist and Lehmann Maupin Gallery, New York

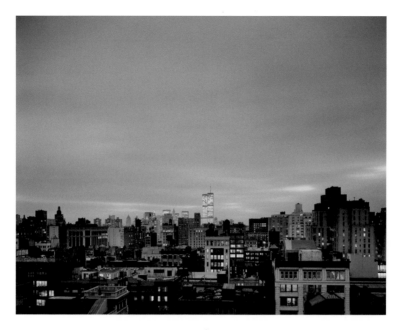

6   Joel Meyerowitz | *The Blue Hour, New York City, 1982,* **1982**
From the series Looking South: New York City Landscapes, 1981-2001 (NIGHT)
© Joel Meyerowitz, 2004, courtesy of Ariel Meyerowitz Gallery, New York

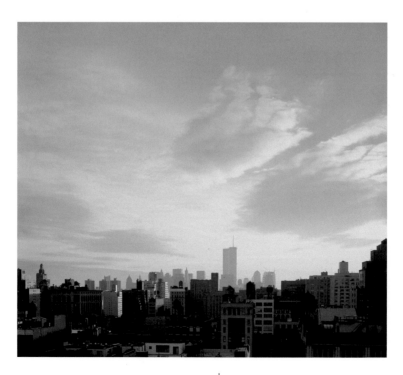

7   Joel Meyerowitz | *New York City, 1989,* **1989**
From the series Looking South: New York City Landscapes, 1981-2001 (DAY)
© Joel Meyerowitz, 2004, courtesy of Ariel Meyerowitz Gallery, New York

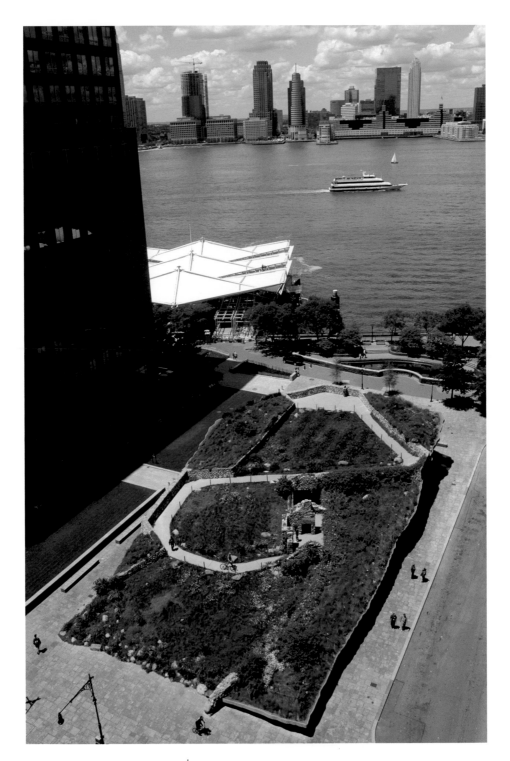

8 Brian Tolle | *Irish Hunger Memorial, installed Battery Park, NYC,* **2002**
Stone, landscaping, glass, illumination, audio, and concrete, 96 x 170 feet
Photo by Nicoleta Coman
Courtesy of the artist

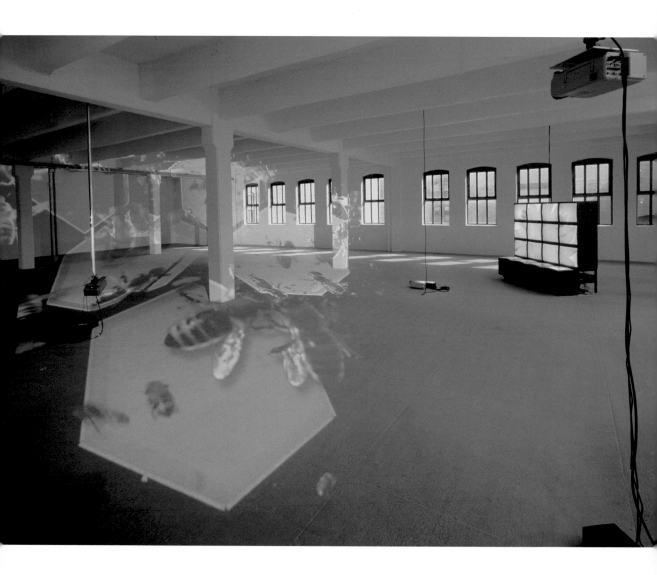

9 Diana Thater | *Knots + Surfaces, Version #1,* **2001**

Installation for 5 LCD video projectors, 16 video monitors, 6 DVD players, 1 VVR-1000 synchronizer, 6 DVDs
unique, + 1 AP
Courtesy of David Zwirner, New York

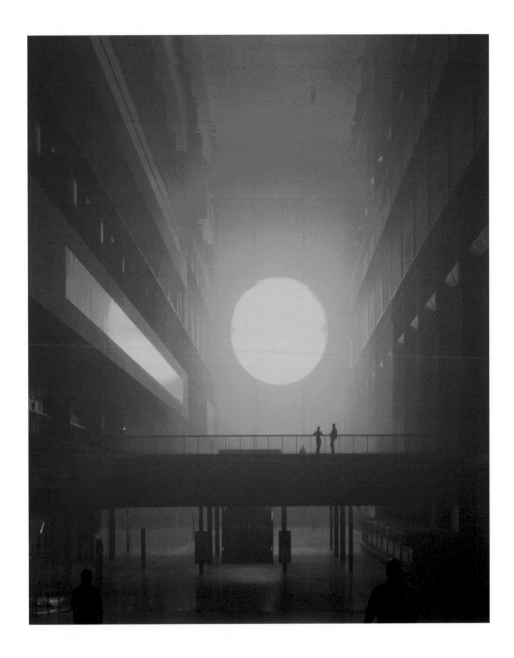

10 Olafur Eliasson | *The Weather Project*, **2003**
Monofrequency lights, projection foil, haze machine, mirror foil, aluminum, and scaffolding, dimensions variable
Installation view at the Tate Modern, London 2003
Photo by Jens Ziehe
© Olafur Eliasson 2003
Courtesy of the artist; Tanya Bonakdar Gallery, New York; and neugerriemschneider, Berlin

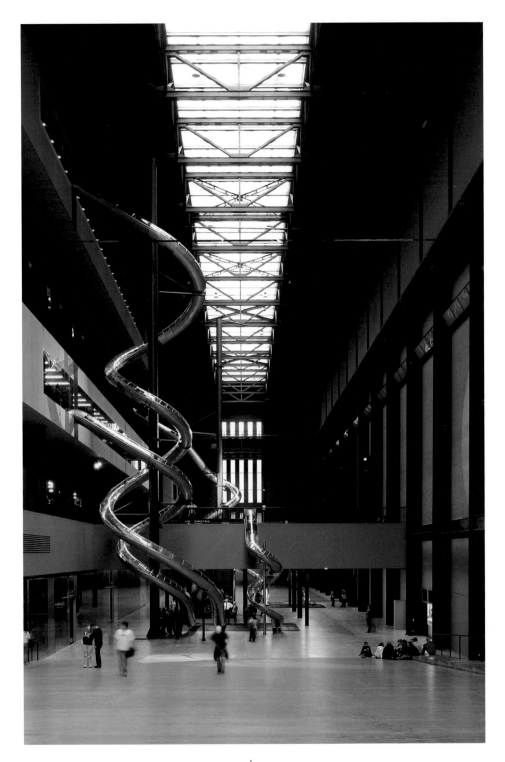

11 Carsten Höller | Œ*Test Site*[1], **2006.**

Installation view ŒUnilever Series : Carsten Höller[1], Turbine Hall, Tate Modern, London 2006
Photo © Attilio Maranzano © VG Bild Kunst, Bonn

Courtesy of the artist; Esther Schipper, Berlin; Casey Kaplan, New York; and Tate Modern, London

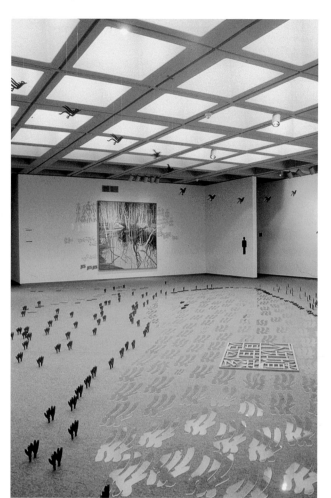

12 Xu Bing | *Reading Landscape*, **2001**
Installation at North Carolina Museum of Art, April, 2001
Courtesy of the artist

13 Ken Aptekar | *Dad is showing me how to develop*, **1997**

Oil on wood, sandblasted glass, bolts, 60 inches square overall; based on Willem van de Velde, the younger Before the Storm, ca. 1700, with text overlay about Aptekar's father teaching him photography
Collection of Ivy & Mark Powell, Aspen, CO
Photo by D. James Dee, 1997
Courtesy of Bernice Steinbaum Gallery, Miami, FL

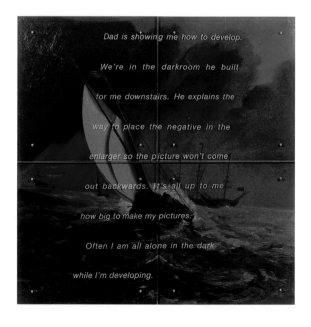

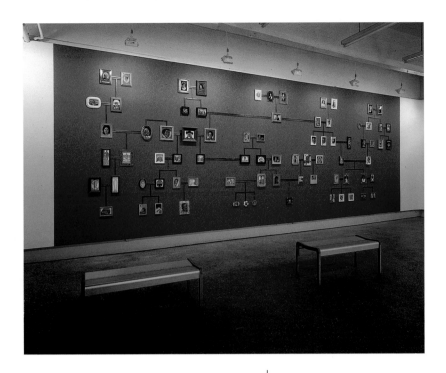

14 Nina Katchadourian | *Genealogy of the Supermarket,* **2005**

Digital prints, frames, wood, wallpaper
Installation view at Sara Meltzer Gallery, New York
Photo by Hermann Feldhaus
Courtesy of Sara Meltzer Gallery, New York

15 Lita Albuquerque | *Stellar Axis: Antarctica,* **2006**

Fiberglass, pigment
Photo by Jean de Pomereu
Courtesy of the artist

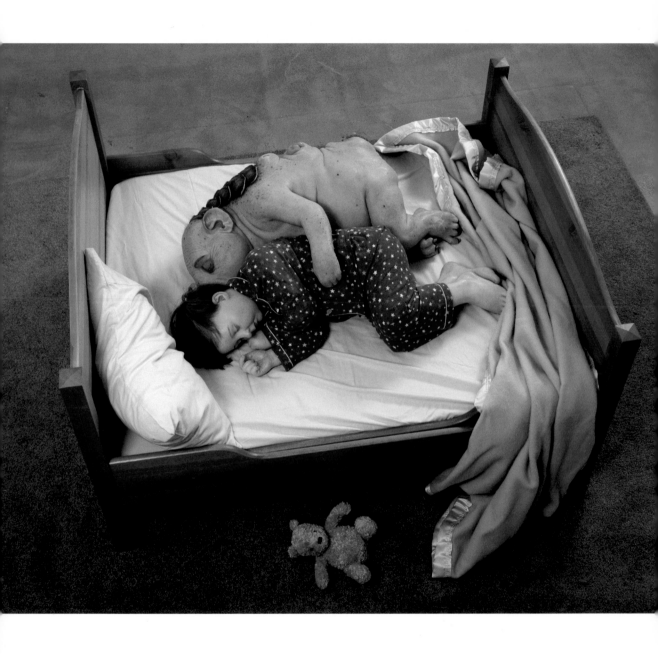

16   Patricia Piccinini | *Undivided,* **2004**

Silicone, fibreglass, human hair, clothing, with bed, and carpet
Lifesize, dimensions variable
Courtesy of the artist

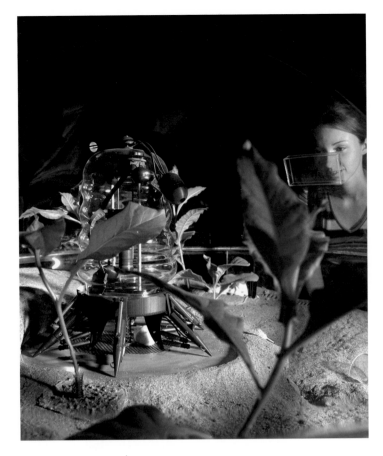

17 **Eduardo Kac** | *The Eighth Day*, **2001 (detail)**
Transgenic artwork with biological robot (biobot), GFP plants, GFP amoebae, GFP fish, GFP mice, audio, video, Internet
Dimensions variable
Courtesy of the artist

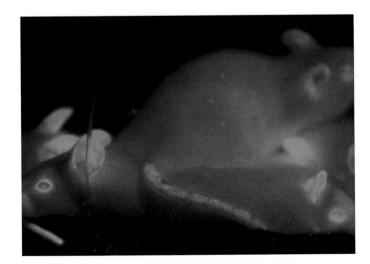

18 **Eduardo Kac** | *The Eighth Day*, **2001 (detail)**
Transgenic artwork with biological robot (biobot), GFP plants, GFP amoebae, GFP fish, GFP mice, audio, video, Internet
Dimensions variable
Courtesy of the artist

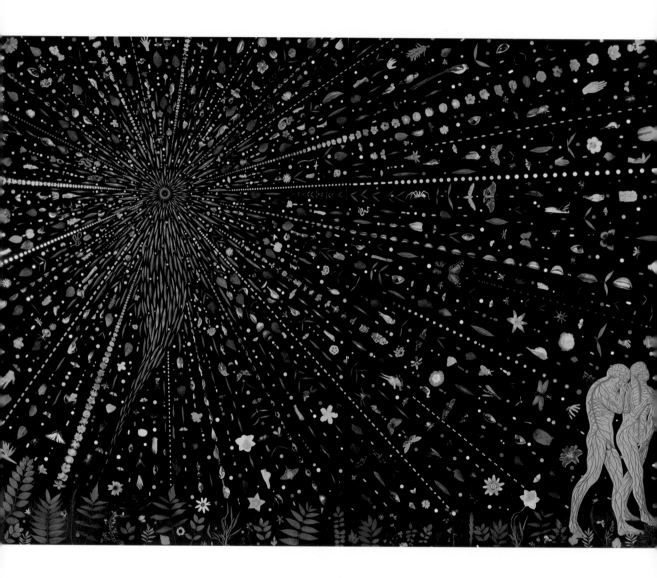

19   Fred Tomaselli | *Untitled [Expulsion]*, **2000**

Leaves, pills, insects, acrylic, photo-collage, resin on wood panel, 84 x 120 inches
Courtesy of James Cohan Gallery

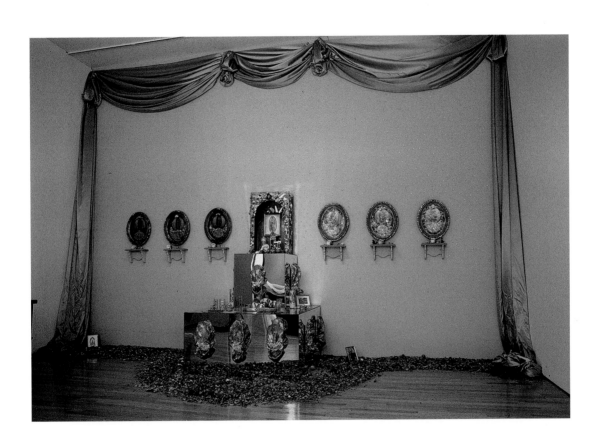

20 Amalia Mesa-Bains | *Queen of the Waters, Mother of the Land of the Dead,* 1992

Mixed media installation
Courtesy of the artist

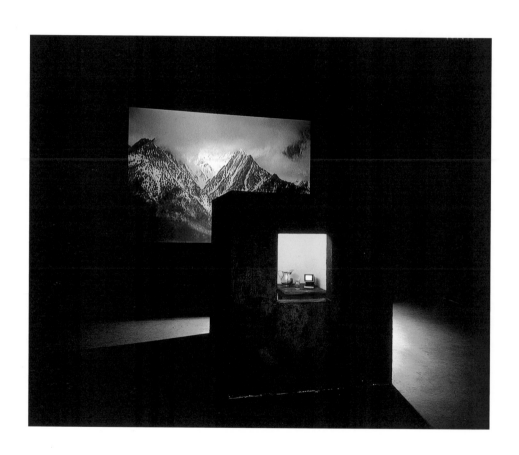

21 Bill Viola | *Room for St. John of the Cross,* 1983
Video/sound installation
Photo by Kira Perov/SQUIDDS & NUNNS

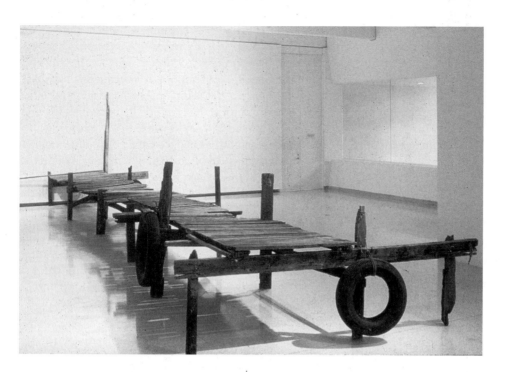

5-11 Kcho (Alexis Leyva Machado) | *El Camino de la Nostalgia (Road of Nostalgia)*, **1994–95**
Mixed-media installation, length of dock approx. 16.5 meters
Courtesy of Marlborough Gallery, New York, © Kcho

these relocations are voluntary, others are involuntary displacements that are due to war, disease, poverty, or persecution, often involving large numbers of people. Pulled up by their roots, displaced people must often cross national borders and even oceans. A forced dislocation is an intense experience with both political and psychological effects.

Displacement is one of the central facts of contemporary culture. Writer and curator Ella Shohat describes "today's morphing, crisscrossing movements across regional and national borders" of "people, capital, digital information, and ecological flow."[32] Powerful art is being made by artists who want to bear witness to displacement. Some of these artists are immigrants themselves who have moved to a new country, often with a new language, and practice their art in a radically altered context. Others identify with a culture that was uprooted earlier in history, forcing large numbers of people to look for a new place to live. The word *diaspora* refers to the "movement, involuntary or otherwise, of large bodies of people, their thoughts and ideas."[33] The world today is dotted with uprooted people who have no state or homeland where they can settle, among them Palestinians and Kurds. British artist Hew Locke, of Guyanese descent, evokes the idea of diaspora in his *Ark* (1992–94), a colorful, lavishly embellished model boat that symbolizes the richness of the ideas and practices that slaves brought with them from Africa to the Americas and that more generally represents the migration of culture that inevitably occurs with all diasporas and emigrations.

Art about displacement may focus on the journey itself, the condition of being in transit between places with different languages, customs, material culture, and ideas—a condition theorist Homi Babha named "in-betweenness." Artists may explore the meaning and location of borders, boundaries, and zones of transition. They may consider the place left behind ("there") or the adopted place ("here") or interactions between both places. The displaced artist retains an emotional connection with the place left behind; indeed, the resonance of the original place is often enhanced and intensified by distance. At the same time, the artist is forging a new hybrid identity that draws on the physical surroundings and cultural climate of the new place.

Contemporary artists who have explored travel, tourism, migration, nomadism, homelessness, and dislocation include (in addition to those already mentioned) Cuban Maria Magdalena Campos-Pons, Chinese-born Hung Liu [2-5], Puerto Rican Pepón Osorio [2-2], Chilean Eugenio Dittborn, Mexican Guillermo Gómez-Peña [2-7], Palestinian Mona Hatoum, and Thai Rirkrit Tiravanija. Imagery in works that are related to the theme of in-betweenness is often *syncretic*, that is, it mixes or juxtaposes multiple cultural references and ideas. Maps and mapping concepts may enter into this work as well as iconic objects suggesting travel and boundaries, such as boats, luggage, footwear, identity documents, and barricades. The provisional quality of place is captured in Japanese artist Yukinori Yanagi's "ant farm" artworks, such as *World Ant Farm* (1990). In this work, 170 plastic boxes connected by tubes each contain the design of a different national flag formed in colored sand. As the ants travel through the tubes from one box to another, they mix the sand and erode the symbols of nationality.

PROFILE: Janet Cardiff

Janet Cardiff, working alone or in collaboration with her husband George Bures Miller, is a pioneer in multimedia art. Her distinctive works immerse viewers in fictive environments where she controls key aspects of what gets seen and heard. Her art has been represented in such high-profile exhibitions as the São Paolo Biennial (1998), the Carnegie International (1999) in Pittsburgh, and the Venice Biennial (2001), as well as numerous exhibitions at smaller museums and galleries, such as Voice and Void (2007) at the Aldrich Contemporary Art Museum in Connecticut.

Among Cardiff's most memorable creations are what she identifies as audio and video "Walks." To experience a "Walk," each participant dons a CD Walkman or looks into the monitor of a camcorder. Once linked to the surrounding environment (via the Walkman or camcorder), the viewer then proceeds to navigate along a route, following directions carefully scripted by the artist. The experience can be both unsettling and familiar, like having a stranger talk intimately in your ear, indicating what to look for and which way to go. A Cardiff "Walk" is a witty and intellectually rich parallel to the guided audio tours that visitors take through museum collections and special exhibitions. Instead of standing within the museum or gallery and looking at discrete works of art, taking a walk with Cardiff means that the viewer follows a path inside a place where everything has been transformed into one extended work of art.

During the Walk, a viewer discovers she or he is inside a setting; some of the objects and architectural details are identified (on the soundtrack) so that they function as props in a dramatic narrative. The narrative, however, is never made explicit. Visual and aural clues (such as the sound of gunshots and rushing footsteps) only hint at a plot. Cardiff develops her art on the philosophy that the best stories leave much for the viewer or reader to imagine. Moving within the Walk, each participant fills in, in his or her own imaginative way, chunks of information that Cardiff leaves out of the unfolding tale.

In a different vein, Cardiff's *Forty-Part Motet* (2001) consists of forty microphones that are placed in an otherwise empty gallery. Each microphone takes the place of a member of a chorus. Seen from a distance, the microphones resemble an arrangement of tall, vertical sculptures, like abstractions of the human form. Hidden inside the microphones are audio speakers that allow each microphone to project the specific sounds made by one particular singer. Coming into a deserted gallery, visitors are surprised and delighted to find themselves surrounded by the sounds of a choral group preparing for a concert. Singers cough. Throats are cleared. Score sheets rustle. Then the singers (one voice per microphone) launch into a full-fledged performance of the polyphonic *Spem in Alium* by the sixteenth-century English composer Thomas Tallis.

The circle of microphones transforms a nearly empty gallery into a theater. With stereophonic accuracy, the re-creation of the performance gives gallery visitors an uncanny illusion of being on stage among the singers. The aural illusion is so complete that *Forty-Part Motet* even seems to transform the physical dimensions of an exhibition gallery into the larger volume of the architectural space where the chorus' actual performance was recorded.

Cardiff's art is not unique in its incorporation of sound and sound effects. In fact, with increasing frequency, viewers of contemporary art find exhibit sites full of sounds as well as sights. For example, the 2002 Whitney Biennial featured a cadre of artists, such as Meredith Monk and Stephen Vitiello, who, like Cardiff, are architects of aural experiences. To achieve her stereophonic illusions, Cardiff employs a recording technology called binaural sound. This sophisticated process allows the listener to discern the specific direction from which sounds come with startling fidelity. As one reviewer of Cardiff's work explained, the result of binaural recording is a "completely spatialized sound environment. . . . [Cardiff allows you] to climb inside" recorded sound.[34] In fact, Cardiff intensifies our experience of sound; our natural tendency to filter out extraneous sound (and to concentrate only on sounds that we expect to be meaningful) is bypassed when we hear Cardiff's soundtrack through headphones.

Other artworks by Cardiff offer the viewer access to totally fictive places. To experience Cardiff's (and Miller's) *The Paradise Institute* (2001), viewers enter through the door of what appears, from the outside, to be a nondescript plywood sculpture, approximately a dozen feet in length and width and about seven feet tall [5-12]. A maximum of sixteen visitors can enter the artwork at one time. Inside, each viewer takes a seat in the simulated balcony of a movie theater (circa 1940s). Donning headphones, each visitor hears ambient noises (on a prerecorded tape). Because the noises are so faithful to what one would expect to hear at the cinema (shuffling feet, the sounds of people taking their seats), disbelief is willingly suspended. The visitor/viewer of *The Paradise Institute* quickly forgets all about wearing headphones and is convincingly transported into the imaginary realm. As the lights go down and the film starts, suddenly, in your right ear, you hear a voice whisper, "I'm worried, I'm afraid I left the stove on."

A film, reminiscent of the film noir genre, appears to be projected onto the screen inside the movie house [5-13]. The soundtrack of the film competes with more ambient sounds from the imaginary audience (a cell phone, for example, starts to ring, the sound seeming to come from the left side of the mezzanine). Each visitor becomes a member of the "cast" in the imaginary story that takes place in the balcony. Cardiff and Miller embed each visitor in their artwork so cleverly that the borders between the film and the film's audience and between the artwork and real life dissolve. *The Paradise Institute* reproduces the multileveled experience of being in a specific place (a movie theater) watching a movie (with

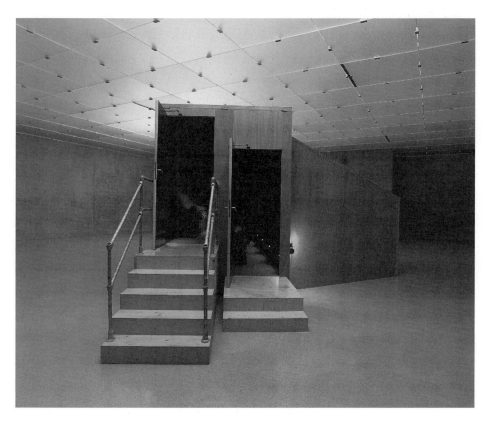

5-12 |anet Cardiff and George Bures Miller | *The Paradise Institute,*
200I (exterior)

Wood, theater seats, video projection, headphones and mixed media, 118 x 698 x 210 inches
Installation view: Hamburger Banhof, Berlin
Courtesy of the artist and Luhring Augustine, NY

its own twisting plot) and sensing a restive audience all around (halfway through
the movie, you hear a person whisper in your ear that she is leaving the theater to
"check on the stove").

As viewers/visitors/listeners to Cardiff's artwork, we find ourselves inside a
sculptural simulacrum of the cinema. We shift back and forth mentally in how we
make sense of the experience. While the overall size of *The Paradise Institute* is
much smaller than an actual theater, the illusion is choreographed (both visually
and aurally) so that all the details and dimensions appear accurate and to scale.
Inside the artwork, we are immersed in a convincing representation of a fictive
environment.

Janet Cardiff's clever, mesmerizing works explore how lived experiences are
anchored in a sense of place. Whether an event is quotidian or mysterious and

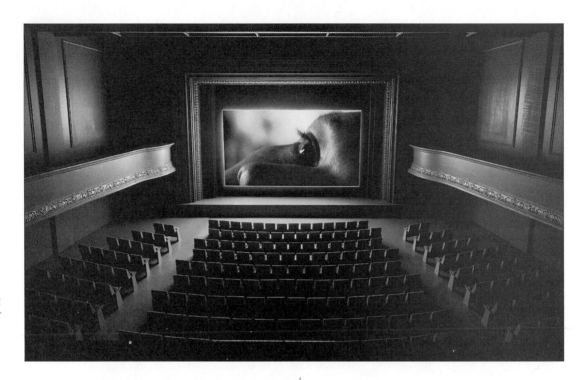

5-13 |anet Cardiff and George Bures Miller | *The Paradise Institute*, **2001** (interior)
Wood, theater seats, video projection, headphones and mixed media, 118 x 698 x 210 inches
Courtesy of the artist and Luhring Augustine, NY

dramatic, the place where the event occurs colors and shapes our understanding of our experience. What did the room look like? From what direction did the sound come from? Our experience of place, its physical and emotional specificity, is the leitmotif of Cardiff's art.

The artist was born in Ontario, Canada in 1957. She currently lives and works with her husband George Bures Miller in Alberta, Canada.

PROFILE: Unilever Series at Tate Modern

The Turbine Hall is a gargantuan space that one enters immediately upon passing through the entrance to Tate Modern, an art museum located on the south bank of the Thames River in London. Tate Modern occupies the former Bankside Power Station, a distinctive building built after World War II to house machinery that generated electricity for the City of London until the power plant closed operations in 1981. Transformed into a museum at a renovation cost in excess of 200 million dollars, the remodeled building reopened as Tate Modern in 2000. The Turbine Hall, named for the massive machines it once housed, occupies half the volume of the museum. (The rest of the museum includes 80,000 square feet of exhibition galleries over seven floors.) The wide-open rectangular Turbine Hall is jaw-dropping in size, 500 feet long and 75 feet wide with a 115-foot ceiling.

The architectural renovation preserved much of the original character of the Turbine Hall as an industrial place, while emptying it of machinery. A few remnants of the original power plant paraphernalia remain, such as a giant mechanical hoist and the ceiling tracks along which it once slid. Entering visitors immediately head down a long slanting concrete ramp into the depths of the cavernous hall. Skylights and great banks of fluorescent fixtures wash light over an interior of metal, glass, and concrete. Halfway down the hall, an overhead pedestrian bridge that can accommodate a crowd bisects the otherwise open interior. Along the full length of every floor on the gallery side of the Turbine Hall, balconies allow visitors to gaze down from different heights into the space.

Beyond its postindustrial references, the remodeled Turbine Hall evokes from an earlier era the grand public shopping arcades where people would gather and stroll. Architects Jacques Herzog and Pierre de Meuron specifically took inspiration from Milan's dramatic arcade, the Galleria Vittorio Emanuele II, built in the nineteenth century. Today, the Turbine Hall, which costs nothing to enter, is one of the most visited public places in London.

Since opening, Tate Modern has become admired for a series that uses the Turbine Hall as a site to show large-scale sculptural installations by individual artists, commissioned one at a time. Each project in the *Unilever Series* (named for the corporate sponsor) remains on public view for about one year, with costs running to approximately 2 million dollars for each installation. The vast scale demands large concepts, and an artist's ideas for the commission can pose considerable technical challenges. Tate Modern and the artist work with expert consultants, many of them structural engineers, to realize the artist's vision. By the end of 2008, nine artists had fulfilled commissions for a Turbine Hall installation: Louise Bourgeois, Juan Muñoz, Anish Kapoor, Olafur Eliasson, Bruce Nauman, Rachel Whiteread, Carsten Höller, Doris Salcedo, and Dominique Gonzalez-Foerster.

The Turbine Hall as a place to create sculpture presents formidable challenges to an artist. Its huge scale can accommodate larger artworks than any other interior site in the United Kingdom, and its sheer physical presence as a work of architecture threatens to dominate any art placed inside its volume. The Unilever Series has become justifiably famous for the inventive, dramatically different ways that artists meet the challenge. As critic Morgan Falconer wrote, "If Tate Modern's Turbine Hall is, as many suggest, the soaring nave of this museum-cathedral, then the competition between artists who are commissioned to fill it every autumn is becoming rather like the great rivalries of the Renaissance."[35]

In this profile, we discuss a few installations in the Unilever Series. In keeping with the focus of this chapter on the theme of place, we emphasize how artists' projects have engaged with the Turbine Hall itself as a distinctive location. Any Unilever commission, of course, also addresses other themes of concern to the particular artist in addition to the theme of place.[36]

Anish Kapoor's monumental *Marsyas* (2002), the third commission in the Unilever Series, was the first to engage the full volume of the Turbine Hall from end to end and top to bottom. Kapoor, who was born in India and lives in London, created *Marsyas* from a single length of 1-millimeter-thick PVC (polyvinyl) membrane, measuring 508 feet by 115 feet, which was stretched into tubular forms over three huge steel rings placed at the ends and midpoint of the Turbine Hall. Architectural in concept, *Marsyas* engulfed visitors within the enormous arched spaces defined by the fabric structure as it snaked between the three huge rings and over the hall's central bridge. The three rings formed openings in the tube, the floor-to-ceiling funnel-shaped opening at one end suggesting a musical horn or an old-fashioned ear trumpet.

Kapoor's title refers to Marsyas, a satyr in Greek mythology who was flayed alive after losing a music contest to the god Apollo. Certainly the blood-red membrane could be imagined metaphorically as the skin of the allegorical musician. When intensely backlit by the strong light in the Turbine Hall, the membrane appeared translucent. According to a review by Alexandra Glanz, much of the visceral impact on astonished visitors derived from "how the organic sculpture connected with the space—how it took and gave space. From all seven floors of the museum, new perspectives could be discovered in the velvety mass, which did not seem to be attached anywhere and which could have been nothing or everything: gramophone, ear, or hymn to the very mystery of skin."[37]

In the next Unilever commission, *The Weather Project* (2003), Scandinavian Olafur Eliasson also took on the full volume of the Turbine Hall, producing a giant artificial glowing sun at the end opposite the entrance [color plate 10]. Eliasson covered the full length of the hall's ceiling in mirrors, which visually doubled the hall's already awe-inspiring height. The artificial sun was actually a giant semicircular translucent disk, which appeared circular in the mirrored ceiling and glowed with hundreds of yellow monofilament lamps. Throughout the day, smoke machines pumped in clouds of mist that diffused the yellow light. Eliasson's theatrical effects muted the distinctive architectural identity of the Turbine Hall, substituting a pretend version of nature, although the hall still exuded its palpable presence as an enormous rectangular volume. Many visitors lay on the floor, transported by the multisensory experience provided by the brilliant indoor sun and hazy atmosphere. Some sought out their tiny reflection in the distant ceiling. The changing formations of reclining people and their collective reflections in turn became part of the spectacle for others gazing from the bridge and balconies.

For his Turbine Hall commission Œ*Test Site* (2006), German Carsten Höller worked mainly with the site's great height and engaged directly with the different levels of the balconies on the gallery floors. From a distance, *Test Site* appeared as a cluster of five large shiny intertwined metal structures that rose in curlicues from the floor to different balconies [color plate 11]. In fact, the five tall sculptures were also slides that whisked riders down their almost vertical ramps and plunked them off on the floor of the Turbine Hall [5-14]. The longest slide, from the museum's

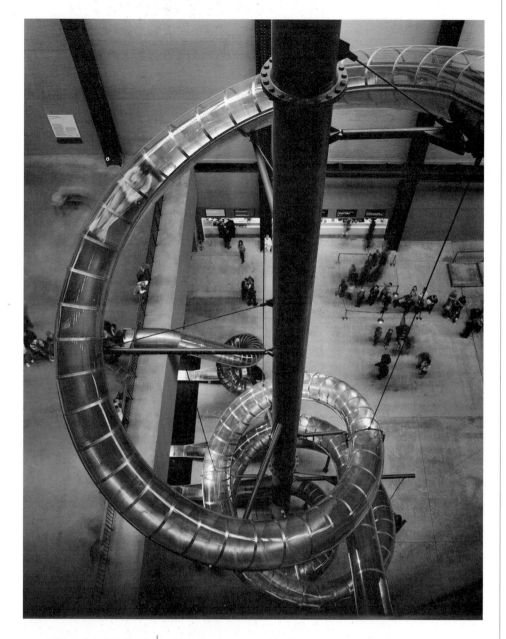

5-14 Carsten Höller | ŒTest Site¹, **2006.**

Installation view ŒUnilever Series : Carsten Höller¹, Turbine Hall, Tate Modern, London 2006.
Photo © Attilio Maranzano © VG Bild Kunst, Bonn
Courtesy of the artists; Esther Schipper, Berlin; Casey Kaplan, New York; and Tate Modern, London

top floor, traveled more than sixty yards while dropping thirty yards. Visitors were thrillingly aware of the height of the Turbine Hall as they made their way up to whichever balcony they chose to use as a jumping-off point, but once in a slide, the experience captured all one's senses.[38]

Originally trained as a biologist, Höller subscribes now to something of an antiscience point of view, expressing doubt and mistrust of modern ideas about technological and rational progress. Tate Modern director Vicente Todoli explained that in addition to offering gallery visitors a funfair-type experience (in which the participant gives up control of her or his own body for a thrilling physical experience), the artwork also offered room for more serious thought as an artistic reconnoitering of "the verticality of the space." Höller further expanded on the artwork's content, asserting that it commented on architectural possibilities, such as the untapped potential for using slides as a physically and emotionally effective means of moving between buildings or floors.[39]

For her Unilever commission *Shibboleth* (2007) [5-15], Colombian Doris Salcedo used none of the hall's vertical volume. Instead she incorporated the entire length of the concrete floor, and its depth as well, by excavating the space below. Indeed, the artwork quite literally merged with the architecture of the Turbine Hall by making an opening for itself in the floor. Working with engineers, Salcedo opened up the long smooth expanse of the concrete with a jagged crack that began relatively modestly at the entrance ramp, then widened into a deep fissure as it zigzagged the full length of the hall, more than five football fields in length. Fissures along

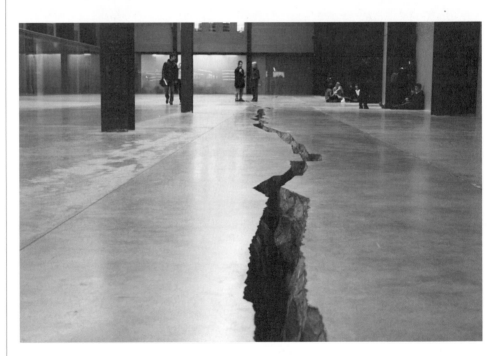

5-15 Doris Salcedo │ *Shibboleth,* **2007**
Concrete and metal, length: 548 ft/ 167m
Installation: Turbine Hall, Tate Modern, London, October 9, 2007 - April 6, 2008
Photo by Cullen Nance
© Doris Salcedo

the crack opened as much as a foot in width and close to half a yard in depth to reveal wavy rocklike substrata embedded with half-buried chain-link wire fence. *Shibboleth* convincingly appeared to be the result of a natural cataclysm, as if an earthquake or massive explosion had split apart the Turbine Hall floor, although Salcedo and her team really constructed all the details. Approaching the dark glass wall at the far end of the Turbine Hall, the reflection extended the lightning-bolt chasm far into a virtual darkened realm.

Shibboleth evoked emotions and ideas beyond its representation of a sundering of the ground, variously suggesting an impending apocalypse, the ecological demise of the planet, or a dark subterranean world hidden by the thin veneer of civilization. As with other installations in the Unilever Series, visitors' interactions with the work became part of the spectacle. Platoons of schoolchildren might be moving around the crack—some leaping across, others just staring or cautiously lowering a hand down into the fissures to touch the jagged edges.

In ancient usage, *shibboleth* refers to a test based on pronunciation of a word that betrays someone as a foreigner to a certain group. A shibboleth thus separates one people from another, as the crack divides the hall. Although not self-evident in the installation itself, Salcedo believes that *Shibboleth* continues her long-term commitment to using art to unmask brutal politics and to represent human suffering and loss inflicted by the powerful on the powerless. (She began by making installations representing effects of war in her native Colombia and went on to consider abuse and trauma in more global contexts.) Salcedo is well aware that the Tate Modern building is a relic of the waning days of the British Empire at the end of the modern industrial era. She described her crack in the building's foundation as revealing a "colonial and imperial history [that] has been disregarded, marginalized or simply obliterated . . . the history of racism, running parallel to the history of modernity and . . . its untold dark side."[40] For Salcedo, *Shibboleth* was intended to expose the schisms that continue to divide rich and poor and developed and postcolonial nations. In this vein of interpretation, Salcedo's artwork and its site-specific location in London fit the connection between sculpture and a monument made thirty years ago by art historian Rosalind Krauss in her influential 1979 essay "Sculpture in the Expanded Field." Krauss wrote, "The logic of sculpture, it would seem, is inseparable from the logic of the monument. By virtue of this logic a sculpture is a commemorative representation. It sits in a particular place and speaks in a symbolical tongue about the meaning or use of that place."[41]

In having a recognizable, ongoing presence, Tate Modern's Turbine Hall exists as more than a background to the artworks commissioned for the Unilever Series. The Turbine Hall's own identity as a specific place colors the design of each installation, as well as visitors' perceptions of the artwork, just as each artwork alters perceptions of the Turbine Hall.

Notes

1. The concept of a "psychically constituted space" is elaborated in the writings of Irit Rogoff and Henri Lefebvre, among others. See, for example, Irit Rogoff, *Terra Infirma: Geography's Visual Culture* (London and New York: Routledge, 2000), especially pp. 20–24.

2. Notable modernist artists who maintained an interest in rendering places include the Europeans Henri Matisse, Georges Braque, Paul Klee, Fernand Léger, Joan Miró, and Yves Tanguy; the Americans Marsden Hartley, John Marin, and Georgia O'Keeffe; and the Canadian Group of Seven.

3. The classic, and still valuable, study of Western landscape art is Kenneth Clark's *Landscape into Art* (Boston: Beacon Press, 1961). For a look at the landscape motif in Chinese art, consult the section "Constructing Landscapes" in *Chinese Art & Culture*, by Robert L. Thorp and Richard Ellis Vinograd (New York: Harry N. Abrams, 2001). William V. Dunning, *Changing Images of Pictorial Space: A History of Spatial Illusion in Painting* (Syracuse, N.Y.: Syracuse University Press, 1991) presents an excellent analysis of variations in the representation of physical space within pictorial space. A classic volume that analyzes the psychic dimensions of place from the perspective of phenomenology, with applications to literature and art, is Gaston Bachelard, *The Poetics of Space* (Boston: Beacon Press, 1969).

4. The history of the representation of space and its changing conceptualization, especially in architecture, is traced in Anthony Vidler, "Interpreting the Void: Architecture and Spatial Anxiety," in Mark Cheetham, Michael Ann Holly, and Keith Moxey, eds., *The Subjects of Art History: Historical Objects in Contemporary Perspective* (Cambridge, England: Cambridge University Press, 1998), pp. 288–307.

5. The use of maps by contemporary visual artists relates to earlier examples of incorporating maps in art, from the paintings of Johannes Vermeer in the seventeenth century to Robert Smithson's plans for earth art projects in the 1960s.

6. Mel Watkin, *Terra Incognita: Contemporary Artists' Maps and Other Visual Organizing Systems* (Saint Louis: Contemporary Art Museum, 2001),n.p. An exhibition brochure.

7. For an analysis of the modernist gallery space, see Brian O'Doherty, *Inside the White Cube: The Ideology of the Gallery Space* (San Francisco: Lapis Press, 1986).

8. Sometimes work made for a specific place is capable of surviving a move to another location. Some artists use the phrase *site sensitive* rather than *site-specific* to refer to such work.

9. Nicolas de Oliveira, Nicola Oxley, and Michael Petry, *Installation Art* (London: Thames and Hudson, 1994), p. 35.

10. For a theoretical analysis of visual artists' work dealing with site specificity and related issues, see Rosalind Krauss, "Sculpture in the Expanded Field," reprinted in Hal Foster, ed., *The Anti-aesthetic: Essays on Postmodern Culture* (Seattle: Bay Press, 1983), pp. 31–42.

11. As quoted in Michael Corris "Para-Cities and Paradigms," *Art Monthly*, March 2001, p. 11.

12. Liz Wells, *Photography: A Critical Introduction* (London: Routledge, 1997), p. 236.

13. Aimee Le Duc, "Zhan Wang" Conceptual Contemplation," *Sculpture* 27, July–August 2008, p. 60.

14. Casey Ruble, "Andreas Gursky," in Katy Siegel, ed., *Everybody Now: The Crowd in Contemporary Art* (New York: Hunter College, 2001), p. 16. An exhibition catalog.

15. Ken Johnson, "West to Eden," *Art in America*, December 1991, p. 88. Johnson's article concerns an exhibition of the work of nineteenth-century American landscape painter Albert Bierstadt.

16. Faye Hirsch, "Frank Moore's Ecology of Loss," *Art in America*, May 2003, p. 129.

17. Eleanor Heartney, exhibition review, *Art in America*, December 1991, p. 121.

18. Richard Martin, ed., *The New Urban Landscape* (New York: Olympia and York Companies, 1989), p. 116.

19. Jeffrey Deitch and Dan Friedman, eds., *Artificial Nature* (Athens, Greece: Deste Foundation for Contemporary Art, 1990),n.p. An exhibition catalog.

20. Toby Kamps, "Small World: Dioramas in Contemporary Art," in *Small World: Dioramas in Contemporary Art* (San Diego, Calif.: Museum of Contemporary Art, 2000), p. 7. An exhibition catalog.

21. Ralph Rugoff, "Bubble Worlds," in *Small World*, p. 16.

22. Anne Ellegood, "Out of Site: Fictional Architectural Spaces," in *Out of Site: Fictional Architectural Spaces* (New York: New Museum of Contemporary Art, 2002), p. 30. An exhibition catalog.

23. Ibid., pp. 7 and 11.

24. David Toop, "A Least Event," in *010101: Art in Technological Times* (San Francisco: San Francisco Museum of Modern Art, 2001), p. 108. An exhibition catalog.

25. Ibid., p. 94.

26. Jonathan P. Binstock, *The 47th Corcoran Biennial: Fantasy Underfoot* (Washington, D.C.: Corcoran Gallery of Art, 2002), p. 74. An exhibition catalog.

27. See Witold Rybczynski, *Home: A Short History of an Idea* (New York: Penguin Books, 1987).

28. Quoted in Martin Lister, "Photography in the Age of Electronic Imaging," in Wells, *Photography: A Critical Introduction*, p. 275.

29. For further discussion of this and other interactive works by Campbell, see Marita Sturken, "The Space of Electronic Time: The Memory Machines of Jim Campbell," in Erika Suderburg, ed., *Space Site Intervention: Situating Installation Art* (Minneapolis: University of Minnesota Press, 2000), pp. 287–296.

30. Deepali Dewan, "Place of Movement," in *No Place (Like Home)* (Minneapolis, Minn.: Walker Art Center, 1997), p. 122. An exhibition catalog.

31. Uta Barth, "The Space of Non-place," in Claire Doherty, ed., *Claustrophobia* (Birmingham,England: Ikon Gallery, 1998), pp. 28-29. An exhibition catalog.

32. Ella Shohat, introduction to Ella Shohat, ed., *Talking Visions* (Cambridge, Mass.: MIT Press, 1998), p. 46.

33. Rohini Malik and Gavin Jantjes, *A Fruitful Incoherence: Dialogues with Artists on Internationalism* (London: Institute of International Visual Arts, 1998), S.V. "diaspora" (in glossary).

34. Aruna D'Souza, "A World of Sound," *Art in America* (April 2002), p. 110.

35. Morgan Falconer, "A Space Odyssey," *Art Review* (October–November 2005): p. 11.

36. The theme of time also figures into the Unilever Series as a whole. Time passing and memories of previous artworks inhabiting the setting affect how returning visitors experience successive commissions in the Turbine Hall.

37. Alexandra Glanz, "Anish Kapoor," *Sculpture* 22 (November 2003): p. 79.

38. Bravely descending into the unknown, one of this book's authors was flabbergasted at the quickening pace of descent and the sense of danger as key body parts (knees, elbows) skimmed a few of the unyielding structural elements along the path.

39. Charlotte Higgins, "Carsten Höller's Slide Show," *Guardian*, October 10, 2006, p. 9.

40. As quoted in Tate Modern gallery brochure for *Shibboleth* (2007), n.p.

41. Rosalind Krauss, "Sculpture in the Expanded Field," reprinted in Paul F. Fabozzi, ed., *Artists, Critics, Context: Readings In and Around American Art Since 1945* (Upper Saddle River, N.J.: Prentice Hall, 2002), p. 285. Krauss used as an example the equestrian statue of Marcus Aurelius "set in the center of the Campidoglio to represent by its symbolical presence the relationship between ancient, Imperial Rome and the seat of government of modern, Renaissance Rome."

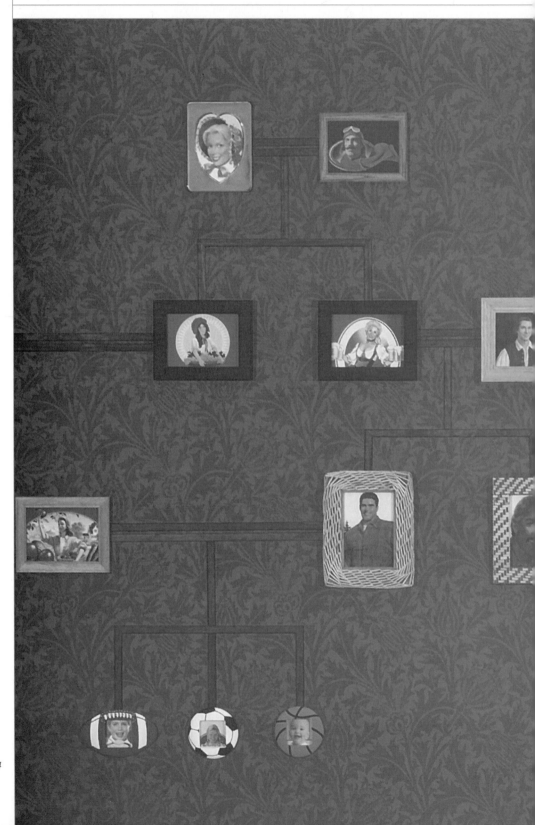

Detail of
Color Plate 14

CHAPTER SIX

Language

Over the past three decades numerous exhibitions have explored language as a theme for art making. As we would expect, the specific inflection or focus within the broad topic of language changes from exhibit to exhibit, sometimes as a matter of individual curatorial interest and, on other occasions, because the organizing principle of an exhibition reflects changes in prevailing trends in the art world. The 1980s and early 1990s witnessed exhibitions showcasing artworks that incorporated language as a strategy in delivering a politically charged message; starting in the 1990s, several exhibitions revolved around more theoretical issues of the relationship of visual to verbal imagery and the relationship of words to representation. Now, in the 2000s we see exhibitions exploring aural language alongside a rising interest in the incorporation of sound in visual art projects.

In 2007 the Aldrich Museum of Contemporary Art, in Ridgefield, Connecticut, presented Voice & Void, an exhibition of artworks that represent or express the human voice. The artworks incorporated the sounds of language in a variety of forms and formats. Julianne Swartz exhibited *Open* (2007), a sculpture created out of an empty wooden chest. Exhibition visitors were allowed to open the chest, which then emitted the sound of people saying "I love you" again and again. The voices gradually increased in volume, continuing until the lid of the chest was closed, stopping the sound. Rachel Berwick's *may-por-e*, a project ongoing since 1997, featured a birdcage containing two real parrots and assorted plant life. Prior to the exhibit, Berwick trained the parrots to speak maypore, a tribal language that was once spoken in Venezuela. Heightening the metaphor of a lost language, the birdcage was veiled behind a sheet of translucent plastic wrapping. Berwick's project focuses attention on the difficulties of any communication: languages change constantly, meanings are lost, and communication is circumscribed by the words and concepts one is taught (the parrots know a vocabulary of only thirty words). In learning a language, are we all parrots, so to speak?

Lorna Simpson's film installation *Easy to Remember* (2001) [6-1] also represents the human voice. (This work was not in Voice & Void.) *Easy to Remember* presents fifteen pairs of disembodied lips arranged in a grid of fifteen screens separately humming the Richard Rodgers's love song of the title. Without accompanying facial expressions,

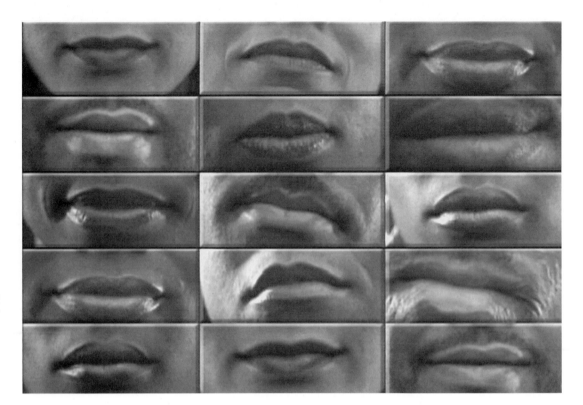

6-1 Lorna Simpson | *Easy to Remember*, 2001

16 mm film transferred to DVD, sound, 2 1/2 minutes
Courtesy of Sean Kelly Gallery, New York

hand gestures, and body postures, we learn little about the individual hummers and how they may be responding to the song's lyrics and melody. Our full understanding seems thwarted by the cropped view. Simpson's artwork also generates, in the minds of viewers who know Rodgers's song, the missing words.

While this chapter's focus is on language *in* art, rather than language *about* art, the two topics cannot be neatly cleaved. Although they often refer to diagrams and illustrations, art historians and critics depend most heavily on verbal communication to discuss and interpret works of visual art.[1] Gavin Jantjes claimed, "Ever since art has been recognized as an autonomous discipline, its central dilemma has been the dominance of the discursive over the visual."[2] The critical reception of all the arts is weighted toward their analysis in words. Artists themselves frame their own creative endeavors in language: many artists regularly compose a written artist's statement to contextualize the interpretation of their own artworks; and some artists seeking even more powerful control over their art's reception have packed their principles and purposes for art in an artistic manifesto.

The current popularity of language as a theme in visual works (and as a means of exploring other themes) stems, in part, from the impact of theories that emphasize how cultural meaning is negotiated within language and other symbolic systems. In the latter half of the twentieth century, works of visual art came to be viewed as "texts" to be examined for internal contradictions, hidden meanings, and implicit ideologies. In the 1980s, visual artists themselves often appeared to be responding to philosophical and linguistic theories about how language works. Artistic strategies of the 1990s and today have moved away somewhat from direct engagement with theory, although language continues to be a popular, powerful medium and vital theme.

Words With Art: A History

Language appears in two primary modes: spoken and written. Written language bears a more obvious relationship to visual art because both have traditionally depended primarily on the sense of sight in order to be perceived. Scholars cannot pinpoint where and when writing originated, but we do know that writing as we know it today was preceded in human development by numerous systems of symbolic communication utilizing tangible devices (such as knots in ropes). We also know that our prehistoric ancestors made pictures and *pictographs*, simplified representations with conventional meanings. (An example of a pictograph is the silhouette of a figure in a skirt that signifies the door to a women's restroom.) Later societies, such as ancient Egypt, developed hieroglyphic writing, in which pictographs are aligned in a sequence to connect together to form a much larger range of ideas. True written alphabets, which are based on a system of symbols that relate, by convention, to the sounds of speech, seem to have appeared only in the past four thousand years.

In contrast to alphabetic writing in contemporary Western societies, the traditional written languages of Asian societies continue to combine visual and verbal representations in an integrated system. Unlike the alphabetic system of English, in which a mere twenty-six letters are used in various arrangements to spell the sounds of words, the Chinese system, for instance, which has been in use for thirty-five hundred years, features an enormous number of characters, each of which conveys a concept. (Most characters are compounds of abstracted shapes with different meanings that are built upon a basic, root element of meaning.) Even speakers of different dialects can understand the same Chinese characters because the characters do not symbolize the sounds of language but the meaning.

Various methods and styles of writing the characters using ink and brushes, called *calligraphy*, developed at different times in China. Calligraphy has been important as a force for cultural unification. In contemporary China, calligraphy remains revered as a form of visual art and an opportunity to display one's poetic sensibility, which is demonstrated by nuanced brushstrokes as well as in the thought that is transmitted. In tracing calligraphy's influence, curator Chang Tsong-zung wrote, "By virtue of the art of calligraphy, words acquired a physical body and demanded attention as material incarnation rather than just conceptual ideas or abstract signs."[3]

As in China and other Asian societies, calligraphy is esteemed as a form of visual art in Islamic cultures. Calligraphy carries the message of the Qur'an, the sacred book of Islam, which records the divine revelations received by the prophet Muhammad. Islamic tradition generally opposes artistic representations of human figures and animals in religious settings and contexts, a circumstance that contributed to the elevation of the art of calligraphy. Even in secular manuscripts, which permitted narrative illustrations, painting was secondary to script.

Skill at handwriting was a hallmark among the educated in Europe at least as far back as the Middle Ages, paralleling, to some degree, the recognition of calligraphy as an art form in China and the Muslim world. Even among German immigrants to America in the late eighteenth and early nineteenth centuries, some were trained in making handwritten documents, such as wedding certificates, that included decorative calligraphic flourishes (known today as *fraktur*).

Writing in English-speaking countries, at the start of our current period, primarily emphasized the semantic meaning of the words and, in the case of poetry, the pattern of the sound of those words. But in the history of world literature, there are numerous instances in which written words have evoked visual qualities (for example, when a poem "paints" a mental picture in words) or have manifested enhanced qualities of visual form. Another strategy is exemplified by composing poems with a distinctive pattern or shape on the page, including shapes that represent objects or figures. Such shaped poetry was a popular pursuit among creative writers in widely different times and places, including ancient Greece, ancient Persia, the Italian Renaissance, and sixteenth-century England.

The tradition of shaped poetry, in which traditional lines of verse are arranged on the page, comes down to us in poems by Guillaume Apollinaire (an early twentieth-century French experimental writer) and in such recent examples as a book of shaped poems by the American writer John Hollander.[4] By the middle of the twentieth century, however, a distinct shift occurred, overshadowing shaped poetry and resulting in a movement known as *concrete poetry*. Concrete poetry broke free of writing strictly in horizontal lines of traditional verse. Starting with the influential work of Eugen Gomringer, a Bolivian-born Swiss, concrete poetry emphasized such aspects of writing as the repetition of letters in nongrammatical patterns, while the choice of typeface and the scale and color of the letters became viewed as strategies to expand the range of language's meaning. The same letter, word, or short phrase might be repeated across the page, creating an abstract shape. Concrete poetry gained wide popularity among experimental writers in the 1950s and 1960s in Europe, the United States, and South America.

Since 1980, visual poetry has continued to attract devoted practitioners, including Richard Kostelanetz (in the United States), Bern Porter (in Ireland), Pierre Garnier (in France), and Alberto Vitacchio and Carla Bertola (in Italy). Contemporary visual artists, such as Americans Kay Rosen [6-2] and Kenneth Goldsmith, have produced paintings and prints that bear strong affinities to the practice of concrete poetry in experimenting with how words can be freed from the traditional linearity of lines of text. Over the past decade, Goldsmith, originally trained as a sculptor, has shifted his creative practice to the generation of projects that draw exclusively from existing texts. In Goldsmith's view, "Writers don't need to write anything more. They just need to manage the language that already exists." To create *Day* (2003), a recent work that overlaps the literary and visual arts, Goldsmith retyped all the words in a single edition of the *New York Times*; to create *Sports* (2008), he transcribed "the radio broadcast of a long and dull Yankees game, ads included."[5] Goldsmith's is an intriguing example of a multidisciplinary practice: is he a writer or a visual artist? With the expanded range of visual qualities now available to us in the presentation of language via electronic technologies, is the distinction between literature and visual art viable any longer?[6]

M-murd-
erer!
st-st-
utter-
edEd

6-2 Kay Rosen | "Sp-spit It Out", #3 out of 5
paintings comprising "The Ed Paintings," 1988
Enamel sign paint on canvas, 32 x 20 inches
© 1988 Kay Rosen, courtesy of the artist

Art With Words: A History

Just as writers have experimented with the visual qualities of language and have developed works that overlap with the concerns of visual artists, visual artists in turn have experimented with the incorporation of language into their work.[7] Illuminated manuscripts of the European Middle Ages, Renaissance fresco cycles based on stories from the Bible, and the emergence, in late eighteenth-century England and the lowlands of northern Europe of a genre known as the "conversation piece" are just a few examples of the verbal and visual commingling. In the latter type of painting, the composition unfolds around a scene of people talking, gesturing, listening, and reacting. Examples linking the visual and verbal abound from around the world, including a long-standing tradition of Chinese ink paintings that incorporate poetic texts in the background area.

In American art in the nineteenth century, the incorporation of words in paintings served multiple purposes. One function was to test artistic skill by attempting painstaking depictions of handwritten notes and lettered signs in *trompe-l'oeil* ("fool-the-eye") paintings, as in the popular paintings of William Harnett. An idiosyncratic use of highly stylized writing can be seen in a wide range of work by nineteenth-century, twentieth-century, and contemporary American folk artists, such as the Reverend Howard Finster.

A range of visual artists in the twentieth century incorporated language into their work. For example, early in the twentieth century, European Cubists, who pioneered the technique of collage, discovered that affixing clippings from newspapers, printed labels, and similar text-based materials to the surface of a painting or drawing was a way of breaking down the distinction between art and life, which has become an important leitmotif in many artists' work over the past hundred years.

Influenced by the Cubists' example, vanguard graphic designers in Europe and the United States in the 1920s and 1930s began to combine typography, photographs, and graphic elements within a single design, often based on the spatial formation of the grid. In late twentieth-century America, graphic designers, such as April Greiman, began to explore emerging digital technologies as a means of combining photo-based images, computer art, and printed text, often in dense layered compositions that resist a quick reading. Inspired by European precedents, some American Modernists, including painters Stuart Davis and Gerald Murphy, created artworks that incorporated words or portions of words. Critics compared the compositional freedom in Davis's renowned abstractions to jazz improvisation. Later abstract artists, such as Cy Twombly and Morris Graves, developed styles of painting that echoed the flow of written script.

American Pop artists, who gained prominence in the 1960s and 1970s, including Roy Lichtenstein and Andy Warhol, expanded the playing field by appropriating the combination of verbal and visual imagery in everyday life, particularly in commercial product designs and the products of popular culture. Lichtenstein, for example, incorporated into his own paintings imagery and dialogue he culled from period comic books, especially those dealing with romance and war stories. Robert Indiana, a still-active pop artist, used words to weigh in on political issues (he was an ardent champion of civil rights) and called attention to the potential to see words in fresh ways, as in his world-famous rearrangement of the word "LOVE" into a stacked pairing of LO above VE. The 1970s saw a burgeoning of photo-realist paintings, prints, and drawings using urban and suburban landscapes as subject matter. Several noted photo-realists, including Richard Estes and Robert Cottingham, included portions of storefront signage, theater marquees, and billboards in their images.

Conceptual artists in the 1960s and 1970s redefined the relationship of visual art to language, building on the breakthrough efforts of Marcel Duchamp (1887–1968), a French Dadaist who moved to the United States during World War I. According to Kristine Stiles, "In 1917, Marcel Duchamp … had already defined an artist as someone able to rethink the world and remake meaning through language, rather than someone who produces handcrafted visual objects for 'retinal' pleasure."[8] Five decades later, Conceptual artists, including Joseph Kosuth, Lawrence Weiner, and Sol Lewitt, carried forward the banner that Duchamp had unfurled; they utilized words as a way of making ideas the central component in their art. In extreme instances, the words themselves became the artwork. Weiner even claimed that anyone who read the words that defined a work of art, and could therefore imagine it, had experienced the art just as fully as someone who saw an actual sculpture or painting. Lewitt, whose geometric wall drawings and sculptures are rooted in both Minimalism and Conceptual Art, emphasized the importance of the written instructions that defined how his artworks were to be created. Rather than draw or paint his art himself, Lewitt often relied on others to follow his written directions to complete a project.

Since the 1960s, a number of artists have employed words, along with photographs and other graphic representations, as a way of documenting a work of art. This *documentation* may take the form of a historical record of the artwork's creation, such as the recording of a live performance event; at other times, the documentation commemorates a static artwork in its completion. Documentation is especially useful for artists who make works that are so large in scale, remote in location, or long in duration that only a limited number of viewers ever experience the actual work. Documentation is a strategy for enlarging the audience and ensuring that the artwork survives, at least in its documented format. Site-specific earthworks and temporary installations are available to us now as charts, captioned photographs, blueprint drawings, and planning documents. In many instances, artists have declared that each image or object of documentation constitutes a work of art in its own right; sales of the documentation can be a strategy for recouping the outlay of funds that made the initial project possible.

Language is a central element in performance art, video, computer-based art, and sound art. These art forms acknowledge that the verbal is as central to life as the visual. Performance art is especially difficult to imagine without the regular use of speech. Many performance artists have perfected an idiosyncratic approach that combines different tones of voice, styles of speaking, dialects, and related gestures (all standard fare in theatrical acting) with a script that makes no or little attempt to develop a plot. A performance artist may focus intensely on the pure flow of words, spinning an ever-shifting intricate net of associations. Variations on this approach are found in the autobiographical monologues recorded by Spalding Gray in the 1980s, such as his *Swimming to Cambodia*, and Miranda July in the 2000s, in various performances that focus on her interpretations of the lives of contemporary women. In *The Swan Tool* (2001) [6-3], July tells the story of a woman working in an insurance company, using a performance, live music, and digital video effects projected onto screens in front of and behind her.

Recent Theories of Language

The exploration of language by visual artists gained renewed prominence after 1980 owing, in part, to the expanding application of concepts from semiotics and linguistics in the analysis of visual culture. *Semiotics*, the branch of philosophy that deals with the study of symbolic signs, and *linguistics*, the study of languages, provide systematic approaches to decoding human communication. Visual art, as a form of communication using representational signs as well as abstract symbols, became a topic caught up in the web of theoretical debates concerning language and the use of signs. Many contemporary artists, in fact, have chosen to make artworks that explicitly refer to or extend the academic discourse about language.

In thinking through the ramifications of a prickly question—Where does the meaning of language reside?—various scholars, philosophers, linguists, and, more recently, artists, art historians, and art critics began to look at language (and other sign systems) as a *structure*. Their conclusion was that meaning resides in (or results from) the condition of language as a system. With respect to language, this approach posits that there is no preexisting meaning that is imported into linguistic form. The meanings made by a given language are generated within and by the operation of that language's system of conventions, including rules of grammar and units of significance that function in

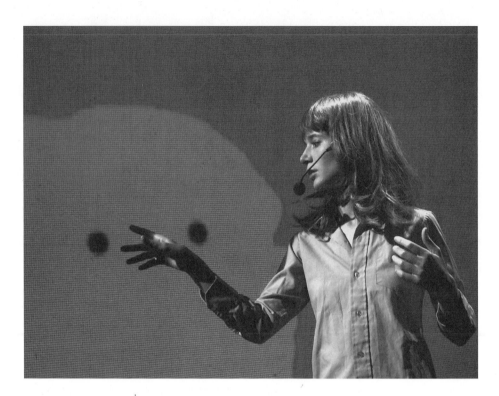

6-3 Miranda July │ *The Swan Tool,* 2001
Performance
Photo by Harrell Fletcher
Courtesy of the artist

relationship to other units. Writings of the Austrian philosopher Ludwig Wittgenstein (1889–1951) were profoundly influential in their emphasis on language as a "game" that a person learns to play by learning the appropriate rules. Knowing the names for words—just like knowing the names for pieces in a game—is not enough to know how to "speak." Another way of saying this is that language *performs* meaning. In the wake of Wittgenstein, scholars and critics applied variations of semiotic analysis to a wide variety of fields of intellectual and creative endeavor, including the production of art within a culture.

To reiterate: a fundamental belief was called into question—language was no longer seen as the pure conveyer of ideas (ideas whose truthfulness could purportedly be measured against a reality external to language itself). Instead, there was a paradigmatic shift that emphasized language as a structured network of meaningfulness, a network of abstract symbols (including letters, words, and punctuation marks) and the rules for using those symbols. Language came to be seen as the all-important context within which thinking was embodied.

The structure of language (phonetic sounds combining into words, the rules of grammar and syntax that govern how words combine into larger units of meaning, and so on) seems so ingrained in the fabric of human beings that some scholars (such as the linguist Noam Chomsky) have argued that the deepest structure of language is hard-wired into us. A simplified version of this concept would state: We humans are born to learn to use language as inherently as a bird is born to fly. This can occur because all languages share underlying traits, and our human brains seem to have adapted (through evolution) a natural propensity for fluency in the language we learn as children.

While the structures of all language bear some similarity, there are and have been myriad languages throughout history and in use today, and within any language there are multiple dialects and individual speakers who each has a different style of speaking (even among speakers of English, pronunciation and vocabulary choices differ). How language functions, how it is structured, how it identifies us as a species, how it distinguishes one group from another—in all these ways language is central to what it means to be human and how we humans make meaning. Because of language's centrality in the process of human thought, contemporary visual artists have found language to be a rich focus for art—as they have aimed to broaden their thematic palette.

The shift in ideas about language, within the field of linguistics, occurred alongside changes in ideas about culture in general (including language, laws, institutions, codes of behavior, customs, and so on). Together, these changes evolved, by the 1960s in France, into an intellectual movement called *structuralism*. Structuralism was based on a strategy for analyzing cultural conditions in terms of an underlying, structural framework. The structural approach employed in the 1960s was heavily influenced by the pioneering work of a Swiss linguist, Ferdinand de Saussure (1857–1913). Saussure's focus on the systemic condition of language was applied to culture as a network of systems of meaning. Furthermore, Saussure understood how language can change over time while always remaining cohesive. Fredric Jameson explained, "Saussure's originality was to have insisted on the fact that language as a total system is complete at every moment, no matter what happens to have altered in it a moment before."[9]

Structuralists were content to assume a neutral stance as they analyzed how language and other symbolic systems work. Then, the structuralist approach was supplanted to a wide degree (starting in France in the 1970s and becoming enormously influential in the United States in the 1980s) with the advent of the more politically engaged concepts of *poststructuralism*. Poststructural thinkers analyzed language and other sign systems as part of the broader power structures of society. Poststructuralists claimed to uncover the ways in which humans are at the mercy of the systems that create and disseminate the texts and images that surround us regularly in our everyday lives. According to poststructuralist theory (a position that was widely influential with the development of postmodernism in the 1970s), our individual subjectivity is a myth: our thought patterns mirror the fractured "maze of competing signs" we are enmeshed in.[10]

Poststructuralists questioned the ingrained habit of "reading" texts, discourses, and visual representations as if they were authoritative sources with fixed, single meanings. Instead, poststructuralists opened various communicative signs to the process of *deconstructing* (also called decoding); deconstructing might involve the critical analysis of a message or image from alternative cultural or theoretical perspectives. Poststructuralists posited that no one can control all interpretations or readings of an image or text, and, just as importantly, no interpretation or reading is solely the work of one author. Even an artist's style, for example, is the result of both the artist and those critics who articulate observations that the original artist could not have intended (for example, by comparing qualities in an artist's style to qualities in the work of artists who worked later in time).

Poststructuralist ideas have resonated strongly with various artists who are involved with feminist and postcolonial issues. Text is often an important component of these artists' work. For example, American Elaine Reichek used needlework samplers to re-present texts by male artists and authors and reformulate their meanings.

The basic idea that meaning can change depending on the context and the viewer's knowledge of conventions has been used effectively to analyze a range of languagelike systems, including body language and the coded display and packaging of consumer objects. Seen in this light, even everyday objects communicate identity, prestige, sexuality, and other hidden meanings. As Howard Singerman wrote, "Always part of a serial chain of identical copies, clothes, cars, computers, and so on are necessarily enfolded in a rationalized and differential system of exchanges that is, according to Baudrillard, not a mirror or a replica of the exchanges of language but the same as it. 'What is consumed is the object not in its materiality, but in its difference—i.e., *the object as sign.*' "[11] Our consumption of a certain article of clothing communicates meaning within the fashion code of our particular social system. A range of contemporary artists have been inspired by the semiotics of body gestures, flags, diagrams, maps, direction signs, and corporate logos of consumer culture, among them Ilona Granet, Ashley Bickerton, Matt Mullican, and Haim Steinbach.[12]

But are we, as social creatures, strictly the product of our cultural education? Although tribal cultures lack sophisticated technologies, linguistic research has established that tribal languages can be as sophisticated in their linguistic complexity as languages spoken anywhere.[13] Our stunning facility to develop language-making skills as children, including our mastery of generating meaningful sentences that we have never heard before, seems to contradict any theory that would posit that learning a language is strictly the product of cultural training. Similarly, an almost exclusive emphasis on culture—and a concomitant disregard of nature's importance—in the analysis of the humanities and the arts can be challenged by the experimental findings of cognitive science, the branch of science that explores how the mind is structured and functions.

Reasons for Using Language

The surge of activity and interest in the use of language in contemporary art has many causes. While the specific reasons for using language are as varied as the artists themselves, some basic trends and influences are in evidence.

As we noted, the development of Conceptual Art, which gained critical mass in the late 1960s and 1970s, resulted in the rapid proliferation in the number of artworks incorporating language as a medium and in the purposeful dematerialization of the artwork. Conceptual Art at that time included plans or descriptions of works of art that might never be realized. While artists in recent decades have moved away from such "pure" forms of Conceptualism, artists still turn to language (in its diverse formats) because words can articulate complex ideas and embody abstractions. Taiwanese conceptual artist Wu Mali created *The Library*, an installation for the Venice Biennale in 1995, in which she put volumes of literature (by earlier authors) through a shredder and displayed the paper fragments in acrylic boxes with the book titles embossed in gold lettering. Wu Mali's action created, in the viewer's mind, the concept of books that no longer exist and simultaneously called into question the enduring value of those books, symbolic of a lost literary canon.

by Austrian-born artist Robert Gschwantner, which expresses his alarm about oil slicks caused by shipwrecks and other industrial disasters. Gschwantner injects oil sludge, used industrial lubricants, and seawater into polyvinyl-chloride (PVC) tubing, which he then weaves into pillows, screens, or large mats. His related series *Peluche* (French for "soft toy") consists of woven and knotted oil-filled PVC mats, rolled up, which resemble the small spiky sea creatures that oil spills decimate.

Artists may collaborate with scientists who share their sense of caution and want other scientists and the public alike to reflect on scientific outcomes and choices. (The interdisciplinary field of bioethics has arisen within the scientific community to focus on philosophical and ethical questions raised by scientific discoveries and practices.) Along these lines, Weather Report: Art and Climate Change, a 2007 art exhibition on view at the Boulder Museum of Contemporary Art in Colorado and at other public locations, fostered dozens of collaborations between artists and scientists. The resulting interdisciplinary artworks drew attention to climate change by addressing such related issues as deforestation, global warming, species extinction, damage to the ozone layer, and ocean pollution. The artist Mary Miss worked with a hydrologist and geologist to envision the magnitude of a feared five-hundred-year flood in the local area. Ultimately Miss affixed three hundred bright blue discs, at the height of the predicted high-water mark, onto structures in heavily populated downtown Boulder. Long-term environmental artists Helen and Newton Harrison relied on the research of a biologist studying the effects of global warming on alpine plants to create *The Mountain in the Greenhouse* (2007) [7-7], an artwork showing plants creeping to higher elevations as their habitat shrinks. Among the other environmentally concerned artists who participated were Kim Abeles, Eve Andrée Laramée, Patricia Johanson, Aviva Rahmani, Agnes Denes, Buster Simpson, Future Farmers, Ellen Levy, and Pierre Huyghe.

Lucy Lippard, the veteran art critic and social activist who curated Climate Change, noted that some works dramatized climate change and others offered solutions. "It remains to be seen which will be more effective, imagining what the change will be like or coming up with ideas for what to do about it," Lippard said.[15] Now in her seventies, Lippard has long believed that art can inspire viewers to take social action.

Activist artists can take an extremely provocative stance. Gregory Green, for instance, made a series of sculptures that replicate, in basement-inventor fashion, primitive prototypes for nuclear, biological, and chemical weapons. All that Green's versions lack are the various fuels (such as enriched uranium) for making the weapons fully functional, although Green "helpfully" provides recipes for mixing explosive materials. The artist, who worked from instruction manuals readily available on the Internet and by mail order, wanted in part to demonstrate how easy it is for terrorists to obtain the knowledge needed to make dangerous weapons. In these and related series of works, Green connects the proliferation of dangerous weapons with science, technology, political ideology, and corporate greed.

With a similar intent, the Critical Art Ensemble (CAE), an art and theater collective founded in 1987, presented participatory performance projects all over the world that were intended to critique various outcomes of emerging biotechnologies and help the public understand the issues. The performances were a form of bio art. CAE performed basic scientific processes in public using biological materials (such as bacteria found in the human digestive track) to educate audiences about genetically altered food and biowarfare. For instance, the art project *Free Range Grains* allowed participants to test food for

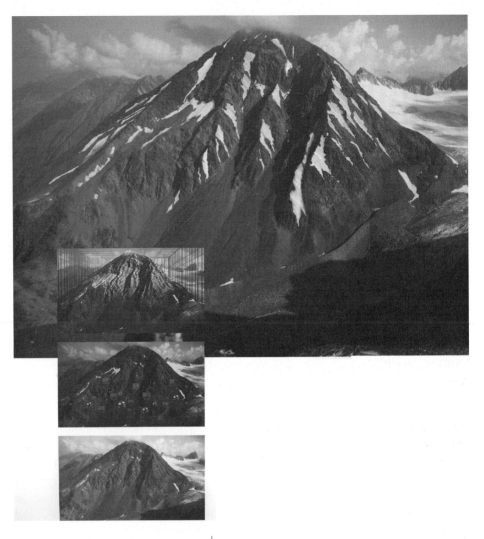

7-7 Helen & Newton Harrison | *Detail from The Mountain in the Greenhouse from Peninsula*
Europe, **2001**
Image from CD-ROM (Flash Player Technology)
duration: approx. 3 minutes
Courtesy of Ronald Feldman Fine Arts, New York

the presence of genetically modified organisms. CAE always used nonhazardous materials legally available to anyone, of the sort routinely used in undergraduate university biology labs. Nonetheless, Steven Kurtz, a founding member of CAE, went from provocateur to terrorism suspect in 2004 when agents from the FBI detained him and accused him of bioterrorism. They seized computers, equipment, manuscripts, and other items from his home, including legally acquired bacteria cultures he was using as art materials. Although the investigation produced no evidence of bioterrorism, the Department of Justice continued to pursue a case based on lesser charges of mail and wire fraud allowable under the USA Patriot Act of 2001; the charges were dropped in 2008.[16]

The Visual Culture of Science

Discoveries in the sciences and related technological developments from computer science and engineering, such as robotics, bioengineering, and artificial intelligence, are highly influential in everyday culture. New scientific ideas and products reach the public not only through written materials, but in a wide range of visual forms from a variety of sources, including scientists themselves, advertising, television programs, the Internet, and science fiction movies. Artists draw inspiration from all these visual sources, sources that are both eye-catching and thought-provoking, two qualities that are highly sought after in the high-stakes world of the contemporary global market for works of art and art events.

Scientific Imaging and Art

Science today generates many powerful images. Scientific images can captivate us in their own right, and they have also affected how visual artists see and think about the fundamental elements of visual art, such as space, texture, movement, and pattern. For example, science has stretched our awareness of scale, which extends from the subatomic to the galactic. Scientific instruments and technologies have yielded images of breathtaking splendor. The Hubble Space Telescope provides pictures of galaxies beyond our own; medical imaging tools show us the hidden interior of the human body and forms of life invisible to the naked eye; instruments on satellites capture real-time images of weather systems moving across continents, as well as track the location of a moving car with a GPS installed.

Scientific images can rival art in their power and authority, posing a philosophical conundrum: If an artist can create an artwork that could pass as a science project, can a scientist produce a work of science that crosses the border into art? The answer appears to be yes. Consider that art historians have marveled at the detailed watercolors and drawings of sponges, protozoa, and sea stars made by the biologist-naturalist Ernst Haeckel (1834–1919) and that the stop-action photographs made by MIT scientist Harold Edgerton in the 1930s and 1940s, including a famous one that captures the path of a bullet exploding through an apple, often appear in texts on the history of photography. Other exceptional scientific images occupy an ambiguous border zone in which their status as art is not clear. For example, in 2000, a widely reproduced "astrophoto" of the Eagle Nebula (a mammoth cluster of stars in the process of formation seven thousand light-years from Earth) was selected as the image on a U.S. commemorative postage stamp honoring the first decade of the Hubble Space Telescope. The image was selected for the stamp because of both its scientific message and its unforgettable visual content. The image shows three column shapes of star matter, each trillions of miles in length.

Scientists adopted photography as soon as it was invented in the mid-nineteenth century and embraced x-ray technology when it was developed in the 1890s. Today physicians and science practitioners in a range of fields use advanced imaging technology, including electron microscopes, ultrasound, magnetic resonance imaging (MRI), satellite images, and CAT scans (a sophisticated form of x-ray), to capture scientific information in a visual form. In addition, scientists use computer-aided rendering programs to translate their data and interpretations into maps, diagrams, and models. Bioimaging in concert with scientific modeling has revolutionized modern medicine and the biological sciences. Physicians no longer diagnose disease primarily by observing external signs and symptoms but employ instruments that see and measure the body's inner workings even at the cellular level. Mona Hatoum is one artist who has used the tools of medical bioimaging. Her video installation *Corps étranger* (1994) [3-8] is a kind of self-portrait focusing on the interior rather than the exterior of the artist's body. The video shows images of the intestines, stomach, and other organs recorded by a camera mounted to medical equipment that technicians inserted into the various orifices of Hatoum's body.

For visual artists, the focus on hidden phenomena and systems operating at the molecular or genetic level contrasts profoundly with the perceptual approach still used in visual art training in most university art programs. Student artists learn much of how they understand the body by direct observation of its contours, surface masses, musculature, and surface attributes, such as hair and skin color, as they attempt to draw it accurately. Historically, however, visual artists also trained by drawing from skulls and models of skeletons, as well as from life, and turned to the study of anatomy to enhance their knowledge. Leonardo da Vinci in the Renaissance and Thomas Eakins in the nineteenth century were so fascinated by interior body structures that they sought permission from civil authorities to observe the dissection of human cadavers.

Artists have depicted the human body and delved into the nature of humanity since prehistoric times, when people first carved small figurines and drew hunters on cave walls. Today bioimaging has made it possible to represent human beings in new ways. Is seeing, as in seeing things with your own eyes, still believing? Or is the surface a lie compared to what is underneath it? Marita Sturken and Lisa Cartwright, coauthors of an introduction to visual culture studies, found "a tension between the idea that truth is self-evident in the surface appearance of things, and the contrasting idea that truth lies hidden elsewhere, in internal structures or systems of the body."[17] American artist Gary Schneider created his installation *Genetic Self-Portrait* (1997–98) in collaboration with scientists using photomicroscopy. The installation juxtaposes photographs of Schneider's ears, hands, and teeth with greatly magnified images of biological samples of the artist's own DNA, chromosomes, cells, sperm, blood, and hair [7-8]. Schneider appears to ask which level of representation, from the surface of his body to his cells to his DNA, identifies him most definitively.

Artists responding to science may use iconic scientific symbols, such as the double helix; copy pictures from x-rays or MRI scans; adapt images of cells magnified by powerful microscopes; or mimic models of molecular structures and genomes. For example, to make her late 1980s series *Viral Landscapes*, British photographer Helen Chadwick superimposed magnified images of her own body's cells over landscape photographs. In the 1990s, American painters Frank Moore and David Wojnarowicz, as well as other artists, made artworks about the impact of AIDS that included molecular images and models of the HIV virus. American sculptor Ronald Jones made an untitled 1989 bronze that, according to the artist, visualizes a human DNA fragment that is carrying cancer genes, while also deliberately evoking a well-known organic abstract sculpture by the modernist Jean Arp. Jones explained, "My sculpture takes hostage Arp's intuitive search for a higher modern form, a utopic or perfect order and perverts it into something distressed and dying, a promise unkept to the culture at large."[18]

In a range of artworks, collaborators Lilla LoCurto and Bill Outcault have explored ways that digital imaging tools can represent the human body. In their three-channel

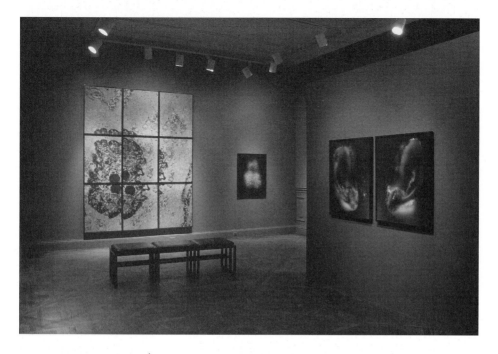

7-8 Gary Schneider | *Genetic Self-Portrait*, **1997/98**
Installation 2000 (detail) International Center of Photography, NYC, NY
From left to right: BUCCAL MUCOSA CELL 1997, DNA DYZ3/DYZ1 1998, HANDS 1997
Installation photo by Adam Eidelberg

animation video *Essay of 1000 Layers II* (2006), the artists manipulate digital data obtained from a full-body scanner that used four lasers to map thousands of points on the surface of each artist's body. Using specialized time-and-motion software, they sliced the scanned figures into topographic layers of varying depths to produce images that lose their human identity and take on the character of three-dimensional calligraphy that changes over time. The artwork is hard to visualize or illustrate because it is multidimensional and exists only in its digital form. By rendering the linear imagery sequentially from multiple angles, the artists represented the traditional three physical dimensions as well as time, and they also produced an effect of simultaneity, mapping each body without a fixed perspective.

Deconstructing the Visual Culture of Science

Artists who mimic or adapt visualizations from science sometimes aim to *deconstruct* the cultural assumptions that underlie them. However objective images generated by science may seem to be, they are *constructed*; they invent, interpret, and translate forms and processes rather than simply reveal them. For instance, the image of the Eagle Nebula discussed earlier, which was incorporated into the design of a postage stamp, is not the utterly factual representation it appears to be. Although the spectacular image looks like a straightforward photograph, the colors in the image are the result of using a computerized process to filter and separate different wavelengths of light. The color choices applied to the wavelengths are abstractions, not existing hues perceptible to the unaided eye.

Scientific images and models, just like works of art, are human products and thus inevitably reflect the assumptions and specialized tools of the researchers who made them. Suzanne Anker and Dorothy Nelkin analyzed the likelihood of distortion in scientific visualizations in their book *The Molecular Gaze*. Discussing medical and scientific reliance on computers and statistical data analysis, rather than direct observation, they stated: "Life on the screen is a reality for science, and measurement is often more important than direct observation. Scientists represent their data produced through sophisticated optical instruments in the form of graphs, charts, formulas, and photographic images. Like artists, they manipulate, alter, and edit these images to contain complexity and emphasize characteristics that effectively illustrate their interpretation of the data."[19]

Paul Vanouse demonstrates the potential for manipulation when translating scientific data into a visual form in *Latent Figure Protocol* (2005–6), a multimedia installation and performance, which he has repeated in several exhibitions. Vanouse works with scientists ahead of time to prepare DNA samples obtained from genetically modified crops and other living things. At the exhibition opening the artist performs a live experiment adapted from a process actually used by scientists to map genomes: Vanouse selects different sizes of DNA samples, inserts them into electrophoresis gel, and then applies different electrical currents to cause the samples to migrate at different rates. The resulting DNA gel images, which mimic low-resolution bitmaps, are displayed near the scientific apparatus used in the experiment.[20] In one version of this experiment, in which Vanouse inserted the DNA of a genetically modified crop into the bands of gels, the electrically manipulated DNA samples formed a copyright symbol as they migrated.

Bioimaging seems to provide objective and authoritative images of biological structures and functions, but the making of scientific images, like the making of artworks, is a culturally dependent process, and the results can take on social and political meanings. A sonogram, for example, is a translation of data that is not inherently visual. It is a computer-generated image in which high-frequency sound waves reflected from tissue are translated into a visual pattern that simulates a photograph; a graph or some other form of abstract notation could have been used to represent the same data. Yet people often treat a sonogram as if it were a realistic image much like a documentary photograph, and they may respond to these images emotionally. A fetal sonogram, in particular, Sturken and Cartwright noted, "takes on the aura of a portrait, a document of the fetus's status as a social being (as a person) and not just a biological entity."[21] Interpreted this way, the "neutral" medical image is deployed in political arguments against abortion.

Scientific Displays and Archives

The general public is able to learn in a visual way about science by visiting natural history museums, museums of science and industry, air and space museums, planetariums, botanical gardens, and zoos, as well as archives and libraries. Within such institutions, specimens from nature (such as taxidermied or live animals, plants, and rocks), scientific instruments, artifacts, documents, photographs, models, renderings, and simulations are arranged into displays, usually with interpretive labels nearby. Some acclaimed contemporary artists create installations that mimic the display techniques of museums, archives, libraries, and related institutions, including institutions with scientific missions. The ideas and results vary greatly depending on the kind of institution the artist is responding to and why.[22]

American artist Mark Dion borrows from museum practices to create displays of his own design into which he often incorporates real scientific specimens and artifacts. Rather than present specimens arranged and labeled according to a rational system of classification (the goal of a traditional scientific display of such material), the artist focuses more on the individuality of the specimens. For example, for an installation that Dion constructed for the 1999 exhibition Weird Science, he selected hundreds of specimens from the reptile and amphibian collection at the Cranbrook Institute of Science. Each specimen had been preserved in formaldehyde in its own glass jar. Dion laid out the jars along an enormous light table that provided the only source of illumination in the gallery. "With fluorescent light traveling through every jar of liquid," wrote curator Irene Hofmann, "each specimen takes on a magical quality—every minor scale, horn, and bump on these animals becomes extraordinary."[23] Dion returned mystery and ambiguity to the public display of modern science, which often can be either a rather dry recitation of information or a funhouse atmosphere. Many critics have noted that Dion's displays of collections have a lot in common with the old-fashioned *Wunderkammern* ("cabinets of wonders"). Before the rise of museums as we know them today, *Wunderkammern* displayed eclectic assemblages of historical artifacts and scientific specimens, which were collected in a haphazard way from all over the world and presented with little, if any, explanation of their original function, meaning, or context.

Artist Hiroshi Sugimoto made a series of black-and-white photographs of dioramas that were constructed for museums of natural history. The photographs heighten the underlying oddity of these detailed, lifelike museum simulations that depict what a particular prehistoric scene might have looked like. Sugimoto's photograph *Permian-Land* (1992), which allegedly shows a prehistoric habitat from the Permian era, is one example of these strange simulacra that the public usually accepts as reasonably accurate depictions of a past world about which we have no detailed record [5-8].

Damien Hirst, who has worked in many media and forms, first became notorious for a series of displays consisting of tanks of formaldehyde containing pickled biological specimens, including a shark, a cow, and a sheep. These specimens were exhibited whole as if in suspended animation or dissected into cross sections to provide a clear view of the insides. Exhibited in art venues, these tanks with their creepy contents provoke some long-standing questions: What makes something art? What distinguishes art from what is not art? And how does the context (an art gallery rather than a science lab or science museum) influence interpretation? Hirst has also created installations that evoke high-tech laboratories and gleaming scientific and medical supply stores. In the setting of an art museum, Hirst's *Pharmacy* (1992) makes our familiar, highly impersonal world of modern medical treatment through chemical prescriptions look strange [7-4]. The installation also invites comparisons of the aesthetic, political, and commercial aspects of the drug industry and the art world.

Science in Popular Culture

Beyond the reports of scientists and the displays in museums, concepts and images emerging from science reach the popular imagination through print media and Internet sites and through films, television shows, novels, video games, comics, and advertisements for consumer products. In popular culture, fictional clones, mutants, and cyborgs inhabit fantastic futuristic worlds and enact extreme scenarios that portray science paradoxically as both a cause of apocalypse and the means to salvation. Some visual artists respond as much or more to representations of science in visual culture as they do to science itself.

Motohiko Odani was inspired by science fiction, children's television, and genetics when he created his video *Rompers* [7-2]. Matthew Ritchie draws from a wealth of sources encompassing science fiction, creation myths, and particle physics to create paintings such as *Self-Portrait in 2064* (2001) [4-6]. Paul McCarthy's sculpture *Mutant* (1993) [3-1] shows a popular culture-inflected version of a transgenic being.

Other art projects have drawn from popular visual culture to create visions of genetic mutation. The aptly titled *Reversed Double Helix* (2003), a two-week installation in Rockefeller Center in New York of sculptural works by Takashi Murakami, featured colorful figures that look like friendly cartoon versions of mutant hybrids. The figures are sculptural versions of Murakami's trademark "Superflat" style, which itself is a hybrid that borrows from both traditional Japanese *nihon-ga* painting and popular Japanese animation and graphic novels (known as *anime* and *manga*). *Cremaster Cycle*, Matthew Barney's group of five epic films, includes many transgenic creatures, such as Barney himself as a kind of satyr in *Cremaster 4* (1994) and the actress Aimee Mullins as a cheetah-woman in *Cremaster 3* (2002) [3-7]. Ancient legends and fairy tales, sci-fi and horror movies, and biology and genetics have all influenced Barney's hybrids.

Classifying Humans in the Genomic Age

Carl Linnaeus (1707–78), the Swedish botanist, zoologist, and physician, established the basic structure of the system of scientific names and categories—the *taxonomy*—that is widely followed to this day in the biological sciences. Linnaeus classified things in nature into three kingdoms (animal, vegetable, and mineral) on the basis of their observable physical characteristics and constructed a hierarchy of ranked subclassifications under the main kingdoms. Although the number of kingdoms and subcategories and many names have changed (or been added) over time, the underlying concept of the Linnaean taxonomy—that creatures could be grouped together according to qualities that are observed and measured—remains an influential model for looking at life forms. Humans, in the original version of this scheme, are part of the animal kingdom but preserve their unique identity with respect to other species of animals.

Nevertheless, the distinction between humans and everything-but-us eroded since the advent of evolutionary biology. As philosopher Christoph Cox noted, "Darwin's theory of natural selection insists that there is a basic continuity in nature, not just among species, but among all living things, who ultimately share a common ancestry."[24] The philosophers Gilles Deleuze and Félix Guattari took the claim even further, arguing that "there are no essential divisions within nature, no absolute differences between minerals, vegetables, animals, and humans. Rather, matter is a vast continuum, a field of virtual forces, intensities, thresholds, and powers that, under particular conditions, is actualized in the things and bodies we know."[25] In a mixed media painting *Human Ancestors* (1997), artist Alexis Rockman appears to parody both Linnaean taxonomy and Darwinian evolution. A portly nude human sits atop the main trunk of a bare tree with branches that support a fantastic range of life forms—some monkeylike, others hybrids of more than one species—all sharing a common ancestor.

New scientific research in genetics is further shaking up basic assumptions about human identity and the relationship between humans and the rest of nature. Today, invisible characteristics, particularly the unique structure of an individual's DNA, serve as the standard of proof of personal identity, which is presented as evidence in courts of law and used to establish biological family relationships.

Researchers in genomics study the DNA molecules that make up genes and the proteins they control to look for the complex structure of genetic information at the cellular level. Genetic code is expressed in symbols, using the letters A, C, G, and T as a form of scientific shorthand for the primary chemicals (adenine, cytosine, guanine and thymine) that comprise the bases in DNA. The human genome is incredibly complex and has 3 billion unique building blocks of DNA, but every organism can be identified in terms of its DNA, from your next door neighbor to an organism of just one cell.

Artist and critic Suzanne Anker became interested in how genetic information is expressed in symbols. For example, a pattern of dots and dashes can be used to represent the complete set of chromosomes of a cell of a living organism. In her installation *Zoosemiotics: Primates, Frog, Gazelle, Fish* (1993) [7-9], Anker presents magnified representations of chromosomes that resemble ancient writing. In related artworks, she has altered the left-to-right way in which chromosome structure is usually presented to create a pattern that reads vertically, similar to Chinese calligraphy. Anker says that

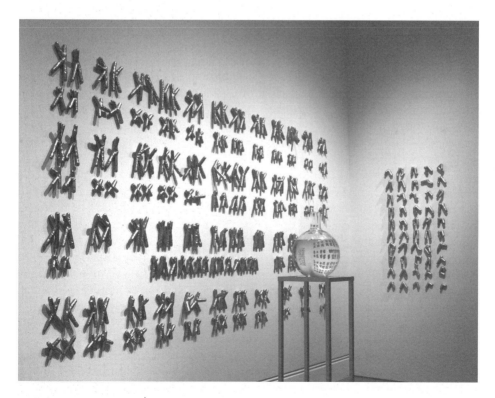

7-9 **Suzanne Anker** | *Zoosemiotics: Primates, Frog, Gazelle, Fish,* 1993

Glass vessel, water, steel, hydrocal, metallic pigment
Courtesy of the artist

she became interested in how the "DNA molecule transmits genetic information from one generation to another, like language transmits information. And then I began exploring the different chromosome structures in various animals—alligator, bird, rat, the primate family, fish. And when I looked at their writing, which I call 'body writing,' they were like different languages."[26]

The linguistic character of genetic coding implies that not only are fundamental characteristics of human nature invisible to the naked eye, existing deep inside the body at the molecular level, but only those specialists who learn this specialized language can make sense of the body's mysteries. Whereas taxonomists used to classify organisms on the basis of observed physical similarities and differences, now they map and compare hidden genetic sequences expressed in complicated, abstract codes. "The genetic code," artist Christine Davis observed, "seemed to be a radical shift from mechanics to communication, from how the body 'works' (blood and guts) to how it 'means' (blocks of letters)."[27] This approach to classifying living things gives priority to the instructions "written" into the chromosomes and defines human identity using linguistic metaphors, such as language, script, code, map, and blueprint.

The emphasis on organisms as information systems has emboldened people to imagine that we may someday control human evolution: If only the structure and sequence of genomes can be completely mapped and genetic codes completely deciphered, then plants, animals, and even humans may be reprogrammed at will to achieve desired characteristics. To many people, including many artists, genetic models of human nature seem to suggest that genes encode most, if not all, human characteristics and behaviors. If there is a gene (or cluster of genes) for weight, height, disease, sexual preference, criminal propensity, mental capacity, and so on, what, if any, role do sociocultural experiences play in forming individual identity? What moral responsibility do humans have for our actions if an intricate mix of chemical compounds is what ultimately determines our personality?

Is Nature Natural?

In contrast to natural selection, a cumulative process that slowly sorts the fit from the unfit and ensures the survival of the fittest organisms, genetic engineering holds out the possibility of controlling the selection process to achieve specific goals. Genomics researchers are identifying genes that are linked to a range of diseases, behaviors, and physical attributes and are experimenting with ways to modify those genes so as to improve our health, rate of aging, emotional state, diet, or physical appearance. Even when manipulating genes with the most benign intentions, such as to ensure that a baby will not develop a grave genetic disease, the life sciences are offering choices that have profound ethical and societal consequences. Do height and physical beauty factor into well-being, for example, and, if so, where is the line between genetic engineering and *eugenics*, a social philosophy that advocates the shaping of a more perfect human race by manipulating hereditary factors? (Eugenics has been used as a justification for such practices as forced sterilization of people deemed genetically defective.)

Inigo Manglano-Ovalle raises the issue of eugenics in his installation *Banks in Pink and Blue* (1999). In this work, two cryogenic sperm canisters of the kind used by commercial sperm banks are color-coded blue and pink. The canisters contain dozens of donated sperm samples that have been separated by the artist's scientific collaborators to select Y or X (male or female) chromosomes. In addition to bringing attention to the potential for selecting a baby's gender, the work raises questions about issues of the ownership and consumer marketing of genetic materials such as sperm.

The human relationship to nature has never been entirely natural. Humans have been intervening in nature since the dawn of history through the practices of agriculture and animal husbandry. People have engaged in the selective breeding of plants and animals for many intersecting reasons: utilitarian (to produce a disease-resistant crop), competitive (to breed a prize-winning racehorse), and aesthetic (to create a new color of tulip). According to David Kremers, a conceptual artist involved in biology, "Biologists estimate that the type of nature we can genuinely refer to as wildlife consists of a mere 2 percent of all life on land. All other life is an artifact of human culture."[28]

Australian Natalie Jeremijenko's *Tree Logic* [7-10], an ongoing sculptural installation begun in 1999 on the grounds of MASS MoCA, provides a wry commentary on bioengineering and our comprehension of what is natural. The root balls of six maple trees were planted in steel containers and then were suspended upside down by heavy cables from a constructed armature, with a drip-irrigation system providing water. The artwork vividly demonstrates that the power of the sun is a stronger force than gravity for the trees; even upside down, the trees grow topsy turvy toward the light, so that over time, their branches curve upward to create a startling form. Curator Laura Steward Heon wrote of this work, "Our perceptions of trees change when we view them as a collection of growth responses rather than as immutable symbols of the natural world."[29]

In another artwork, *Onetree*, begun in 1999, Jeremijenko acquired one hundred genetic clones of a single walnut tree and had them planted throughout San Francisco and at selected international sites. According to the artist, "Because the trees are biologically identical, they will render the social and environmental differences to which they are exposed in subsequent years. The trees' slow and consistent growth will record the unique experiences and contingencies of each public site."[30] Jeremijenko suggests that no form of life has an essential, unchanging nature; all organisms dynamically adapt to their local environment. Jeremijenko also insinuates that agribusiness cannot turn a plant into a completely manufactured, controlled product.

Traditional selective breeding practices influenced evolution without raising widespread social or ethical concerns. Today the pace of genetic mutation is accelerating, as cloning and DNA sequencing techniques are systematically applied to many plants and animals in biotechnology labs. We consume genetically modified food every day, and it is a matter of considerable debate whether genetically modified organisms (GMOs) are a boon to agribusiness at the expense of consumers' health. Advocates point out that GMOs have the potential to solve world hunger. Naysayers fear health risks from exposure to GMOs in food, worry about the potential of GMOs to hybridize with non-modified plants, and fear a loss of biodiversity.

Alexis Rockman, an artist who is concerned about the ethical and environmental implications of unregulated biotechnology, reminds us that genomics is a science and an industry. Rockman's painting *The Farm* (2000) [7-11] shows a world in which the demands of agribusiness override the integrity of animals and plants. On the left are familiar farm animals; on the right imagined bioengineered versions of the same animals. Rockman also depicts modifications that have already occurred in labs, such as vegetables bred to have a squarish shape so they can be packaged efficiently and, at the

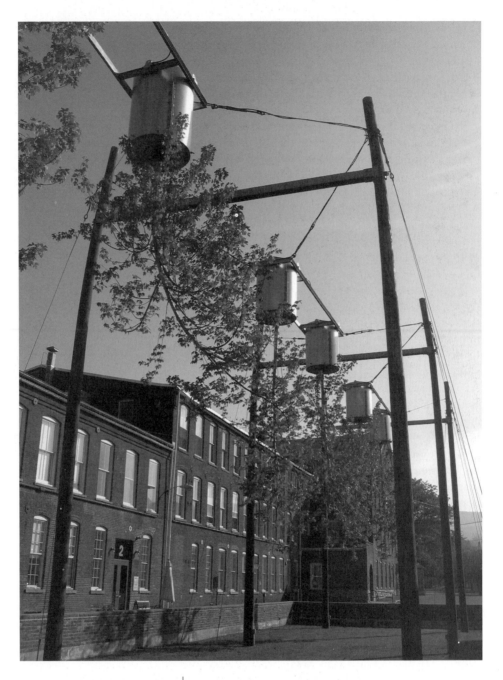

7-10 Natalie Jeremijenko | *Tree Logic*, **1999**

Six Flame Maple trees (Acer ginnala), telephone poles, stainless steel planters and
armature, aircraft cable, drip irrigation system
MASS MoCA, North Adams, MA

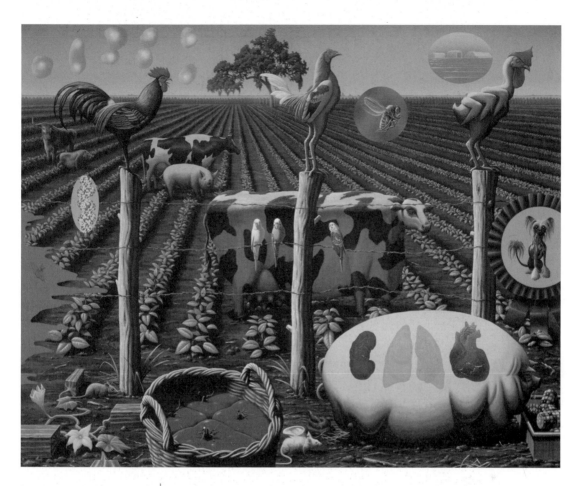

7-11 Alexis Rockman | *The Farm,* 2000

Oil and acrylic on wood
Courtesy of Leo Koenig Inc.

bottom center, a mouse with a human ear on its back (echoing an actual experiment at Massachusetts General Hospital in which scientists grew tissue-engineered cartilage in the shape of an ear on a mouse).

Genetics experiments that are aimed at changing animal and plant genomes, even producing new organisms that combine traits across species boundaries, are especially unsettling. German Thomas Grünfeld began a series called *Misfits* in 1989 in which he constructed his own versions of cross-species creatures by combining parts from two or three different taxidermied animals, such as one with the narrow face of a sheep and the stocky body of a St. Bernard dog [7-12]. The hybrids appear to be the strange results of genetic lab experiments. Other versions of transgenics illustrated in this chapter include Motohiko Odani's girl-reptile hybrid [7-2] and Patricia Piccinini's lifelike simulations of transgenic creatures [7-14 and color plate 16].

As humans use biotechnology to intervene more often in the organic world, many questions arise: How much manipulation can take place before we decide that something

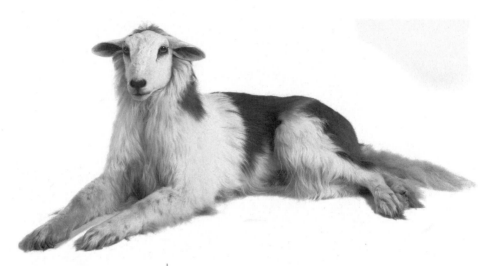

7-12 Thomas Grunfeld | *Misfit (St Bernhard)*, **1994**
Taxidermy, plexiglas, and wood vitrine
© 2008 Artist Rights Society (ARS), New York / VG Bild-Kunst, Bonn

natural has become artificial? Is a new species created in a lab still natural as long as all its components are organic? What does individual identity mean in an age of cloning and robotics? Is it appropriate to implant animals with human genes? Who "owns" life when gene sequences can be patented? What responsibility do humans have when they intervene in nature? For example, if Piccinini's humanlike transgenic creatures were real, what right to life would they have?[31] A few of the many other artists who are working with the images and issues of bioengineering are Christine Borland, Bradley Rubenstein, Bryan Crockett, Eva Sutton, and Marta de Menezes.

Marveling at the Universe

While numerous contemporary artists critique, parody, or sound the alarm about scientific activities, other artists celebrate how science has added to our knowledge of the universe and made us feel awe at its beauty and vastness. This attitude toward science has an ancient lineage, at least as we imagine our forebears' motives. For example, on the basis of empirical observations of the temporal rhythm of the lunar cycle, we now see Stonehenge as a combination of planetarium, public sculpture, and sacred site. Perhaps we romanticize the emotions our prehistoric forbearers might have felt as they contemplated the place of their known world within a larger, mysterious cosmos. Nevertheless, humans seem motivated to make sense of the universe by both a curiosity about how things work and an appreciation of beauty.

Artist Josiah McElheny shows this dual concern in his sculpture *An End to Modernity* (2005) [7-13]. The form of the artwork embodies two distinct concepts. First, the large (twelve-by-fifteen-foot) glass and metal sculpture resembles an over-the-top 1960s chandelier, and its starburst form specifically pays homage to the historic chandeliers at New York City's Metropolitan Opera house. Second, McElheny's sculpture represents the big bang theory of the origin of the universe as we know it today. According to this theory, an explosive expansion of space in all directions changed the universe from an impenetrable, opaque dark mass to star-lit transparency. An aluminum orb at the sculpture's center represents the earliest stage of this transformation. The silvery rods that radiate like spokes from the sphere have different lengths that represent the relative passage of time. Bursting from their ends are glass clusters representing clusters of galaxies that formed during later phases of the big bang. Thus the outer periphery of the sculpture represents the universe now. As an abstraction *An End to Modernity* encapsulates our current scientific understanding of the universe and at the same time inspires us with its elegant form.

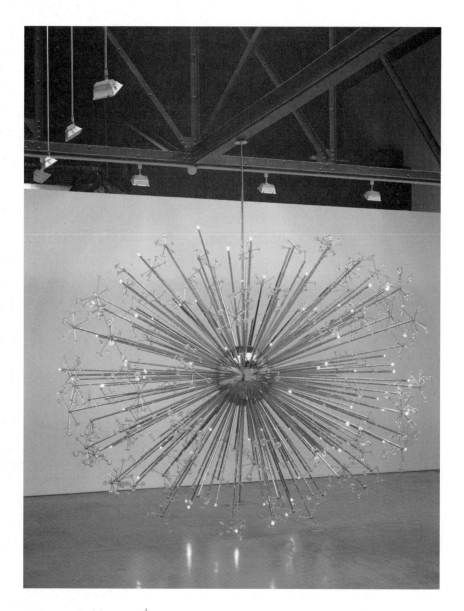

7-13 Josiah McElheny | *An End to Modernity*, **2005**

Chrome-plated aluminum, electric lighting, hand blown glass, steel cable and rigging, 16 feet diameter
ARG#MJ2005-001
Photo by Tom Powell
©Josiah McElheny, courtesy of Andrea Rosen Gallery, NY

PROFILE: Patricia Piccinini

Patricia Piccinini represented Australia at the 2003 Venice Biennale with an installation entitled *We Are Family* that consisted of six sculptural groupings. One of these groupings, *The Young Family* (2002) [7-14], shows a sowlike creature lying on her side while three small offspring nestle and suckle at her exposed teats. *The Young Family* is a convincingly realistic construction of silicon, acrylic resin, and mixed mediums.[32] These creatures resemble no ordinary breed of barnyard animal but incorporate a jarring combination of traits: human eyes and flesh (including wrinkles, moles, and sagging flesh), primate arms and hands, and snout, floppy ears,

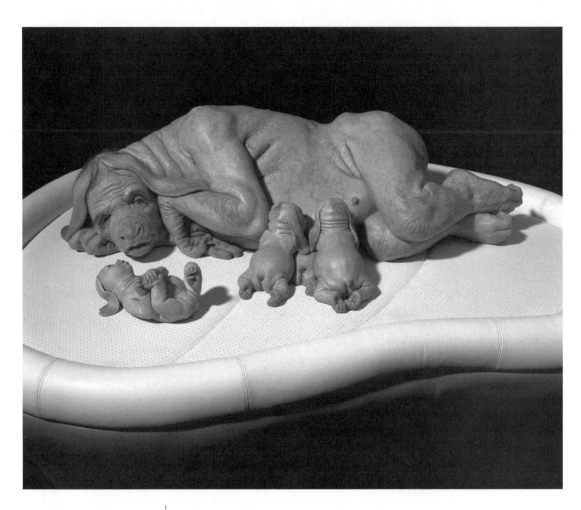

7-14 Patricia Piccinini │ *The Young Family*, **2002**

Silicon, polyurethane, human hair, leather, plywood 80 x 150 x 110cm
Courtesy of the artist

and a stubby tail of uncertain animal origins. With eyes brimming with feeling, the weary-looking mother appears disturbingly self-conscious; she is a sentient being occupying a body invented in a laboratory.

Piccinini has gained international attention for her highly realistic silicon-based sculptures, as well as videos and digitally manipulated photographs that show a menagerie of unnerving and intelligent-looking creatures that appear to be hybrids of humans and other animals. These artworks provocatively refer to *transgenics*, a rapidly growing field of research that involves combining genetic material from different sources to create plants, animals, and other organisms with modified or new traits. Bioengineering using recombinant DNA technology gives researchers the potential of pushing the evolutionary process in new directions (beyond ensuring the survival of the fittest). Transgenic research experiments proceed at a pace much faster than natural evolution and provide strategies for melding the characteristics of different organisms, including different species. The potential of using this scientific tool to engineer new life forms raises urgent moral and philosophical questions, especially when human genetic material is involved. Piccinini's transgenic creatures visually fracture the mental categories that keep humans and other species distinct and separate. They challenge the basic belief in a common, inviolable human identity, which is one of the last bastions of *essentialism*—the belief that members of a group, in this case the human species, share unchanging traits that define all members as one and separate them from all other creatures. Instead, as scholar Kim Toffoletti noted, Piccinini's imagery, with its seamless fusing of human and animal, "raises the fundamental question of what constitutes identity, difference, and being in a posthuman age."[33]

Piccinini steers clear of making polemical pronouncements, but her sculptures visualize scenarios that have revolutionary implications. They not only challenge us to reconsider what it means to be human, but reopen the issue of fundamental rights tied to human identity. Since the Enlightenment, this issue had seemed to be resolved, both scientifically and philosophically (although not politically in every society)—every human being, of any status, had the same worth and was entitled to the same basic rights. But what if we live in a world that includes semihumans? As people, we have no taboos against eating many species of animals, we force animals to do work for us, we use their fur and skin in clothing, and we confine them for our convenience. Would we do similar things to beings that are part human? Use them to perform household chores? Breed them to create a supply of biological organs that could be transplanted into humans? Even eat creatures like the transgenics in Piccinini's *The Young Family*? Would we grant them some human rights but not others and give them limited political power? And what if they rebelled against being used for these "human" purposes?

In her series *Nature's Little Helpers* (2004–05), Piccinini invented several new species that were designed hypothetically to assist humans in various ways. Some of these transgenics supposedly were created with the benevolent intention of protecting real-life endangered species, although, as Piccinini stated, "There is a clear paradox in the work in that it suggests that we intervene to fix a situation caused by our intervention in the first place." [34][Piccinini imagined other helpers that were designed to provide care for human offspring, such as the doglike creature with a humanoid face in *Undivided* (2004) [color plate 16], who protectively cuddles a pajama-clad human child in a small bed. The weird creature is simultaneously in the process of birthing other small creatures that emerge from pouches along its spine. Piccinini stated that we should consider "our relationship with the things we create, in this case my helper creatures." She added, "I am as interested in the emotional outcomes of such transformations as I am in the conceptual or ethical."[35] The question arises, What would be the fate of these transgenic bodyguards once their purpose was achieved? Piccinini uncovers the ethical and emotional complexities that underlie our relationships to genetically engineered animals and suggests that scientists who create new life forms and release them to become part of the ecosystem of the earth have both "parental" and social responsibilities.

The emotional impact of Piccinini's sculptures comes from their verisimilitude: we almost accept them as actual flesh and blood. Piccinini's believable visualizations are examples of *hyperrealism* in art: the artist employs such meticulous craftsmanship and incredible detail in rendering textures and colors that the artworks convince us of a nonexistent reality. Piccinini's artworks connect with the ideas of the French cultural theorist Jean Baudrillard, who maintained that technologically advanced cultures create many hyperreal *simulations* of things that do not exist. Baudrillard argued that viewers of an endless array of simulations lose their ability to separate reality from fantasy. We react emotionally to Piccinini's transgenics precisely because of their hyperreality; we relate to them as real creatures in their own right rather than as artistic representations. And as Piccinini creates more and more hyperreal visualizations of fantastic life forms that biotechnology may usher in, we also start to see them as normal. As such images are circulated more and more widely, seeing becomes believing.

Piccinini's hyperreal simulations blur the line between fiction and reality and bring a fantastic, and morally perplexing, future closer. As we collectively forge a new world, her art seems to advise us to be prepared to confront and embrace the strange—the strangely familiar, the strangely touching, even the strangely beautiful.

Patricia Piccinini was born in Sierra Leone in 1965 and emigrated to Australia in 1972 with her family. She studied economic history before enrolling in art school. Today she lives and works in Melbourne.

Eduardo Kac is internationally known for his work as a *bio artist*, meaning that he adopts the same tools and techniques as scientists working in biology and other life sciences. Bio artists manipulate actual biological and genetic materials to make art. In this profile, we discuss a few of this interdisciplinary artist's bio-art projects that examine relationships among humans, animals, other organisms, machines, and communications systems, including the Internet.

Kac adopted the term *transgenic art* in 1998 to describe artists' appropriation of "wet lab" bioengineering techniques from genetics and cell biology to create transgenic organisms that are exhibited as art. Kac's own transgenic art projects resonate powerfully because the bioengineered organisms he produces do not exist solely as artworks; they are living organisms (which may live only as long as the artwork is on view). Unlike the simulations of life forms manufactured by Patricia Piccinini (the subject of the previous profile), Kac's bio-art creations are truly alive.

Kac defines transgenic art as "a new art form based on the use of genetic engineering techniques to transfer synthetic genes to an organism or to transfer natural genetic material from one species into another, to create unique living beings."[36] In his transgenic works, Kac taps into our curiosity as well as our anxiety about the forces that are being unleashed as scientists experiment with creating new life forms. Scientists are bioengineering organisms ranging from bacteria to higher mammals. They are creating transgenic products that include industrial enzymes; pharmaceuticals; agricultural crops, such as golden rice; and transgenic animals, such as lab mice that are used to study disease and GloFish that are sold as pets. No one fully can predict where such research will take us.

Kac named his interactive transgenic installation *Genesis* (1999) after the first book of the Old Testament, the sacred scripture of the Hebrews that makes up the first half of the Christian Bible. The opening chapters of Genesis tell the story of the divine creation of the world, including God's creation of the first humans, Adam and Eve. Kac based the installation on a sentence from the biblical text that reads: "Let man have dominion over the fish of the sea, and over the fowl of the air, and over every living thing that moves upon the earth." The sentence proclaims a worldview that places man at the top of a hierarchy, with supremacy over everything else alive on earth. Kac's *Genesis* challenges that message of human dominion in an evolving installation that mixes languages and codes, biological materials, telecommunications, genetic engineering, human agency, and chance. Commissioned by Ars Electronica in 1999, Kac's *Genesis* has been exhibited in almost forty different venues over the past ten years.[37]

Kac created a new synthetic "artist's gene" (as he calls it) for *Genesis* through a process of successive translations: he translated the English sentence (itself already a translation from ancient Hebrew) into the dots and dashes of Morse code, then converted the Morse code into the four chemical bases of genetics—A, C, G, and T—using a conversion principle he devised. Kac uses the resulting DNA sequence of base pairs to create the synthetic gene, which he mixes into bacteria, thus producing a transgenic combination of synthetic and natural genes. During an installation, Kac displays the transgenic bacteria in a petri dish under ultraviolet lights. Gallery visitors, as well as remote participants who are linked via the Internet and a Webcam, can manipulate light levels, thus causing actual, biological mutations in the multiplying bacteria. If the now mutated DNA sequences are translated back into English, the sentence changes meaning in unpredictable ways. A sculptural diptych that is included in the installation shows this process of translation and its reversal carved in granite stones that mimic the Rosetta Stone [7-15]. Kac's *Genesis* suggests that potentially anyone can alter life; at the same time, human agency causes the mutations that destroy words such as *man* in the biblical proclamation.

The stakes rise when genetic manipulation is practiced on higher mammals. With *GFP Bunny* (2000) Kac attempted to give visual embodiment to the ethically controversial practice of manipulating the genome of a mammal. He commissioned scientists in a biology lab in France to inject the fertilized egg of an albino rabbit with a GFP (green fluorescent protein) gene from a type of jellyfish. (This technology already was widely used by research scientists for a range of purposes, such as producing glowing mice used to study embryo morphology.) The rabbit that was born, named Alba, fluoresces green under a specific blue light.

7-15 **Eduardo Kac** | *Encryption Stones*, **2001**
Laser-etched granite (diptych), 20" X 30" (50 X 75cm) each
Collection of Richard Langdale

In Kac's mind *GFP Bunny* was more than the individual bioengineered animal as a form of aesthetic object that occasionally glowed; the artwork encompassed Alba as a living transgenic social subject who would be integrated into an ongoing network of relationships with other animals, the human public, and the artist. Kac's intention was that he and Alba would live together in an art gallery for a brief period as an installation and then he would bring Alba home to Chicago to reside permanently with Kac and his family, but this plan was thwarted when the lab decided not to release Alba.

With his project, *The Eighth Day* (2001) [color plates 17 and 18], Kac moved beyond the concept of introducing a transgenic creature such as Alba into an existing social environment. Now he imagined an entire ecosystem of transgenic organisms cohabiting an environment together. *The Eighth Day* was a temporary bio-art version of an environment in which every living thing had been bioengineered. The project came to fruition at Arizona State University (ASU) in fall 2001 after two years of collaboration between Kac and ASU developmental biologists, engineers, artists, and specialists in interactive media. The centerpiece of *The Eighth Day*, exhibited in a darkened room, was a clear acrylic hemisphere four feet in diameter that functioned as a large terrarium. Inside it, a variety of transgenic organisms lived together for the duration of the exhibition: amoebas, tobacco leaves, zebra fish, and mice that were all bioluminescent because they had been artificially bioengineered to have the GFP jellyfish gene, like Alba. The genetic modification was relatively simple but visually dramatic.

In the *Eighth Day* Kac also incorporated a "biobot." Part machine, part organism, the biobot had electronic "eyes" that functioned as a camera and a colony of GFP amoebas inserted inside its "head," giving it a semblance of a primitive biological brain. As the amoebas mutated during the exhibition, the biobot altered its pattern of motion. Visitors to the gallery could peer through the dome or bend down for a closer look through light filters attached to the sides. Remote viewers on the Web could see inside the dome through the biobot's camera eyes or gaze at the bioengineered environment from outside via digital cameras in the gallery.

Dan Collins, an intermedia artist who helped supervise *The Eighth Day* for ASU, wrote that this striking visual display showing very different organisms all bioengineered with the same foreign gene provided "partial proof that we are all, finally, connected. In point of fact, these various organisms could not 'accept' the jellyfish gene unless they were fundamentally produced out of the same chemical building blocks. This is not fiction; this is concrete fact." Collins argued that the work also contains a paradox: because the green glow of the different organisms marks them visually as transgenic (and thus serves as an "index of alterity," in his words), we human onlookers can cast the living organisms in the role of the Other and thereby retain our sense of difference from them. [38]

Kac's transgenic projects have a powerful impact. They provoke us to consider the differences and commonalities of art and science, the excitement an artist or scientist feels in creating something new (or "playing God"), the morality of experimenting with living things, and the stunning idea that all forms of life, including new transgenic organisms that are created by human design, are the same at the most basic level.

Eduardo Kac was born in 1962 in Rio de Janeiro, Brazil. His early career unfolded in Brazil in the 1980s. Since then, he has spent many years in Chicago, first as a student and then on the faculty at the School of the Art Institute of Chicago.

Notes

1. Stephen Wilson, *Information Arts: Intersections of Art, Science, and Technology* (Cambridge, Mass.: MIT Press, 2002), p. 55.

2. For a timeline of discoveries and developments in genetics, see Ricki Lewis with Bernard Possidente, "A Short History of Genetics and Genomics," in Marvin Heiferman and Carole Kismaric, *Paradise Now: Picturing the Genetic Revolution* (Saratoga Springs, NY: Tang Museum at Skidmore College, 2001), pp. 110–115. An exhibition catalog.

3. Quotations are from the artist's talk on June 24, 2007, at the Indianapolis Museum of Art in conjunction with the opening of Easterson's one-person exhibition *Nature Holds My Camera*.

4. Extensive information about *Stellar Axis* is available at the project website: http://www.stellaraxis.com.

5. In developing the definition of science and related sections, the authors are indebted to the suggestions of Professor Alan Jones (School of Engineering and Technology, Indiana University-Purdue University, Indianapolis), and to Dr. James D. Robertson (a geophysicist in Fort Worth, Texas) for his insightful editing and additions.

6. This is a simplification of what, in real scientific projects, can be organized as an extremely complicated iterative process.

7. The polling process and results by country are explained in JoAnn Wypijewski, ed., *Painting by Numbers; Komar and Melamid's Guide to Art* (New York: Farrar, Straus, and Giroux, 1997). Information about a World Wide Web version of the *People's Choice* project is available online at Dia's website: http://www.diacenter.org/km/usa/usa.html.

8. Steven Shapin, "What Else Is New? How Uses, Not Innovations, Drive Human Technology," *New Yorker*, May 14, 2007, p. 148.

9. More information about the Hyperbolic Crochet Coral Reef Project can be found at the project's website: http://www.theiff.org.

10. Quoted in Heiferman and Kismaric, *Paradise Now*, p. 70.

11. Jonathan Moreno, "Science Progress, the Phrase and the Title: What We're All About," 2007, Science Progress, http://www.scienceprogress.org/2007/10/science-progress-the-phrase-and-the-title (accessed April 5, 2008).

12. Portions of the remainder of chapter 7, Science, appeared previously in Jean Robertson, "Art on the Edge of Science," in Betsy Stirratt, ed., *Human Nature* (Bloomington: School of Fine Arts Gallery, Indiana University, 2007), pp. 7–25. An exhibition catalog. The material has been revised for this book and is used with the permission of the School of Fine Arts Gallery.

13. Thomas Kuhn, *The Structure of Scientific Revolutions* (Chicago: University of Chicago Press, 1962).

14. Laura Steward Heon, *Unnatural Science* (North Adams, Mass.: MASS MoCA, 2000), p. 12. An exhibition catalog.

15. As quoted in Claire Dederer, "Looking for Inspiration in the Melting Ice," *New York Times*, September 23, 2007, Arts and Leisure section. Lucy Lippard has championed many causes in her decades as a critic and curator. In addition to supporting art that addresses ecological concerns, Lippard has long recognized art that gives voice to women and minorities.

16. Information about the prolonged bioterrorism investigation, which has been a nightmare for Steven Kurtz, can be found online at http://www.caedefensefund.org. Robert Ferrell, a professor of human genetics who collaborated with Kurtz, was also a target of the investigation. Ferrell, who is gravely ill, pled guilty to lesser charges in fall 2007 to avoid a lengthy trial.

17. Marita Sturken and Lisa Cartwright, *Practices of Looking: An Introduction to Visual Culture* (Oxford and New York: Oxford University Press, 2001), p. 298.

18. Quoted in Heiferman and Kismaric, *Paradise Now*, p. 66.

19. Suzanne Anker and Dorothy Nelkin, *The Molecular Gaze: Art in the Genetic Age* (Cold Spring Harbor, N.Y.: Cold Spring Harbor Laboratory Press, 2004), p. 187.

20. For more information about Vanouse's *Latent Figure Protocol*, see the artist's website, http://www.contrib.andrew.cmu.edu/~pv28/electart.html.

21. Sturken and Cartwright, *Practices of Looking*, p. 293.

22. Artists who respond to museum practices are also discussed in chapter 5, Place.

23. Irene Hofmann, *Weird Science: A Conflation of Art and Science* (Bloomfield Hills, MI: Cranbrook Art Museum, 1999), p. 16. An exhibition catalog.

24. Christoph Cox, "Of Humans, Animals and Monsters," in Nato Thompson, *Becoming Animal* (North Adams, Mass.: MASS MoCA, 2005), p. 20. An exhibition catalog.

25. Ibid., p. 23.

26. Bettyann Holtzmann Kevles and Marilyn Nissenson, "Picturing DNA: An Interview with Suzanne Anker," *Genomic Art*, July 23, 2006, JGS, Inc., http://www.genomicart.org/genome~Anker.htm (accessed April 7, 2008).

27. Artist's statement in Heiferman and Kismaric, *Paradise Now*, p. 56.

28. David Kremers, 2003, *Wonder/Controversy: An Experimental Book* (Pasadena: Biological Imaging Center, California Institute of Technology), p. 3, http://quad.bic.caltech.edu/~kremersd/wonder/start.html (accessed April 7, 2008).

29. Heon, *Unnatural Science*, p. 21.

30. Artist's statement in Heiferman and Kismaric, *Paradise Now*, p. 64.

31. In chapter 3, The Body, we discuss the increasing appearance in new art of hybrid bodies, including cyborgs and mutants.

32. The sculptor Sam Jinks, who usually works on the fabrication of Piccinini's sculptures, assists the artist in achieving the high degree of realism.

33. Kim Toffoletti, *Cyborgs and Barbie Dolls: Feminism, Popular Culture and the Posthuman Body* (London and New York: I. B. Tauris, 2007), p. 134. Toffoletti is particularly interested in the issue of gender difference and "its potential dissolution in a world of new biotechnologies and reproductive practices."

34. Interview with the artist in *Becoming Animal: Contemporary Art in the Animal Kingdom* (North Adams, Mass.: MASS MoCA, 2005), p. 104. An exhibition catalog.

35. Artist's statement in *Patricia Piccinini: Nature's Little Helpers* (New York: Robert Miller Gallery, 2005), unpaginated. An exhibition catalog.

36. Eduardo Kac, 2008, Transgenic Art. http://www.ekac.org/transgenic.html (accessed May 11, 2008). Originally published in *Leonardo Electronic Almanac* 6 (December 1998).

37. The coauthors have seen *Genesis* twice—at the Henry Art Gallery, Seattle, in 2002 and at the School of Fine Arts Gallery, Indiana University, Bloomington, in 2007.

38. Dan Collins, "Tracking Chimeras: *The Eighth Day*," in Sheilah Britton and Dan Collins, eds., *The Eighth Day: The Transgenic Art of Eduardo Kac* (Tempe: Institute for Studies in the Arts, Arizona State University, 2003), pp. 100–101.

Spirituality

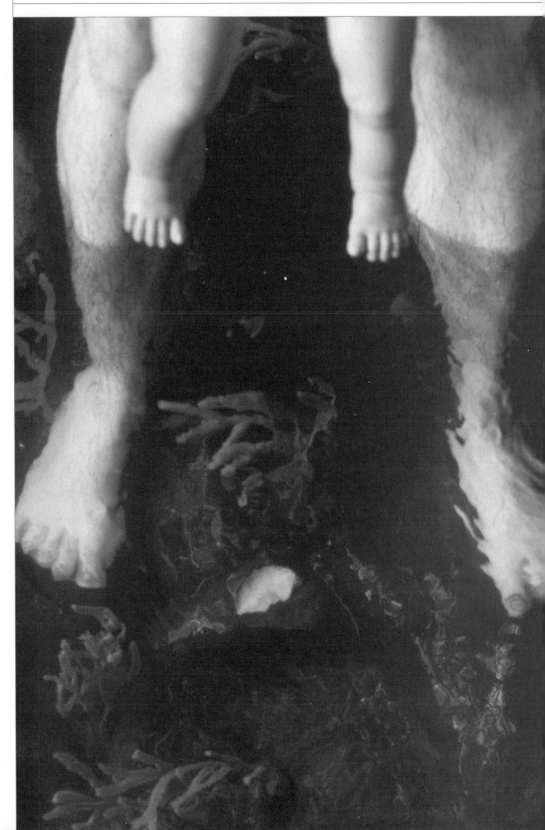

Detail of 8-7

CHAPTER EIGHT

Spirituality

This chapter—focusing on spirituality—explores arguably the most contentious thematic topic that our book raises.[1] With spirituality, we focus on a theme that many in the art world (and from all walks of life) call into question at the most bedrock level. For doubters, spirituality in general and religions of any denomination may be dismissed as outmoded patterns of thinking, belief systems that were formulated to provide teleological explanations and were attempts to control the future, impart moral values, and uphold power relationships.

Among the contested issues swirling around spiritual matters, one of the most prominent in the United States during the period under discussion has been the prickly debates that pit a belief in divine creation against a belief in scientific models. The debates are often framed in such a manner as to make opposing positions seem mutually exclusive. In our opinion, artist Fred Tomaselli has taken up the issue and offers an artistic alternative (albeit one that will not fit within all viewers' beliefs) in his enormous multimedia work *Untitled (Expulsion)* (2000) [color plate 19]. The work includes, in the lower right corner, a painted version of the Judeo-Christian motif of Adam and Eve, presented in the Bible as the first man and woman. Tomaselli borrows the pose of the figures from a fresco by the early Italian Renaissance painter Masaccio. The surface of the artwork is covered with a thick, glossy coating of resin that is reminiscent of the heavily varnished look of old master paintings. Significantly, Tomaselli depicts the male and female figures in the process of their expulsion from the Garden of Eden, an episode that is depicted repeatedly in the history of Western art. Adam and Eve have fallen from a state of grace and are being driven from Paradise to make their way on Earth. In Tomaselli's version of the decisive event—the start of earthly human history—the pair is expelled in a blinding flash of eternal light, as shown by a complicated starburst pattern that covers a jet-black night sky. According to Gregory Volk, "A concentration of energies on the left made of small paint marks hovering above real leaves (the ensemble is Tomaselli's rendition of God) gives rise to this patterned explosion. . . . Everything occurs everywhere."[2]

Tomaselli's artwork appears to meld together a religious story of creation with a symbolic representation of key aspects of the latest scientific theorization of both the origin of the universe (as we know it in its physical manifestation) and the creation of species by evolution. In theories of the big bang, the mass and energy of the entire universe exploded outward from a single monumentally concentrated point. Tomaselli's artwork shows these lines of force, light, and energy radiating outward and transforming (evolving) into the myriad forms of nature that we know. The last to appear is the pair of humans, in the extreme lower right corner.

The emotional impact on the figures of Adam and Eve is a compelling combination of awe, grief, and vulnerability (note how Eve, and only Eve, covers her sex with her hands). The figures have turned their backs on the beauty unfolding around them and propelling them forward. The entire universe, as depicted from its point of origin outward, appears as one instantaneous *now*; in addition, the image diagrams a temporal dimension as time flows forward, away from the beginning flash.

In the five centuries prior to the period under discussion, the vast majority of artworks made by artists in the West, like Tomaselli's, drew on the tradition of Western art history, coupled with the traditional iconography of Christianity if the artwork was to reference religion at all. Since 1980, concurrent with the dramatic increase of culturally diverse artistic voices, we find many more examples of contemporary artists working in the West who draw from a much wider range of artistic and religious traditions. Shahzia Sikander, for example, often combines imagery drawn from both Muslim and Hindu iconography, along with abstract and imaginary motifs in her paintings [8-1]. Born in Pakistan, Sikander has concentrated much of her artistic practice on creating superbly crafted, contemporary versions of miniature painting, a style that reflects her Pakistani heritage. Sikander mixes these disparate sources to construct a springboard for addressing a range of problematic cultural issues, such as intolerance of homosexuality.[3]

Artworks that explore aspects of spirituality include, in addition to those that focus on contested issues, an array of works that signal an undiluted sense of faith and optimism. Visitors to the Royal Academy of Arts in London in the fall of 2000 encountered examples of both doubt and belief as they found themselves looking at works by thirteen of the foremost contemporary artists in the world. The curators invited each artist to fill one gallery with work on the theme of the Apocalypse. Taking the book of Revelation (a Christian text written almost two thousand years ago and attributed to Saint John the Divine) as its literary godfather, the exhibit, titled Apocalypse, presented visions of beauty and horror. It was not mere coincidence that the exhibit coincided with the first year in the new millennium.

Many of the artists' contributions to Apocalypse explored specific spiritual ideas and issues. Mariko Mori, born in Japan, showed her *Dream Temple* (1999), a complex, multipart artwork combining computer graphics, 3-D surround sound, architecture, and virtual reality. Visitors who entered the octagonal structure of the temple, modeled after a temple completed in Japan in 739 A.D., found themselves engulfed by a luminous video projection that covered all the surrounding surfaces. Mori's imagery, including abstract force fields of light interspersed with mystical scenes in nature (a forest, a waterfall), offered viewers a glimpse of enlightenment, a taste of the eternal present that the artist believes is available to us now via cutting-edge technology.

In addition to Mori's optimistic creation, Apocalypse also confronted viewers with critiques of contemporary religion and gut-wrenching visions of a world gone awry. Jake and Dinos Chapman, from England, displayed *Hell*, featuring hundreds of tiny victims caught up in a hellish scene of Nazi brutality. The Chapmans' work of art

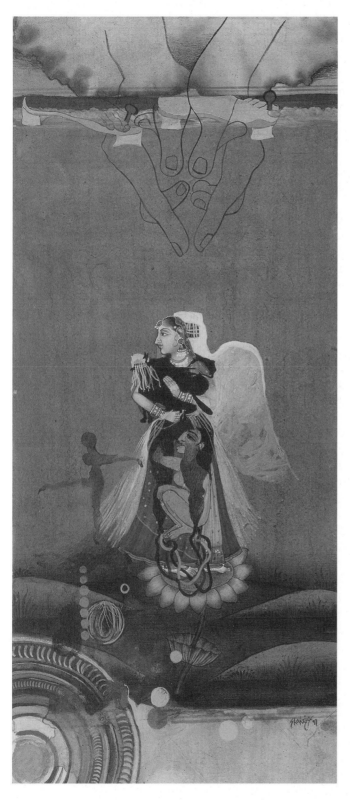

Order I, **1996–97**

Vegetable color, dry pigment, watercolor, tea on
hand-prepared Wasli paper, 17 1/2 x 12 inches
Courtesy of Brent Sikkema, NYC

condenses the history of concentration camps into a metaphor for apocalyptic horror and the damnation that humans have heaped on each other.

That the possibilities for interpretation of both Mori's and the Chapmans' works are multileveled and open ended is a key aspect of the power and mysterious delight they provide as works of art. The Chapmans' *Hell*, for instance, raises intriguing philosophical issues: why and how can we as viewers take pleasure in looking at a work of art that denotes pain and suffering in others? Does it change the equation if the figures in the artwork are fictional or represent factual people?[4] At what, if any, level do we insist on a congruency between the morality represented in a work of art and the morality that we subscribe to in the real world of flesh and blood?

A particularly controversial piece in the show was Italian-born Maurizio Cattelan's *La Nona Ora (The Ninth Hour)* (1999) [8-2]. Cattelan's work consisted of a red-carpeted exhibition gallery, empty except for a life-size and lifelike sculpture of the pope lying on the floor, clutching the cross. The pontiff is pinned beneath a meteorite roughly half his size; by the evidence of shards of glass nearby, the stone from outer space appears to have fallen on him through the skylight overhead. Cattelan's meteorite appears like a divine message, perhaps sent to awaken us to the fallibility of organized religion, or, paradoxically, could the meteorite signify that God is not dead (contrary to the claims of secular thinkers): who else would have such miraculous aim? To knowledgeable viewers, Cattelan's meteorite could also symbolize the Western art world's predominantly critical stance toward the artistic expression of sincere belief in any organized religion.

Collective doubt is a key ingredient in our present cultural condition. As a society, we are inclined to doubt the singularity of grand narratives, including religion and spirituality. In the preceding chapter, we discussed the doubts that the public and contemporary artists have raised concerning scientific progress. In the case of science, however, doubt almost never results in total disbelief. In the case of spirituality, doubt may lead to total disbelief: disbelief in a deity, disbelief in any divine forces in the universe.

Yet, spirituality and religion (as manifested in diverse forms around the globe) exert an undeniable influence on world affairs and on everyday personal life. Throughout the three decades that this book examines, wars with religious differences at their core have been waged in many regions of the world. The moral debates surrounding many of the subjects of potential scientific research (such as stem cell research) involve clashing worldviews involving religious beliefs and belief in the neutrality of science.

Today the majority of Americans still espouse fundamental spiritual beliefs. A nationwide survey, conducted in 2007 by the Pew Forum on Religion and Public Life, summarized responses to survey questions: "absolutely believes in God" (71 percent of U.S. adults) and "believes many religions can lead to eternal life" (70 percent of U.S. adults).[5] Residents of many other countries might respond with even higher rates of consistency—avowing fundamental beliefs in spiritual truths and subscribing to a specific religious doctrine.

Spirituality and Religion

Definitions of religion and spirituality vary widely in contemporary culture. We reserve the term *religion* for institutionalized formal practices with a recorded history, established traditions, and shared rituals and doctrines. Common features of most religions are the belief in an immortal divine being (a deity) or multiple divine beings and the

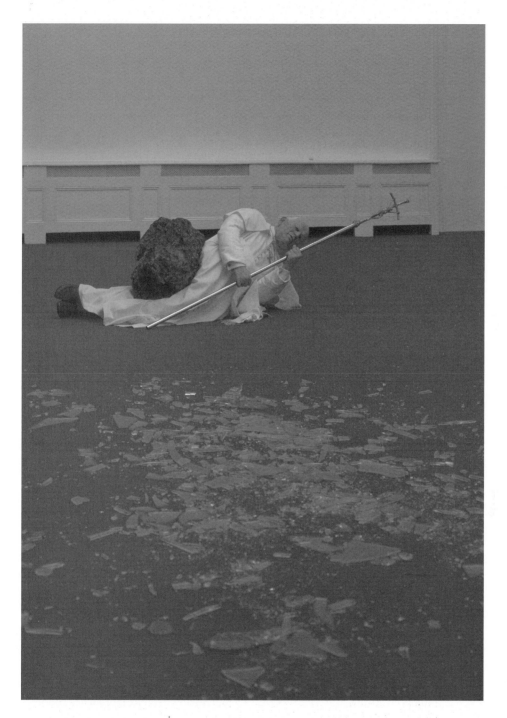

8-2 Maurizio Cattelan | *La Nona Ora, (The Ninth Hour),* **1999**

Mixed media, Lifesize

Courtesy: Marian Goodman Gallery, New York

belief that the deity (or deities) has some degree of influence over reality. Long-standing organized religions include Christianity, Judaism, Buddhism, Hinduism, and Islam. We use the word *spiritual* to refer to the common yearning to belong to something greater than the self, the desire to probe the source of life and the nature of death, and the acknowledgment of ineffable, intangible forces at work in the universe. People who do not participate in a formal religion may nevertheless recognize a powerful spiritual dimension to their life. As curator Susan Sollins put it, "whether or not we participate in formal religious practice, the human condition seems to demand that we explore the spiritual, question our existence and a possible afterlife; we ponder our connections to the world around us, and examine experiences that seem to be inexplicable."[6]

A Short History

If we look back through history, we discover that art and spirituality have had a strong bond throughout human existence, that they have frequently been intertwined and mutually reinforcing. Spiritual art has addressed humanity's most profound needs and life's greatest mysteries; beliefs about death and an afterlife, the nature of the universe and humanity's place in it, and the moral codes that guide private and public behavior have all been explored in art. Art has told the stories of specific religious traditions, given visual form to ideas of divinity, and provided devotional objects and settings (churches, synagogues, mosques, temples) for religious worship and rituals. Ancient examples include the gigantic carved Buddhas at Polonnarua in Sri Lanka, Hagia Sophia in Istanbul, the Mayan pyramids at Chichen Itza in Mexico, and the Egyptian pyramids at Giza.

In the West, Christianity dominated the production of art from the third to the seventeenth century, and the iconography of Christian art (based on stories from the Old and New Testaments, especially the life of Christ and the Crucifixion) is familiar to many viewers of art, whether or not they are Christians. Other great world religions, notably Hinduism and Buddhism, have likewise relied on art to portray gods, holy people, and religious narratives. Judaism and Islam have historically been opposed to images (icons) made for religious purposes. Instead, the religious art of these faiths has focused on abstract symbolism and the embellishment of religious texts through calligraphy and other means.

Different religious belief systems have shaped the art of different civilizations in ways that often contrast dramatically. For instance, some religious traditions and practices are more rational and some more mystical. The art of the former tended to instruct the faithful in a logical, easily understood way, while the art of the latter provided arcane symbols or ecstatic visions that were meant to overwhelm viewers with a sense of mystery and emotion. Moreover, no religion has remained static; one religion can emphasize different artistic approaches in different historical circumstances. For example, the schism that divided Christianity into Catholic and Protestant churches in the sixteenth century was reflected in the contrasting artistic approaches found in Catholic and Protestant countries of Europe during the Baroque era. Nor is any religion monolithic. There are many sects within each of the major religions, each of which has its own interpretations of their faith, including ideas about the role of art in religion.

In mainstream cultures in the West, from the Enlightenment onward, the worlds of art and of religion grew apart. Many secular institutions that supported and exhibited art arose, and the leadership of churches as patrons of visual art declined. The Constitution of the new United States of America, through the First Amendment (ratified in 1791), mandated the separation of church and state; thus governments in the United States have never promoted religious art. Moreover, beginning with the arrival of the Puritans in New England, North America served as a haven for religious groups who were fleeing persecution elsewhere; as a result, tolerance of religious differences is built into the social fabric of the country. Historically in the United States, the most openly identified religious artists have tended to come from the margins of society or from the ranks of folk artists.

Philosophical doubts about a divinely created universe and skepticism about the validity or relevance of organized religions were voiced openly in the nineteenth century and culminated in German philosopher Friedrich Nietzsche's famous pronouncement "God is dead" (made in 1882). At the same time in the West, increased exposure to religions from other parts of the world inspired new beliefs. Some alienated individuals became atheists, while others turned to religions that borrowed from many traditions or adopted beliefs that were anchored in nature, which was seen as a vital, pantheistic force.

The philosophical and literary concept of *the sublime*, first popularized in Europe in the eighteenth century by the writings of Edmund Burke, gave a name to the quasi-religious veneration of nature.[7] Burke distinguished the philosophical concepts of the beautiful and the sublime; according to Burke, the sublime was a powerful sensation felt by the viewer in the presence of the vast—a feeling that combines a sense of awe, horror, and supreme aesthetic pleasure. Following Burke's influence, the term *the sublime* began to be used for any experience that induced awe or terror, overwhelming the mind and senses, much as a religious fervor can overwhelm believers. The sublime reaction was induced by extraordinary and grand phenomena. When the concept was attached to nature, the sublime described an awed reaction to viewing mountain vistas, vast oceans, extraordinary thunderstorms, blizzards, magnificent sunsets, and the like.

Subsequent to Burke, German philosophers, including Immanuel Kant and Arthur Schopenhauer, further refined the concept of the sublime and its distinction from the pleasing finitude of form that characterizes beauty. Kant, for instance, emphasized the boundless magnitude of nature, beyond our ordinary capacity for human comprehension, as a quality in inducing the feeling of the sublime. In the context of analyzing video work by Bill Viola (see the profile), Cynthia Freeland employed the concept of the sublime in the Kantian sense, as follows: "when we are faced by something vast or powerful like a mountain range or storm, what Kant calls our faculties of sensibility and imagination become overwhelmed. They cannot take it all in. But on the other hand, we have another cognitive faculty, reason, which feels uplifted by the experience. Reason, which is also the source of morality and freedom for humans, somehow identifies with the vast object. But this does not involve actual cognition, which is done by yet another faculty, understanding. No faculty is adequate to the sublime experience. It is as if instead reason makes an intuitive leap to embrace the sublime object without actually conceptualizing or recognizing it—and we ride a resultant surge of energy."

While the specific concept of the sublime received relatively little attention from the middle of the nineteenth to the middle of the twentieth centuries, it again came under scrutiny in the past few decades. French philosopher Jean-François Lyotard, for example, considered the sublime in his writings in the 1970s and 1980s. Lyotard, whose critique of the universal claims of the meta-narratives of culture impacted the development of postmodernism in both Europe and the United States, considered the sublime as an important example that demonstrated the limitations of rationality.

In nineteenth-century America, belief in the sublime was transposed into *transcendentalism*, whose adherents believed in an ideal spiritual reality that transcended the material world.[8] This philosophy was associated with writers, including Henry David Thoreau and Ralph Waldo Emerson, who viewed nature, especially the American wilderness, as closer to God than more civilized places. American "earth artists" in the 1960s and 1970s continued this transcendentalist strain of reverence for the natural world. Some of them created site-specific outdoor works that evoked the feeling of prehistoric religious sites, such as Stonehenge in England or Serpent Mound in Ohio.

Throughout most of the twentieth century, religion in art largely went silent in Europe and the United States. If you review art histories and art criticism of the period, you do not find much use of the word *religion* until late in the century. With some exceptions, including Georges Rouault, Max Beckman, Salvador Dali, and Graham Sutherland, art with recognizable religious iconography no longer commanded the attention of the most innovative or prestigious artists. Frequently, however, notable artists continued to express metaphysical ideas, feelings about spirituality, or a yearning for a utopian future, often using a more coded or private language.[9] Scholarly and critical analyses of modern art tended to focus on the designs, colors, and techniques that artists were using and to downplay spiritual content when it was present, unless the artist was regarded as eccentric (as in the case of Marc Chagall, for example).

The most powerful refuge of spiritual art in the twentieth century was nonobjective art. Some artists who were making completely abstract works were on a quest to see if art could inspire a transcendental state akin to the sublime feeling that nature could inspire. They hoped that viewers would experience a spiritual revelation or, at least, a deeply meditative feeling while gazing at abstract surfaces or forms. Wassily Kandinsky and Barnett Newman are older examples of such artists. A more contemporary example is Brice Marden, who nudged his characteristic formalist abstractions in a spiritual direction with a series of paintings titled *Annunciation* (1978–80). The significant current of spirituality running through modern abstract art was finally highlighted and studied in 1986 in a groundbreaking and influential exhibition, The Spiritual in Art: Abstract Painting, 1890–1985, curated by Maurice Tuchman for the Los Angeles County Museum of Art, and its accompanying catalog.[10]

In recent decades in the United States, religion and art have often come head to head. The "culture wars" that erupted after 1980, for example, included protests against exhibitions with artworks that some people regarded as sacrilegious or demeaning to their religious beliefs or sacred symbols. If governmental funds were involved, protesters lobbied federal, state, and city governments to prevent the display of the art. In one notorious incident in 1989, protesters challenged the use of funds from the National Endowment for the Arts for a grant to photographer Andres Serrano, whose photograph *Piss Christ* (1987) depicted a plastic crucifix suspended in urine. A similar controversy occurred ten years later, when then-mayor of New York, Rudolph Giuliani, led the opposition to an exhibition from England at the Brooklyn Museum titled Sensation. Giuliani singled out as blasphemous Chris Ofili's *The Holy Virgin Mary* (1996), a painting of a black Madonna that incorporated balls of dried elephant dung.[11]

Widely publicized controversies such as these give the impression that contemporary art and religion are adversaries. As critic Eleanor Heartney noted: "Despite Western culture's rich tradition of great religious art, the contemporary world tends to see art and religion as enemies. Whenever the two are mentioned together, it tends to be in the context of some controversy or scandal, in which artists are accused of . . . heaping their contempt on religion. . . . And even within the art world, there seems to be considerable discomfort with the notion that faith and avant-gardism might share any common ground."[12]

Nevertheless, increasingly since the 1990s, contemporary art has openly addressed religion and spirituality, and some influential curators and critics are paying attention to this theme. Artists are again asking soul-searching questions about the meaning of life—its mysteries, miracles, and moral lessons—and art's role in the cosmos. Ahead of the curve, in her 1991 book *The Reenchantment of Art*, critic Suzi Gablik called for a spiritual and ethical renewal in American culture and for art that would support that goal. In Gablik's view, "we cannot heal the mess we have made of the world without undergoing some kind of spiritual healing."[13] Heartney is another critic with a keen interest in spiritual issues. She has written extensively about contemporary artists who were raised as Catholics, including Serrano and Ofili as well as Kiki Smith, David Wojnarowicz, Joel-Peter Witkin, Robert Gober, and Janine Antoni, and how their work is inflected with religious ideas (whether or not they continue to practice their faith). A number of significant exhibitions that included works by these and other artists signaled the new climate of acceptance of the theme of spirituality.

The reasons for the renewed interest in spiritual themes are many. For one thing, the controversy surrounding contemporary artworks that some viewers find offensive has focused attention on religious iconography in recent art. Unexpectedly, it has had the effect of making art about spiritual beliefs seem hip and avant-garde. Real-world upheavals and the migrations of large numbers of people all over the world in the past thirty years have also brought spiritual themes to the forefront as many spiritual traditions have intermingled. Moreover, as the twentieth century drew to a close, a trend toward end-of-the-millennium art surfaced; this art asked questions about the future of the planet and where we are heading as individuals, as societies, and as a species. Some artists framed their questions in a spiritual way or sought spiritual answers. The German Neo-Expressionist Anselm Kiefer, for example, explained, "I think a great deal about religion because science provides no answers."[14] We might have expected the end-of-the-millennium mood to abate once we entered the twenty-first century, but dramatic world events, including wars, terrorism, and ecological disasters, have prolonged this period of spiritual questioning.

A Few Strategies

Visual artists who seek to articulate the theme of religion or spirituality must, like artists dealing with any theme, embody their artistic vision in material forms. These forms promote potential meanings, which take shape in the minds of viewers.

Manipulating Forms, Materials, and Processes

Some forms have spiritual implications because of their repeated use in religious or sacred practices. For example, altars and shrines are traditional forms that a number of contemporary artists, such as Christian Boltanski, Pepón Osorio, and Amalia Mesa-Bains, have used to create a spiritual context. For example, Mesa-Bains, a Chicana, has made altarlike installations honoring Mexican women of the past, including the painter Frida Kahlo and the actress Dolores del Rio, as well as the Virgin of Guadalupe, a beloved religious figure in Mexico [color plate 20]. Likewise, the *reliquary*, a container for sacred relics, has been used by artists, such as Betye Saar and Paul Thek, who have turned all kinds of objects into fetishes by placing them inside reliquary forms. The *triptych*, a picture made up of three parts, is a shape that recurs throughout the history of Christian art; this form has served as a symbol of the sacred triad Father, Son, and Holy Ghost and of heaven, earth, and hell. A 1982 exhibition entitled Contemporary Triptychs, organized by David S. Rubin, documented contemporary artists engaged with the three-panel form, both flat and as a folding screen.[15] Pyramids, ziggurats, and labyrinths are additional shapes that often evoke spiritual implications.

As with particular forms, the use of certain physical materials can signal religious or spiritual content. Luxurious materials, such as gold or precious jewels, or colors with symbolic significance can indicate to the initiated that an image or object holds sacred meaning. The gold background in Chris Ofili's *The Holy Virgin Mary* recalls the traditional gold ground of Christian icon paintings, a representation of the sacred space of heaven. At the same time, Ofili's incorporation of elephant dung within the artwork sparks mixed messages. To the artist, the dung is an African symbol of fertility; to Mayor Giuliani, the dung is excrement, an insult to the beliefs of practicing Catholics.

Some artists treat natural materials as invoking the transcendent in and of themselves; they may move out into nature to create site-specific works or bring natural materials, such as rocks, honey, beeswax, and flowers, into galleries. Artists such as Cherokee Sara Bates and German Wolfgang Laib choose natural materials because of their belief in the close connection between nature and the sacred. Laib does not profess allegiance to a particular religion but has studied the writings of Jalaluddin Rumi (a thirteenth-century Sufi poet and theologian), Saint Francis of Assisi (a Christian monastic who venerated animals and nature), and Indian mystical texts from both Buddhism and Jain, all of which inform his approach to art as a kind of ascetic ritual practice deeply attuned with nature. One of Laib's forms is a "pollen square," made by carefully sifting specks of bright yellow pollen onto a square or rectangle of transparent paper covering a designated area of gallery floor (the squares can measure from five to fifteen feet on a side). Laib spends six months each year harvesting pollen from dandelions, buttercups, hazelnut trees, pine trees, and mosses, garnering just four to six jars of pollen each year for his labor. According to writer Clare Farrow, Laib's repetitive labor of pollen gathering "is not simply about material gain, nor is the repetition a negative aspect of the process, as one might imagine: for the act of doing something again and again brings about a state of equilibrium and intense concentration bordering on meditation."[16]

The incorporation of ritual, ceremony, and other forms of highly patterned behavior into the practice of art can bestow on the artist the role of high priest or shaman. German Joseph Beuys is a well-documented example of an artist in the 1960s and 1970s who welcomed this role. Beuys orchestrated a range of ritualistic activities, some involving only himself, others involving large numbers of other people. His influence is still widely felt today. Contemporary artists noted for working with ritualistic activities include, to name a few, Laib, Marina Abramovic, Tehching Hsieh, Linda Montano, and Ron Athey, although these artists would not consider themselves shamans.

Artists who create performances, videos, and installations, which involve the temporal dimension, have been especially protean in exploring ritual expression. Performances and installations that have a repetitive, meditative quality or an element of endurance and bodily ordeal are used in a cathartic manner to transport artists and viewers out of the realm of ordinary perception into a state of heightened awareness. For example, in our profile on Bill Viola, we analyze the spellbinding video/sound installation *The Crossing* (1996) [8-13 and 8-14], in which a man becomes engulfed over and over in a torrent of water on one side of the work and in fire, on the other. Typically, contemporary audiences never fully achieve a state of altered consciousness. At some point, we inevitably turn away from the artwork and back to our everyday lives. But while we stand and let the flow of sounds and images surround us, we may feel we are on the threshold of a spiritual awakening.

The use of transient forms, such as installation and performance, and unstable materials, such as plants and liquids, lend themselves to spiritual messages about the impermanence of life and the fragility of human existence. Felix Gonzalez-Torres's "spills" of piled candies, which diminish and are replenished as viewers take away candies and other candies are added, serve as death-haunted metaphors for life's passage and the value of engaging with the present. According to critic Anne Morgan, the use of transient forms and materials "reflects a spiritual truth common to many spiritual paths about the importance of direct experience, of being fully present, of fully experiencing the 'now'."[17]

The use of ephemeral materials and the performance of ritualistic activities in contemporary art relate to the transitional state that appears to be characteristic of contemporary cultures. Cultural critics have focused on how, when, where, and why whole cultures may be moving away from the acceptance of (or subjugation by) one grand worldview, such as modernism or colonialism. We live in a "post" age: the present state is in transition away from previous worldviews. The future is not yet codified, and boundaries are fuzzy and porous. Theorists use the term *liminal* to refer to this state of transition, which includes mental shifts as well as physical changes (*limen* means "threshold" in Latin). The term is borrowed from the writings of the early twentieth-century Dutch ethnologist Arnold van Gennep, who described as "liminal" the transitional phase through which a person moves when he or she is experiencing a change in status. Historically, a rite of passage, such as a wedding, is associated with a significant change in status; the ritual delivers the initiate safely from one state to another and supports the person during the mentally and physically unstable liminal stage.[18] In related fashion today, ritualistic artworks may help artists and viewers navigate the instabilities of our current cultural moment.

Manipulating Meanings and Minds

In the Western world in recent decades, there has been a revival of recognizable religious symbols, icons, and stories in art, often involving ones that borrow from the Christian tradition.[19] In using these elements, artists evoke the mythological, emotive, and psychological power of familiar stories and iconography. In British sculptor Anthony Gormley's *A Case for an Angel II* (1990), for instance, a hollow figure with huge wings attached represents the angel of the title as well as a coffin. Mike and Doug Starn's *Triple Christ* (1985–86), a photographic work, borrows from Phillipe de Champaigne's seventeenth-century painting *The Dead Christ*. The Starns sliced apart and reassembled photographs of the painting to accentuate the physical pain inflicted on Christ's body during the Crucifixion.

Looking beyond Christianity, African American artists, such as Alison Saar, have created contemporary sculptures that recall African fetishes. Shahzia Sikander (from Pakistan)[8-1], discussed earlier in the chapter, and Phyllis Bramson (from the United States) are artists who have combined representations of religious figures and icons from many religions in postmodern pastiches. Historical religious iconography has also been used ironically, or without any basis in faith, for example, in the appropriations of religious kitsch statuary by Jeff Koons.

Other artists, linking the natural world with the spiritual, have made works that recall the veneration of animals. These artists have used actual animals and animal parts as artistic material or representations of animal forms. Native American artists Jaune Quick-to-See Smith and Duane Slick completed suites of paintings and prints devoted to the coyote, an archetype of the shape-shifting trickster in some Native American traditions. A suite of bronze sculptures by Kiki Smith shows a transmogrifying human emerging from the side of an animal [8-3].

In addition to using iconography drawn from the stories of specific religions, artists use more general symbols and metaphors to express spiritual emotions and ideas. Light, both represented and real, continues to serve as a potent symbol of the divine and sacred, and the contrast of light and darkness expresses the ideas of polarity, paradox, and mystery as it has throughout human history. Contemporary expressions involving

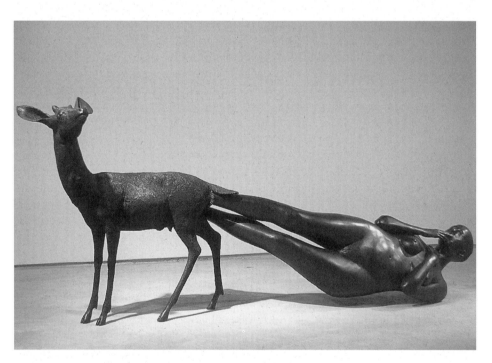

8-3 Kiki Smith | *Born*, **2002**

Bronze, 39" x 101" x 24" (99.1cm x 256.5cm x 61 cm)
Edition of 3 + 1 AP
© Kiki Smith, courtesy of PaceWildenstein, New York

light range from Gerhard Richter's abstract geometric design for a stained-glass window, commissioned and now installed (2007) in the Cologne Cathedral, to Bill Viola's use of fire in his video works, to James Turrell's *Skyspace* (2000) at Live Oaks Friends Meeting House in Houston, Texas, that uses a retracting roof to open a space in the ceiling that reveals the sky's changing light and color. Turrell's choreography of celestial light in his ongoing Roden Crater Project in Arizona provides visitors to this remote and monumental earth work inside an extinct volcano with an unforgettable transcendent experience.

Contemporary artists continue to make use of abstraction as a vehicle for transcendence, offering nonobjective artworks as a focus for ecstatic or meditative spiritual experiences. As Anne Morgan explained, "The potential for artwork to manifest some form of mystical communication that transcends our ordinary reality is great. Abstraction lends itself naturally to this goal, since many of the concepts of spirituality are by nature abstract (such as 'infinity')."[20] In addition to Richter, Turrell, and Laib, contemporary artists who have created abstract works that invite spiritual reflection include James Lee Byars, Agnes Martin, Anish Kapoor, Shirazeh Houshiary, Ron Janowich, and Christian Eckart. Not all these artists discuss their art in spiritual terms. For example, Agnes Martin disavowed any specific religious connection in her nonobjective paintings and drawings, yet, according to Helen Tworkov, she spoke "of drawing 'daily sustenance' from Taoism. . . . [Her] work is an invitation to enter a contemplative space, a space that requires the mind to slow down, dispense with commentary, and take on a posture of receptivity—in other words to assume the attitude of an acolyte."[21]

Martin's art is an excellent example of how thematic content is indissolubly linked to form. By composing her work on a grid, Martin draws viewers into a realm of endlessness: a dense pattern of horizontal rectangles appears to repeat infinitely, and this sense of infinite space registers as timelessness. Other contemporary artists have employed intense patterning to induce a rapt mindset in the viewer. American painter Alex Gray, for instance, creates views of the human body of dizzying complexity in which the interior is revealed as an intricate web of veins. Fred Tomaselli [color plate 19] and the noted American folk artist Howard Finster likewise utilize dense patterning or symmetry to effect a transformation in the viewer's mind. These patterns have the effect of slowing down looking, overwhelming the senses, and opening the door to a dreamlike consciousness. Their work has an affinity with religious art that uses intensely detailed, symmetrical designs to induce a hallucinatory state in the minds of viewers, as in the intricate Tantric paintings of Buddhism and Hinduism. The use of symmetry itself may draw the viewer into a meditative state, perhaps because the symmetrical form suggests stability and the eternal.

Shirazeh Houshiary, who was born in Iran and lives in London, makes abstract art with a transcendental purpose from a position of faith in a particular religious tradition. Houshiary practices Sufism, a mystical branch of Islam that began in the eighth century. According to architectural historian Kenneth Frampton, Houshiary's Sufism "means that she maintains her Islamic beliefs but has taken on additional ascetic tasks and exercises whose goal is communion with the deity through contemplation and ecstasy." Houshiary studies the teachings of Rumi, "where the significance of 'becoming,' through transcendent exercises, dancing and whirling, leads to divine enlightenment."[22] She makes abstract sculptures, sculptural installations, and drawings that are inspired by Sufi philosophy, Rumi's poetry, and geometric symbolism. Her piece

Turning Around the Centre (1993) [8-4] consists of four cubes encased in lead; embedded in the top of each cube is a square whose indented form is lined with gold leaf. The golden squares represent the dancer (the whirling dervish of Sufism) transcending the material world on Earth (symbolized by the lead) and achieving enlightenment. In analyzing her artistic goals, Houshiary said, "The journey to find out the nature of matter takes you to amazing places, because it is about going deep within your own being and trying to know what you are composed of. I'm not trying to understand who I am in relation to name, culture, and all that. Those things I can describe and understand and finish with, but I cannot understand the magic, the mystery of existence. I can feel it. The nature of being, of existence, is more powerful than anything I know."[23]

Even when their art contains no explicit religious references, numerous artists approach art making itself as a quasi-mystical experience or a kind of awareness practice. Calling for extreme devotion and a willingness to slip free of the bonds of prosaic, earthly responsibilities, the creative process transports the creator into another realm. Likewise for some viewers, the process of appreciating the finished artwork can be a transporting experience. Artists and viewers may look to art for contemplative, emotional, or revelatory experiences that are similar to those provided by religion. Meanwhile, others are skeptical about the ability of art to provide an experience of transcendence or are critical of the reasons why such aesthetic transcendence may be sought. For example, valuing art as a higher calling in and of itself may result in a willingness to avoid tackling problems in the here and now. "Art as religion is the programme of the dispossessed," according to Doreet LeVitte Harten.[24]

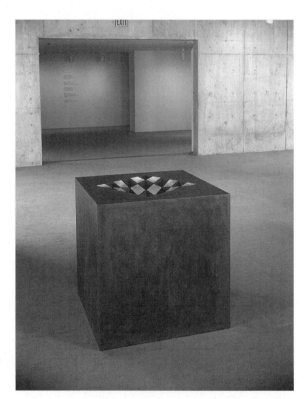

8-4 **Shirazeh Houshiary**

Turning Around the Centre, **1993**

Four parts
Lead and gold leaf, 100 x 100 x 100 cm each
Installation: University Gallery, University of
Massachusetts, Amherst, Nov. - Dec. 1993
Courtesy of Lisson Gallery

Finding Faith and Harboring Doubt

For our discussion, we define *faith* as a belief in the tenets of a religion or, more generally, as a belief in a divine universe. Faith requires no reasoning or proof; faith is an acceptance. *Sistah Paradise's Great Walls of Fire Revival Tent* (1993) [8-5], a large-scale work of fiber art by American Xenobia Bailey, provides a contemporary example of spiritual faith. Bailey hand-crocheted a structure over nine feet tall out of yarn. The form, derived from a Yoruban headdress, symbolizes the Yoruban belief that the head is the sacred center of the body. In this work, Bailey grafts together an African religious concept and a personal belief in the power of women as conjurors and spiritual healers; the composite is an expression of faith in a spiritual power beyond the earthly realm.[25]

Of course, we would expect art based on faith to be part of art on spiritual themes. Artists who do not believe in or care to evaluate the notion of a divinely created universe usually make art about something else. On the other hand, some nonbelievers have explored their atheism and its implications through artworks. For instance, Bruce Nauman's neon piece *One Hundred Live and Die* (1984), which has one hundred blinking electronic messages that each contain the word *LIVE* or *DIE*, is, in Wendy Doniger's view, "a digital, binary, on/off commentary on an existence without any anchors in religious belief." Nauman is saying that death is final and we are alone in "our existential and purposeless journey."[26]

The poles of spiritual certainty on the one hand and absence of faith on the other are insufficient for describing the full range of contemporary art that has been made about spiritual beliefs. Many contemporary artists are conflicted about the existence, definition, or role of the sacred. Artists who are raising spiritual issues often do not know exactly what they believe, and their art suggests ambivalence or a search for answers; seldom is the artist's outlook one of pious certainty. According to Harry Philbrick, a key organizer of the exhibition Faith in 2000, art about religion can be "built upon the armatures of doubt implied by a fall from faith."[27]

Robert Gober, who does not practice the religion of his upbringing (Catholicism), attempted to come to terms with the absence of religion in his life in an untitled installation that was displayed in 1995–97. The work features a life-size statue of the Virgin Mary that is punctured by a culvert pipe through her torso and flanked by two open suitcases [8-6]. Viewers peer beneath a grate in each suitcase into a make-believe grotto built under the floor where the legs of a man and child appear to be bathing in a tidal pool [8-7], in a reference to the Christian rite of baptism by water. Besides noting the Christian references, curator Dean Sobel offered a psychoanalytic interpretation, noting that "this dual-level installation also explores the dynamic between the conscious world (what is immediately apparent) and the subconscious (those things lurking beneath the surface)."[28]

One reason that artists are drawn to the themes of religion and spirituality even when they harbor doubt is that they are interested in morality and ethics. Like everyone else, artists have ideas about ethical behavior, or how people should behave toward each other, toward animals, and toward the planet. Religions provide explanations of good and evil as well as codes of moral conduct and stories that model moral and immoral behavior. Nonbelievers, as well as believers, have used religious iconography to make moral points or to reference another culture. Artists may reference a religion in order to criticize all or

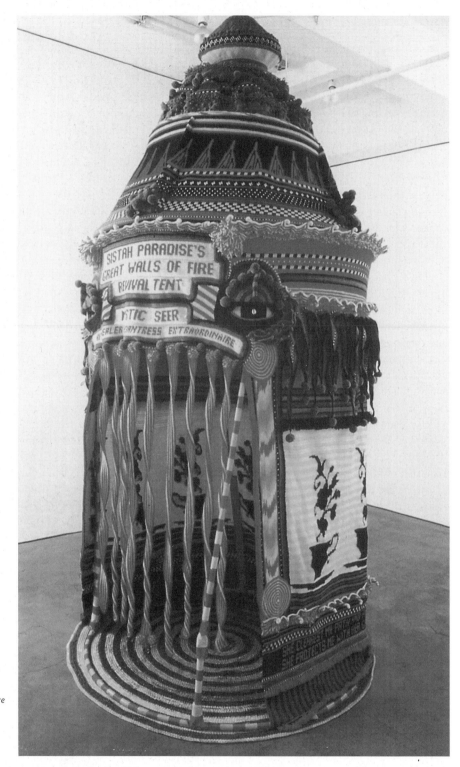

Xenobia Bailey

Sistah Paradise's Great Wall of Fire Revival Tent, **1993**
Acrylic and cotton yarn, hand crocheted, 112 x 63 inch diameter
Courtesy of Stefan Stux Gallery, NY

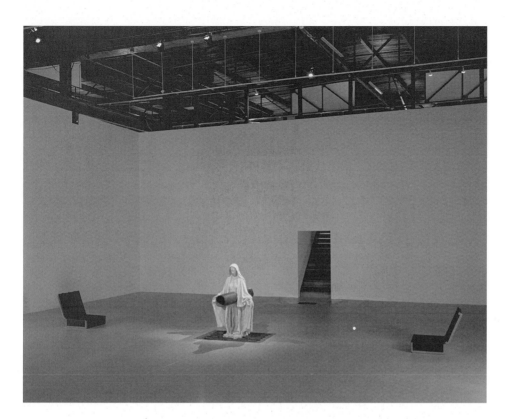

8-6 Robert Gober | *Installation view of Untitled,* **1995–97**
At the Geffen Contemporary at the Museum of Contemporary Art, Los Angeles, September 7 - December 14, 1997
Photo by Russell Kaye
Courtesy of Robert Gober and Matthew Marks Gallery, New York

some of the moral codes promulgated by its leaders. For instance, the New York–based artist collective Gran Fury, active from 1988 to 1994, made posters and billboards deploring the Catholic Church's teachings on homosexuality, AIDS, and birth control. Their images were graphic and direct; one billboard-sized work featured images of the pope alongside an erect penis wearing a condom. This work did not challenge the entire Catholic faith, just its official doctrine regarding one important area of behavior, sexuality.

Other contemporary artworks that are intended to encourage ethical behavior have no obvious religious iconography. Much activist art falls into this category. The maker wants to convince viewers to think about an issue and take action and sometimes even change their daily behavior. Activist artists have strong moral positions, but we do not necessarily know from the artworks what part, if any, spirituality or religious doctrine plays in guiding their beliefs.

Expressing Religious Identities

Violence and armed standoffs all over the world between groups who claim allegiance to different religions demonstrate the continuing importance of religious identity. The

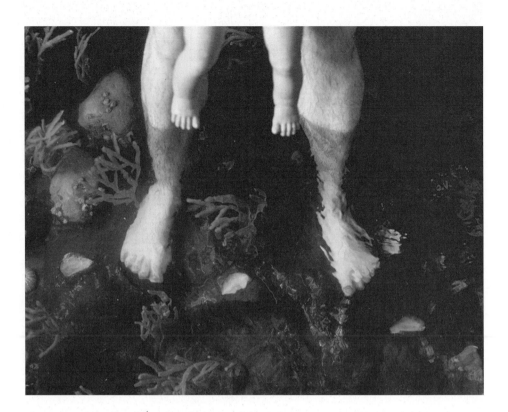

8-7 Robert Gober | *Installation view of Untitled,* 1995–97
At the Geffen Contemporary at the Museum of Contemporary Art, Los Angeles, September 7 - December 14, 1997
Photo by Russell Kaye
Courtesy of Robert Gober and Matthew Marks Gallery, New York

role of art in establishing and preserving religious identity is horribly evident whenever one group destroys religious monuments of a rival group in an attempt to eradicate the beliefs and culture the art represents. In 2001, for instance, the Afghan Taliban, then the theocratic government of Afghanistan, destroyed two great Buddhas and frescoes at Bamiyan following a Taliban decree ordering the destruction of all pre-Islamic statues and sanctuaries in the country.

Despite attempts to build barriers between religions, throughout history people of different religions have interacted and mingled, voluntarily, by happenstance, and by force. Religious identities do not remain static, but are remixed and reformed by historical events and encounters. For example, the Catholic religion of the European colonizers and the indigenous religions of colonized peoples in Mexico, Latin America, and the American Southwest have interacted since the seventeenth century. The art of these regions reflects the dynamism of changing religious identities. From the outset of this forced encounter, the Baroque style of the Counter Reformation and indigenous forms were melded into artistic hybrids that expressed a syncretism (a cross-cultural interaction) of religious ideas, beliefs, and practices.[29] The work of numerous contemporary Latino artists continues to reflect a religious syncretism. For instance, Mexican Nahum Zenil makes works on paper exploring his combined Catholic and Indian heritage.

Zenil's *Ex Voto (Self-Portrait with the Virgin of Guadalupe)* (1987) pairs a devotional image of the Virgin of Guadalupe, who is the patron saint of Mexico (hence a dual symbol of religious and national identity), with a bleeding heart pierced by a knife, the latter a reference to ancient Aztec beliefs as well as to Catholicism.

Contemporary artistic expressions of religious history and identity, including the history of religious tolerance and intolerance, can be conflicted. Manuel Ocampo, born and raised in the Philippines, was trained to copy Catholic religious paintings. He explores the violent legacy of Spanish colonialism in his homeland in *Heridas de la Lengua* (Wounds of the Tongue) (1991), a painting replete with Catholic references, including a Madonna and child. In the central image, "a knife-wielding figure engages in a bloody act of self-decapitation," as Margo Machida described it. Ocampo's concept, Machida explained, is that if "a Filipino/a severs any of the components of his or her complex identity, all that will be accomplished is the painful mutilation of one's psyche."[30]

On the other hand, encounters between different religions and spiritual practices can have a positive effect, enabling individuals to select and combine beliefs, rituals, and forms in creative and meaningful ways. Many individuals have forged hybrid spiritual practices in this way.[31] Betye Saar, an African American who works with mixed media and incorporates many symbols in her assemblages, stated, "I am a Christian, but I am interested in Hinduism, Buddhism, paganism, and alternative religions such as Santería and Voodoo. What I really want is a sort of holistic bonding between formal religions so that another essence, another kind of quality comes out."[32]

When two or more religions are fused into a new one with communal rituals and beliefs that are practiced by many people, the hybrid may become recognized as a separate religion. For example, Santería is a syncretic religion born of the *mestizaje* (cross-cultural interaction and mixing) of Yoruba religion and Catholicism. Santería is practiced today in Cuba and other parts of the Caribbean, as well as in many places in the United States and South America, particularly among Latinos of African descent.[33] Well-known past artists who explored Santería aesthetics in their work include the Cubans Wilfredo Lam (1902–82) and Ana Mendieta (1948–86). Another Cuban, José Bedia (see the profile), who migrated to the United States in 1993, is a current artist influenced by the Afro-Cuban religions Santería and Palo Monte as well as by Native American religions.

Often art expressing a communal religious identity is as much or more about cultural, ethnic, and national identity and history. For example, Iranian-born Shirin Neshat makes film installations about the impact of a fundamentalist Islamic political theocracy on Iranian culture (see profile in chapter 2, Identity). In addition to exploring religious implications, she considers the effect of the fundamentalist revolution on Iranian national identity.

Art that refers to Jewishness provides a good example of how art that references a religious group can be about ethnic identity as well as spiritual beliefs. Too Jewish? Challenging Traditional Identities, a 1996 exhibition organized by the Jewish Museum, New York, raised the question of where Jewish artists fit into Judaism. In addition, according to curator Ori Soltes, the exhibition raised "the myriad cultural, as opposed to religious, questions of a Judaism interfacing with the secular yet Christian American world."[34] The works of Deborah Kass, Ken Aptekar, Archie Rand, Cary Leibowitz, Elaine Reichek, Allan Wexler, and other artists in Too Jewish? consider stereotypes of Jews, anti-Semitism, attitudes about the ethnic Jewish body, Jewish feminism, and issues of consumerism. Some of the works that were exhibited offer new forms of ritual that support spiritual practices in the contemporary age.[35]

Finally, some contemporary art concerning religious identity attempts to deconstruct stereotyped views of the spiritual beliefs and practices of a particular group. To cite one widespread example, both mainstream media and the arts frequently romanticize Native Americans as inherently spiritual, as if having been born Native American necessarily makes one a kind of shaman or spiritual who is adept with special magical abilities, such as the power to talk to animals. John Feodorov, an American of mixed Navajo and Russian descent living in Seattle, takes a humorous look at such mythologizing in mixed-media works such as *Totem Teddies*, which feature toy bears decked out with consumer trinkets. Feodorov's 2000–2001 installation *The Office Shaman* included plastic dolls wearing business suits covered with feathers and beads and audible chants that, according to Lynn M. Herbert, "sound traditional—they have the right tone, the right ring—but as you listen, you realize that they are repeating motivational slogans often found posted in the workplace."[36]

Facing Death, Doom, and Destruction

Through history, spiritual teachings all over the world have dealt with the dark side of life, including sin, death, and destruction. These teachings often address the impermanence of life by providing an explanation of what happens after death and prescribing behavior on earth that will help the individual be accepted into the unseen world of the spirits. Spiritual art gave visual form to fears about the transience of life and beliefs about an afterlife and supported rituals of mourning. Art historian Richard B. Woodward wrote, "The ancient Greeks, however heroic, mourned the fragility of life. Hindu and Buddhist teachings explain that the things of this life are illusory and obscure the truth, the ultimate reality. The art of African cultures often focuses on the cycle of life and the transition from the world of the living to the realm of the ancestors."[37]

The term *vanitas* refers to art that is intended to remind us that life and its pleasures are fleeting. Vanitas still-life paintings, which were especially popular in seventeenth-century Holland, depict objects, such as skulls, decaying fruit, and hourglasses with the sand running out, as symbols of the inescapability of death. Although the term is European, variations on the theme are found in artworks worldwide. John B. Ravenal, who curated a 2000 exhibition at the Virginia Museum of Art on this topic in contemporary art, noted, "The theme of *vanitas* concerns one of life's fundamental tensions, between the enjoyment of earthly pleasures and accomplishments and the awareness of their inevitable loss. This bittersweet notion has long inspired some of Western civilization's most profound works of art and literature."[38]

Vanitas and other themes related to death and destruction, including expressions of loss and mourning, are widespread in contemporary art. The ongoing nuclear threat, the AIDS epidemic, terrorism, wars, and ecological disasters have all influenced the production of art with apocalyptic content and a strong tone of elegy. For example, in a series of paintings called *Atmosphere*, American Ross Bleckner employs traditional symbols of death and mourning, such as skeletons, candelabras, and urns full of flowers, "as a direct means of expressing his pain and fury over AIDS, the atomic threat and the inescapability of death."[39] In addition to using traditional vanitas motifs, today's artists use temporary forms, such as installation and performance, and materials that are ephemeral or fragile to evoke disease, mortality, decay, and death. American Zoe Leonard's *Strange Fruit (for David)* (1992–97), an installation of 295 pieces of fruit skins stitched back together, memorializes artist and gay rights activist David Wojnarowicz, who died of AIDS in 1992. While "strange fruit" is a reference to Wojnarowicz's homosexuality, the shriveled, sewn fruit skins recall religious relics and symbolize the notion of the body's decay. Mexican Gabriel Orozco uses an actual human skull in *Black Kites* (1997) [8-8] to evoke death directly. Orozco also includes more oblique symbols; for instance, his graphite drawing of black-and-white squares on the skull suggests a chessboard, "recalling that game's traditional symbolism of the conflict between dualities, including life and death."[40]

Art dealing with death and destruction need not contain references to religion or spirituality, of course. American Frank Moore painted a postnuclear landscape in *Wizard* (1994) that offers no vision of an afterlife; the mood of fear may reflect an absence of spiritual faith. American Lucinda Devlin has photographed a series of death chambers in prisons throughout the United States. She frames electric chairs, gas chambers, and lethal injection devices in a deadpan documentary manner that is in chilling contrast to the subject matter.

Mingling the Sacred and the Secular

As we have seen repeatedly, fine art and other arenas of visual and popular culture meet and mingle constantly in contemporary life. Art that takes religion as its theme is no exception to this pattern. One manifestation of the intermingling of religion and secular culture occurs when artists borrow religious imagery for a decorative or frivolous purpose. Jeff Koons, for example, has appropriated and enlarged popular religious statuettes of saints and cherubs. Koons's *Ushering in Banality* (1988), for instance, is a five-foot-long carved and painted sculpture showing a pig flanked by two angels and a little boy. While many sophisticated art viewers would interpret this work as containing an ironic critique of commercialization, Koons claims that he simply takes pleasure in the kitsch imagery. In other cases, artists place secular forms and icons from popular culture in a religious context. Ghanian artist Kane Kwei (1924–1991) built whimsical fantasy coffins in the shapes of automobiles, airplanes, and animals [8-9] that represent the secular interests of the deceased. As Kwei's heartfelt art proves, not all art related to the rituals of death needs to be somber in tone.

The line between the religious and the secular, or the sacred and the profane, is not always clear-cut. Artists may deliberately transgress boundaries laid down by religious authorities to challenge their validity. It can be argued that Serrano and Ofili, both raised as Catholics, combined religious imagery (a crucifix and a Madonna) with profane elements (urine and dung) in part to challenge contemporary Catholic ideas about what is sacred and what is sacrilegious, or taboo. From this perspective, Serrano and Ofili are advocating an extreme religious position that the Christian belief in incarnation—God made flesh—includes the idea that excrement is part of God's world. Eleanor Heartney argued that a Catholic perspective in particular lends itself to conflicting views about whether the human body is an ideal reflection of God or a profane vehicle of temptation, impurity, and sin. According to Heartney, "although by no means the exclusive domain of Catholics, such themes as the extremes of human sexual expression, the

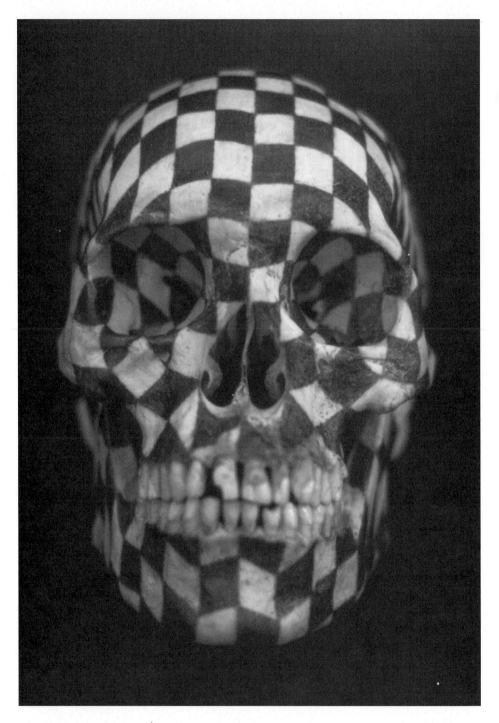

8-8 Gabriel Orozco | *Black Kites,* 1997
(Papalotes negros)
Graphite on skull, 8-1/2 x 5 x 6-1/4 in. / 21.6 x 12.7 x 15.9 cm
Inv.#5475
Courtesy of Marian Goodman Gallery, New York

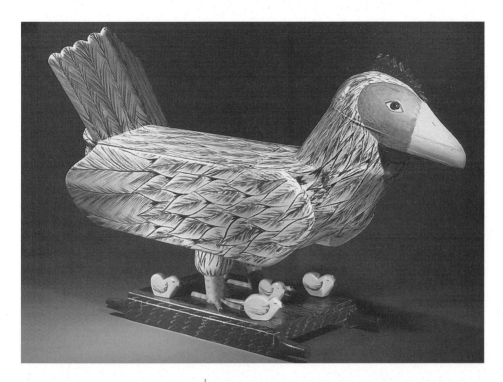

8-9 Workshop of Kane Kwei | *Hen with chicks fantasy coffin made by workshop of*
Kane Kwei, **1988–91**

Wood, cloth and paint, 54 x 25 x 104 inches
© The Children's Museum of Art
Photograph courtesy of the Indianapolis Museum of Art / Hadley Fruits, photographer

horrors of decaying flesh and death, and the forthright depiction of the body's excre-
tions and physical processes are especially well-suited to the Catholic imagination."[41]

Within this subtheme, a number of artists have borrowed liturgical forms of display to represent secular heroes, newsmakers, and cult figures from popular culture.
Elayne Goodman, from Mississippi, used dozens of images of Elvis Presley as well as
simulated relics (hair and fingernail clippings) to create her *Altar to Elvis* (1990) [8-10].
(The spontaneous altars of photographs, flowers, and texts that spring up in public
places when a famous personality dies provide a vernacular version of this kind of
artistic practice.) Similarly, Jeffrey Vallance, an artist born in California, has made fake
replicas of the sweat-stained scarves that Presley ritualistically handed out to fans at
his concerts.

The motives for appropriating religious forms and iconography may be straightforward. Amalia Mesa-Bains, for instance, sincerely wishes to honor the women who are
the subjects of her altars [color plate 20]. Goodman and Vallance, in contrast, appear to
be gently mocking the cultlike devotion of many Elvis fans. They may be asking viewers
to ponder the boundary between religious worship and secular idolatry. What are the
consequences of the transfer of devotion from divine to human idols? What does it mean
when a society's gods and heroes are personalities who exist in the material world?

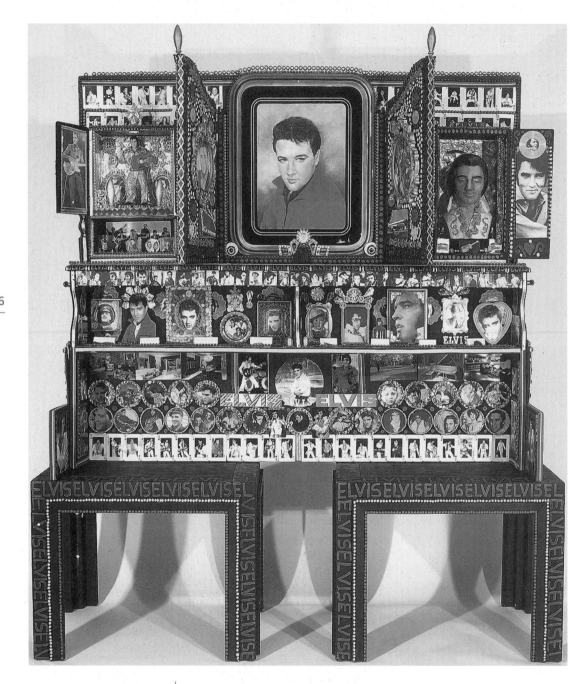

8-10 Elayne Goodman | *Altar to Elvis*, **1990**

Mixed media: wood construction with attachments, collage, Elvis collectibles,
fake relics, posters and prints, buttons, braids, sequins, 74 x 66 x 22"
Collection of the artist, Columbus, Mississippi
Photo by Carlos Studios, Columbus, Miss.
Courtesy of Elayne Goodman

Imagery that explores a mingling of the sacred and the secular is not necessarily concerned with popular culture. The Brazilian photographer Sebastião Salgado and the Israeli video artist Michal Rovner are among those contemporary artists who reveal a sense of the mystical in the most profane of human circumstances. The art critic Richard Cork ascribed a "biblical undertow" to Salgado's riveting photos of exhausted men laboring in Brazilian goldmines; the teeming scenes of workers climbing wooden ladders appear like events from the Old Testament. In our view, a similar description applies to Rovner's friezes of out-of-focus, anonymous figures lined ghostlike along a distant, bleak horizon during wartime in the Middle East.

The critic Thierry de Duve argued that in contemporary secular societies, "entertainment has replaced religion . . . but *religiousness* is still there."[42] Humans now experience religious feelings, such as devotion or awe, in secular public domains including museums, rock concerts, sports arenas, and shopping malls. Given this trend, some may wonder whether art will continue to have the power—and the audience—to speak profoundly about humanity's deepest concerns. The directions that contemporary art will take in the future will depend on myriad forces, forces that intertwine the world and the art world. Advances in the cognitive sciences may yet yield fresh insights, supported by experimental evidence, of underlying relationships of consciousness, the body, aesthetic experience, and spirituality. Who knows? In any case, our own belief is that contemporary artists in the future will continue, as they have for the preceding *twenty-five thousand years,* to soak in all that is unfolding in the world around us and to create works that challenge us to rethink that world and our relationship with the universe.

The graphic power of José Bedia's mixed-media drawings, paintings, and site-specific installations captivate viewers in a glance. In many of his art works, linear elements lock elongated figures within a pattern as eye-catching as a spider's web. Bedia often creates monumental wall drawings that are done primarily in black, accompanied by objects that are culled from either pop culture or nature, such as a toy boat or pair of antlers. To access the deeper symbolic associations contained in his imagery, however, viewers find it valuable to learn something of the influences the artist has embraced. Bedia is Cuban; his heritage blends diverse ethnic traditions, including Hispanic, Native American, African, Afro-Cuban, and European. Early in his career, he developed an interest in ethnographic studies, but since his maturation as an artist, his work flows primarily out of his internalization of ideas "concerning the relationship of human beings with the world, from Afro- and Indo-American viewpoints."[43]

A frequent motif in Bedia's art is the representation of a journey. A journey may be represented explicitly (by a boat or a bridge, for instance), or a journey may be shown implicitly (with a labyrinth or passage of paint that appears to glow, thus marking an inner spiritual transformation). In Bedia's imagery, a mystical journey represents the process by which knowledge is gained. Gaining knowledge provides the opportunity for a metaphysical transformation; such a transformation is the dramatic center of many important works of art and literature of South and Central America.

Spiritual or transforming journeys are central to Bedia's art as well as to his own autobiographic experiences. Starting in the 1970s, as a teenager in Havana, Bedia accompanied his mother on visits to a priest of Palo Monte. Palo Monte is a religious faith transposed to the Caribbean by black slaves who were brought from central Africa in the eighteenth and nineteenth centuries; as a religion, Palo Monte claims a sacred connection between the world of humans and of animals. "The name of the faith refers to 'trees of the sacred forest,' for the classical Kongo religion of Central Africa focuses on special spirits or saints, *bisimbi*, and ancestors, *bakulu*, and both are believed to reside in the forests beyond the city."[44] Since his indoctrination into Palo Monte in the early 1980s, Bedia has devoted much of his art to a representation of reality as seen through the Palo Monte belief system. Words are incorporated frequently into his imagery to pinpoint the specific issues (such as the frailty of life) that the artwork directs the viewer to consider. Words, inserted as titles or captions, are often snippets of Palo songs and expressions—*mambos*—some profoundly spiritual, others political and topical, often in reference to the challenges and injustices stemming from colonialism. In addition to incorporating Palo Monte words, Bedia's art may utilize ritual objects and altarpiece forms to evoke the religious practices of the Kongo that were brought to the New World by slaves. (In central Africa, altars can represent the face of the gods.)

The Palo Monte religion, an Afro-Cuban religion, contains "parallels with Native American cultures and religions such as the Nahuatl, Lakota, Sioux or Navajo."[45]Bedia recognized these affinities intuitively and then confirmed them through research in anthropology texts. In 1985 the artist traveled to the Rosebud Sioux Reservation in South Dakota, where he lived with a shaman. Among the Sioux, immersed in a North American Plains Indian culture, Bedia intensely explored art and artifacts in which "every element, color, and image carries a specific symbolic reference."[46]The shaman instructed Bedia in ritualistic practices, such as the sweat lodge in which spiritual regeneration occurs through self-purification. Bedia's own creative practice has since incorporated imagery (such as pipes for smoking and concentric patterns) that is derived from the cosmologies of the North American Plains Indians. An example of this influence is seen in *Mira, Mamita, Estoy Arriba, Arriba* (1991) [8-11]; the shape of this artwork, painted on a canvas adorned with found objects, echoes the dried leather hide, known as

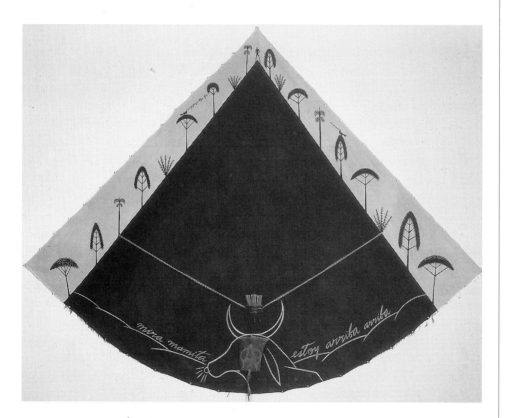

8-11 José Bedia | *Mira, Mamita, Estoy Arriba, Arriba,* 1991

Acrylic on canvas with found objects, 73 x 94 1/2 inches
Collection of the Bacardi Art Foundation
Courtesy of the artist

parfleche, on which Native American pictographs were drawn. The image itself takes the triangular shape of a teepee. The entire work depicts a mysterious animal (a symbol of shamanistic power) anchoring an iconic forest; the silhouette of a man, small but significant, stands at the apex of the scene.

Immersing himself in other Native American traditions (including Aztec and Mayan traditions of Mexico), Bedia has found inspiration for his simplified, almost cartoonlike forms. Among these preliterate cultures the realms of people, animals, and nature interpenetrate on physical and metaphysical planes. In various artworks that the artist has produced over the past two decades, figures often gesture to a void, while their eyes glow or stare at empty spaces, signifying the hidden dimensions that lie behind the façade of everyday existence.

The artist claims that his use of symbolism is authentic, that his work is anchored in his own firsthand knowledge of actual traditions. In an interview published in 1999, he explained, "I don't invent anything. For example, the sand symbols. I learned what each thing represents from a medicine man in Montana."[47] Drafted into the Cuban army in 1986, Bedia traveled to Africa; in Angola, he studied African religious beliefs that are ancestral to the Palo Monte and Santería traditions of Cuba. According to the artist, while he may duplicate an altar within the process of creating an artwork, the resulting artwork is not a sacred altar. The artwork cannot function in a truly spiritual way because the artist would never place "the sacred elements of his religion in a secular art installation."[48]Such an artwork is never consecrated.

Among Bedia's most powerful artworks are those the artist has created by painting or drawing directly on gallery or museum walls, attaching or adding other materials to complete the installation. An example of this creative strategy, *Las Cosas Que Me Arrastan* (The Things That Drag Me Along) (1996) [8-12] includes a double-headed figure being "dragged" forward through the space of the gallery, attached by chains to a collection of found objects. Each head is defined by a jaw protruding in a way that is characteristic of many of Bedia's figures. On the enormous figure's chest are pasted photographs of an iron cauldron and sweat lodge, symbols of the Afro-Cuban and Plains Indian faiths, respectively. Pulling the figure are a "team" of altars, each representative of some aspect of the range of Bedia's knowledge of sacred rituals. At the front, a miniature bull marches forward on crutches; the animal is on a spiritual journey. The bull symbolizes the strength to cross boundaries in search of knowledge. Such a quest is the primary goal in all that the artist undertakes and all that his art represents. The entire artwork functions further as a collection of talismanic images and objects that may lead the viewer along the path of enlightenment as well.

Born in Havana in 1959, Bedia left Cuba permanently in 1990. He spent three years in Mexico, after which he migrated to the United States in 1993, where he settled in Miami, choosing that city for its close ties to Hispanic culture.

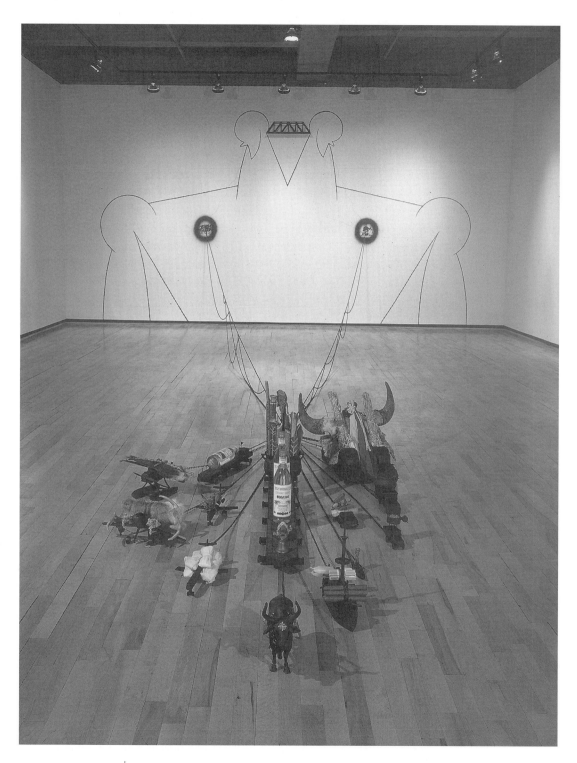

8-12 | José Bedia | *Las Cosas Que Me Arrastran (The Things That Drag Me Along)*, 1996

Wax, crayon, acrylic, found objects. Approximately 10 x 20 x 30 feet
Collection of the Bacardi Art Foundation
Courtesy of the artist

In front of or surrounded by one of Bill Viola's videotapes or video/sound installations, most viewers stand transfixed. In *Five Angels for the Millennium* (2001), we watch scenes of a figure ascending and descending into a pool of water at night; in *The Crossing* (1996), installed in a darkened gallery, we see a two-sided projection of a solitary man striding forward from a distance. Upon nearing, he comes to a stop, and then, on one side of the suspended screen, the man becomes engulfed in rising flames [8-13]; simultaneously, on the other side of the screen, the same figure becomes engulfed in a rapidly building torrent of water [8-14] After he is totally immersed on both sides, the cascade of water and blazing fire die out. The man has disappeared. Then, the cycle repeats. In describing this work, the artist wrote, "The two traditional natural elements of fire and water appear here not only in their destructive aspects, but manifest their cathartic, purifying, transformative, and regenerative capacities as well. In this way, self-annihilation becomes a necessary means to transcendence and liberation."[49]

The overall effect of these examples of Viola's work can confound us. Why? First, there is the issue of the function and meaning of his choices of specific images. We may be tempted to assume that the artist is using images from nature symbolically: a pool of water (in *Five Angels for the Millenium*), perhaps standing for purity, and the night sky, perhaps standing for the vast knowledge we have yet to learn. We have had practice interpreting such natural symbols in poems, movies, novels, and private walks in the woods; we are primed by culture to translate the rich potential of nature's symbolism.

However, in deriving the core of his imagistic vocabulary from nature, Viola moves beyond a symbolic interpretation. Viola intends the video imagery not as mere representation or symbol, but as reification. The image does not carry the meaning of an external subject; it becomes the subject itself. And it does so on two key levels. First, "Time, life, death, space and the individual in Viola's work are never concepts or events translatable to other languages, but languages in themselves, places of immanence of meanings which cannot be articulated."[50] Second, Viola's video imagery becomes a world unto itself that parallels and embodies those aspects of the human condition upon which the work concentrates attention. To put this into the terms of a specific work, in *The Crossing* the immersion in water is that—an immersion; the immersion creates transmogrification, not on a metaphoric or symbolic level but on the phenomenological level. The video event is the event. Viola's concern is not principally with the figure (the actor) in the imagery, but with our (the audience's) relationship to the imagery. We become immersed in the event of the total artwork.

In many of his works Viola concentrates our attention on the transformation of imagery from the beautiful to the awesome. We watch this occur in *The Crossing* as the rush of water builds from a glittering trickle to a frightening torrent. At the dramatic ending of the cycle—when the figure has melded with the infinite power of water and fire—he (the man in the artwork) disappears into the cosmos, and we (the viewers in the gallery) are in the midst of experiencing the sublime.

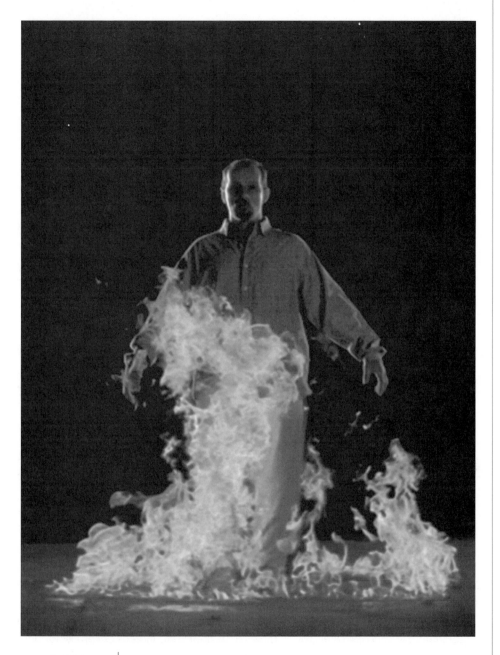

8-13 Bill Viola │ *The Crossing,* 1996
Video/sound installation
Photo by Kira Perov

What is the sublime? As discussed in chapter 8, Spirituality, the sublime is a powerful experience that combines disparate feelings. Cynthia Freeland applied the term
in a careful analysis of several examples of Bill Viola's video works. As she explained,
"The sublime was overwhelming, something that might sweep one away with its vast

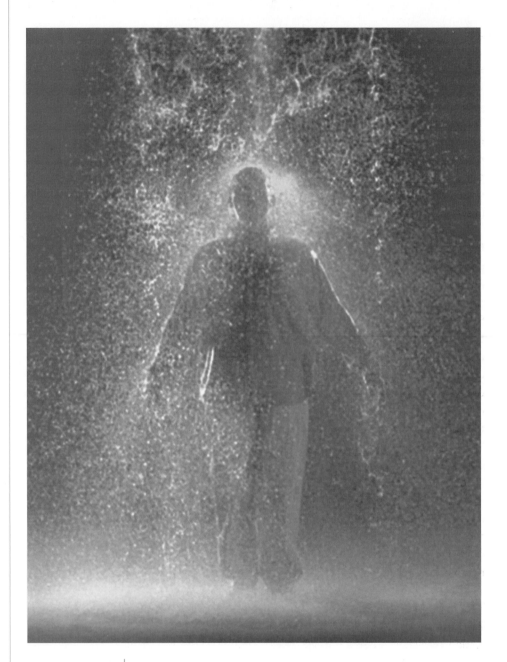

8-14 Bill Viola | *The Crossing, 1996*
Video/sound installation
Photo by Kira Perov

size or power. Whereas the beautiful was smooth and soft, the sublime was rough and jagged. Stormy oceans and jagged mountains were typical examples."[51]

A signature device in many of Viola's videotapes and installations is the slowing of time; Viola elongates the duration of an event to allow our mind to catch up with our sensory perceptions. (In addition to slowing time, in Viola's body of work there are also examples when time is rapidly speeded up and Viola's keen interest in exploring the limits of human perception is manifest.)[52] Seeing and hearing a slowed-down sequence of images and sounds—ocean waves, for instance—we have time to marvel at, and meditate on, what it is we are experiencing in the present moment. This slowed-down and focused way of thinking becomes a spiritual exercise for the viewer. The water concentrates our attention on our relationship to the water, as an aspect of reality: the water and we, in the midst of watching the water, are unified in the temporal flow. Understanding this unification provides us with a gateway for understanding our unification with the whole of reality as our minds expand in greater and greater circumferences of thought. At the least, we believe that Viola's work aims for this deep (if swift) connection of viewer and video, sound, gallery, meaning, and reality.

That Viola would ask us to consider a transcendent plane of meaning confounds us because the quest for a vivid spiritual connection is relatively rare in the current art world. In the West, an uncritical embrace of the spiritual realm lost currency during the heyday of modernism. Further disengagement came during the dismantling of grand narratives in the late twentieth century. Art historian James Elkins has written on the difficulties and rarity of creating serious visual art today that celebrates, embodies, or explores religion or spirituality without irony or a critical stance.[53] Viola's creations do not aim for a scientific, economic, or political understanding of nature by providing data and observing patterns. Viola entices us to set aside a secular mindset and embrace a new paradigm of meditative spirituality. His works are informed by a broad, though eclectic, knowledge of global traditions of religion (including Zen Buddhism and Sufi and Christian mysticism), literature, philosophy, and natural science. Viola also draws on personal experiences, such as his near drowning when he was a child. His goal in making the work is not to contribute to the perfection of society (as an artist focusing on nature from an ecological perspective might) but to the perfection of the individual. A particularly confounding aspect of his work is that Viola manages to draw viewers into a meditative state—in which we are both inside ourselves and standing outside ourselves simultaneously in contemplation of life's enduring mysteries—within a relatively short time in the rather crowded urban public space of an art museum.

The effects we describe can be experienced clearly in any number of examples. The video and sound installation *Room for St. John of the Cross* (1983) [color plate 21], for instance, consists of a darkened gallery within which a mural-size video projection of distant mountain peaks covers one wall. The sound of roaring wind fills the gallery's interior; the projected mountains shake on the wall (the result of purposefully unsteady filming); in the center of the gallery stands a black cubicle. The cubicle measures slightly less than the height of an adult: it is built to the recorded dimensions of the cell in which Saint John, a sixteenth-century Christian mystic, was imprisoned during the Inquisition. Gallery viewers must stoop to peer inside the cell's window. During the nine months of his captivity, Saint John was released from his cell only to be tortured; in solitary confinement, he produced lines of ecstatic, visionary poetry. In Viola's installation, visitors listening at the window hear excerpts from the poems, spoken in barely audible Spanish, that include visions of flying over the mountainous landscape. A single writing table sits inside the cramped cell; on the table, a much smaller image of a single mountain is projected on a small monitor.

Exploring *Room for St. John of the Cross*, the viewer ponders her or his role in the implied drama. Is one a witness? possibly even a torturer? Could the viewer also "be" Saint John? The darkness of the gallery isolates each of us so that we each become the saint in solitary meditation. The tiny mountain on the monitor, a point of calm within the cell, functions like a Zen koan, providing a focus for meditative engagement. Alexander Puhringer explained, "Viola views his work as a kind of individual exercise. But what makes it transcend the private realm is the way it is treated. Of decisive importance here is the fact that Viola—in William Blake's sense—grants every person the ability of having visions and being in contact with the divine imagination."[54] Viola choreographs the entire scene so that viewers/listeners are not merely captivated by the experience but are also transported. From this spiritual perspective we see the mountain. The mountain landscape moving on the wall is the mountain, and the still mountain on the monitor in the cell is also the mountain. One does not symbolize the other. The mountain is not a symbol of escape or endurance. The mountain is the mountain. Existence is being.

Another interesting aspect of Viola's work, given its spiritual import, is the reliance on the medium of video, a technology related to television, perhaps the most commercialized of all contemporary media. For Viola, time is the fundamental element of video. The flow of time in video parallels the dynamic, continual changes that take place in reality. Thus form and content blend seamlessly. Viola analyzes the relationship of medium to motif: "Most important, it is the awareness of our own mortality that defines the nature of human beings. . . . As instruments of time, the materials of video . . . have as a part of their nature this fragility of temporal existence. Images are born, they are created, they exist, and, in the flick of a switch, they die."[55] Reality is in flux; transformation and transition occur incessantly. In Viola's *Tiny Deaths* (1993), the imagery consists of a group of anonymous figures, whose poses mimic those of the museum audience. In the video imagery, each figure glows for a period of time and then slowly loses contrast, turning luminescent before finally disappearing.

In the mid-1990s, Viola began to create video versions of iconic Renaissance paintings (such as *The Greeting*, based on a visitation scene by the sixteenth-century Italian painter Jacopo Pontormo). In Viola's versions, the stillness of the imagery is revealed as an ever so slowly changing video image. The greatest mystery of all, in Viola's art, appears to be time itself. Time is change, and in time all will change. Viola's work is most compelling because it confronts and compels viewers with a secular outlook to consider questions to which there is no secular or scientific answer: Why do we live? Why do we die? What is the meaning of time?

Bill Viola was born in 1951 in Flushing, New York. He received a bachelor of fine arts degree from Syracuse University. Viola and his wife and collaborator, Kira Perov, currently live in Long Beach, California.

Spirituality

Notes

1. Chapters 2 through 7 delve into themes that contain hotly contested issues. However, no educated reader would disavow the relevance of the subject at the core of a previous theme. Who would question that time and place are concepts that refer to fundamental aspects of our shared reality? No educated reader—or viewer of art—would call into question that humans possess bodies and language. While many vehemently criticize the influence and direction of scientific exploration and may take a moral stand for or against issues of identity, no one reasonably disagrees that science and identity refer to subjects—the patterns of natural and social behavior—that really exist (even though we cannot claim to know, or that there ever will be, an ultimate truth about either).

2. Gregory Volk, "Fred Tomaselli's Hybrid Sublime," in *Fred Tomaselli* (New York: James Cohan Gallery, 2000), p. 5. An exhibition catalog.

3. Lynn M. Herbert, "Shahzia Sikander," in *Art: 21: Art in the Twenty-First Century* (New York: Harry N. Abrams, 2001), pp. 93–99.

4. For intriguing discussions of these and related issues, see Alex Neill and Aaron Ridley, eds., *Arguing About Art: Contemporary Philosophical Debates*, second edition (London: Routledge, 2002), pp. 233–371.

5. Pew Forum on Religion and Public Faith, U.S. Religious Landscape Survey, results released in February 2008. See "Survey: My Way Isn't the Only Way to Earn Salvation," *Indianapolis Star*, June 24, 2008, p. A1 and A6.

6. Susan Sollins, "Extending Vision," in *Art: 21*, p. 9.

7. Edmund Burke, *A Philosophical Inquiry into the Origin of Our Ideas of the Sublime and Beautiful* (London: Oxford University Press, 1990).

9. For example, Andy Warhol's *Gold Marilyn Monroe* (1962), an image of Marilyn Monroe's head floating against a gold background, has been interpreted as an instance of the artist's coded religiosity.

10. See Maurice Tuchman, ed., *The Spiritual in Art: Abstract Painting, 1890–1985* (New York: Abbeville Press, 1986). An exhibition catalog.

11. For an analysis of the controversy around Serrano's *Piss Christ*, see Linda Weintraub, *Art on the Edge and Over: Searching for Art's Meaning in Contemporary Society 1970s–1990s* (Litchfield, Conn.: Arts Insights, 1996), pp. 159–164. For a discussion of the Sensation show at the Brooklyn Museum, see David Halle, "The Controversy over the Show Sensation at the Brooklyn Museum, 1999–2000," in Alberta Arthurs and Glenn Wallach, eds., *Crossroads: Art and Religion in American Life* (New York: New Press, 2001), pp. 139–187.

12. Eleanor Heartney, "Art Between Heaven and Earth," in *Faith: The Impact of Judeo-Christian Religion on Art at the Millennium* (Ridgefield, Conn.: Aldrich Museum of Contemporary Art, 2000), p. 57. An exhibition catalog.

13. Suzi Gablik, *The Reenchantment of Art* (New York: Thames and Hudson, 1991), p. 12.

14. Anselm Kiefer, quoted in Axel Hecht, "Macht der Mythen," *Art: Das Kunstmagazin, Wiesbaden*, March 1984, p. 33; cited in Mark Rosenthal, *Anselm Kiefer* (Philadelphia: Philadelphia Museum of Art; Chicago: Art Institute of Chicago; Munich: Prestel Verlag, 1987), p. 27. An exhibition catalog.

15. David S. Rubin, *Contemporary Triptychs* (Claremont, Calif.: Pomona College, 1982). An exhibition catalog.

16. Clare Farrow, "Wolfgang Laib: More Than Myself," in *Parkett* 39 (March 1994): p. 78. Several articles in this issue of *Parkett* are devoted to Laib's work.

17. Anne Morgan, "Beyond Post Modernism: The Spiritual in Contemporary Art," *Art Papers* 26, no. 1 (January–February 2002): p. 32. Morgan is talking specifically about the site-specific installations of Ann Hamilton.

18. For a succinct summary of van Gennep's definition of a liminal state, see Stuart Morgan and Frances Morris, *Rites of Passage: Art for the End of the Century* (London: Tate Gallery, 1995), p. 12. An exhibition catalog.

19. The entire issue of CAA's *Art Journal* for Spring 1998 was entitled "The Reception of Christian Devotional Art"; this publication included a range of examples of contemporary art that incorporated symbolic or metaphoric references to Christianity. For example, within the imagery of Derek Jarman's *The Garden . . .*, a pair of young male lovers *together* represent Christ. See *Art Journal* 57, no. 1 (Spring 1998): p. 73, and Derek Jarman's artist statement, p. 76.

20. Morgan, "Beyond Post Modernism," p. 32.

21. Tworkov, quoted in ibid.

22. Kenneth Frampton, "Shirazeh Houshiary," in Richard Francis, ed., *Negotiating Rapture* (Chicago: Museum of Contemporary Art, 1996), p. 176. An exhibition catalog.

23. Shirazeh Houshiary, "From Form to Formlessness: A Conversation with Shirazeh Houshiary," by Anne Barclay Morgan in *Sculpture* 19, no. 6 (July–August 2000): p. 29.

24. Doreet LeVitte Harten, "Creating Heaven," in *Heaven* (Stuttgart, Germany: Hatje Cantz; New York: Distributed Art Publishers, 1999), p. 11. An exhibition catalog.

25. For a detailed analysis of Bailey's work, see Dorothy Desir-Davis, "Xenobia Bailey: Paradise Under Construction," in Salah M. Hassan, ed., *The Art of Contemporary Africana Women Artists* (Trenton, N.J.: Africa World Press, 1997), pp. 19–26.

26. Wendy Doniger, "Bruce Nauman," in Francis, ed., *Negotiating Rapture*, p. 156.

27. Harry Philbrick, "Creating *Faith*," in *Faith*, p. 15.

28. Dean Sobel, *Interventions: New Art in Unconventional Spaces* (Milwaukee, Wisc.: Milwaukee Art Museum, 2000), p. 13. An exhibition catalog. This installation is now broken up; one of the grates is in the collection of the Milwaukee Art Museum.

29. For examples of how this syncretism played out in one South American country, see Edward J. Sullivan, ed., *Brazil: Body & Soul* (New York: Guggenheim Museum, 2001). An exhibition catalog.

30. Margo Machida, "Out of Asia: Negotiating Asian Identities in America," in *Asia/America: Identities in Contemporary Asian American Art* (New York: Asia Society Galleries and New Press, 1994), p. 76. An exhibition catalog.

31. Contemporary artists who express spiritual ideas in their art that draw from a variety of religions include Xenobia Bailey, Shahzia Sikander, Betye Saar, Alison Saar, Bill Viola, Pepón Osorio, Sonya Y. S. Clark, Ernesto Pujol, and Cao Guo-Qiang.

32. Quoted in Amei Wallach, "Art, Religion, and Spirituality: A Conversation with Artists," in Arthurs and Wallach, eds., *Crossroads*, p. 239.

33. For a discussion of Santería and its impact on the visual arts, see Arturo Lindsay, ed., *Santería Aesthetics in Contemporary Latin American Art* (Washington, D.C.: Smithsonian Institution Press, 1996).

34. Ori Soltes, "Contexts: Jews and Art at the End of the Millennium," in *Faith*, p. 111.

35. See Norman L. Kleeblatt, ed., *Too Jewish? Challenging Traditional Identities* (New York and New Brunswick, N.J.: Jewish Museum and Rutgers University Press, 1996). An exhibition catalog.

36. Lynn M. Herbert, "Regarding Spirituality," in *Art: 21*, p. 88.

37. Richard B. Woodward, foreword to *Vanitas: Meditations on Life and Death in Contemporary Art*, by John B. Ravenal (Richmond: Virginia Museum of Fine Arts, 2000), p. 7. An exhibition catalog.

38. Ravenal, *Vanitas*, p. 13.

39. Burkhard Riemschneider and Uta Grosenick, eds., *Art at the Turn of the Millennium* (Köln, Germany: Taschen, 1999), p. 74.

40. Ravenal, *Vanitas*, p. 15.

41. Eleanor Heartney, "Postmodern Heretics," in *Art in America* 85, no. 2 (February 1997): p. 37.

42. Thierry de Duve, "Come on, Humans, One More Stab at Becoming Post-Christians!" in *Heaven*, p. 74.

43. Arturo Lindsay, "The Presence of Africa in the Visual Art of Cuba," in Arturo Lindsay, ed., *Santería Aesthetics in Contemporary Latin American Art* (Washington, D.C.: Smithsonian Institution Press, 1996), p. 247.

44. Robert Farris Thompson, "Sacred Silhouettes," *Art in America* 85 (July 1997): p. 66.

45. Cecilia Fajardo, "José Bedia: American Chronicles," *Art Nexus* 26 (October–December 1997): p. 105.

46. Louis Grachos, introduction to *José Bedia: La Isla—el Cazador y la Presa (The Island—the Hunter and the Prey)* (Santa Fe, N.Mex.: Site Santa Fe, 1997), p. 2. An exhibition catalog.

47. As quoted in Sherry Gaché, "José Bedia: Only the Most Valuable Things," *Sculpture* 18, no. 5 (June 1999): p. 48.

48. Lindsay, "The Presence of Africa," p. 216.

49. Bill Viola, "The Crossing," in *Bill Viola* (New York: Whitney Museum of American Art, 1998), p. 65. An exhibition catalog.

50. Celio Montolio, "The Unspoken Language of the Body," in *Bill Viola* (Klagenfurt, Austria: Ritter, 1994), p. 183. An exhibition catalog.

51. See Cynthia Freeland, "Piercing to Our Inaccessible, Inmost Parts," in Chris Townsend, ed., *The Art of Bill Viola* (London: Thames & Hudson, 2004), p. 35. In this essay, Freeland provides a useful analysis of the history of the concept of the sublime as the complexities, nuances, and emphases in its definition have undergone significant changes from the philosophical writings of Edmund Burke and Immanuel Kant, in past centuries to the contemporary formulations by Jean-Francois Lyotard, Arthur Danto, and Elaine Scarry. See pp. 25–45.

52. Viola's video installation *Interval* (1995) features the sequential projection of imagery on two facing walls. The streams of paired imagery, under the control of a computer-programmed switcher, move through a cycle of being projected one after another at an increasingly rapid pace, ultimately exceeding our capacity to track their alternating projections.

53. James Elkins, *On the Strange Place of Religion in Contemporary Art.* (New York and London: Routledge, 2004).

54. Alexander Puhringer, foreword to *Bill Viola* (Klagenfurt, Austria: Ritter, 1994), p. 11.

55. Bill Viola, "Putting the Whole World Back Together: Bill Viola in Conversation with Otto Neumaier and Alexander Puhringer," in ibid., p. 152.

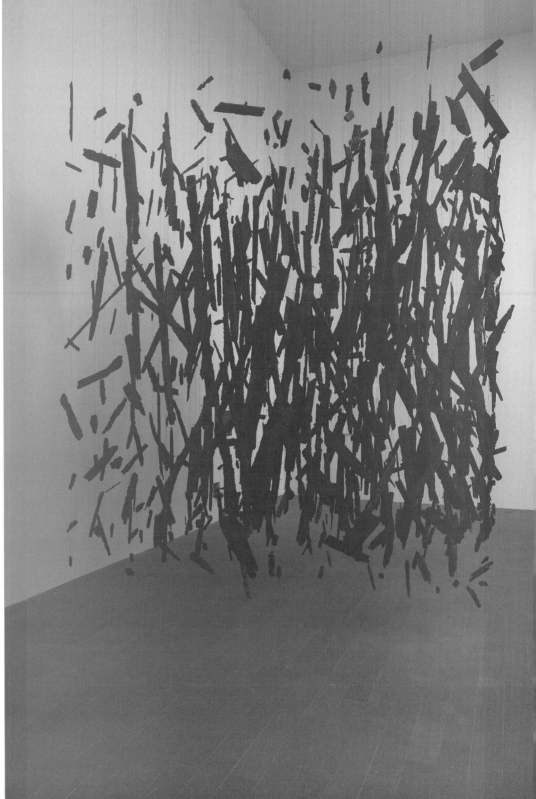

Detail of 4-13

Timeline

This timeline covers the twenty-nine-year period 1980 through 2008. Each year includes a sample of key events in three broad categories: world events, art, and pop culture. The events within any single year are not listed in strict chronological order because so many of the events (such as the duration of a war or the run of a movie) overlap. Readers are invited to consider the interplay of historical forces that characterize the current era. Such influences are, of course, not one directional. World events and occurrences in popular culture strongly influence the work of visual artists, and, we believe, the achievements of artists also influence, in subtle and sometimes not-so-subtle ways, the development of culture and the course of history.

This timeline, like all timelines, is far from exhaustive. What the reader should be able to glean from even this highly selective listing is a small taste of the intersecting flows of culture and nature. History, as mapped in the time line, records events and achievements in at least three broad categories of patterns: patterns that are highly predictable (e.g., without preventive actions, global warming and the growth of the world's population will inevitably continue), patterns that are predictable only in large statistical pools of data (e.g., earthquakes will occur each year, but exactly where is unpredictable), and patterns that are idiosyncratic (e.g., events looked at on an individual level—such as a particular rock star dying in an automobile accident). Together these patterns create a larger overall pattern that gives the passage of time a texture or flavor (with some predictability and some chance occurrences, some tragedies and some trivialities, and so on). The flavor of reality that this timeline offers remains highly selective, but that it has a flavor at all is, we believe, symptomatic of how anyone's view of reality is a social construction.

Timeline

	1980	1981	1982	1983
ART	Anselm Kiefer and Georg Baselitz represent Germany at the Venice Biennale • Pablo Picasso: A Retrospective, Museum of Modern Art, New York • Women's Images of Men, Institute of Contemporary Arts, London • John Berger publishes *About Looking* • Keith Haring starts drawing on New York City subway station walls • French intellectual Roland Barthes dies • Death of Austrian Expressionist Oscar Kokoschka	Postmodernism begins to be applied as a concept to the visual arts in the U.S. • Thomas Ruff's first solo exhibition opens in Germany • Major German Neo-Expressionists are featured in gallery exhibits in New York • A New Spirit in Painting, Royal Academy of Arts, London • Death of International Style architect Marcel Lajos Breuer	Vietnam Veterans Memorial, designed by Maya Lin, dedicated in Washington, D.C. • Michael Graves designs the Humana Building in Louisville, Kentucky • Jenny Holzer exhibits her first Truisms work using LED in *Messages to the Public*, Times Square, New York • Transavantguardia Italia/America, Galleria Civica Modena • Extended Sensibilities: Homosexual Presence in Contemporary Art, New Museum of Contemporary Art, New York	Philip Johnson's postmodern AT&T building, New-York • Edward Larrabee Barnes's IBM building, New-York • Whitney Biennial features fourteen women artists out of forty-six total • *Temporary Contemporary*, Museum of Contemporary Art, Los Angeles • Death of U.S. engineer and architect Buckminster Fuller • Death of Abstract and Surrealist painter Joan Miro
POP CULTURE	Martin Scorsese's *Raging Bull* • George Lucas's *Star Wars: Episode V-The Empire Strikes Back* • Alfred Hitchcock, Hollywood's king of suspense, dies at age 80 • Ted Turner founds the Cable News Network (CNN) • John Lennon and Yoko Ono's *Double Fantasy* • **December 8** John Lennon shot dead in New York City • South African novelist J.M. Coetzee publishes *Waiting for the Barbarians* • Death of French existentialist Jean-Paul Sartre • Nintendo's first electronic game • Sony introduces the Walkman • Pac-Man launched	Hugh Hudson's *Chariots of Fire* • Steven Spielberg's *Raiders of the Lost Ark* • First MTV video airs • Primetime TV soap opera *Dallas* cliffhanger "Who shot J.R.?" • Death of Rastafarian reggae singer Bob Marley • Death of U.S. composer Samuel Barber • Death of songwriter Hoagy Carmichael • Toni Morrison's *Tar Baby* • Salman Rushdie's *Midnight's Children* • Prince Charles and Lady Diana Spencer wed • IBM introduces its first personal computer, the IBM PC	Ridley Scott's *Blade Runner*, an adaptation of-Philip K. Dick's *Do Androids Dream of Electric Sheep?* • Steven Spielberg's *E.T., the Extra-Terrestrial* • Richard Attenborough's *Gandhi* • Comedian John Belushi dies of an overdose • *Cheers* TV sitcom debuts • *Lifestyles of the Rich and Famous*, hosted by Robin Leach, debuts • Death of jazz pianist Thelonius Monk • Alice Walker's *The Color Purple* • Gabriel Garcia Marquez's *Chronicle of a Death Foretold* • Compact Disc (CD) audio system launched • Satellite TV introduced	Lawrence Kasdan's *The Big Chill* • Adrian Lyne's *Flashdance* • George Lucas's *Star Wars: Episode VI-Return of the Jedi* • Popular TV programs include *M*A*S*H* and *Magnum P.I.* • Death of American playwright Tennessee Williams • Michael Jackson's *Thriller* • Death of blues singer and songwriter Muddy Waters • Death of Russian-born U.S. choreographer George Balanchine • Death of American heavyweight boxer Jack Dempsey • *Time* magazine names the PC as "Man of the Year"
WORLD EVENTS	First automatic defibrillator is implanted into a human heart • U.S. space probe *Voyager 1* reaches Saturn • **May 18** Mount Saint Helens erupts • Former Hollywood actor Ronald Reagan wins election against incumbent Jimmy Carter • The Green Party forms in Germany • Shipyard strikes in Poland lead to the Solidarity trade union movement • Death of Yugoslavian president Joseph Tito • Iran-Iraq War begins when Iraqi armed forces invade western Iran • Deng Xiaoping takes power-in China • Congress Party under Indira Gandhi wins Indian general elections • South Africa raids guerrilla bases in Angola	U.S. launches first space shuttle, *Columbia* • AIDS (acquired immune deficiency syndrome) identified • **March 30** Assassination attempt on U.S. president Ronald Reagan • Sandra Day O'Connor becomes the first female U.S. Supreme Court justice • Socialist François Mitterand elected president in France • Assassination attempt on Pope John Paul II • Clashes between the PLO and Israel in Lebanon begin • Israeli air strike destroys nuclear reactor in Iraq • **October 6** Egyptian president Anwar Sadat assassinated by a member of his own armed forces • China limits families to one child • World population reaches 4.5 billion	First permanent artificial heart, the Jarvik-7, is implanted • Insulin manufactured from bacteria becomes the first commercial product of genetic engineering • 2,075 couples, members of the Unification Church ("Moonies"), wed in a mass ceremony in Madison Square Garden, New York • Falklands War between Britain and Argentina • Israel invades Lebanon • New government under Chancellor Helmut Kohl forms in West Germany • In Poland, the labor union Solidarity is outlawed • Soviet president Leonid Brezhnev dies	Sally Ride becomes the first woman in space • Human immunodeficiency virus (HIV) identified • First successful live human embryo is implanted • President Reagan calls the Soviet Union the "Evil Empire" and proposes the Strategic Defense Initiative (SDI), "Star Wars" • British prime minister Margaret Thatcher wins a-second term • U.S. invades Granada • U.S.S.R. downs South Korean jet KAL 007, killing all 269 passengers • Writer Arthur Koestler, proponent of voluntary euthanasia, takes his life • Oil tanker runs aground off Cape Town, South Africa, causing severe pollution • Blowout in the Nowruz oil field in the Persian Gulf spills an estimated 600,000 tons of oil

1984	1985	1986	1987
Primitivism in 20th Century Art: Affinities of the Tribal and the Modern, Museum of Modern Art, New York • Art and Ideology, New Museum of Contemporary Art, New York • Frederic Jameson's influential essay "Postmodernism, or The Cultural Logic of Late Capitalism" is published • French philosopher Michel Foucault dies • Death of U.S. photographer Ansel Adams	The Art of Memory/The Loss of History, New Museum of Contemporary Art, New York • The Saatchi Gallery opens in London • Katharina Fritsch's first solo exhibit opens in Cologne, Germany • Peter Halley, Alfredo Jaar, and the Starn Twins are featured in their first solo exhibits in New York • Rosalind Krauss publishes The Originality of the Avant-Garde and Other Modernist Myths • Death of Russian-born artist Marc Chagall • Death of French artist Jean Dubuffet, developer of Art Brut	The Spiritual in Art: Abstract Painting, 1890–1985, Los Angeles County Museum of Art • Arthur C. Danto publishes The Philosophical Disenfranchisement of Art • Andreas Huyssen publishes After the Great Divide: Modernism, Mass Culture, Postmodernism • Death of German sculptor and performance artist Joseph Beuys, at age 64 • Death of British sculptor Henry Moore • Death of U.S. painter Georgia O'Keeffe	The Museum of Women in the Arts is founded in Washington, D.C. • The NAMES Project AIDS Memorial Quilt is displayed in Washington, D.C., on the Mall • Barbara Kruger and Sherrie Levine become first female artists to join Mary Boone Gallery roster • Influential photographer Peter Hujar dies • King of Pop Andy Warhol dies at age 59 of a heart attack following a routine surgery
James Cameron's The Terminator, starring Arnold Schwarzenegger • Rob Reiner's mock documentary This Is Spinal Tap • (the artist formerly known as) Prince releases Purple Rain • Madonna releases Like a Virgin • Death of swing master Count Basie • Singer Marvin Gaye is shot dead by his father in a violent argument • The term cyberspace is coined by William Gibson in Neuromancer • Czech novelist Milan Kundera publishes The Unbearable Lightness of-Being • Death of writer Truman Capote	Robert Zemeckis's film Back to the Future • Akira Kurosawa's film Ran • Death of filmmaker and actor Orson Wells • Actor Rock Hudson dies from AIDS • Motion picture industry designs the new advisory rating PG-13 • Samplers begin to transform pop music production • Live Aid concert at Wembly Stadium, London, and in Philadelphia • Isabel Allende's The House of Spirits • Nintendo Entertainment System is introduced in the U.S. • The cellular telephone system is introduced in Britain • Microsoft Windows 1.0 released	Oliver Stone's film Platoon • David Lynch's film Blue Velvet • Spike Lee's She's Gotta Have It • Death of actor Cary Grant • The Oprah Winfrey Show is syndicated nationally • Margaret Atwood publishes The Handmaid's Tale • Art Spiegelman publishes Maus: A Survivor's Tale • Death of French author Simone de Beauvoir • Death of playwright Jean Genet • Apple's Macintosh introduces the mouse, windows, and onscreen icons to personal computers	Adrian Lyne's film Fatal Attraction • John Boorman's Hope and Glory • Bernardo Bertolucci's The Last Emperor • Wim Wender's Wings of Desire • Death of comedian Jackie Gleason • "Good Night," the first "shorts" episode of The Simpsons airs • Michael Jackson releases Bad • Death of kitsch piano king Liberace • Reggae musician Peter Tosh is shot dead in Jamaica • Toni Morrison's Beloved • Tom Wolfe's The Bonfire of the Vanities • Disposable contact lens marketed
Genetic fingerprinting is developed • President Ronald Reagan wins another term in election against Walter Mondale; Geraldine Ferraro is the Democratic Party's nominee for vice president • Miners' strike in Britain • British prime minister Margaret Thatcher agrees to return Hong Kong to China in 1997 • October 31 Prime minister of India Indira Gandhi is assassinated • December 3 Pesticide leak from Union Carbide factory at-Bhopal, India, kills 2,500 • Archbishop Desmond Tutu is awarded the Nobel Peace Prize • Three million die of famine in Ethiopia	Synthetic skin is introduced • Bifocal contact lens are marketed • British scientist Joe Farman publishes the discovery of an ozone hole over Antarctica • The wreck of the Titanic is found by underwater robotics • Israel withdraws from Lebanon • French government intelligence agents sink Greenpeace ship Rainbow Warrior in Aukland, New Zealand, harbor; the environmental group was protesting France's nuclear weapons tests in the Pacific • Mikhail Gorbachev comes to power in the U.S.S.R. • South Africa abolishes laws forbidding interracial marriage	January 28 The space shuttle Challenger explodes on take-off, killing the entire crew, including teacher Christa McAuliffe • Core unit of the Mir space station launched • Six million participate in Hands Across America, a project to raise money for the homeless • U.S. bombs Libya • Iran-Contra Scandal surfaces; profits from illegal arms sales to Iran were given to Contra rebels fighting the elected Sandinista government in Nicaragua • Jacques Chirac is elected French prime minister; Socialists are defeated in elections • April 26 Chernobyl nuclear power plant disaster in the Ukraine when a reactor explodes • U.S. imposes sanctions on South Africa with the Anti-Apartheid Act • Desmond Tutu is appointed Anglican archbishop of South Africa	Glass fiber optic cable laid across the Atlantic • Construction of the Channel Tunnel between France and Britain begins • President Ronald Reagan uses the word AIDS in a public address • Lieutenant Colonel Oliver North testifies at the Iran-Contra congressional hearings in Washington, D.C. • October 19 Black Monday collapse of the stock markets of London and New-York • Prime minister Margaret Thatcher wins a third consecutive term • U.S. and Soviet Union sign the Intermediate Nuclear Forces Treaty for reducing nuclear weapons

	1988	1989	1990	1991
ART	I.M. Pei's pyramid extension to the Louvre in Paris opens • Griselda Pollock publishes *Vision and Difference: Femininity, Feminism, and the Histories of Art* • Jean-Michel Basquiat dies of a heroin overdose at age 27 • Death of Romare Bearden • Death of Italian car designer Enzo Ferrari • Death of sculptor Louise Nevelson • Death of abstract sculptor Isamu Noguchi	Andres Serrano's *Piss Christ* (1987) is debated by the U.S. Senate; a bill passed prohibits the National Endowment for the Arts from funding artworks deemed obscene • Robert Mapplethorpe: The Perfect Moment, Washington, D.C. • Magiciens de la Terre presents the subject of "globalism" at the Centre Georges Pompidou, Paris • Richard Serra's *Tilted Arc* is removed from the Federal Plaza in Lower Manhattan • Death of Spanish Surrealist Salvador Dali • Photographer Robert Mapplethorpe dies at age 42	High and Low: Modern Art and Popular Culture, the Museum of Modern Art, New York • The Decade Show: Frameworks of Identity in the 1980s is presented at the Museum of Contemporary Hispanic Art, the New Museum of Contemporary Art, and the Studio Museum in Harlem • Jenny Holzer becomes the first woman to represent the U.S. at the Venice Biennale, where she wins the grand prize • Keith Haring dies from AIDS at age 31	Pleasure and Terrors of Domestic Comfort is presented at the Museum of Modern Art, New York • Dislocations is presented at the Museum of Modern Art, New York • Degenerate Art: The Fate of the Avant-Garde in Nazi Germany opens in Los Angeles • Sculptor Anish Kapoor wins the Turner Prize • Painter Carlos Alfonzo dies from AIDS at age 41 • Death of U.S. painter Robert Motherwell • Death of Swiss artist Jean Tinguely
POP CULTURE	Giuseppe Tornatore's film *Cinema Paradiso* • John Waters's film *Hairspray* • Barry Levinson's film *Rain Man* • Robert Zemeckis's film *Who Framed Roger Rabbit?* • George Michael releases *Faith* • Singer Roy Orbison dies of a heart attack at the age of 52 • Stephen Hawking publishes *A Brief History of Time* • Gabriel Garcia Marquez publishes *Love in the Time of Cholera* • U.S. track athlete Florence Griffith Joyner wins three gold medals at the Olympic Games in Seoul, Korea; Canadian Ben Johnson is disqualified for using steroids before the 100-meter race	Spike Lee's film *Do the Right Thing* • Martin Scorsese's film *The Last Temptation of Christ* • Michael Moore's *Roger and Me* • Steven Soderbergh's *sex, lies and videotapes* • Popular TV shows include *Roseanne* and *The Wonder Years* • Death of comedian Lucille Ball • Salman Rushdie publishes the novel *The Satanic Verses*; the Iranian government accuses him of blasphemy against Islam and issues a death sentence • Death of Irish dramatist and author Samuel Beckett • Nintendo's Game-Boy is introduced	Kevin Costner's film *Dances with Wolves* • Francis Ford Coppola's film *The Godfather Part-III* • Martin Scorsese's film *GoodFellas* • *Beverly Hills 90210* debuts • Death of singer and entertainer Sammy Davis-Jr. • American blues guitarist Stevie Ray Vaughan dies at the age of 35 in a helicopter crash • Poet Anthony E. Hecht publishes *The Transparent Man* • Naomi Wolf publishes *The Beauty Myth* • Baseball legend Pete Rose is banned from the game for gambling on professional sports • Tim Berners-Lee writes the first World Wide Web program	Zhang Yimou's film *Raise the Red Lantern* • Jonathan Demme's film *Silence of the Lambs* • Ridley Scott's film *Thelma and Louise* • Nirvana's *Nevermind* • Queen's member Freddie Mercury dies from AIDS • Death of jazz musician Miles Davis • Douglas Coupland's *Generation X: Tales for an Accelerated Culture* • Death of Theodor Geisel, creator of Dr. Seuss • Earvin "Magic" Johnson announces his retirement from the NBA after testing HIV positive • Norplant contraceptive implants are introduced in the U.S.
WORLD EVENTS	First transatlantic fiber optic cable processes 40,000 phone calls simultaneously • DNA fingerprinting is used in forensics • Global warming fears increase; a UN resolution calls climate a "common concern of mankind" • George Bush wins the U.S. presidential election against Democratic candidate Michael Dukakis • Panamanian dictator Manuel Noriega is indicted on drug charges • Iran-Iraq War ends as the Iranian economy collapses • Mikhail Gorbachev becomes president of the reformed Soviet government • Soviet troops withdraw from Afghanistan • Nelson Mandela's 70th birthday is marked by world protests over his continued imprisonment in South Africa	First communications between commercial E-mail and Internet • U.S. launches the *Magellan* and *Galileo* probes to explore Venus and Jupiter; *Voyager 2* reaches Neptune • **March 24** Exxon Valdez oil tanker runs aground in Prince William Sound, Alaska, spilling 11 million gallons • **October 17** Earthquake in San Francisco bay area, collapsing a double-tiered freeway bridge; • Panama declares war on U.S. • **November 9** The Berlin Wall falls • Death of Iranian leader Ayatollah Khomeini • Death of Emperor Hirohito of Japan • **June 3** Tiananmen Square massacre in Beijing, China • F. W. de Klerk becomes president of South Africa	The *Hubble* space telescope is sent into orbit • Beef products are banned in Britain over concern about Mad Cow disease, bovine spongiform encephalopathy (BSE) • Margaret Thatcher resigns as British prime minister; John Major takes office • Germany is reunited to form the Federal Republic of Germany, led by chancellor Helmut Kohl • Communist Slobodan Milosevic is elected president of Serbia • Conflict between Serbs and Albanians in Kosovo, Yugoslavia • Iraq invades Kuwait • Boris Yeltsin is elected president of Russia • Collapse of the U.S.S.R. • Mikhail Gorbachev is awarded the Nobel Peace Prize for his role in helping to end the Cold War • **February 11** Nelson Mandela is released after 27 years' imprisonment	Precision-guided munitions, called "smart bombs," are used in the Persian Gulf War • President George Bush signs the Strategic Arms Reduction Treaty in Moscow • Anita Hill accuses U.S. Supreme Court nominee Clarence Thomas of sexual harassment • **March 3** Black motorist Rodney King is beaten by four white Los Angeles police officers; a witness' videotape of the incident prompts national debate on race and police brutality • Cholera outbreak hits Peru and spreads to Brazil • The Warsaw Pact is dissolved • Slovenia and Croatia declare independence from Yugoslavia • South African government announces repeal of apartheid laws • Civil war in Somalia • World population reaches 5.5 billion

1992

Helter Skelter: LA Art in the 1990s is presented at the Temporary Contemporary of the Museum of Contemporary Art, Los-Angeles • Mining the Museum, an installation by artist Fred Wilson, is presented at the Maryland Historical Society • Post Human, FAE Musée d'Art Contemporain, Pully/Lausanne • Death of British painter Francis Bacon • Death of artist and composer John Cage • Death of U.S. painter Joan Mitchell • David Wojnarowicz dies from AIDS at age 37

1993

The U.S. Holocaust Memorial Museum, designed by James Ingo Freed, opens in Washington, D.C. • The 1993 Biennial Exhibition, presented at the Whitney Museum of American Art, explores issues of race, class, and sexual identity • Roy Lichtenstein, Solomon R. Guggenheim Museum • The Return of the Cadavre Exquis, the Drawing Center, New York • Sculptor Rachel Whiteread wins the Turner Prize • Death of U.S. painter Richard Diebenkorn

1994

The Andy Warhol Museum opens in Pittsburgh • Michelangelo's restored Sistine Chapel frescoes are unveiled at the Vatican • Sculptor Antony Gormley wins the Turner Prize • Black Male: Representations of Masculinity in Contemporary American Art, Whitney Museum of American Art, New York • Andres Serrano, Works, 1983–1993, Institute of Contemporary Art in Philadelphia • Death of critic Clement Greenberg at age 85 • Death of U.S. sculptor Donald Judd

1995

In a Different Light: Visual Culture, Sexual Identity, Queer Practice, University Art Museum in Berkeley, California • The Masculine Masquerade, MIT List Visual Arts Center • Africus 95 is the first Johannesburg Biennale • Sense and Sensibility: Women Artists and Minimalism in the Nineties, the Museum of Modern Art, New York • Longing and Belonging: From the Faraway Nearby, presented at SITE Santa Fe, explores issues of identity in global culture

---

Neil Jordan's *The Crying Game* • Régis Wargnier's film *Indochine* • Alfonso Arau's *Like Water for Chocolate* • Spike Lee's film *Malcolm X* • Comedian Johnny Carson retires as host of *The Tonight Show*; he is replaced by Jay Leno • Francis Fukuyama publishes *The End of History* • Death of scifi writer Isaac Asimov • The term *virtual reality* is coined by Jaron Lanier • The National Space and Air Museum opens an exhibit of Star Trek memorabilia, including the ears of Mr. Spock

Chen Kaige's film *Farewell My Concubine* • Jane Campion's *The Piano* • Tran Anh Hung's *The Scent of Green Papaya* • Steven Spielberg's *Schindler's List* • *X-Files* premieres • Death of actor Raymond Burr, known for his role as Perry Mason • Tony Kushner's *Angels in America: A Gay Fantasia on National Themes* opens on Broadway • Death of jazz trumpeter and bebop pioneer Dizzy Gillespie • Alan Lightman publishes *Einstein's Dreams* • Poet A. R. Ammons publishes *Garbage*

Robert Zemeckis's *Forrest Gump* • Quentin Tarantino's *Pulp Fiction* • King of pop Michael Jackson weds Lisa Marie Presley • Kurt Cobain, lead singer of Nirvana, kills himself with a shotgun • Death of U.S. jazz singer and band leader Cab Calloway • The Woodstock 25th anniversary concert, Saugerties, New York • Sherwin Nuland publishes *How We Die* • At age 47, George Foreman reclaims the world heavyweight boxing title by defeating 27-year-old Michael Moorer • Death of Jacqueline Kennedy Onassis

Idrissa Ouedraogo's *Africa, My Africa* • Joel and Ethan Coen's *Fargo* • Danny Boyle's *Trainspotting* • *Superman* star Christopher Reeve is paralyzed after falling from his horse • Death of Jerry Garcia of The Grateful Dead • Death of baseball great Mickey Mantle • The computer program Aaron, developed by Harold Cohen, produces the first "original" artworks, exhibited at the Boston Computer Museum • Tamagotchi virtual pets introduced in Japan

---

Democrat Bill Clinton wins presidency in election against Republican incumbents and billionaire independent candidate H. Ross Perot • **April 29** Riots break out in Los Angeles after the four police officers charged for the Rodney King beating are acquitted • European community signs the Treaty of European Union • Boutros Boutros Ghali is appointed secretary general of the United Nations • Yugoslavia dissolves into independent republics; massacres in Bosnia and Croatia • U.N. imposes sanctions on Serbia • U.S. military intervenes in Somalia in an effort to distribute food supplies

February 26 The World Trade Center in New York is bombed, killing 6, injuring more than 1,000 • North America Free Trade Agreement (NAFTA) between Mexico, U.S., and Canada • The Brady Act, imposing slight gun control, passes in the U.S. • The Waco headquarters in Texas is stormed by federal agents; 82 people are killed in a fire • President Clinton orders the military to lift ban on homosexual servicemen • Homosexuality is decriminalized in Ireland • Oslo Peace Accord signed by Israel and the PLO • U.S. troops withdraw from Somalia • U.N. forms war crimes tribunal for genocide committed in the former Yugoslavia • Czechoslovakia becomes the separate Czech Republic and Slovakia

President Clinton is investigated for his involvement with the Whitewater Development Corp in Arkansas • Death of former U.S. president Richard Nixon • O.J. Simpson is charged with the murders of Nicole Brown Simpson and Ronald Goldman • More than 20,000 Cubans leave for the U.S. when the Cuban government lifts restrictions on departure • Channel Tunnel connects Britain and France • Homosexual age of consent lowered to 18 in Britain • Britain and Ireland sign a declaration of peace • Russian forces invade Chechnya • Nelson Mandela is elected president of South Africa in the first fully democratic elections • Massacres in Rwanda's civil war

AIDS affects over 1 million worldwide • U.S. space shuttle *Discovery* docks with Russian space station *Mir* • **April 19** Oklahoma City's Alfred P. Murrah Federal Building bombed • **October 16** The Million Man March, led by Muslim leader Louis Farakhan, draws 400,000 African-American men to the Mall in Washington, D.C. • Referendum in Quebec narrowly votes to remain part of Canada • Assassination of Israeli prime minister Yitzhak Rabin • Aum Shinrikyo cult members release nerve gas in Tokyo subway trains, killing 12 and injuring over 5,000 • Thousands of Hutu refugees are killed by Tutsi forces in Rwanda • Ebola outbreak in Zaire

Timeline

	1996	1997	1998	1999
ART	Stelarc performs Ping Body, an "Internet Activated Performance," Art Space in Sydney, Australia; the audience participating via the Internet control the movements of the artist's body • The AIDS Memorial Quilt is displayed on the Mall in Washington, D.C. • Distemper: Dissonant Themes in the Art of the 1990s, Hirshhorn Museum and Sculpture Garden, Washington, D.C. • Death of sculptor Dan Flavin • Felix Gonzalez Torres dies of AIDS at age 38	Edwardo Kac has an identification microchip implanted in his leg in his "intracorporeal" artwork • The Basilica of Saint Francis of Assisi is damaged by an earthquake in Italy • Rrose is a Rrose is a Rrose: Gender Performance in Photography, Solomon R. Guggenheim Museum, New York • Sensation, Royal Academy, London • Death of Willem de Kooning • Death of Roy Lichtenstein • Italian fashion designer Gianni Versace is shot dead	Frank Gehry's Guggenheim Museum opens in Bilbao, Spain • The Art of the Motorcycle, Solomon R. Guggenheim Museum, New York • Mark Rothko, The National Gallery of Art, Washington, D.C. • Jackson Pollock, the Museum of Modern Art, New York • Painter Chris Ofili is awarded the Turner Prize • Death of designer Ferdinand Porsche	Inside Out: New Chinese Art, San Francisco Museum of Modern Art and the Asian Art Museum of San Francisco • Regarding Beauty: A View of the Late Twentieth Century, Hirshhorn Museum and Sculpture Garden, Washington, D.C. • William Kentridge is awarded the Carnegie Prize at the Carnegie International, 1999/ 2000 • New York City mayor Rudolph Giuliani threatens sanctions against the Brooklyn Museum of Art's exhibition Sensation: Young British Artists from the Saatchi Collection
POP CULTURE	David Cronenberg's film Crash • Anthony Minghella's film The English Patient • Roland Emmerich's film Independence Day • Popular TV shows include ER and Friends • The U.S. Congress requires television manufacturers to equip new sets with v-chips, hardware that allows parents to block out violent programming • Prince Charles and Princess Diana divorce • Death of comedian George Burns • Death of jazz singer Ella Fitzgerald • Death of poet and essayist Joseph Brodsky	Paul Thomas Anderson's film Boogie Nights • James Cameron's film Titanic • Death of actor Jimmy Stewart • South Park debuts on cable TV • In an episode of the TV sitcom Ellen, actor Ellen DeGeneres becomes the first star in a prime time series to "come out" as a homosexual • **September 6** Princess Diana's funeral becomes the most-watched televised event in history • Death of beat poet Allen Ginsberg • Death of French oceanographer Jacques Cousteau • Volkswagen redesigns the Beetle • Intel launches the Pentium II chip	The Coen brothers' film The Big Lebowski • Peter Weir's The Truman Show • CBS airs footage of assisted suicide advocate Dr. Jack Kevorkian administering lethal drugs to a terminally ill patient • Saturday Night Live veteran Phil Hartman is shot to death by his wife • Pop singer George Michael comes out as a homosexual • Death of singer Frank Sinatra • Track legend Florence Griffith Joyner dies at age 38 • The FDA approves the use of Viagra for the treatment of male impotence	Sam Mendes's film American Beauty • Spike Jonze's film Being John Malkovich • Daniel Myrick and Eduardo Sanchez's Blair Witch Project • David Fincher's film FightClub • Andy and Larry Wachowski's film The Matrix • Barbie makes her movie debut in the blockbuster Toy Story 2 • Death of film director Stanley Kubrick • Death of baseball legend Joe Dimaggio • Japan's Pokemon cards and video games dominate the toy market
WORLD EVENTS	U.S. launches Pathfinder probe to explore Mars • President Clinton wins a second term, defeating opponent Bob Dole • "Unabomber" Theodore Kaczynski is arrested • Death of counterculture exponent Timothy Leary • Rally of nearly 200,000 school children at the Lincoln Memorial in Washington, D.C., in protest of Congress's cuts in social and educational programs • Yasser Arafat is elected president of Palestine • Benjamin Netanyahu is elected prime minister of Israel	Scottish geneticist Ian Wilmut announces his successful cloning of a sheep; the clone is named Dolly • Timothy McVeigh is convicted of the Oklahoma City bombing and sentenced to death • Britain turns Hong Kong over to China • Tony Blair is elected British prime minister • BSE crisis in Britain; beef on the bone is banned • Taliban forces seize power in Afghanistan • Death of Chinese leader Deng Xaioping • European Union bans tobacco ads • Death of Mother Theresa of Calcutta • The World Trade Organization is established	The first component for the International Space Station is launched • NASA announces there is enough frozen water on the moon to support a colony • "Unabomber" Theodore Kaczynski is sentenced to life without parole; over 17 years, his mail bombs killed three people and injured 29 • U.S. Congress votes to impeach President Clinton on charges of perjury and obstruction of justice in the investigation of his alleged affair with White House intern Monica Lewinsky • The Euro currency is introduced by the European Union • Peace deal in Northern Ireland • India and Pakistan each conduct nuclear arms tests • World's longest suspension bridge opens in Japan	Y2K: computer technicians anticipate failure of the two-digit date system • U.S. Senate acquits President Clinton of charges in the Lewinsky scandal • **April 21** Teenagers Eric Harris and Dylan Klebold, armed with automatic weapons, enter Columbine High School in Littleton, Colorado, killing 13 students and teachers; • **November 20** Riots break out in Seattle, Washington, during the meeting of the World Trade Organization • U.S. turns over control of the Panama Canal to Panama • Vladimir Putin becomes Russian prime minister after President Boris Yeltsin resigns • Nelson Mandela steps down as the president of South Africa to be succeeded by Thabo Mbeki

ART

2000

The Tate Modern opens in London • Deborah Willis publishes *Reflections in Black: A History of Black Photographers, 1940 to the Present* • The American Century: Art and Culture, 1950–2000, Whitney Museum of American Art, New York • Death of sculptor George Segal

2001

Spectacular Bodies, Hayward Gallery, London • Alberto Giacometti, Museum of Modern Art, New York

2002

Gerhard Richter is presented at the Museum of Modern Art, New York • Eva Hesse is presented at the Museum of Modern Art, New York • Death of celebrity photographer Herb Ritts • Death of painter Larry Rivers

2003

The Lois and Richard Rosenthal Center for Contemporary Art, designed by Zaha Hadid, opens in Cincinnati • Philip Guston is presented at the San Francisco Museum of Modern Art

POP CULTURE

2000

Cameron Crowe's *Almost Famous* • Ang Lee's film *Crouching Tiger, Hidden Dragon* • Lars von Trier's film *Dancer in the Dark* • Wong Kar wai's film *In the Mood for Love* • Steven Soderbergh's film *Traffic* • Napster, a leader in the digital media sharing industry, faces a legal battle over online copyrights • The "I Love You" computer virus, the most destructive in digital history, affects computer networks worldwide, including the British Parliament, the U.S. Central Intelligence Agency, and the Pentagon

2001

Jean-Pierre Jeunet's film *Amelie* • Ron Howard's film *A Beautiful Mind* • Peter Jackson's adaptation of J. R. R. Tolkien's *The Lord of the Rings: The Fellowship of the Ring* • David Lynch's film *Mulholland Drive* • Death of cartoon animator Bill Hanna • Death of Beatle George Harrison • Death of blues musician and performer Ron Taylor • Death of *Hitchhiker's Guide to the Galaxy* author Douglas Adams

2002

Peter Jackson's film *The Lord of the Rings: The Two Towers* • George Lucas's film *Star Wars: Episode II-Attack of the Clones* • Alexander Sokurov's *Russian Ark* • Hayao Miyazaki's *Spirited Away* • Discount chain Kmart files for Chapter 11 bankruptcy protection • Death of Queen Mother Elizabeth at age 101 • Death of Bugs Bunny and Porky Pig animator Chuck Jones

2003

Peter Jackson's film *The Lord of the Rings: The Return of the King* • Sofia Coppola's film *Lost in Translation* • Jacques Perrin's film *Winged Migration* • Popular TV "reality" shows are *American Idol* and *Survivor* • Death of Fred Rogers, creator and host of the PBS children's show *Mister Rogers' Neighborhood* • Death of actor John Ritter, known for his role as Jack Tripper in the sitcom *Three's Company*

WORLD EVENTS

2000

Human DNA sequence established • U.S. District Court finds Microsoft in violation of antitrust laws • President Bill Clinton leaves office; in his eight-year term, he passed measures to protect 58 million acres of national forest and set aside eight million acres of land as new national monuments • The IRA disarms; Britain restores the Northern Ireland Parliament • The first-ever Concorde jet crashes near Paris, killing 113 people • Vojislav Kostunica is elected Yugoslav president, ousting Slobodan Milosevic • Russian nuclear sub *Kursk* sinks in the Barents Sea, killing 118 crew members • The 13th International AIDS Conference in Durban, South Africa, considers strategies for controlling surging AIDS rates in developing countries • World population exceeds 6 billion

2001

September 11 Terrorists destroy the World Trade Center in New York City and damage the Pentagon in a coordinated hijack attack; an estimated 3,000 are killed • Government officials in Washington, D.C., New York, and Florida receive letters laced with deadly anthrax spores; the incidents lead to new fears of biological terrorism • Enron files for bankruptcy • Former Yugoslav president Slobodan Milosevic surrenders to Serbian authorities; he is tried by the UN war crimes tribunal at The Hague, charged with crimes against humanity in Croatia and Kosovo and genocide in Bosnia • U.S. bombs Afghanistan • The Buddhas of Bamiyan are destroyed by the Taliban • Mad Cow disease spreads within Europe • **November 18** Leonid Meteor Shower • George W.-Bush is inaugurated president after a controversial election against Democrat Al Gore and Green candidate Ralph Nader

2002

Odyssey space probe maps the surface of Mars using thermal emission imaging; the probe identifies ice deposits • There are an estimated 42 million AIDS cases worldwide • The Euro becomes the common currency in 12 European Union nations • Former President Jimmy Carter receives the Nobel Peace Prize • President Bush establishes the Homeland Security Department • A jury in Birmingham, Alabama, convicts former Ku Klux Klan member Bobby Frank Cherry of the 1963 murders of four girls at the 16th Street Baptist Church bombing • Yucca Mountain in Nevada is approved for use as a nuclear waste depository • Hu Jintao replaces Jiang Zemin as general secretary of the Chinese Communist Party • North Korea confirms it is developing nuclear arms, in violation of a 1994 international treaty

2003

Scientists at the University of Illinois develop a copy of a human jaw joint with stem cells from rats • **February 1** Space shuttle *Columbia* breaks apart re-entering the earth's atmosphere, killing all seven aboard, including Colonel Ilan Ramon, Israel's first astronaut • China launches its first manned spacecraft, the *Shenzou 5* (Divine Vessel) • U.S. Senate outlaws partial birth abortion • Supreme Court ruling in *Lawrence v. Texas* overturns sodomy laws in 13 states, establishing equal rights for homosexuals • **March 19** U.S. leads massive air strikes against Iraq; international opponents stage demonstrations • **August 14** Blackout of power grids in Ontario and eight Northeast and Midwestern states; it is the biggest power failure to hit North America • Arnold Schwarzenegger is elected governor of California • Iraqi leader Saddam Hussein is captured by U.S. forces • The deadly respiratory illness, Severe Acute Respiratory Syndrome (SARS), sweeps Asia

	2004	**2005**	**2006**	**2007**

ART

2004
Controversy over the Dia Art-Foundation's proposed restoration of Robert Smithson's *Spiral Jetty* (1970) in the Great Salt Lake • Death of influential theorist Jacques Derrida, best known for his "deconstruction theory" • Death of painter Agnes Martin

2005
Turkey opens its first museum of modern art in Istanbul • Philip Johnson, architect and founding director of the Museum of Modern Art's department of architecture, dies • Patrick Caulfield, British pop artist, dies • Art historian Linda Nochlin receives a lifetime achievement recognition from the College Art Association • Thelma Golden becomes director of the Studio Museum in Harlem • Robert Gober's *Untitled (Leg)*, created in 1990, sells at auction for more than $900,000

2006
Exhibition Legacies: Contemporary Artists Reflect on Slavery opens at the New York Historical Society • The 400-year anniversary of the birth of the renowned Dutch painter Rembrandt is celebrated with special exhibitions at numerous museums • A painting of Dora Maar by Pablo Picasso sells at auction for $95.2 million

2007
The first American museum survey of Australian artist Patricia Piccinini is held • The Whitney Museum in New York presents an exhibition of Lawrence Weiner, including key examples of his art incorporating language • Picasso's *Les Demoiselles d'Avignon* is selected by a *Newsweek* poll as the most influential work of art of the past 100 years • Damien Hirst's diamond skull reportedly sells at auction for $100 million

POP CULTURE

2004
• Lifestyle expert Martha Stewart is convicted of obstructing justice in an investigation into the sale in 2001 of nearly 4,000 shares of ImClone, a biotech company founded by Stewart's friend Sam Waksal • Death of actor Christopher Reeve, who became a campaigner for stem cell research after he was paralyzed

2005
Live 8 concerts raise awareness about global poverty • Harold Pinter, British playwright, wins the Nobel Prize for Literature • The highest-grossing movie is *Star Wars: Episode III—Revenge of the Sith* at $380 million • *Brokeback Mountain* is a hit movie • Popular books published during the year in the United States include *Freakonomics*, by Steven Levitt, and *The Year of Magical Thinking*, by Joan Didion

2006
Former vice president Al Gore releases his documentary *An Inconvenient Truth* about global warming • Barbaro wins the Kentucky Derby • The Album of the Year is U2's *How to Dismantle an Atomic Bomb* • American pop singer James Brown, known as the godfather of soul, dies • Italy wins the World Cup championship in soccer

2007
Author Norman Mailer dies • Newspaper columnist Art Buchwald dies • Racehorse Barbaro dies • Swedish filmmaker Ingmar Bergman dies • Barry Bonds passes Hank Aaron for the record of most home runs in baseball history; his record is controversial because of allegations of steroid use • The Mitchell Report, analyzing the steroid scandal in baseball, is published • The final episode of *The Sopranos* airs on HBO

WORLD EVENTS

2004
Spirit rover transmits images of Mars surface • A new security system, the U.S. Visitor and Immigrant Status Indicator Technology (US VISIT), requires international travelers to be photographed and fingerprinted • U.S. Central Intelligence Agency chief weapons inspector David Kay resigns in the face of an investigation of intelligence reports presented before the U.S.-led war against Iraq; the agency found no evidence of chemical, biological, or nuclear weapons in Iraq • Violent demonstrations in Haiti call for the removal of President Jean Bertrand Aristide • Afghanistan adopts a new constitution that establishes a presidential system and national assembly and gives equal rights to women • **March 11** Terrorists bomb three train stations in Madrid, killing 190, injuring more than 600 • Avian flu (Bird flu) spreads in Asia • **September 1–3** At least 320 people are killed, many of them children, in a siege of a school in Beslan, Russia by Chechen separatists

2005
The world's population reaches 6.4 billion • The U.S. population reaches 296 million • A relief effort is mounted to help Southeast Asian countries devastated by a massive tsunami that struck late in 2004 • Pope John Paul II dies; Benedict XVI becomes the pope • Islamic militant terrorists detonate a bomb in London, killing fifty-two • The Irish Republic Army declares it will seek a united Ireland only through peaceful means • Angela Merkel becomes the first woman elected chancellor of Germany • George W. Bush begins his second term as U.S. president • Hurricane Katrina, the costliest and one of the deadliest natural disasters in U.S. history, strikes the country at the Gulf Coast. Emergency efforts are disorganized

2006
The world's population reaches 6.5 billion • The U.S. population reaches 300 million • According to the United Nations, in 2006, 40 percent of the world's population lives on less than $2 a day • Saddam Hussein is hanged in Baghdad, convicted by an Iraqi court of genocide • A Danish newspaper publishes cartoons of Muhammad provoking protest among Muslims worldwide • President Bush signs a law renewing the Patriot Act. • President Bush vetoes legislation to expand stem-cell research • The New Horizons spacecraft is launched to study Pluto • Pluto is reclassified as a dwarf planet • South Africa legalizes same-sex marriage • Pioneering feminist Betty Friedan dies • Scientists report the discovery of a 375-million-year-old fossil of a fish with rudimentary limbs, adding weight to the theory of evolution

2007
The world's population exceeds 6.6 billion people • Bill Gates, with $59 billion, is the richest American • The European Union expands to twenty-seven nations, adding Romania and Bulgaria • Nancy Pelosi becomes the first woman to serve as Speaker of the U.S. House of Representatives • Scientists identify five planets circling a star forty-one light-years away from Earth • Tony Blair steps down as prime minister of Great Britain • Boris Yeltsin, former president of Russia, dies • Scientists report success using human skin cells to create embryonic stem cells • Greenhouse gases continue building in the Earth's atmosphere reaching 380 parts per million of carbon dioxide in the atmosphere • The Iranian president reports that Iran has the ability to enrich uranium on an industrial scale • More than thirty killed in a Virginia Tech University shooting rampage

Take Your Time: Olafur Eliasson, a survey of Scandinavian Eliasson's art, including large installations and sculpture, opens at the San Francisco Museum of Modern Art • Altered States, a large survey of work by Chinese Zhang Huan, is presented at the Asia Society in New York • Robert Rauschenberg dies • A benefit auction of contemporary art raises more than $40 million to help fight AIDS in Africa • Italian performance artist Giuseppina Pasqualino di Marineo (Pippa Bacca) is killed while engaged in an art project to promote peace in the Middle East

English pop singer Amy Winehouse wins five Grammy Awards • China hosts the summer Olympic games • Comedian George Carlin dies • Apple, Inc., introduces the Macbook Air, the world's thinnest laptop • Tiger Woods wins his fourteenth major golf tournament

Senator Barack Obama secures the nomination as the presidential candidate of the Democrat party after a close primary contest with Senator Hillary Clinton • A committee of Spain's Parliament votes to extend some basic "human" rights to the great apes • Senator John McCain is the Republican nominee for U.S. president • Stock markets around the world fall as fears of a U.S. recession grow • Fidel Castro resigns as president of Cuba • A large earthquake kills over 68,000 people in China • The U.S. Supreme Court rules that the Second Amendment guarantees citizens the right to keep a loaded gun for self-defense at home • Conflict continues in the Darfur region of Sudan, with more than 300,000 estimated killed in the past five years • The U.S. Congress authorizes a $700 billion bailout to rescue faltering financial institutions and businesses amid a worldwide financial crisis • Senator Barack Obama is elected President of the United States, the first African American to achieve the presidency

Selected Bibliography

Chapter One: The Art World Expands

Benezra, Neal, and Olga M. Viso. *Distemper: Dissonant Themes in the Art of the 1990s*. Washington, D.C.: Hirshhorn Museum and Sculpture Garden, Smithsonian Institution, 1996. An exhibition catalog.

Bonami, Francesco, ed. *Universal Experience: Art, Life, and the Tourist's Eye*. Chicago: Museum of Contemporary Art; New York: Distributed Art Publishers, 2005. An exhibition catalog.

Davies, Hugh. *Lateral Thinking: Art of the 1990s*. San Diego, Calif.: San Diego Museum of Contemporary Art, 2002. An exhibition catalog.

Harris, Jonathan. *The New Art History: A Critical Introduction*. London and New York: Routledge, 2001.

Harrison, Charles, and Paul Wood. *Art in Theory 1900–2000: An Anthology of Changing Ideas*. New eds. Malden, Mass.: Blackwell, 2003.

How Latitudes Become Forms: Art in a Global Age. Minneapolis, Minn.: Walker Art Center, 2003. An exhibition catalog.

King, Elaine, and Gail Levin, eds. *Ethics and the Visual Arts*. New York: Allworth Press, 2006.

Kocur, Zoya, and Simon Leung. *Theory in Contemporary Art Since 1985*. Malden, Mass.: Blackwell, 2005.

Lovejoy, Margot. *Postmodern Currents: Art and Artists in the Age of Electronic Media*. 2nd ed. Upper Saddle River, N.J.: Prentice Hall, 1997.

Neill, Alex, and Aaron Ridley, eds. *Arguing About Art: Contemporary Philosophical Debates*. Second Edition. London and New York: Routledge, 2002.

"The 1980s, Part One." Special issue, *Artforum*, March 2003.

"The 1980s, Part Two." Special issue, *Artforum*, April 2003.

Senie, Harriet, and Sally Webster, eds. *Critical Issues in Public Art: Content, Context, and Controversy*. New York: HarperCollins, 1992.

Stiles, Kristine, and Peter Selz, eds. *Theories and Documents of Contemporary Art: A Sourcebook of Artists' Writings*. Berkeley and Los Angeles: University of California Press, 1996.

Tawadros, Gilane, ed. *Changing States: Contemporary Art and Ideas in an Era of Globalisation*. London: Institute of International Visual Arts, 2004.

Tribe, Mark, and Reena Jana. *New Media Art*. Köln, Germany: Taschen, 2006.

Vitamin P: New Perspectives in Painting. London and New York: Phaidon, 2002.

Chapter Two: Identity

Anderson, Walter Truett. *The Truth About the Truth: De-confusing and Re-constructing the Postmodern World*. New York: Putnam, 1995.

Asia/America: Identities in Contemporary Asian American Art. New York: Asia Society Galleries and New Press, 1994. An exhibition catalog.

Berger. Maurice, ed. *White: Whiteness and Race in Contemporary Art*. Baltimore, Md.: Center for Art and Visual Culture; New York: Distributed Art Publishers, 2004. An exhibition catalog.

Butler, Judith. *Gender Trouble: Feminism and the Subversion of Identity*. London and New York: Routledge, 1993.

Carson, Fiona, and Claire Pajaczkowska, eds. *Feminist Visual Culture*. New York: Routledge, 2001.

Chiu, Melissa, Karin Higa, and Susette S. Min *One Way or Another: Asian American Art Now*. New York: Asia Society; New Haven, Conn.: Yale University Press, 2006. An exhibition catalog.

Comic Release: Negotiating Identity for a New Generation. New York: Distributed Art Publishers, 2002. An exhibition catalog.

Freestyle. New York: Studio Museum in Harlem, 2001. An exhibition catalog.

Hassan, Salah M., ed. *Gendered Visions: the Art of Contemporary Africana Women Artists*. Trenton, N.J. and Asmara, Eritrea: Africa World Press, 1997. An exhibition catalog.

ID: An International Survey on the Notion of Identity in Contemporary Art. Eindhoven, the Netherlands: Stedelijk Van Abbemuseum, 1996. An exhibition catalog.

Lippard, Lucy R. *Mixed Blessings: New Art in a Multicultural America*. New York: Pantheon Books, 1990.

Malik, Rohini, and Gavin Jantjes, *A Fruitful Incoherence: Dialogues with Artists on Internationalism*. London: Institute of International Visual Arts, 1998.

Nottage, James H., ed. *Diversity and Dialogue: The Eiteljorg Fellowship for Native American Fine Art*. Indianapolis, Ind.: Eiteljorg Museum of American Indians and Native American Art, 2007. An exhibition catalog.

Reckitt, Helena, ed. *Art and Feminism*. London and New York: Phaidon Press, 2001.

Shiner, Eric C., and Reiko Tomii, eds. *Making a Home: Japanese Contemporary Artists in New York*. New York: Japan Society; New Haven, Conn.: Yale University Press, 2007. An exhibition catalog.

Shohat, Ella, ed. *Talking Visions: Multicultural Feminism in a Transnational Age*. New York: New Museum of Contemporary Art; Cambridge, Mass.: MIT Press, 1998.

Profile: Nancy Burson

Atkins, Robert. "Nancy Burson: Making Faces." *Contemporanea* 24 (January 1991): pp. 54–59.

Burson, Nancy, and Michael L. Sand. *Seeing and Believing: The Art of Nancy Burson*. Santa Fe, N.Mex.: Twin Palms Publishers, 2002. An exhibition catalog.

Busselle, Rebecca. "A Defining Reality: The Photographs of Nancy Burson." *Aperture* 136 (Summer 1994): pp. 73–75.

Friis-Hansen, Dana. *Nancy Burson: The Age Machine and Composite Portraits*. Cambridge, Mass.: MIT Press, 1990. An exhibition catalog.

Herbert, Lynn. *Faces: Nancy Burson*. Houston: Contemporary Arts Museum, 1992. An exhibition catalog.

Robertson, Jean, and Craig McDaniel. "Facing Up to Nancy Burson." *New Art Examiner* 25, no. 4 (January 1998): pp. 36–41.

Profile: Shirin Neshat

Bailey, David A. and Gilane Tawadros, eds. *Veil: Veiling, Representation and Contemporary Art*. Cambridge, Mass.: MIT Press, 2003.

Kontova, Helena. "Marina Abramovic, Vanessa Beecroft, Shirin Neshat: Modern Nomads." *Flash Art* 40 (July–September 2007): pp. 102–107.

Neshat, Shirin. "Shirin Neshat: Interview." By Arthur C. Danto. *Bomb* 73 (Fall 2000): pp. 60–67.

Shaw, Wendy Meryem K. "Ambiguity and Audience in the Films of Shirin Neshat." *Third Text* 57 (Winter 2001–02): pp. 43–52.

Van Hoof, Marine. "Shirin Neshat: Veils in the Wind." *Art Press* 279 (May 2002): pp. 34–39.

Wallach, Amei. "Shirin Neshat: Islamic Counterpoints." *Art in America* 89 (October 2001): pp. 136–143, 189.

Zabel, Igor. "Women in Black." *Art Journal* 60, no. 4 (Winter 2001): pp. 16–25.

Chapter Three: The Body

Body. Melbourne and New South Wales, Australia: Bookman Schwartz and Art Gallery of New South Wales, 1997. An exhibition catalog.

Brand, Peg Zeglin. *Beauty Matters*. Bloomington: Indiana University Press, 2000.

Brettle, Jane, and Sally Rice, eds. *Public Bodies–Private States: New Views on Photography, Representation and Gender*. Manchester, United Kingdom, and New York: Manchester University Press, 1994.

Broude, Norma, and Mary D. Garrard, eds. *The Expanding Discourse: Feminism and Art History*. New York: HarperCollins, 1992.

Deitch, Jeffrey. *Post Human*. Pully and Lausanne, Switzerland: FAE Musée d'Art Contemporain; New York: Distributed Art Publishers, 1992. An exhibition catalog.

Ebony, David. *Curve: The Female Nude Now*. New York: Universe, 2003.

Hall, Donald. *Corporal Politics*. Cambridge, Mass.: MIT List Visual Arts Center; Boston: Beacon Press, 1992. An exhibition catalog.

Jones, Caroline, ed. *Sensorium: Embodied Experience, Technology, and Contemporary Art*. Cambridge, Mass.: MIT List Visual Arts Center and MIT Press, 2006. An exhibition catalog.

Kristeva, Julia. *Powers of Horror: An Essay on Abjection*. New York: Columbia University Press, 1982.

McDonald, Helen, *Erotic Ambiguities: The Female Nude in Art*. London and New York: Routledge, 2001.

McEvilley, Thomas. *Sculpture in the Age of Doubt*. New York: Allworth Press, 1999.

Miglietti, Francesca Alfano. *Extreme Bodies: The Use and Abuse of the Body in Art*. Milan: Skira, 2003.

Mulvey, Laura. "Visual Pleasure and Narrative Cinema." *Screen*, Autumn 1975, and reprinted in Mulvey, *Visual and Other Pleasures*. Basingstoke, United Kingdom: Macmillan, 1989.

Rogers, Sarah J. *Body Mécanique: Artistic Explorations of Digital Realms*. Columbus: Wexner Center for the Arts, The Ohio State University, 1998. An exhibition catalog.

Stirratt, Betsy, and Catherine Johnson, eds. *Feminine Persuasion: Art and Essays on Sexuality*. Bloomington: Indiana University Press, 2003. An exhibition catalog.

Thompson, Barbara, ed. *Black Womanhood: Images, Icons, and Ideologies of the African Body*. Hanover, N.H.: Hood Museum of Art, Dartmouth College, in association with University of Washington Press, Seattle, 2008. An exhibition catalog.

Warr, Tracey, ed. *The Artist's Body*. London: Phaidon Press, 2000.

Profile: Renée Cox

Cox, Renée. *Renée Cox: American Family*. New York: Robert Miller Gallery, 2001. An exhibition catalog.

Hobson, Janell. *Venus in the Dark: Blackness and Beauty in Popular Culture*. New York: Routledge, 2005.

Liss, Andrea. "Black Bodies in Evidence: Maternal Visibility in Renée Cox's Family Portraits." In Marianne Hirsch, ed., *The Familial Gaze*. Hanover, N.H.: University Press of New England, 1993, pp. 276–290.

Myers, B. E. "What Is My Legacy? Transient Consciousness and the 'Fixed' Subject in the Photography of Renée Cox." In Salah M. Hassan, ed., *Gendered Visions: The Art of Contemporary Africana Women Artists*. Trenton, N.J., and Asmara, Eritrea: Africa World Press, 1997, p. 32.

Profile: Zhang Huan

Chiu, Melissa, ed. *Zhang Huan: Altered States*. New York: Asia Society, 2007. An exhibition catalog.

Dziewior, Yilmaz, ed. *Zhang Huan*. Hamburg, Germany: Hatje Cantz, 2003. An exhibition catalog.

Erickson, Britta. *On the Edge: Contemporary Chinese Artists Encounter the West*. Stanford, Calif.: Iris & B. Gerald Cantor Center for Visual Arts, 2005. An exhibition catalog.

Minglu, Gao, ed. *Inside Out: New Chinese Art*. Berkeley and Los Angeles: University of California Press, 1998. An exhibition catalog.

Chapter Four: Time

Appel, Dora. *Memory Effects: The Holocaust and the Art of Secondary Witnessing*. New Brunswick, N.J.: Rutgers University Press, 2002.

Doubletake: Collective Memory and Current Art. London: South Bank Centre and Parkett Publishers, 1992. An exhibition catalog.

Friedel, Helmut, ed. *Moments in Time: On Narration and Slowness*. Stuttgart, Germany: Hatje Cantz; New York: Distributed Art Publishers, 1999.

Gangitano, Lia, and Steven Nelson, eds. *New Histories*. Boston: Institute of Contemporary Art, 1996. An exhibition catalog.

Herkenhoff, Paulo, Roxana Marcoci, and Miriam Basilio. *Tempo*. New York: Museum of Modern Art, 2002. An exhibition catalog.

Hughes, Alex, and Andrea Noble. *Phototextualities: Intersections of Photography and Narrative*. Albuquerque: University of New Mexico Press, 2003.

Huyssen, Andreas. *Twilight Memories: Marking Time in a Culture of Amnesia*. New York: Routledge, 1995.

Kleeblatt, Norman L., ed. *Mirroring Evil: Nazi Imagery/Recent Art*. New York: Jewish Museum; New Brunswick, N.J.: Rutgers University Press, 2002. An exhibition catalog.

Making Time: Considering Time as a Material in Contemporary Video and Film. Lake Worth, Fla.: Palm Beach Institute of Contemporary Art, 2000. An exhibition catalog.

Rush, Michael. *New Media in Late Twentieth-Century Art*. New York: Thames & Hudson, 1999.

Saltzman, Lisa. *Making Memory Matter: Strategies of Remembrance in Contemporary Art*. Chicago: University of Chicago Press, 2006.

Thomspon, Nato, ed. *Ahistoric Occasion: Artists Making History*. North Adams: Mass MoCA Publications, 2007. An exhibition catalog.

Toll, Nelly. *When Memory Speaks: The Holocaust in Art*. Westport, Conn.: Praeger Publishers, 1998.

Profile: Brian Tolle

Blackwell, Josh. "Brian Tolle at Shoshana Wayne," *Art Issues* 63 (Summer 2000): p. 49.

Kaizen, William. "Brian Tolle," *Bomb* 77 (Summer 2001): pp. 56–63.

Owens, Craig. "The Allegorical Impulse: Towards a Theory of Postmodernism." In Charles Harrison and Paul Wood, eds., *Art in Theory: 1900–2000*, pp. 1025–1032. Malden, Mass.: Blackwell, 2003.

Richardson, Lynda. "Like Potato Fields, His Memorial Lies Fallow." *New York Times*, May 14, 2003, p. B2.

Servetar, Stuart. "Ouverture: Brian Tolle." *Flash Art* 189 (Summer 1996): p. 124.

Weaver, Thomas. "Brian Tolle: Overmounted Interior." *Sculpture* 15, no. 7 (September 1996): pp. 64–65.

Profile: Cornelia Parker

Button, Virginia. *The Turner Prize 1997*. London: Tate Gallery, 1997. An exhibition catalog.

Cornelia Parker: A Meteorite Lands. Manchester, United Kingdom: Ikon Gallery, 2002. An exhibition catalog.

Corrin, Lisa G. *Cornelia Parker*. London: Serpentine Gallery, 1998. An exhibition catalog.

Ferguson, Bruce, and Jessica Morgan. *Cornelia Parker*. Boston: Institute of Contemporary Art, 2000. An exhibition catalog.

Jahn, Andrea, ed. *Cornelia Parker—Perpetual Canon*. Stuttgart, Germany: Württembergischer Kunstverein, 2005. An exhibition catalog.

Chapter Five: Place

Bachelard, Gaston. *The Poetics of Space*. Boston: Beacon Press, 1969.

Bender, Susan and Ian Berry. *The World According to the Newest and Most Exact Observations: Mapping Art and Science*. Saratoga Springs, N.Y.: Tang Teaching Museum and Art Gallery, Skidmore College, 2001. An exhibition catalog.

Davies, Hugh. *Blurring the Boundaries: Installation Art, 1969–1996*. San Diego, Calif.: Museum of Contemporary Art, 1996. An exhibition catalog.

Deitch, Jeffrey, and Dan Friedman, eds. *Artificial Nature*. Athens, Greece: Deste Foundation for Contemporary Art, 1990. An exhibition catalog.

De Oliveira, Nicolas, Nicola Oxley, and Michael Petry. *Installation Art*. London: Thames and Hudson, 1994.

Doherty, Claire, ed. *Claustrophobia*. Birmingham, United Kingdom: Ikon Gallery, 1998. An exhibition catalog.

Dunning, William V. *Changing Images of Pictorial Space: A History of Spatial Illusion in Painting*. Syracuse, N.Y.: Syracuse University Press, 1991.

Enwezor, Okwui, "A Question of Place: Revisions, Reassessments, Diaspora," in *Transforming the Crown: African, Asian & Caribbean Artists in Britain 1966–1996*. New York: African Diaspora Institute, 1997, pp. 80–88.

Grynsztejn, Madeleine, *About Place: Recent Art of the Americas*. Chicago: Art Institute of Chicago, 1995.

Kastner, Jeffrey, ed., *Land and Environmental Art*. London: Phaidon, 1998.

Kwon, Miwon, *One Place After Another*. Cambridge, Mass.: MIT Press, 2002.

Lippard, Lucy, *The Lure of the Local: Senses of Place in a Multicentered Society*. New York: The New Press, 1997.

Martin, Richard, ed., *The New Urban Landscape*. New York: Olympia & York Companies, 1989.

McMaster, Gerald, ed. *Reservation X: The Power of Place in Aboriginal Contemporary Art*. Quebec: Canadian Museum of Civilization; Seattle: University of Washington Press, 1998.

No Place (Like Home). Minneapolis, Minn.: Walker Art Center; New York: Distributed Art Publishers, 1997. An exhibition catalog.

O'Doherty, Brian. *Inside the White Cube: The Ideology of the Gallery Space*. San Francisco: Lapis Press, 1986.

Out of Site: Fictional Architectural Spaces. New York: New Museum of Contemporary Art, 2002. An exhibition catalog.

Reiss, Julie H. *From Margin to Center: The Spaces of Installation Art*. Cambridge, Mass.: MIT Press, 1999.

Rogoff, Irit. *Terra Infirma: Geography's Visual Culture*. London and New York: Routledge, 2000.

Rybczynski, Witold. *Home: A Short History of an Idea*. New York: Penguin Books, 1987.

Small World: Dioramas in Contemporary Art. San Diego, Calif.: Museum of Contemporary Art, 2000. An exhibition catalog.

Storr, Robert, *Mapping*. New York: Museum of Modern Art, 1994. An exhibition catalog.

Suderburg, Erika, ed. *Space, Site, Intervention: Situating Installation Art*. Minneapolis: University of Minnesota Press, 2000.

Vidler, Anthony. "Interpreting the Void: Architecture and Spatial Anxiety." In Mark A. Cheetham, Michael Ann Holly, and Keith Moxey, eds., *The Subjects of Art History: Historical Objects in Contemporary Perspective*, pp. 288–307. Cambridge, United Kingdom: Cambridge University Press, 1998.

Profile: Janet Cardiff

Betsky, Aaron. "Janet Cardiff." In *010101: Art in Technological Times*. San Francisco: San Francisco Museum of Modern Art, 2001, pp. 052–053. An exhibition catalog.

Cardiff, Janet. "Inexplicable Symbiosis: A Conversation with Janet Cardiff." By Carolee Thea. *Sculpture* 22, no. 1 (January–February 2003): pp. 52–57.

D'Souza, Aruna. "A World of Sound." *Art in America* 90, no. 4 (April 2002): pp. 110–115, 161.

Kimmelman, Michael. "Janet Cardiff" in "Art in Review." *New York Times*, November 30, 2001, p. E36.

Lerner, Adam. "Janet Cardiff and George Bures Miller." In Jonathan P. Binstock, *The 47th Corcoran Biennial: Fantasy Underfoot*. Washington, D.C.: Corcoran Gallery of Art, 2002, pp. 42–45.

Profile: Unilever Series at Tate Modern

Blazwick, Iwona, and Simon Wilson, eds. *Tate Modern: The Handbook*. London: Tate Publishing, 2000.

De Salvo, Donna. *Anish Kapoor: Marsyas*. London: Tate Publishing, 2002. An exhibition catalog.

Grynsztejn, Madeleine. *Take Your Time: Olafur Eliasson*. San Francisco: San Francisco Museum of Modern Art; New York: Thames and Hudson, 2007. An exhibition catalog.

May, Susan. *Olafur Eliasson: The Weather Project*. London: Tate Publishing, 2004. An exhibition catalog.

Morgan, Jessica. *Test Site: Carsten Höller*. London: Tate Publishing, 2006. An exhibition catalog.

Salcedo, Doris. *Doris Salcedo Shibboleth*. London: Tate Publishing, 2007. An exhibition catalog.

Chapter Six: Language

Bee, Susan, and Mira Schor, eds. *M/E/A/N/I/N/G: An Anthology of Artists' Writings, Theory, and Criticism*. Durham, N.C.: Duke University Press, 2000.

Bowman, Russell. "Words and Images: A Persistent Paradox." *Art Journal* 45 (Winter 1985): pp. 335–343.

Colpitt, Frances, and Phyllis Plous. *Knowledge: Aspects of Conceptual Art*. Santa Barbara: University Art Museum, University of California, 1992. An exhibition catalog.

Drucker, Johanna. *The Century of Artists' Books*. New York: Granary Books, 1995.

A Forest of Signs: Art in the Crisis of Representation. Los Angeles: Museum of Contemporary Art; Cambridge, Mass.: MIT Press, 1989. An exhibition catalog.

Hapkemeyer, Andreas, and Peter Weiermair, eds. *photo text text photo: The Synthesis of Photography and Text in Contemporary Art*. Bozen, Italy: Museum für Moderne Kunst; Frankfurt am Main, Germany: Frankfurter Kunstverein, 1996. An exhibition catalog.

Hughes, Alex, and Andrea Noble, eds. *Phototextualities: Intersections of Photography and Narrative*. Albuquerque: University of New Mexico Press, 2003.

Lauf, Cornelia, and Clive Phillpot. *Artist/Author: Contemporary Artists' Books*. New York: American Federation of Arts and Distributed Art Publishers, 1998.

Lyons, Joan, ed. *Artists' Books: A Critical Anthology and Sourcebook*. Rochester, N.Y.: Visual Studies Workshop Press, 1987.

Selected Bibliography

McDaniel, Craig, Matthew Brennan, and Renée Ramsey, eds. *Is Poetry a Visual Art?* Terre Haute: Indiana State University, Turman Art Gallery, 1993. An exhibition catalog.

Perverted by Language. Greenvale, N.Y.: Hillwood Art Gallery, Long Island University/C.W. Post Campus, 1987. An exhibition catalog.

Spector, Buzz, ed. *Verbally Charged Images.* Chicago: *WhiteWalls: A Magazine of Writings by Artists* 10/11, (Spring–Summer 1984).

Stiles, Kristine. "Language and Concepts." In Kristine Stiles and Peter Selz, eds., *Theories and Documents of Contemporary Art: A Sourcebook of Artists' Writings*, pp. 804–816. Berkeley and Los Angeles: University of California Press, 1996.

Vesna, Victoria. *Database Aesthetics: Art in the Age of Information Flow.* Minneapolis: University of Minnesota Press, 2007.

Word and Meaning: Six Contemporary Chinese Artists. Buffalo, N.Y.: University at Buffalo Art Gallery, 2000. An exhibition catalog.

Words and #s. Dayton, Ohio: Museum of Contemporary Art, Wright State University, 1991. An exhibition catalog.

Wye, Deborah. *Thinking Print: Books to Billboards, 1980-95.* New York: Museum of Modern Art, 1996. An exhibition catalog.

Profile: Nina Katchadourian

Berry, Ian. *Nina Katchadourian: All Forms of Attraction.* Saratoga Springs, N.Y.: Frances Young Tang Teaching Museum and Art Gallery at Skidmore College, 2006. An exhibition catalog.

Richard, Frances, Daniel Rosenberg, and Lytle Shaw. *Talking Popcorn, Paranormal Postcards, and Indecision on the Moon.* New York: Debs and Co., 2001. An exhibition catalog.

Rosenberg, Daniel. "One Small Step (for Nina Katchadourian)." *Art Journal* 61, no. 3 (Fall 2002): pp. 32–39.

Volk, Gregory. "Nina Katchadourian at Sara Meltzer." *Art in America* 94, no. 1 (January 2006): p. 114.

Profile: Ken Aptekar

Bryson, Norman. "The Viewer Speaks." *Art in America* 87, no. 2 (February 1999): pp. 98–101.

Kaplan, Janet. "Ken Aptekar." In "Give & Take Conversations." *Art Journal* 61, no. 2 (Summer 2002): pp. 71–74.

Sangster, Gary. "Ken Aptekar." In *43rd Biennial of Contemporary American Painting.* Washington, D.C.: Corcoran Gallery of Art, 1993, pp. 34–35. An exhibition catalog.

Chapter Seven: Science

Anker, Suzanne, and Dorothy Nelkin. *The Molecular Gaze: Art in the Genetic Age.* Cold Spring, N.Y.: Harbor Laboratory Press, 2004.

Ede, Siân, ed. *Strange and Charmed: Science and the Contemporary Visual Arts.* London; Calouste Gulbenkian Foundation, 2000.

Heiferman, Marvin, and Carole Kismaric, eds. *Paradise Now: Picturing the Genetic Revolution.* Saratoga Springs, N.Y.: Tang Teaching Museum and Art Gallery, Skidmore College; New York: Distributed Art Publishers, 2001.

Heon, Laura Steward. *Unnatural Science: An Exhibition.* North Adams: Mass MoCA Publications, 2000. An exhibition catalog.

Hoffman, Irene. *Weird Science: A Conflation of Art and Science.* Bloomfield Hills, Mich.: Cranbrook Art Museum, 1999). An exhibition catalog.

Levy, Ellen K. "Art Enters the Biotechnology Debate; Questions of Ethics." In Elaine A. King, and Gail Levin, eds., *Ethics and the Visual Arts*, pp. 199–216. New York: Allworth Press, 2006.

Obrist, Hans Ulrich, and Barbara Vanderlindnen, eds. *Laboratorium*. Antwerp: Antwerpen Open and Roomade; New York: Distributed Art Publishers, 2001. An exhibition catalog.

Smith, Marquard, and Joanne Morra, eds. *The Prosthetic Impulse: From a Posthuman Present to a Biocultural Future*. Cambridge, Mass.: MIT Press, 2006.

Stirratt, Betsy, ed. *Human Nature*. Bloomington: School of Fine Arts Gallery, Indiana University. 2007. An exhibition catalog.

Thompson, Nato, ed. *Becoming Animal: Contemporary Art in the Animal Kingdom*. North Adams: Mass MoCA Publications; Cambridge, Mass.: MIT Press, 2005.

Wilson, Stephen. *Information Arts: Intersections of Art, Science, and Technology*. Cambridge, Mass.: MIT Press, 2002.

Profile: Patricia Piccinini

Patricia Piccinini: Nature's Little Helpers. New York: Robert Miller Gallery, 2005. An exhibition catalog.

Thompson, Nato. "Patricia Piccinini." In Nato Thompson, ed., *Becoming Animal: Contemporary Art in the Animal Kingdom*, pp. 98–105. North Adams, Mass.: MASS MoCA; New York: Distributed Art Publishers, 2005. An exhibition catalog.

Toffoletti, Kim. "Origins and Identity in a Biotech World." In *Cyborgs and Barbie Dolls: Feminism, Popular Culture and the Posthuman Body*, pp. 133–159. London and New York: I. B. Tauris, 2007.

Profile: Eduardo Kac

Britton, Sheilah, and Dan Collins, eds. *The Eighth Day: The Transgenic Art of Eduardo Kac*. Tempe: Institute for Studies in the Arts, Herberger College of Fine Arts, Arizona State University, 2003.

Kac, Eduardo, ed. *Signs of Life: Bio Art and Beyond*. Cambridge, Mass.: MIT Press, 2006.

Kac, Eduardo. *Telepresence and Bio Art: Networking Humans, Rabbits, and Robots*. Ann Arbor: University of Michigan Press, 2005.

Chapter Eight: Spirituality

Apocalypse: Beauty and Horror in Contemporary Art. London: Royal Academy of Arts, 2000. An exhibition catalog.

Baldessari, John, and Meg Cranston. *100 Artists See God*. New York: Independent Curators International, 2004. An exhibition catalog.

Baas, Jacquelynn, and Mary Jane Jacob, eds. *Buddha Mind in Contemporary Art*. Berkeley and Los Angeles: University of California Press, 2004.

Elkins, James. *On the Strange Place of Religion in Contemporary Art*. New York and London: Routledge, 2004.

Faith: The Impact of Judeo-Christian Religion on Art at the Millennium. Ridgefield, Conn.: Aldrich Museum of Contemporary Art, 2000. An exhibition catalog.

Francis, Richard, ed. *Negotiating Rapture: The Power of Art to Transform Lives*. Chicago: Museum of Contemporary Art, 1996. An exhibition catalog.

Gablik, Suzi. *The Reenchantment of Art*. New York: Thames and Hudson, 1991.

Heartney, Eleanor. *Postmodern Heretics: Catholic Imagination in Contemporary Art*. New York: Midmarch Press, 2004.

Herbert, Lynn M. "Regarding Spirituality." In *Art: 21: Art in the Twenty-First Century*. New York: Harry N. Abrams, 2001.

Kleeblatt, Norman L., ed. *Too Jewish? Challenging Traditional Identities*. New York: Jewish Museum; Brunswick, N.J.: Rutgers University Press, 1996. An exhibition catalog.

Lipsey, Roger. *An Art of Our Own: The Spiritual in Twentieth-Century Art*. Boston: Shambhala, 1988.

Morgan, Anne. "Beyond Post Modernism: The Spiritual in Contemporary Art." *Art Papers* 26, no. 1 (January–February 2002): pp. 30–36.

Ravenal, John B. *Vanitas: Meditations on Life and Death in Contemporary Art* (Richmond: Virginia Museum of Fine Arts, 2000). An exhibition catalog.

Tuchman, Maurice, ed. *The Spiritual in Art: Abstract Painting 1890-1985*. Los Angeles: Los Angeles County Museum of Art; New York: Abbeville Press, 1986. An exhibition catalog.

Profile: José Bedia

Bettelheim, Judith. "Palo Monte Mayombe and Its Influence on Cuban Contemporary Art." *African Arts* 34, no. 2 (Summer 2001): pp. 36–49, 94–95.

Gaché, Sherry. "José Bedia: Only the Most Valuable Things." *Sculpture* 18, no. 5 (June 1999): pp. 42–49.

José Bedia: La Isla—el Cazadcor y la Presa (The Island—the Hunter and the Prey). Santa Fe, N.Mex.: SITE Santa Fe, 1997. An exhibition catalog.

Lindsay, Arturo, ed. *Santería Aesthetics in Contemporary Latin American Art*. Washington, D.C.: Smithsonian Institution Press, 1996.

Mosquera, Gerardo. "Juan Francisco Elso: Sacralisation and the 'Other' Postmodernity in New Cuban Art." *Third Text* 41 (Winter 1997–98): pp. 74–84.

Sullivan, Edward. "Fantastic Voyage: the Latin American Explosion." *ARTnews* 92, no. 6 (Summer 1993): pp. 134–37.

Thompson, Robert Farris. "Sacred Silhouettes." *Art in America* 85 (July 1997): pp. 64–71.

Profile: Bill Viola

Bill Viola. Klagenfurt, Austria: Ritter, 1994. An exhibition catalog.

Bill Viola: Slowly Turning Narrative. Philadelphia: Institute of Contemporary Art; Richmond: Virginia Museum of Fine Arts, 1992.

Ross, David A., and Peter Sellars. *Bill Viola*. New York: Whitney Museum of American Art, 1998. An exhibition catalog.

Townsend, Chris, ed. *The Art of Bill Viola*. London: Thames and Hudson, 2004.

Index

Note: *Italicized* page numbers indicate illustrations. **Boldface** page numbers indicate initial occurrences of terms. References preceded by the word "color" indicate color plates.